Religion in 50 More Words

Religion in 50 More Words: A Redescriptive Vocabulary provides a succinct historical, social, and political examination of some of the key words used in the modern study of religion. Differing from the first volume's more theoretical focus, this volume analyzes more common first order descriptive terms that are used throughout the field, inviting readers to theorize their traditional vocabulary. Topics covered include:

- Atheism/Theism
- Conversion
- Cult
- Evil
- Fundamentalism
- Idol
- Magic
- Pilgrimage
- Ritual
- Sacrifice

Religion in 50 More Words submits such terms to a critical interrogation and subsequent redescription. This paves the way for a collective and more critical reframing of the field. The volume, along with *Religion in 50 Words*, provides an indispensable resource for students and academics working in the field of religious studies and cognate disciplines.

Aaron W. Hughes is the Philip S. Bernstein Professor in the Department of Religion and Classics at the University of Rochester, USA.

Russell T. McCutcheon is University Research Professor and Chair of the Department of Religious Studies at the University of Alabama, USA.

"*Religion in 50 More Words* marks a turning point in the academic study of religion. Aaron Hughes and Russell McCutcheon offer both scholars and the general public a comprehensive and provocative entrée into the challenging theories that are fundamentally altering the way 'religion' is conceived and treated both in universities and in settings that determine public policy. In clear, substantial and detailed discussions, the authors show that religion and the vocabulary related to the term do not refer to mysterious, universal and timeless principles, but rather point to compelling contingencies of history, power and politics. This is a book that will shake up a field in serious need of renewal."

Naomi Goldenberg, University of Ottawa, Canada

"While their first volume (*Religion in 50 Words*) interrogated critical themes and theories within the academic study of religion, this book tackles the field's many attempts (and failures) at establishing a *lingua franca*. This second testament, which can be read alone or as a companion to the first volume, outlines the often-overlooked histories, uses, and effects of words commonly deployed by students and scholars of religion. Rather than offering their readers a definitive summary, Hughes and McCutcheon provide us with the tools to take up a clearer understanding and more precise application of those concepts and terms that punctuate the academic study of religion."

Rebekka King, Middle Tennessee State University, USA

"In this volume, two well-known scholars of the critical study of religion take readers on a journey through familiar terms on religion, shaking up many certainties. The result is an equally thought-provoking as entertaining read!"

Anne Koch, University College of Education, Linz, Austria

Religion in 50 More Words
A Redescriptive Vocabulary

Aaron W. Hughes and
Russell T. McCutcheon

LONDON AND NEW YORK

First published 2022
by Routledge
2 Park Square, Milton Park, Abingdon, Oxon OX14 4RN
and by Routledge
605 Third Avenue, New York, NY 10158
Routledge is an imprint of the Taylor & Francis Group, an informa business
© 2022 Aaron W. Hughes and Russell T. McCutcheon

The right of Aaron W. Hughes and Russell T. McCutcheon to be identified as authors of this work has been asserted by them in accordance with sections 77 and 78 of the Copyright, Designs and Patents Act 1988.

All rights reserved. No part of this book may be reprinted or reproduced or utilised in any form or by any electronic, mechanical, or other means, now known or hereafter invented, including photocopying and recording, or in any information storage or retrieval system, without permission in writing from the publishers.

Trademark notice: Product or corporate names may be trademarks or registered trademarks, and are used only for identification and explanation without intent to infringe.

British Library Cataloguing-in-Publication Data
A catalogue record for this book is available from the British Library

Library of Congress Cataloging-in-Publication Data
Names: Hughes, Aaron W., 1968- author. | McCutcheon, Russell T., 1961- author.
Title: Religion in 50 more words : a redescriptive vocabulary / Aaron W. Hughes and Russell T. McCutcheon.
Description: Abingdon, Oxon ; New York, NY : Routledge, 2022. | Includes bibliographical references and index. |
Identifiers: LCCN 2021025782 | ISBN 9781032052212 (hardback) | ISBN 9781032052229 (paperback) | ISBN 9781003196631 (ebook)
Subjects: LCSH: Religion—Terminology. | Religion—Terms and phrases.
Classification: LCC BL31 .H8435 2022 | DDC 200.3—dc23
LC record available at https://lccn.loc.gov/2021025782

ISBN: 978-1-032-05221-2 (hbk)
ISBN: 978-1-032-05222-9 (pbk)
ISBN: 978-1-003-19663-1 (ebk)

DOI: 10.4324/9781003196631

Typeset in Times New Roman
by codeMantra

Contents

List of consultants ix
Acknowledgments xi

Introduction: a user's guide 1

1 Afterlife 11

2 Animism 17

3 Atheism/Theism 23

4 Church 29

5 Civil Religion 35

6 Commentary 41

7 Conversion 46

8 Creation/Endtimes 52

9 Cult 58

10 Dialogue 62

11 East/West 67

12 Emic/Etic 73

13	Evil	78
14	Founder	84
15	Fundamentalism	88
16	God	94
17	Hagiography	98
18	Icon	104
19	Idol	109
20	Immanence/Transcendence	114
21	Initiation	119
22	Liberation	126
23	Magic	131
24	Meditation	137
25	Monotheism/Polytheism	142
26	Myth	148
27	Mysticism	154
28	Nones	161
29	Paganism	167
30	Piety	172
31	Pilgrimage	177
32	Prayer	183

33	Priest/Prophet	188
34	Reformation	194
35	Renunciation	201
36	Ritual	206
37	Sacrifice	212
38	Salvation	218
39	Sect	223
40	Sexuality	228
41	Shamanism	234
42	Soul	239
43	Spirituality	245
44	Symbol	251
45	Syncretism	257
46	Theology	265
47	Totem	271
48	Tradition	276
49	Understanding	282
50	Value	288
	Appendix: a word on etymologies	295
	Index	297

Consultants

Mustafa Alıcı, Faculty of Theology, Erzincan University, Turkey

Matthew Baldwin, Department of Religion and Philosophy, Mars Hill University

Carmen Becker, Institute for the Study of Religion, Leibniz University, Germany

Emily Crews, University of Chicago College, University of Chicago, USA

Martin Lund, Department of Society, Culture, and Identity, Malmö University, Sweden

Gerhard van den Heever, Department of Biblical and Ancient Studies, University of South Africa

David G. Robertson, Department of Religious Studies, The Open University, UK

Edith Szanto, Department of Religious Studies, University of Alabama, USA

Jeri Wieringa, Department of Religious Studies, University of Alabama, USA

Zhu Xiaohong, Department of Religious Studies, Fudan University, Shanghai, China

Acknowledgments

Writing such a volume had been in the back of our minds for quite some time. We recall our friend, Willi Braun, reporting how Jonathan Z. Smith had once told him that he wished that he had written a book akin to Raymond Williams's *Keywords: A Vocabulary of Culture and Society* (1976), the very book that has inspired us here. It was more formally conceived when we were nearing the end of writing what is now the first volume, *Religion in 50 Words*, as we realized there was so much more to address than we had examined in that book's manuscript. We then proposed it to Routledge's Rebecca Shillabeer in the Fall of 2020—to whom we are grateful for contracting this follow-up book, as well as expressing our appreciation for the input of the anonymous reviewers whose comments again have helped to make it a better volume. Then, throughout the Spring of 2021, the book that you now hold was another ideal sort of COVID-19 writing project for both of us—Aaron still in New York state on the southern shores of Lake Ontario and Russell still in Tuscaloosa, Alabama—given that we were each mostly working away from our offices or offering hybrid courses, and awaiting our turns, in each state, to be vaccinated. With university libraries now open but limited in some services and hours, we were again reliant to a large degree either on periodically carting a box of books home or, more likely than not, the many online resources to which each of our university's libraries luckily subscribe (e.g., electronic journals and a variety of other research databases). And so, while many of us who joined book clubs long ago probably still own that old blue, photo-reduced two-volume *Oxford English Dictionary* (complete with the rectangular magnifying glass stored in a little drawer at the top) there is nothing now quite like the full entries and embedded links for over 600,000 words (including plenty of examples of various historic and contemporary usages) that are now available at the online OED. We should also acknowledge how useful Google's various digital resources have become, between scholarly articles that are searchable via Google Scholar, the partial or, in many cases, complete scans of recent and historic books and manuscripts that are part of Google Books, not to mention its Ngram Viewer initiative, which searches and then graphs the frequency of word and phrase usage from 1500 to 2019, along with links to examples of such usage as found in its archive of already scanned materials. These were all among the now handy resources on which we relied while mostly working away from our offices—tools that we do not take for granted given that we are each old enough to easily imagine them as not existing at all. We certainly recall the days of heading to the reference room to flip through the pages of the American Theological Library Association's (ATLA) thick, semiannual volume, *Religion Index One: Periodicals*, in search of the details on articles and authors. Thus, tackling a follow-up project like this at a time such as this is certainly something that would have been unthinkable to a previous generation of scholars. Our indebtedness to those working in the digital humanities therefore needs to be noted—an indebtedness that hopefully makes apparent just how closely integrated so-called traditional humanistic scholarship now is with the digital realm; after all, an awful lot of behind-the-scenes work with computer code, not to mention all those people who have scanned all of those books' pages (sometimes leaving more than just hints of their trace via the scans of gloved hands that pop up every now and then) helped us to learn more about how precursors to this or that word somehow made its way into English sometime in the twelfth or thirteenth century.

Along with acknowledging the importance of these resources, we would also again like to mention a variety of colleagues, near and far, who, though no less immersed in a rather unusual COVID-19 semester of their own, each agreed to join the project as consultants (with their names listed at the opening of the volume). Not only did some read early drafts of many of the entries that follow, offering feedback that helped us to revise much of what is to come, they were all invited to read and comment on the completed manuscript, prior to its submission to the publisher. We recognize that, even though we are coauthors, each bringing different expertise to bear, we hardly exhaust that growing subfield that some now call critical religion. Recruiting colleagues who also identify with the attitude of this approach, to provide input of their own, therefore helps to make the volume all the stronger, we think, by being more representative and therefore, we hope, more useful to readers (whether they are students or colleagues). We are therefore grateful for the time and energy that our consultants each put into this project.

Introduction
A user's guide[1]

> [A]cademic subjects are not eternal categories...
> Raymond Williams, *Keywords: A Vocabulary
> of Culture and Society*

Scholarly analyses are only as good as the words in our possession and scholars' agreement on how they are used and what they do. Words function as the basic tools that we use to name things, to bring features of the world that catch our attention or our curiosity into sharper focus, and to construct a set of narratives about them and their relationships to other things, all of which are often passed on from generation to generation. But words may also do more than just name things that are already out there; they may very well constitute or, as some scholars say, individuate items from their hectic background, making it possible for us to distinguish and thereby talk about something that, lacking the word (and, yes, all that goes with it) we might not have even noticed. Yet we rarely reflect carefully on our choice of words or consider them to be not just tools but also historical artifacts with a past, with implications, and even with limits; instead, scholars often prefer to assume that their words are as natural as that which they use them to name. We ignore all this, however, at our own peril—especially when that "we" names a group of scholars who see themselves as occupying a common field, with a common focus, and a shared pursuit. It is especially challenging in the field that we, the authors, share; since the European-inspired academic study of religion is, at most, about a hundred and fifty years old, and because it was preceded by many generations of theological speculation, there is—despite the appeals of many to the contrary—much room for confusion and slippage. The book that follows, the second in a series, is meant to confront that slippage, head-on, by focusing on our words. Not just any words, of course, but some of those that have created and continue to define the academic study of religion.

DOI: 10.4324/9781003196631-1

2 Introduction: a user's guide

Although we are both critical of some of the work now carried out by those who count themselves as members of this field (notably named a discipline in some parts of the world—the terms come with implications), we hope that each of our previous works have also made evident that we are both mindful of the importance of understanding the history of the field—after all, where it came from, as the old saying goes, helps us to understand where it might be going. It is for that reason that the rationale for this book, intended as a primer for a vocabulary necessary for what some are now calling a critical study of religion (more on that below), is explicitly rooted in another little book, first published fifty years ago by Eric J. Sharpe (1933–2000), the noted historian of our field. His 1975 book, *Comparative Religion: A History* once counted among a small number of required readings for students of religion in our own academic generation. But the book that we have in mind here is probably lesser known these days: his *Fifty Key Words: Comparative Religion* (1971), a small volume appearing in a series that was also devoted to such other titles as theology, philosophy, the Church, sociology, and the Bible. The books that appeared in the series along with Sharpe's certainly tell us something about an earlier moment in the field's history (there is, for example, no volume on the Qur'an, let alone one devoted to the Synagogue or the Temple). Moreover, the words that he decided to cover in his volume signal an obvious deference to Christianity—and, more than likely, a particular type of Protestantism—which may not have been obvious at the time, but certainly cannot go unnoticed today. Such "keywords" for the entire field of comparative religion therefore included the likes of: creation, divination, eschatology, evil, heaven and earth, incarnation, judgment, mana, priest, prophet, revelation, salvation, sanctuary, scripture, shaman, and worship. Moreover, these words often are used as having matter-of-fact definitions and little about them (let alone the wider assumptions that drive their use) is scrutinized or questioned. This means that the messiness of such words—their investments in ideology or class structure, for example, pointing to heated debates over how they have been used and what they do or do not name and accomplish—is overlooked, thereby naturalizing how they happen to be used now (along with the interests of their users). Neat and simple definitions are given, reinforcing popular usage, with which most readers might just nod their head and keep reading. All the words (and the assumptions on which they are premised) are left standing at the end of the book in much the same manner that they had before. That is not the goal of this book.

Take Sharpe's entry on God, as but one, quick example. The opening sentence reads as follows: "It is a truism to say that the question of belief in God or the gods is determinative for most historical religions…"

But is it really a truism? Not anymore, we would suggest, if ever it actually was. The longstanding assumption that religion is best or properly defined as having something to do with a god, despite still being widely shared to this day (such as almost any dictionary definition of religion, let alone scholars who continue to assume as much), is hardly the only way of defining religion. This should be obvious to anyone acquainted with the variety of definitions that are out there in the literature. In fact, once common debates on whether Buddhism is or is not a religion (dating to at least the nineteenth century) hinged on taking this definition as self-evident—a debate that quickly evaporates if one opts to define religion in some other way, as the opium of the people, following Karl Marx, for instance. The classification of religions into certain subcategories, such as that once common designation "historical religions"—namely those that can be traced back several centuries or millennia to what are claimed to be historical figures and events—was largely driven by Christian scholars prioritizing their own familiar themes and then looking for them elsewhere, in the unfamiliar. To this we could also add the still prominent idea of "world religions," including various subtypes (like so-called Eastern and Western religions) or even Sharpe's own use of the once popular term "the great religions." All of these categories are now seen by many scholars as highly problematic for a wide variety of reasons and thus in need of careful rethinking (which might result in their removal from our common vocabulary). Case in point: as recently as the mid-1970s scholars still routinely classified all religious traditions simply into "Christian" and "non-Christian," much as Sharpe did in his volume, leaving us in no doubt concerning the self-invested manner in which scholarship on religion often proceeds. And as for the emphasis on this thing called belief in the aforementioned quotation—a word often assumed to correspond to some internal set of assumptions or propositions that can be enumerated or stated by means of what many would call a creed or simply a statement of belief, whose recitation is often thought to signal one's membership in a group—well, it is no longer so obvious. As the terms that follow reveal in some detail, the complexity of our terminology—and thus the things they name—are often presented to us as being far simpler and easier than they might actually be.

With this problem of simplicity and ease in mind, we should also note that, in our reading, the goal of many scholars of religion is either to chronicle (and thereby merely describe) how people already talk about themselves and their worlds or to arrive at some sort of mutual understanding amidst the different religions. The latter is on particular display in the discourses associated with interreligious or interfaith dialogue, something that has become one of the hallmarks of contemporary religious studies (at least in some of its guises). Although we distance ourselves from such versions of the field, we find the ongoing tendency to take the people whom we study for granted instructive. For we maintain that one of the central problems of the field is that scholars of religion (many of whom are still from, and were therefore trained in, North America and Europe, often arriving at the field via prior theological interests or investments of their own) have long taken a certain sort of common sense or even folk vocabulary for granted. This is precisely what Sharpe did with those discourses on god, belief, etc.—simply adopting such terms and using them *as if* they also constituted a scholarly vocabulary or cross-cultural utility. Addressing this problem is at the heart of the entries that follow.

Consider again Sharpe's entries, among which, of course, was also such classic comparative religion topics as: ancestor-worship, animism, comparative method, initiation, myth, phenomenology of religion, ritual, tabu, totem, and so on. Taken as a whole, the entries largely present topics of relevance to but one religion—to wit, Christianity—that just happens to be familiar enough to many in the field (at least fifty years ago). His readers would of course see no difficulty in raising them to the status of cross-cultural, comparative categories, reasoning that, for example, if "we" had priests and prophets, well, "they" probably do too. For instance, in the country where we are both employed as professors, the federal authorities routinely discuss the tax implications for those non-profits designated as churches, thereby using a term of obvious, local significance to Christians as if it can easily carry the weight of cross-cultural difference, thereby standing in also for mosques, temples, synagogues, gurdwaras, and so on. While we do not wish to be so crass as to liken a previous generation's work as being akin to someone from, say, England, arriving ashore in India, a few hundred years ago, and asking someone there "What's the name of your Bible?" we nonetheless see this as being not so far off from where the field once was and, lamentably, where it still might be, at least in some of its versions and for some of its members. In many ways this is understandable, to be sure, since research has long established that each of us confronts the unknown by means of models that we then generalize and extend from the already known.

But—or so we have both long argued, and as we hope to demonstrate in our own volume devoted to keywords here—scholarship requires us to do something other than merely adopting, even if later stretching, one local discourse and then using it *as if* it was a scholarly discourse capable of providing a systematic model for understanding the world around us.

This point strikes us as still eluding many in the field. This might not be that surprising, after all, since, generally speaking, it is often *their* shared local vocabulary that is being stretched and thus *their* common sense that is being extended to other cultures and societies. Perhaps these problems would have been painfully obvious to readers of Sharpe's volume if he had instead adopted a viewpoint dominant in some *other* part of the world, one that was alien to his readers' local understanding. What would have happened, for example, if he had written in the voice of someone unfamiliar with North America or Britain and who was, say, local to somewhere like Saudi Arabia and therefore brought up taking "things Muslim" for granted, or, let's say again, the voice of an author from South Korea or someone from ... (you get our point, we hope). Such a writer, hoping to reach readers in the English-speaking market, many of whom undoubtedly take "things Christian" for granted, could certainly not just start generalizing from *their* local context as a way to talk about what they thought was *our* universal. They would use, for example, such terms as "hadith" or "hajj" (terms no less technical, let alone local, than "god" and "belief") as if they were natural and then use them to name concepts assumed to be similar in other religions. In fact, in writing that very sentence we were tempted, as is customary in scholarly writing, to italicize those two Arabic terms since they are, after all, foreign words. Yet, most scholars never consider italicizing the word church, used above, despite the fact that the term is both technical and foreign as well, inasmuch as it is used by a specific subgroup of people we happen to study and derived from a much earlier proto-Germanic word. So that instinct to mark the difference or historicity *of just some words*, or the temptation to take certain locals for granted, betrays the very point that we are trying to make here. A major argument that weaves throughout all that follows is that the field of religious studies can do so much better than simply reproducing and using mostly Christian terms as if they were naturally extendable and evidenced all around us. To cite one more example from Arabic, jihad is frequently described as a subset of "Just War Theory," and hadith as a species of "Commentary," "Text," or "Canon"—all terms well established in Christian discourses. Perhaps readers, upon finishing this book, will come to understand why we see such approaches as anything but scholarly.

  The question, then, is *what is scholarly*, and how, in deriving a vocabulary capable of doing scholarly work, we might accept but also build on the assumption that all of us are rooted in some local context. We do not write here, as Sharpe and many of our other predecessors did, assuming that we are each somehow objectively floating outside reality as we carefully describe its inner workings. In fact, we are aware of very few who do assume that today, making the object of those continued critiques of the presumed neutrality of the study of religion a red herring. Nothing might make the problem with that once dominant position more obvious than co-writing with someone else, as we have done before and as we are pleased to be doing once again here, for we each come to the blank page and the various rewrites of draft entries with our own history, assumptions, aims, style, etc. So how can we *retool*, and not just stretch, our inevitably local words along with the local interests of which they are representative and which they help to achieve, doing so in a way that is capable of giving voice to both of our curiosities? Might we even just invent some new words of our own, or devise brand new uses for old words, to do the new sorts of work that we both hope to accomplish? After all, words, like academic subjects, did not simply fall to us from the heavens, already made; instead, they are the tools that our predecessors devised and defined, with the aim of doing specific work that they wanted done, and which were then passed along to us inasmuch as we shared in those labors. But these words—and the scholarly narratives that they produce—also limit us, potentially preventing us from seeing or imagining outside of the terms of reference they have created. What if we wanted to do something new, and something different? What if we were not content with Sharpe's introduction defining our field as "the (as far as possible) objective study of religious beliefs and practices, ancient and modern, along historical and analytical lines"? Surely, we would need new tools. Is it possible, in other words, to develop a new way of talking about the world, in the pursuit of different ends—a way that can be adopted by those who, *regardless of their own local setting*, might also wish to talk about the world in a way that not only looks for similarities and differences across local settings and times but also tries to offer an account of sameness and difference?

This is the place, then, to be a little more specific about what we mean by a *critical* study of religion, and how it can be informed by the vocabulary that follows. By that term we do not mean, of course, to criticize religion or the people who identify as religious (whatever they may mean by that)—we are not here to inform people how to perform their own rituals properly or the correct way to tell the stories that they tell. Indeed, our work has never been critical of religion or the religious, if by that one means intervening in debates and practices that scholars usually examine when they say they study religion; rather, we have often been critical of the scholarly moves and frames used by scholars to study them in an academic context—studies that sometimes, in our view, improperly intervene in disputes taking place among the people being studied, thereby taking sides or normalizing just some of the claims or practices while exoticizing yet others. In fact, it would be quite unfortunate if being "critical of religion" was the take-away from this volume—we might caution that those in disagreement with the version of the field we recommend may be tempted to characterize our work in just that way, making it all the easier to dismiss. Now, we do indeed recognize that there are those who use the designation in this manner, aiming to find what they represent as *better* ways of being religious, as judged from this or that set of values or interests; this, however, is not our approach. Instead, our aim is to steer entirely clear of such judgments, aiming, instead, to place ourselves in a tradition that develops and uses technical tools capable of studying religion—which includes even calling something religion to begin with!—as something thoroughly human. We therefore study, if we frame it a little differently, what people designate *as* religious and whatever its opposite might be (after all, being designated as something presupposes those other things that are not). As will become evident soon, many of the terms we use to carry out this work operate in complex relationships with their opposites—much as up presupposes down and cold is meaningless without an idea of what it means to be hot—as ways of charting territory and identity. Things get interesting, of course, when this way of mapping our world bumps up against things that are rather more complicated and ambiguous than such paired concepts can manage—like the often-cited person standing on the threshold of the room, neither in nor out, thereby confounding the rules for behavior either inside or outside of the room. In our reading, religious acts—as well as designating just some acts *as* religious—are nothing more or less than part of the spectrum of ordinary human behaviors and human creations, and thus something that can be scrutinized as can be any other human claim, action, or institution. In a word, a critical approach places this thing called religion—however one defines the term—firmly within the changeable and contestable landscape of history and culture (words that, like many we have been using here, are themselves also tools that need to occupy our attention). Should one consider religion to be something more or other than that, then there are plenty of other books and intellectual pursuits to follow in achieving those other ends. But those are not ours.

But with this final point in mind—i.e., seeing the study of religion, and claims that something is religious, as an historical and cultural effect—we come to the second, rather more influential, book that we also have in mind in tackling this shared project, one first published the year after Sharpe's own volume. That other book is *Keywords: A*

Vocabulary of Culture and Society (1976), by Raymond Williams (1921–1988), a Welsh literary theorist known for his work linking literary works to practical issues of ownership and power. In doing this, he went against how others had traditionally studied literature, literariness, and the supposedly ethereal meaning thought by many to lurk within a story or a poem. His *Keywords* (which, unlike Sharpe's book, is still in print and in use) has been helpful to scholars well beyond literary or culture studies—indeed, scholars such as us. In tracking down the derivation and various modern uses of terms that we commonly use in studying groups of people, Williams's entries steer clear of making normative claims (that is, this is how we must use this or that word) and instead make plain the sometimes happenstance twists and turns taken by our words along with their sometimes unintended effects. In so doing, he draws attention to our way not just of talking *about* the world but, more than this, our way of *constituting* a world that we see to be worth talking about in either this or that way—doing so by being cognizant of how words work in relation to yet other words, constituting a vocabulary, which is so much more than a mere list. From aesthetic to consumer, ethnic, family, hegemony, modern, private, tradition, and work, Williams helps readers to do just what we hope to do in a rather less ambitious volume that is aimed primarily, but certainly not exclusively, at our own scholarly field, namely, to investigate clusters of words while *retooling* or, in a word, *redescribing* (yet another word that will deserve some attention) those familiar terms that many students and scholars often use without giving them much thought. In so doing, we show the assumptions and interests that they entail and the linguistic, methodological, and theoretical relations they imply, all in hopes of furthering a scholarly and critical discourse devoted to studying claims about a thing in the world that many of us, for good or ill, call "religion." (For more on a discursive approach to the study of religion see Jay Johnston and Kocku von Stuckrad's co-edited volume, *Discourse Research and Religion: Disciplinary Use and Interdisciplinary Dialogues* [2020].)

Each entry in our book therefore follows Williams's lead by first identifying where our terminology comes from (what we might call historicizing our discourse). In addition, we then move on to demonstrating the various ways in which scholars have used or still employ these terms, making evident the larger conversations—and, sometimes, disagreements—enabled by saying one wishes to understand religion as opposed to explain it. We will not shy away from making recommendations of our own for future use for some of these terms but, to get there, we also aim to be fair in making readers aware of who has been using these terms in order to do what sort of work. Even if readers do not wish to follow our lead, we hope nonetheless to nudge their work along by acquainting them with their tools' sources and, just as importantly if not more so, their implications. That there are far more terms than just the fifty that we have selected—some with the help of the anonymous reviewers who gave us feedback on the idea earlier on—should be obvious. (Williams's own book, for example, had fifty just by the time he made it to F in his alphabetical table of contents.) But we have to start somewhere and, ideally, we would like to keep it all succinct enough to offer a book that is affordable, that can be readily used, and that can prompt the sort of debate that keeps a scholarly field healthy and dynamic. Our choices were certainly not arbitrary, and we hope that many of the terms will, as in Williams's own book, be recognized as operating within clusters—though, of course, we have also included some that are simply representative of noteworthy trends or developments in the current field and thus something deserving of a reader's attention. To highlight these clusters, at the end of each entry we provide a list of the other terms in the book that are directly relevant to the term under discussion. For the sake of convenience, we also list those relevant terms in the first volume, *Religion in 50 Words*. Hopefully, those who see unfortunate gaps in our table of contents will fill them in with some etymological digging of their own, finding forgotten uses for terms and suggesting ways of their own to revise them or, in some cases, maybe recommending that we just retire them altogether.

The present study therefore seeks to provide a succinct historical, social, political, and institutional examination of many of the interconnected key technical terms that together comprise the architecture of the modern study of religion, all of which is aimed at both students and colleagues in the field. Our goal, then, is to get at the historic beginnings, common uses through time, and current significance and utility of many of the basic technical terms used within the current field of religious studies. These are the terms that both students and scholars routinely deploy to create a domain in which to think about, describe, and analyze their data. In submitting these terms to a critical interrogation and subsequent redescription, we hope to facilitate further a collective reframing of the field. Though, as we just noted, our ideal audience is students and scholars in religion, we also trust that this volume will be of interest to readers in other academic fields who routinely choose to study religion in their own work, but who may lack the technical training offered by the academic study of religion.

One final word, before we begin: as will be evident from a quick look at the table of contents, this is not a book like Ron Geaves's pocket-sized

10 *Introduction: a user's guide*

Keywords in Religious Studies (2006)—with succinct entries often used when describing and comparing religions (such as his asceticism, flagellant, Gaia, initiation, neo-pagan, penance, and schism—many of which, by the way, also lean heavily on Christian sources). It is also not a book in the style of the many edited handbooks that are now available (with Mark C. Taylor's *Critical Terms for Religious Studies* [1998] being the first of these modern resources to be published), each with multiple authors providing an often uneven overview of the literature on this or that topic. Nor does it merely present a collection of religious terminology, as in a phenomenological lexicon of first order terms, what one would find in a dictionary of world religions. For, as important as such comparative terms as church, myth, ritual, and tradition may be for carrying out some of our work, we decided to pull the camera back considerably further in our first volume and instead focus there on the far more general and, we hope, shared theoretical vocabulary that all students and scholars in our field may wish to hone and employ, whether they study people or texts, actions and objects, or institutions. Regardless of the group, historic period, or region that we each study, we would hope that all scholars are engaged in definition and description, distinguishing religious from non-religious things, and studying how these items or actions intersect with other aspects of the human—and that such scholars are up to the task of fine-tuning their vocabulary and their tools as a way of improving their work. In this follow-up volume, however, we zoom in a little more and address the field's more common, comparative vocabulary.

We are therefore inviting readers of this follow-up volume to examine the fact that many of us somehow just apparently seem to know that a scholar of religion ought to be able to use such terms as karma, mitzvah, Tao, sin, and gurdwara, thereby qualifying each *as* distinctly religious and therefore seeing them all as somehow inherently related to each other. And to examine the ease of making those associations (for these associations are indeed made by us) we will need a whole new critical vocabulary—or at the very least a new way of using some of our old words.

Note

1 Like the Acknowledgments and the Appendix, this introduction largely mirrors directly the Introduction to *Religion in 50 Words*; although some may wish to use these two volumes together, we anticipate yet other readers coming across only one of the two books, thus prompting us to provide these same, hopefully helpful, resources in both volumes.

1 Afterlife

Virtually all of those social formations commonly known as religions offer their adherents some narrative that purports to give an account of what happens to them after death. More often than not, such claims about an afterlife often involve a variation on the theme of a promise of some type of beneficial continued existence for the righteous and an inferior future or maybe even outright punishment for the unrighteous. In fact, one could argue that claims about some sort of existence beyond death—and thus the existence of an immaterial source that outlives the physical body—is, for many, seen as a defining trait and thus a necessary condition for something even to be designated as a religion. Thus, we witness debates that took place amongst early European scholars of religion as to whether or not the groups they called Buddhist, whose goal seemed less about attaining an afterlife than the extinction of impermanence, was in fact a religion rather than, say, a philosophy. Regardless, the afterlife—alternatively called "life after death," "the world-to-come," "rebirth," "the next life"—tends to refer to a post-corporeal existence in which some part deemed to be definitive of or essential to the identity of an individual (variously known as soul, spirit, consciousness, atman, or even self) is believed to continue living, in some fashion, long after the demise of the physical body, which is often (though not always, e.g., the Protestant denomination known as the Seventh Day Adventists) maintained to be non-essential. According to some so-called monotheistic systems, the dead are believed to go to a specific place when they die—e.g., heaven or hell—based upon the actions done and beliefs held in this life. So-called Asian religions, in contrast, are often grouped together inasmuch as they are seen to focus less on such notions and instead emphasize reincarnation in this or other worlds when people die, but with that rebirth again determined by the person's actions and deeds in the previous life.

DOI: 10.4324/9781003196631-2

Thus, the question becomes: how do scholars study differing conceptions of the afterlife about which some people make claims when no one has had a direct experience of or encounter with that afterlife? One common way to go about such study, at least historically, has been to compare and contrast what scholars usually term beliefs in the afterlife, showing where such beliefs are similar and where they depart from one another—possibly inferring something from such comparative work. Not unlike the study of experience in the study of religion more generally, there is an unstated assumption that ideas can be true if religious people report them (especially if these reports exhibit cross-cultural similarity), even in face of a lack of empirical verifiability. We see this, for example, in the California State University (East Bay) scholar, Christopher M. Moreman, and his book, *Beyond the Threshold: Afterlife Beliefs and Experiences in World Religions* (2008), which, while historical, also describes itself as practical: "even though we cannot know for sure what happens to us after death, our understanding of the afterlife can have a profound impact on how we live."

The claims of Moreman, himself a scholar of religion, notwithstanding, it should be clear that the "afterlife"—or, more properly, claims about the afterlife—is less about happenings after death, something that should fall outside of the purview of critical scholarship, than it is about the ways in which the living think about that over which they have little or no control. Discourses about death and what is supposed to happen to those on the other side of it, thus become a convenient way to exert control over people's lives while they are alive and in the present. What better way, for example, for elite classes to get others to fall in line than to tell them that, if they do not do what is required of them, they will be punished in the next life or when they experience rebirth? In like manner, we could point to Karl Marx (1818–1883) and his famous statement in the Introduction to the "Contribution to the Critique of Hegel's *Philosophy of Right*" (1844): "Religion is the sigh of the oppressed creature, the sentiment of a heartless world, and the soul of soulless conditions, it is the opium of the people" (see Robert C. Tucker's edition of *The Marx-Engels Reader* [1978]: 53). Here, Marx famously argues that the collection of beliefs, practices, and institutions known as religion provide the underprivileged with a hope or a promise that if they do as they should, i.e., follow the bourgeois class that seeks to alienate them from their means of production and instead not try to communalize such means, then they will be rewarded in a future life with all they lack in this one. Marx, of course, was highly critical of such a sentiment because, on his reading, it meant that people were too often prepared to accept their poor working and living conditions in this world for the hope that things would be different in another one, the so-called afterlife. To rephrase: while a lottery ticket may provide one with hope for a better future, it does nothing to change one's present, material circumstances.

It is difficult to understand etymologically the term "afterlife" since all those a scholar of religion may study have their own word for the concept. Rather than examine the meanings of terms such as *olam ha-ba* ("the world to come" in Hebrew), *samsara* ("the cycle of life and death" in Sanskrit), or *jannah* ("world to come" in Arabic, i.e., the afterlife), we will look solely and explicitly at the etymology of the English term for which scholars generally see these others as equivalents. In this context, "afterlife" has a fairly simple derivation, since it comes from the combination of two words "after" and "life," namely the period that occurs after we are alive. Although it gains considerable prominence across the mid- to late-twentieth century, it is attested as early as the end of the sixteenth and beginning of the seventeenth century, where, in addition to its current meaning, it could also refer to "the later part or parts of a person's life." Thus, we read in William Cornwallis's (1579–1614) *Essayes*: "My after life ... is not without profit" (I. xv. sig. 18). Even in writings from this time period, in ones that would today easily be classed as religious, it has this sense of one's "later years." For example, in the *Life of God*, Henry Scougal (1650–1678), a Church of Scotland Minister, could write that the "lessons which afflictions teach us, are then most advantageous when we learn them betimes, that we have the use of them in the conduct of our after lives" (quoting Sermon III in John Jebb's collection of Scougal's sermons, *Piety Without Asceticism Or, The Protestant Kempis* [1836], 2nd ed., 153).

Coinciding with this earlier meaning, we also encounter our more familiar usage. As early as 1598, for example, we read in the opening to the dedication of the Elizabethan playwright Christopher Marlowe's (1564–1593) posthumously published poem, *Hero & Leander* (1598): "The impression of the man, that hath beene deare vnto vs, liuing an afterlife in our memory, there putteth vs in mind of farther obsequies" (quoting an 1821 edition). From this sense, the afterlife can then take on any number of characteristics—be it positive or negative—that fit the need of the interpreter or the group in question. This, for example, could rather easily enable those who wanted to emphasize, say, the chosen few—such as those Protestant denominations (e.g., those traced to the influential writings of the French theologian and so-called reformer, Jean Calvin [1509–1563]) that believe that God has already predestined some people to be saved and relegated others to eternal damnation. Or it could lead to additional theologizing, such as done in the Roman Catholic Church, that some people spend time in purgatory after death—occupying some sort of vague middle space between heaven and hell—and that they could eventually be purified and thus released through the payment, by the living, of "indulgences" to Church authorities. Or, in the case of Buddhism, which, as noted above, lacks the idea of a permanent self or soul, it could equate with the idea of some sort of spiritual energy that could be reborn into others or eventually released into an existence indescribable in contemporary terms.

The question now is how does the afterlife—or perhaps better, conceptions of or claims about the afterlife—play out in the academic study of religion? Since most members of the field tend to adopt a fairly descriptive methodology, there is a tendency simply to chronicle what people think the afterlife consists of, perhaps even with the implicit notion that such beliefs are somehow true or at least true to the people making the claims. This often takes the form of some statement like the following: "Jews believe that when the Messiah returns, the souls of the dead will be re-corporealized, the exiles will be ingathered in the 'holy land,' and then the messianic era will reign supreme." Left out of such discussion, of course, is what fate will be met by non-Jews. We witness such an approach to the world religions in Moreman's aforementioned *Beyond the Threshold: Afterlife Beliefs and Experiences in World Religions*. He argues that it is important not only to understand the way various religions and religious people understand *the* afterlife (it is, incidentally, often referred to in the singular and with the definite article), but how they *experience* it. He writes that "[m]y aim ... has been to fill that need in addressing the beliefs of major traditions and how experiences of the afterlife are incorporated or not into these religions" (ix). In this passage, Moreman seems to imply—in good phenomenological fashion—that there exists a universal concept of the afterlife that is somehow manifested in the various "world religions." The critical student of religion here will see (as late as 2008, no less!) how the work of the University of Chicago historian of religion, Mircea Eliade (1907–1986), is still alive and well in the field. For religions, at least for Moreman as indeed for Eliade as well, can subscribe to some of the characteristics of a universal type (i.e., morphology in Eliade's language) without ever fully exhausting them.

We see something similar in the collection titled *Death and Afterlife: Perspectives of World Religion* edited by Hiroshi Obayashi (1992), whose table of contents also reveals the field's still current debt to earlier, and now outdated and troublesome, structures and categories. It is divided into three sections: "Death and Afterlife in Nonliterate and Ancient Religions"; "Death and Afterlife in Western Religions"; and "Death and Afterlife in Eastern Religions." In his editorial introduction, Obayashi writes:

> Questions about human life need not have a single true answer to be intellectually worthwhile and stimulating. Neither do they have to be scientific (about biological organisms, for example) to be able to claim their legitimate place in the domain of academic inquiry.
>
> (ix–x)

Into this ambiguity, he situates death and the concomitant notion of the afterlife. Though we all have experiences with death, since we all have had loved ones who have passed away, less certain is what happens to us after our own death. He argues, quite legitimately, that how we structure what comes after life is ultimately based on what we encounter or are told to encounter in this life. Problems set in, however, when he puts such claims on a quasi-evolutionary scale, in which early people were "unable to understand death" whereas so-called Eastern and Western religions (a division still prominent but highly problematic) have more abstract and complex ideas about the afterlife.

More recent years, especially in the subfield known as the cognitive science of religion (CSR), have witnessed studies on the relatively widely reported phenomenon of Near Death Experiences (NDE). Here, the idea is that by comparing and analyzing the reported experiences of people who have had a NDE we can learn something about what is assumed to be a uniform religious experience of the afterlife. Those who claim to have had a NDE, for example, commonly report being transported to a different "realm" or "plane of existence." Recent neuroscientific research has hypothesized that while an NDE is ultimately a subjective event, the result of "multisensory integration," they bear resemblances to religious accounts. See the useful overview in Adriana Sleutjes, A. Moreira, and B. Greyson, "Almost 40 Years Investigating Near-Death Experiences: An Overview of Mainstream Scientific Journals," *Journal of Nervous and Mental Disease* 202 (2014): 833–836. What a "resemblance" consists of, for the researcher, is equally subjective, of course, and thus problematic from an analytic point of view—at least if it is used as evidence of an objective state. Thus, how we get from the study of such experiences to a better sense of an actual afterlife, i.e., something real as opposed to some form of wish fulfilment or narrative of power over one's peers, is not entirely clear.

Unlike such speculative and often faulty comparative approaches to death and afterlife, we have more useful and rigorous analytic studies available. In his *Life After Death: A History of the Afterlife in Western Religion* (2004), Alan Segal (1945–2011) informs his readers that his goal is neither to study death and the afterlife nor is it to teach his readers how to cope with it. On the contrary, it is to "show the connection between visions of the afterlife and the early scriptural communities who produced them" (3). He does this by examining the numerous maps—both literal and metaphorical—that premodern communities created of the afterlife with an eye towards understanding those communities' (or select members') very real and living ideals and realities. Or, in his *Afterlife: A History of Life after Death* (2016), the cultural historian Philip C. Almond uses the "afterlife" as a trope to examine how writers have tried to confront not only their own mortality, but also the fragility of the times and places in which they lived.

Studies such as these, that use the "afterlife" as a trope, a cultural construct, or as a map to understand the ways in which actors construct their social worlds—in the present as opposed to some other existential or metaphysical domains—would seem to offer the critical scholar a way forward that is much more productive and promising than arguing that the afterlife is a reality. If we, as scholars, simply reproduce the ideas that an afterlife is how a divine being(s) rewards the righteous or punishes the unrighteous, then we miss a real opportunity to understand how discourses of the afterlife are, in fact, discourses of the social worlds that people now inhabit. This is not unlike how studying discourses on the future, whether in so-called religious or science fiction literature, whether utopian or dystopian, are *always* about the present when they were conceived. In this regard, narratives of the afterlife are narratives of power that try to convince others that what one does here and now somehow influences one's status in another world. When redescribed in this manner, the afterlife is less about what comes *after* this life, but the political and material conditions *within* this one.

In this volume see: church, East/West, priest/prophet, salvation, sect, soul, theology

In *Religion in 50 Words* see: authority, belief, cognition, comparison, description, experience, faith, ideology, methodological agnosticism, phenomenology, power, redescription

2 Animism

Despite the fact that the *HarperCollins Dictionary of Religion* describes animism as "an obsolete term employed to describe belief systems of traditional peoples that appear to hold that natural phenomena have spirits or souls," it continues to be used by scholars to name either distinct items or a phase whose study is said to tell us something about religion in general. Indeed, its brief entry warns against its continued use either as a cross-cultural, comparative category or as the name of a stage of so-called religious evolution (1995: 51–52). Nevertheless, we still see it, e.g., in the British scholar Graham Harvey's book *Animism: Respecting the Living World* (2005) and the UK social anthropologist Katherine Swancutt writing for the online *Cambridge Encyclopedia of Anthropology* where she refers to the term as a "style of engaging with the world and the beings or things that populate it" and "an immanent rather than transcendent form of sentience" (see the opening and closing paragraphs to the entry). We also witness in the American philosopher's Stephen T. Asma's online 2020 *Aeon* essay, "Ancient Animistic Beliefs Live on in Our Intimacy with Tech." It seems clear that, despite the above warning, the category shows no signs of being dropped from our scholarly vocabulary any time soon. Its longevity can be linked to two seemingly divergent traditions. While one is a contemporary holdover from its well-known roots in the Victorian-era, the other is part of a renewed interest—by scholars and practitioners alike—in an aspect of what is now called Indigenous religious traditions or Indigenous faiths. (On the so-called old animism see Harvey's comments in his opening chapter in his aforementioned *Animism*; on what is now called the new animism, of which Harvey's work is a useful example, see both Darryl Wilkinson's 2017 essay "Is There Such a Thing as Animism?" in the *Journal of the American Academy of Religion* 85/2: 289–311 and Isabel Laack's 2020 essay, "The New Animism and Its Challenges to the Study of Religion" in *Method & Theory in the Study*

DOI: 10.4324/9781003196631-3

of Religion 32/2: 115–147). Despite "animism" now being used by some to name but one more member of the larger family of world religions, a critical scholar may wish to heed that earlier caution and, instead, propose that studying how the term is used—both historically as well as today—tells us much about the people who are using it and the way that they think it is best to account for what they see as similarities and differences among people.

Although it may be a relatively unfamiliar word for some readers today, in the late nineteenth century "animism" was a shorthand for a popular theory on the origins of religion. It referred particularly to the "wide human propensity to understand human beings, and often nature more broadly, as bodies animated by spirits" (citing Pamela E. Klassen's article "Medicine" in the multi-authored *The Oxford Handbook of the Study of Religion* [2016], 402). The term was used at a time when scholars proposed a variety of competing views on how religion might have arisen, in the earliest phases of our species, without divine intervention, often attracting the attention of a fairly large reading public throughout Europe. This interest—one that was clearly linked to colonial-era reports of what were then seen as the exotic and strange customs of peoples elsewhere on the globe, along with the similarities across cultures that struck early researchers as surprising but obvious and therefore in need of study—presupposed what was then the relatively new theory of biological evolution. This, of course, was credited to the work of the English naturalist, Charles Darwin (1809–1882), such as his books *On the Origin of Species* (1859) and *The Descent of Man* (1871). By the late 1870s, his theory was extended to understand how entire social groups, and not just individuals, might also change over time. As defined in the 1966 teacher's edition of the widely used *1865 to the Present: A United States History for High Schools*, Social Darwinism—a movement once closely associated with the English scholar, Herbert Spencer (1820–1903)—was the preferred term to name the view that "those who succeeded and made riches did so because they were the fittest and most capable" (39). Though, we should also recognize that, as early as 1896, the implications of this once widely used approach was judged to be "pernicious," at least as argued by the Italian political economist Achille Loria (1857–1943) in an essay published in June in the French journal, *Revue International de Sociologie*. Today, of course, many would instead simply label it as racist. The notion of higher vs. lower races along with civilized vs. primitive people would become entrenched in scholarship, to say nothing of international politics and governance, all of which was informed by the supposedly scientific presumption that the irresistible pull of evolutionary forces (the so-called survival of the fittest) had teased these groups apart, resulting in some being seen as naturally superior as opposed to those that were sadly inferior. That biological evolutionary theory (i.e., random mutations that may or may not make an organism more or less suited to any given environment) makes little sense in such social applications did not prevent many of our intellectual predecessors from ranking and therefore prioritizing societies, doing so hardly in a disinterested manner. Quite clearly, the approach was driven by assumptions about their own group's norms, predictably represented as being at the pinnacle of human history and accomplishment, and thus used as the basis for judging others. For a survey of early Social Darwinist scholarship, see Paul Crook's 1996 survey, "Social Darwinism: The Concept," *History of European Ideas* 22/3: 261–274.

It is out of this intellectual and colonial context that the theory of animism first arises—a term whose frequency of use in English begins to rise dramatically in the last third of the nineteenth century. We see the term used as early as in the work of the Bavarian physician, Georg Ernst Stahl (1659–1734), a proponent of what was once known as Vitalism—the study of the hypothetical principle that gives life to things. Today, however, the term "animism" is mostly associated with the British scholar, Edward Burnett Tylor (1832–1917), among the early scholars to whom the academic discipline of Anthropology traces its beginnings. Since so many of these colonial-era scholars designated the curious practices of others *as* religious, subsequent scholars of religion often include them in their own field's history. Tylor, like so many of his contemporaries, was interested in explaining religion, i.e., identifying its origins or, as we might also phrase it, its natural cause not just in the life of the individual but as a pan-human phenomenon. Derived from the Latin noun *anima*—a root that is today also found in such words as "animal" or "animation"—meaning breath, and, by extension, life along with its presumed source (e.g., soul), the term seems to have entered English from the prior French *animisme*, itself dating to the late eighteenth century. In his once influential, two volume book, *Primitive Culture: Researches Into the Development of Mythology, Philosophy, Religion, Art, and Custom*, a book still in print today on account of its historical importance, Tylor uses the term to refer to what he calls "the doctrine of Spiritual Beings." In so doing, he opts to avoid using the then more common term "spiritualism" (given its association with seances, etc.—what Tylor refers to as "a modern sect, who indeed hold extreme spiritualistic views" [1871, vol. 1, 385]). He goes on: "Animism characterizes tribes very low in the scale of humanity," though it is a tendency continuing throughout all human history (what such early scholars called a survival—some act or belief that outlasted the context in which it originally made sense to do or hold), leaving its traces even in modern beliefs. Thus, Tylor argued that he had uncovered not only the unifying essence of all religion—and here we read his still famous, minimalist definition of religion as "belief in spiritual beings" (385)— but also the natural cause of all religion. The origin of this belief provides the account of why people are religious, something that then demands other theories to account for how this belief system complicates over time, eventually being entrenched in elaborate and highly structured rituals and institutional systems.

To be precise, Tylor placed the origin of this belief system in very early human pre-history, in a speculative moment where his idea of our evolutionarily early ancestor (a so-called savage poet and philosopher, as he called them [327]) must have mistaken a dream for a reality. Such a cognitive mistake was part of an attempt, or so Tylor reasoned, on the part of that early problem-solver to make sense of their puzzle over how, upon waking, they could be both there and here. This would have led to the postulation of the existence of an immaterial substance that must inhabit, but can also exist apart from, the physical body—a belief widely chronicled, Tylor argues, across time and throughout the present day. And so, in competition with other early theories on the natural origins of religion, animism was proposed as a theory of religion. On other early theories of religion consider the role of what even earlier scholars called the fetish (a term borrowed from Portuguese)—"a word of sinister pedigree," William Pietz observes in a series of essays published in *Anthropology and Aesthetics* between 1985 and 1988 (see vols. 9: 5–17; 13: 23–45, and 16: 105–124). Or what others located in the supposed belief in mana or power (a term of Polynesian origins), as argued by another early anthropologist, Robert Ranulph Marett (1866–1943).

Perhaps the opening caution about continuing to use this term "animism"—let alone cognate terms like "fetish," "mana," or "totem"— makes more sense now. Today there are significant problems not just with the social evolutionary assumptions that once informed its use but also because Tylor's tale of early humans waking from dreams is read by the next scholarly generation as an utterly speculative story that cannot be confirmed or disconfirmed, and thus hardly scientific. This criticism makes the onetime scholarly preoccupation with determining pre-historic origins a rather significant problem to subsequent scholars, notably those who adopted functionalist methods concerned not with ancient origins but with the present effects of, or purposes for, the behaviors or institutions they studied.

Despite such criticisms, the interest to determine the essential origin of religion—something assumed to be shared across all religions, then and now—persists. It persists, moreover, whether that presumed core or kernel is studied naturalistically (i.e., seen as being the result of prior psychological, sociological, or economic factors, to name just three) or theologically (i.e., seen as being a human response to some sort of divine stimulus). What is more, the assumption that religions continue to evolve is still prevalent. It is captured, for example, in an early article by the influential American sociologist Robert N. Bellah (1927–2013), "Religious Evolution," which was first presented as a public lecture at the University of Chicago in 1963 and later published in *American Sociological Review* 29/3 (1964): 358–374) and then in his book *Religion in Human Evolution* (2011); in this regard, see also Ina Wunn's essay, "The Evolution of Religions" in *Numen* 50/4 (2003): 387–415. We could also point to the now large body of work that falls in the subfield known as the cognitive science of religion (CSR), in which an evolutionary framework is widely assumed. Though the simplistic and profoundly self-serving models of over one hundred years ago have become far more sophisticated, such work is, as Bellah himself acknowledged in the closing to his earlier essay, "an extremely risky enterprise" (1964: 374), especially given how the posited origin can often take on heightened authority, as if it informs the very essence of something, which is often assumed to be uniform over time, as if it somehow defies historical circumstance and thus change.

Perhaps it makes sense, then, that despite its earlier problems, the idea that religion is, at its heart, animistic, eventually reappears—the so-called new animism mentioned earlier—but this time with a dramatically different inflection. Animism can now be associated with what yet other scholars (and practitioners) take to be a previously ignored, under-valued, yet enduring and important feature of those beliefs and practices that are now sometimes termed Indigenous. While early theories of religion aré now understood often to have denigrated such people's beliefs and practices, seeing them either as a simplistic forerunner to modernity or sometimes as a degraded form, today the world religions textbook genre has, in many cases, been enlarged to include an opening chapter on such groups, which may indeed inadvertently reproduce longstanding evolutionary assumptions. Indeed, a scholarly specialty has developed around their study, whether in the past or among those seen as their descendants today (e.g., the Indigenous Religious Traditions program unit at the American Academy of Religion; see also Mary N. MacDonald's essay "The Primitive, the Primal, and the Indigenous in the Study of Religion" in the *Journal of* the *American Academy of Religion* 79/4 [2011]: 814–826). Unlike previous eras, however, what is now known as the new animism is seen as the "more careful and nuanced" study of local, non-globalized traditions, free of condescending and misleading colonialist assumptions, of how religion is "expressed in indigenous lifeways" (citing Harvey 2005, 20; see also Isabel Laack's essay, "The New Animism and Its Challenges to the Study of Religion" in *Method & Theory in the Study of Religion* 32/ 2 [2020]: 115–147).

Here we return to our opening. As Wilkinson has argued in his above-mentioned article, "Is There Such a Thing as Animism?" (2017), claims about animistic beliefs and practices are, as with all scholarly tools, based on metaphors that scholars develop and then use to try to understand people and practices other than their own. As he importantly specifies: "[m]y critique of the new animists is not that they are using the category of animism as 'merely' a metaphor; *rather the problem is that they are treating metaphorical terms as if they were literal*" (307; italics added). Despite the fact that it is sometimes adopted as a term of self-designation by the people we may study, the term "animism" serves our purposes, as observers, necessarily existing at a distance from some essential or enduring quality in the beliefs or actions so named. Thus, studying the term's use—regardless who uses it and to what effect—may tell us far more about the people who employ it than the people whose practices are given the name.

In this volume see: cult, East/West, idol, magic, totem

In *Religion in 50 Words* see: belief, classification, culture, environment, essence, explanation, indigeneity, origin, primitive, religion

3 Atheism/Theism

Atheism, which in theory stands in stark opposition to religion, like many of the terms examined here is rather complicated with a lengthy history and in possession of a number of overlapping meanings. In its broadest sense it refers to an absence of belief in the existence of God or gods. An atheist is, at least when understood in this manner, someone who believes neither in God/gods nor, by extension, in organized religion. Historically, this would make such an individual an enemy of religion and, potentially, society more generally. The latter is the case because the profession of some type of religious beliefs—let alone dominant religious beliefs—often seems to be an entry requirement for social standing. Immediately, then, a critical scholar should see the term as doing work that involves identity and social classification that revolves around status and membership. Because of this, scholars should be cautious of just how it is employed in their work, carefully noting who employs it and for what purposes. Perhaps because it is thought to signal the opposite of religion, it might come as little surprise that the term has had a rather strange history in the field of religious studies. On the one hand, the field has historically tended to avoid the study of atheism and atheists because both seem to stand opposed to the so-called sacred. Recent years, however, have seen an interest among scholars of religion to examine these terms, especially when they are understood as members of the so-called "nones," that is, people who claim to have no religious affiliation, reported to be a growing class of people.

When applied to how one is supposed to study religion, which is ultimately still an open question of methodology for many in the field today, we frequently encounter the term "methodological atheism," which implies that, in their work, the scholar of religion ought to deny the possibility that the objects of religious faith are true or real. Such a methodological position tends to stand in stark opposition to many in

DOI: 10.4324/9781003196631-4

the field who instead see it as their job simply to describe the beliefs and practices of religious practitioners, doing so as if they were somehow real or at the least real to the people who report such beliefs. This often involves carefully detailing beliefs and practices as if they actually provided some sort of mediation with a different (i.e., spiritual) world. Instead of such "methodological atheism," which seems to be normative in other fields and disciplines throughout the Humanities and Social Sciences, there is instead a tendency, as Tim Fitzgerald notes in his *The Ideology of Religious Studies* (2000), to support traditional theological claims that religion comprises a distinct and thus special category for study. While an atheistic approach to the study of religion ought to mean reduction, explanation, and redescription of acts and beliefs traditionally understood as religious to be distinctly human products and byproducts, there is instead a desire in large parts of the field simply to reproduce the claims that social actors regularly make about their world. The field of religious studies, in short, seems afraid of atheism—be it actual atheists who deny the sacred, given that it runs counter to some scholars' claim that religion is a pan-human phenomenon, or as a method that seeks to reduce claims of this sacred to such other human domains as sociology, economics, psychology, etc.

Since "atheism," carrying the common a- prefix that signals a negative, is inextricably linked with "theism," like any term that is based on a binary, its meaning is as much generated by its opposite as it is by understanding its own semantic range. In order to understand atheism, then, we must pair it with its opposite, which signals, in its most general form, a belief that one or more deities or divine beings exists. This dialectic between atheism and theism—not unlike other binary pairs, such as East/West, sacred/profane, private/public, etc.—works on the fact that each of the two words, when paired, gives meaning to the other, often in such a manner that neither needs to be defined explicitly as long as each can be understood as being the opposite of the other, though paradoxically all the while being defined by it. This provides us with an example of what some scholars now refer to as "the deferral of meaning"—recognizing that meaning is a product of relationships of similarity and difference. Atheism, in other words, is imagined as the opposite of the term theism, just as the latter is regarded as the opposite of the former. Often added to the mixture is a third term, "agnostic," itself of relatively modern provenance (late-nineteenth century), at least when compared to the other two, which many in religious studies find to be less off-putting, since it refers to the position claiming that nothing of any certainty can be known of immaterial things, especially of the existence or nature of God. Atheism, theism, and agnosticism can be seen as referring to three different religious orientations as much as they do to three different methodological approaches to the study of religion. Theism often translates into a fairly sympathetic approach to the religious beliefs and practices of others, which animates a theological approach. Atheism, in contrast, often translates into a more cynical approach in which the beliefs of others are not to be believed and described accurately so much as they are to be reduced or translated to other, non-religious, issues or factors. Agnosticism, it is argued, tends to fit somewhere in between—often comprising the stance of scholars in the field who often adopt what they name as a methodologically agnostic stance which avoids posing questions of truth in their work.

Etymologically, the English term comes from the French *athéisme*, itself based on the Greek "a" (i.e., the negative particle) and *theos*, the word for god. By the sixteenth century, atheism came to refer to a general disbelief in or otherwise denial of the existence of a God. But, as Lucien Febvre (1878–1956) argues in his *The Problem of Unbelief in the Sixteenth Century* (1985; French original 1942), the term was so vague that it could be used as a convenient label to put on anyone with whom one disagreed. More specifically, the term could also be used in the sense of disregarding one's duty to God, that is, a general sense of godlessness. In both the Greek original and its English iteration, the term is often used pejoratively to denote outcasts in the sense that "atheists" are sometimes (1) those thought to reject the gods worshiped by the larger society, (2) those who were forsaken by the gods, or (3) those who had no commitment to belief in the gods. One of the earliest attestations is in the English translation of Philip Sidney and Arthur Golding's *A woorke concerning the trewnesse of the christian religion* (1587): "Athisme, that is to say, vtter Godlesnes" (355, citing the 1976 edition). In such a quotation we clearly see the equation between the term in question and the depravity associated with "godlessness." To bring out the juxtaposition with theism, proper belief in deities, and the behavior toward them (obviously in the context of Christianity with which it is often equated), we might consider Lord Shaftesbury's *Moralists* (1709), wherein we read: "I consider ... that to be a settled Christian, it is necessary to be first of all a good Theist. For Theism can only be oppos'd to Polytheism, or Atheism" (i. ii. 28).

The term "atheism" was used with considerably more regularity in the first half of the nineteenth century than it is today. In that earlier period, again showing the binary with "theism," we see how atheism was a useful category to elucidate its opposite: orthodox belief. Thus, in 1800 in a treatise titled, *Christianity and Atheism Compared in a*

Discourse, Eliezer Cogan (1762–1855), an English scholar and Anglican divine, informs readers that:

> You fhrink back with a fecret and indefinably horror from the idea of atheifm; and not without reafon. It is a fyftem, (if a fyftem it can be called), which divefts a man of dignity, robs him of the inftruments of virtue, and plunders him of hope.
>
> (21, quoting the original edition)

He goes on to add that the worst type of such "atheifm" is that which is speculative, which "may, and probably will, conduct to atheifm of practice; a species of atheifm, I am forry to add, not confined to thofe who deny in for the being of a God" (21). Such beliefs and practices, needless to say, can be put in neat counterpoint with those of one's own religion. In the same work, which again attests to the utility and overlapping nature of the term, Cogan accuses fellow Christians who do not worship God in the same true and authentic manner as he does of being "atheifts." In like manner, in the ninth edition of his *A Sketch of the Denominations of the Christian World; Accompanied with a Persuasive to Religious Moderation, to which is prefixed an account of the Atheism, Deism, Theophilanthropism, Judaism, Mahometanism and Christianity, adapted to the present times* (1804), John Evans writes, quoting a certain Archbishop Tillotson:

> For some ages before the reformation, Atheism was confined to Italy, and had its chief residence in Rome. All the mention that is of it in the history of those times, the Papists themselves give us, in the lives of their own popes and cardinals, excepting two or three small philosophers, there were retainers at the court. So that this atheistical humour amongst Christians was the spawn of the gross superstition and corrupt manners of the Romish church and court.
>
> (4)

Also interesting is the fact that Evans assigns "atheism" as a sect or denomination on a level that is similar to Deism, Judaism, and/or "Mahometanism." As a final example, consider that in a sermon titled, "A Spital Sermon Preached at Christ Church, Upon Easter Tuesday, April 15, 1800," Dr. Samuel Parr seeks to show the difference between atheism and superstition:

> Superstition is never expofed to the dreary vacuities in the foul, over which Atheifm is wont to brood in folitude and filence; but

Atheifm is fometimes haunted by forebodings fcarcely lefs confufed, or lefs unquiet than thofe by which Superftition is annoyed.
(97)

In these select examples, chosen from literally hundreds, the narrative is always the same: atheism, to be feared for its corrupting influence on both the minds of individuals and the good of society more generally, desires (and it is often presented as a malevolent and active force) to subvert the natural order. The latter, of course, is imagined to coincide with whatever denomination of Protestant Christianity the particular scholar or clergy member happens to ascribe.

This idea of the pernicious effects of atheism became even more pronounced in the early decades of the twentieth century when, in liberal democratic political discourses, it became increasingly connected to "communism." Once again, we see how "atheism" can be deployed as a device to signal that those who hold the position are somehow "not like us." Writing just prior to World War II, for example, Bagsar M. Bagdoyan writes that if "you can succeed inoculating atheism into anybody's head you can destroy at least ninety-five per cent of the moral and ethical principles for which that individual would be standing" (26). Likewise, we read in *Sources of Modern Mass Atheism in Russia* (1954) by Edmund Taylor Weiant (1924–2004), former professor of Foreign Languages at Queens University in Charlotte, NC, and onetime head of the Far Eastern Desk at Radio Free Europe/Radio Liberty (a US government-funded organization that broadcasts and reports news, information and analysis to countries in what some still refer to as Eastern Europe along with Central Asia and the Middle East): in Russia, "atheism spread from one generation to the next, this becoming traditional and inheritable. Christianity, the victim of this train of events, has been feeling more of the lash and now finds itself in the situation of having to recede" (127).

Recent years have seen a set of new trends in the study of atheism, in which it is no longer simply seen as a pernicious moral force or as that to which some version of theism can be compared. For we now see titles such as *Atheism: A Very Short Introduction* (2003), *The Handbook of Atheism* (2013), *Atheism: The Basics* (2018), and *A Companion to Atheism and Philosophy* (2019). In all of these titles we witness the lack of belief elevated to an object of study in its own right and, at least in such academically respected titles, we find none of the pejorative assertions of times past. Increasingly in such literature, however, atheism is presented as a "worldview," as noted above, which would seem to elevate it—as also witnessed in several examples cited above—to something on par with a religion (inasmuch as it is claimed to provide an orientation toward making the world meaningful and thus navigable for people). The aforementioned *Oxford Handbook of Atheism*, for example, has chapters devoted to "Atheism, Gender, and Sexuality," "The Visual Arts," "Jewish Atheism," "The Islamic World," and so on—all topics that would be at home in a book dealing with any other religion. In terms of religious studies, the role of atheism, at least broadly understood, has increasingly gravitated towards those now commonly referred to as "the nones." Although this term receives a separate chapter below, it suffices to mention in the present context that this group refers to those who claim to have no religious affiliation (answering "none of the above" on religiosity surveys). Indeed, they are often referred, paradoxically, as now being one of the largest "religious" groups in the United States. Despite many descriptive studies of the non-religious now appearing in print (a group far larger than just self-professed atheists, of course), in his *The Critical Study of Non-Religion: Discourse, Identification and Locality* (2020), Christopher R. Cotter sets out to do as the title suggests: to outline a critical apparatus that allows us to examine non-religious subjects, especially in the context of the United Kingdom, as a way to avoid reverting to the standard position that religion is somehow unique or that it has to be studied using some sort of special methodology. At stake for Cotter is not whether someone is or is not an atheist (let alone agnostic), but the ways that such labels—or, perhaps better, socially formative categories—are used by various social actors, including institutional agencies, to identify and categorize. Issues of identification and how various social actors actually use such terms as a way to locate themselves and their beliefs (or lack thereof) in relation to others is certainly a much more productive way for a critical scholar to proceed than simply, as many of the examples witnessed above from the early nineteenth century do, denoting "atheism" as something real, substantial, and pernicious to the body politic.

In this volume see: civil religion, emic/etic, god, myth, nones, soul, spirituality, theology, tradition

In *Religion in 50 Words* see: belief, classification, critical, definition, faith, method, methodological agnosticism, orthodoxy, secular

4 Church

There is a tendency to assume religion is tantamount to an inner sentiment, often referred to as a religious experience, that is only secondarily projected into the world, via either symbols or actions. The traditional challenge of studying religion revolves around how the observer can access these inner feelings and motivations in such a manner that describes and then compares them cross-culturally with the aim of inferring some possible pan-human nature or even origin. Many such studies have focused on the social gatherings that so-called religious people regularly hold, with the assumption that the supposedly private experiences are believed to animate people's observable actions and their organizations. This is, for example, one of the reasons that the category ritual is among the most fundamental units of study in the history of the field. Such behaviors are assumed to be learned and repetitively practiced in institutionalized settings, making these social locales among the most important places where scholars have traditionally studied religion. Sociologists often go so far as to develop indices of religiosity that are mainly based on measuring the frequency of attendance at such ceremonies by, for example, basing claims on how religious someone is on the extent of their affiliation and participation. If we add to this the obvious and longstanding influence of Christianity throughout the history of the modern field, then it makes sense why this term "church" has played such a foundational role in the history of the field. This has often involved a preoccupation with studying various types of Christianity, notably the various forms of Protestantism, as if they were an authorized prototype for all other religions. Despite being a local term relevant to a specific sub-group of people, the term "church" is frequently used by both English-language scholars and portions of the general public as if it is also the generic name for the place where religious people routinely gather to meet and perform their ceremonies, all part of an activity more often than not termed worship. Indeed, consider that this latter term has its origins in Old English, as a compound term to denote a state or condition of having value (worth + ship), initially a noun used to name a person of standing and authority, e.g., it still in use as an honorary title in nations influenced by British history and law ("Your worship"), used when addressing a magistrate or a mayor. The frequent use of this term "church," then, to name such meeting places provides another entry into a series of problems in the study of religion—from those concerning how many scholars conceptualize religion to how they often unwittingly universalize, and thereby naturalize, what are actually historically or regionally discrete particulars that are incapable of bearing the cross-cultural weight.

The term "church" is certainly well established in English. Both the noun and adjective date to early Old English, well over one thousand years ago, involving an array of different spellings over time (e.g., from "ciirice" and "kyrice" to "cherich" or "chureche" in Middle English and even "choorch" and "chu'ch" in some local variants as late as the early nineteenth century). The term is derived from Germanic roots, themselves believed to have been influenced by the ancient Greek *kýrios*, meaning something akin to lord or even master—English translations of the Greek New Testament routinely translate it as the uppercase Lord. In continuous use, the term tends to mean one of two things: (1) the specific building where Christians gather for their ceremonies, something that presupposes a nuanced vocabulary to distinguish a cathedral or basilica, on the one end of size and complexity, from a mere chapel, at the other; or, more generally, (2) designating the collectivity of all Christians, thus the sometimes use of the uppercase "Church," as in the Roman Catholic Church, the Eastern Church, or the Church of England. "Christendom" was once popularly used for an even wider application, implying a pan-national civilization, though today's designation "Christianity," seemingly its modern synonym, has firmly been placed within the larger world religions paradigm, seeing it as a religion and not a so-called civilization. For example, in the English translation of Martin Luther's (1483–1546) tract, *An Open Letter to the Christian Nobility of the German Nation Concerning the Reform of the Christian Estate* (1520) we see both "Church" and "parish-church" used to convey these two different senses (see 133 of C.M. Jacobs's 1915 translation, compared to the original German edition published by Valentin Schumann). Moreover, the verb, to church, comes into use in the mid-fifteenth century, used to refer to an action performed in that setting, See, for example, the onetime Christian practice of blessing or churching a married woman recently recovered from childbirth.

Eventually "churching" signifies the institutionalization of something, such as the so-called churching of America, a phrase used in scholarship to refer to the increasing membership in, and thus identification with, such institutions. We see this, for instance, in the title of Roger Finke and Rodney Stark's sociological study, *The Churching of America, 1776–2005: Winners and Losers in our Religious Economy* (2005).

For reasons specified from the outset, early scholars thought it natural to extend this now commonsense designator to the customs of other peoples. Their familiarity with Christianity prompted them to look for all sorts of analogues and points of similarity when confronted with the unfamiliar ways of others, all in an effort to establish just what "our" relationship ought to be to "them." While looking through the ethnographic record arriving in European centers of learning from a variety of colonial outposts, scholars went searching for, among other things, beliefs in a so-called high god, which enabled them to develop a vocabulary of polytheism and monotheism. Nineteenth-century scholars also came up with the category of dying and rising gods, along with references to saviors whose exploits were conveyed in equivalents to the canon already known as the Bible. In the latter, for example, they placed the text known as the *Bhagavad Gita*, a small portion of the much larger ancient Sanskrit epic, *The Mahabharata*, has long been termed "the Hindu Bible," both today, in some renderings, as well as in scholarship from over one hundred years ago. This effort to know "the other" in terms of the local makes sense, of course, especially if we adopt the rather uncontroversial assumption that human beings have no choice but to employ familiar categories, associations, and assumptions when confronting novel and therefore unanticipated information. That such prototypes should be held loosely, however, with scholars recognizing that their models inevitably are historically-specific, conceptual tools which are therefore limited and bound to fail when stretched too far, is too often forgotten or ignored.

Thus, we come to the problem of too quickly designating what others might refer to as, to name but two, their *gurdwara* (Sikhism) or *mandir* (Hinduism), as simply being "their church." Even within Christianity the designation means many different things. It can refer to anything from the area around the altar and thus the focus of ritual activity when the weekly worship ceremony takes place to the physical building in which a host of weekly social activities take place, from education programs run by the congregation itself to various extracurricular activities throughout the day and evening. Thus, the traditional "going to church," likely conveying one's participation in a Christian ceremony, utterly fails to capture the complex roles of this architectural structure *within Christianity alone*. How much more problematic, then, is it to assume that the word easily names what yet others might call their *mosque* (in Islam)?

Scholars have not completely failed to recognize this, of course, mobilizing such other English words as "temple" and "shrine" to name other people's meeting places that fail to sufficiently overlap with what scholars themselves mean by a church. This is especially the case when such places are not sites for the collectivity to routinely meet on regular ritual occasions (as in a roadside shrine periodically and briefly visited by a lone pilgrim) or when the site defied what eventually became familiar distinctions in the European world between sacred and secular functions and thus when the building was also the location of governmental authority. Again, we see how a specific but often undisclosed theory of religion drives our choice of terminology, with "church" easily being distinguished from, say, a town hall. Sometimes such alternative terms as "temple" were invoked somewhat pejoratively, as if protecting "church" from unworthy comparisons to what were seen to be the inferior actions and institutions of others. Yet, at other times, and we think here of the US Tax Code, the term "church" is universalized out of what is portrayed as practical convenience, so that it is expanded to refer to an entire family of such non-profit religious institutions. "The term is not used by all faiths," the Internal Revenue Service (IRS) realizes, in the introduction to its *Tax Guide for Churches and Religious Organizations* (2015. 1);

> however, in an attempt to make this publication easy to read, we use it in its generic sense as a place of worship including, for example, mosques and synagogues …. [T]he use of the term church throughout this publication also includes conventions and associations of churches as well as integrated auxiliaries of a church.

Here, we might note as an aside that, for tax purposes in the US, all churches are religious organizations but not all religious organizations are churches. However, amidst the practicality something else is happening. It should be clear that a variety of historical factors privilege Christians, and their associations constrain the IRS from even thinking of elevating another no less local term, say, *synagogue* (as in a Jewish meeting place) to stand in for the entire family's name in the tax code. This, no doubt, would be seen as inappropriate and preferential—something no less present in the case of "church." Though it often goes undetected in the latter case inasmuch as it represents and contributes to a taken-for-granted Christian dominance in American society. In fact, so successfully have some of these terms been used to refer to other people's structures that English-speaking scholars would have trouble understanding the so-called temple in ancient Jerusalem as anything but a temple, going so far as to date ancient Hebrew chronology by this name, i.e., Second Temple Judaism (a period stretching from the sixth century BCE to first century CE).

What should be clear is that, whether we see it or not, such seemingly simple terms as "church" come with assumptions and theoretical—sometimes even theological—baggage. It is the critical scholar's task to be as self-conscious as possible and, when needed, to develop categories reflective of their scholarly interests that exist at a distance from the various ways that the people under study may discuss their own worlds. We might question whether *église* (French for church) could do the theoretical work demanded of it by no less a scholar than the sociologist Emile Durkheim (1858–1917), as in when he famously argued in the close of chapter 1 of *Les Formes Élémentaires de la Vie Religieuse* (1912) that (in translation):

> A religion is a unified system of beliefs and practices relative to sacred things, that is to say, things set apart and forbidden—beliefs and practices which unite into one single moral community called a Church [i.e., *Église*] all those who adhere to them.

Notably, the term is uppercase in the original, likely hoping to have the local term do new, cross-cultural work in his definition. To use a different example, to show the problem behind this type of thinking: if by "soul" someone implies an immaterial essence that not only outlives the physical body but which is then judged by God and then admitted either to a place called heaven or hell, then a term signifying such an obviously Christian view will surely be of little use when stretched to name a no less ethereal substance but which is claimed either to be reborn repeatedly or possibly be extinguished into emptiness. So too, we must ask how much work "church" can do for a scholar or whether—much as in coining "ritual specialist" instead of looking for "ministers," "pastors," and "priests" in other religions—it should be removed from a critical vocabulary and theorized as being among the various devices and sites a group's members regularly use to reproduce an image of themselves. What's more, lacking a defensible theory for precisely why certain groups are distinct or unique—thereby leading to scholars employing a very particular term for the places where they gather—scholars of religion may simply resort to discussing the meetings places that, like any group, the people they study use when, for a variety of reasons, they assemble in person.

In this volume see: afterlife, civil religion, cult, emic/etic, evil, God, icon, idol, magic, pilgrimage, prayer, soul

In *Religion in 50 Words* see: authority, classification, definition, identity, sacred/profane, world religions

5 Civil Religion

Discussions of religion tend to focus on specific religions (e.g., those groups known as Hinduism, Islam, Shinto, etc.) and, less frequently, on those things that, in one or another way, are perceived to be *like* religion. In this latter context we might situate "civil religion," a term which refers to what have been understood as the secular values of a nation-state that are expressed or legitimized through such traditionally non-religious concepts as the national flag, national holidays, reciting pledges or oaths, etc., while commemorating events in the history of the nation that are seen to be special, perhaps commemorating them by means of such things as monuments (e.g., at battlefields, national cemeteries, or in the name of heroic ancestors). Though separate from churches—broadly understood as any religiously-affiliated institution—the latter symbols, actions, or sites often play a role in promoting and otherwise maintaining what an earlier generation of scholars referred to as a civic or civil religion. This relationship can either be close, especially in countries with a national church (such as England and its Church of England) or it can be more informal (e.g., when synagogues put American and Israeli flags on the podium in the US). In the case of England we see the very close connection between those groups and institutions known as religion, on the one hand, and the nation's civil religion, on the other, when, for example, there occurs the coronation of a new king or queen (the head of both the state and the church), in which widespread civic celebrations throughout the country culminate in a grandiose ceremony overseen by the head of the Anglican Church, known as the Archbishop of Canterbury, at Westminster Abbey. The question, of course, is whether this is a civil or a religious ceremony. Or perhaps both?

Civil religion, or so its advocates have argued, is not simply reducible to nationalism, though it certainly plays a large role in maintaining its effectiveness. In modern liberal democracies it often involves the invocation of God in public or in political speeches (e.g., the common political refrain: "God bless America") or public prayers or the reading of religious texts on public occasions. Oftentimes, however, such invocations are presented as generic enough so as to seem to be inclusive of many different religions represented within the nation—though such presentations are bound to frustrate yet other members of the group, inasmuch as their own preferred religious symbolism seems minimized or even slighted.

Etymologically, the adjective added to religion, "civil," is in part a borrowing from the Old French and in part from the prior Latin. The adjective originated as a legal term used to refer to those laws that refer neither to criminal nor canon (i.e., Church) law, but to those involving relations between ordinary citizens. Among the earliest compound uses of this term—as early as the late fourteenth century—is with "war," i.e., "civil war," which refers to conflict or warfare occurring *within* a society or community, including between inhabitants of the same country or state, or between the populace and the ruling power. Theologically, "civil" could also be used to refer to being virtuous or ethical but otherwise lacking the faith required for good and proper Christian belief. In this sense "civil" refers to those morals believed to derive either from reason or inclination as opposed to, for example, divine grace. Thus we read in the English clergyman, Robert Bolton's (1572–1631) *A Discourse About the State of True Happinesse* (1611): "He which reaches but to ciuill honesty, comes farre short of being in Christ, and consequently of true happinesse" (17). When the adjective is subsequently compounded with "religion," however, we get the sense of something—often something otherwise seen as secular and thus not religious at all—that *resembles* a religion in some fashion. We, thus, read in the second book of *Remarks Upon a Late Discourse of Free-thinking* (1713), by the English scholar of the classics, Richard Bentley (1662–1742): "But as to the Civil Religion, Socrates never oppos'd it, but always countenanc'd it both by discourse and example. His precept to his Scholars about matters of Worship was to govern themselves ... by the Custom of the Country" (33).

We should, of course, be aware that when the adjective "civil" is *not* appended to the noun "religion" the latter does not somehow cease to be civil. On the contrary, we could easily make the case that all religions are preeminently about imaging a community (to paraphrase the title of Benedict Anderson's [1936–2015] well-received book, *Imagined Communities* [1983], which argues that nations are socially constructed communities imagined by those who perceive themselves as part of that group). Religion, in other words, cannot be separated from the civil, the civic, and thus the social and the political. The crucial difference between "religion" and "civil religion," however, is that the latter is explicitly connected to the modern nation-state, whereas the former is often perceived by practitioners and many scholars alike as some sort of primordial identity or affection only later attached to or subsumed within the state. Civil religions are, thus, widely regarded as invented or created in service of the nation, thereby drawing upon dimensions of existing religions that are often imagined as authentic, with the aim of using but also transcending them in the name of national cohesion (e.g., "God bless America" or "God save the Queen"). It is in this latter aspect that the collection of symbols, ceremonies, and rhetorics known as civil religion serves, either officially or unofficially, as the basis for national identity and civic life. We could very well add, however, that if this is true for a civil religion, then it is surely the case for all religions. This, then, naturally leads to the question that we must ask for all of the terms examined here: who is employing the term? And, even more importantly, what sort of intellectual work do they see the term as performing?

The term itself was widely used by the influential French philosopher Jean-Jacques Rousseau (1712–1778), especially in his still read book, *The Social Contract* (1762). Near the end of the work, Rousseau attempted to define the central elements of such a religion and emphasized how important it was for the creation and subsequent maintenance of a healthy body politic. Within this context, the object of civil religion was to foster sociability and a desire to engage in the performance of public duties amongst a nation's citizens. Such a religion, Rousseau argued, should be relatively simple and include, among other things: a belief in a perfect God, the affirmation of a concept of the afterlife, and the idea that the just will be rewarded therein while the wicked punished, along with an over-arching belief in religious tolerance. All of this helped, at least for Rousseau, to secure for the citizens of a nation-state the perceived sanctity of the social contract (or agreements between citizens) and the civil laws that maintained it. Rousseau also maintained that the religious beliefs of individuals should *not* be the business of the state insofar as they did not impede the functioning of its own civil religion. Ultimately, the value of promoting a civil religion was seen as its ability to unite divine love with the laws of one's country, with the end result that citizens will pray for their homeland and thereby sustain the body politic and its national interests (both domestic and foreign). We, thus, see in civil religion the manner in which religion is constructed and imposed from the top down as a source of communal virtue. In this sense we are able to witness how religion—not regarded as grounded in and reflecting some vague notion of the "sacred"—has a predominantly social function.

Whenever we talk about the social function of religion the name of the early French sociologist, Emile Durkheim (1858–1917), is never far behind. Certainly, in his *The Elementary Forms of the Religious Life* (1912), Durkheim laid out the foundation for the idea that claims about a god—and religion, more generally—are to be understood as symbolic claims about society itself, with religious claims functioning as ways that members represent their group and its needs to themselves. Durkheim was also a proponent of the idea of a universal secular religion. Indeed, the American sociologist Robert N. Bellah (1927–2013), perhaps the most well-known modern theorist of the notion of civil religion, referred to Durkheim as the "high priest and theologian of the civil religion of the Third Republic" (see his *Emile Durkheim on Morality and Society* [1973], x). In a chapter titled, "Durkheim's Political Sociology: Civil Religion, Nationalism and Cosmopolitanism," Marcela Cristi argues that Durkheim's political sociology was also open to a global and cosmopolitan vision, which she locates in his idea of moral individualism, "a notion that transcends both the individual and a given nation-state" (in A. Hvithamar, M. Warburg, and B. Jacobsen's edited book, *Holy Nations and Global Identities* [2009], 48). Although Durkheim never used the term "civil religion," others, most notably Ruth A. Wallace (1932–2016), have argued that in his more obscure writings—such as a little essay he wrote with the title "The School of Tomorrow" in F. Buisson and F.E. Farrington's edited volume, *French Educational Ideals of Today* (1919)—he emphasized that public schools are critical in implementing civil religion and national solidarity. See, in this regard, Wallace's essay, "Emile Durkheim and the Civil Religion Concept," *Review of Religious Research* 18/3 (1977): 287–290.

As already suggested, likely the most influential use of civil religion as a way to analyze the nation was provided by Robert Bellah. In a well-known article, "Civil Religion in America" (*Daedalus* 96/1 [1967]: 1–21), he argues that, existing alongside the various religions and denominations in the US, there also exists another variety, what he calls a "religious dimension" that "has its own seriousness and integrity and requires the same care in understanding that any other religion does" (1). He examines references to God in political speeches (he had John F. Kennedy's inaugural presidential speech January 20, 1961 in mind). While we might be tempted simply to write such invocations off as mere rhetorical flourishes, Bellah argues that they are, in fact, indicative of deep-seated values and commitments that are not made explicit in the course of everyday life. That Kennedy's speech did not mention Jesus or Moses or Muhammad (or anything else attached to a particular tradition for that matter) and that he did not mention any particular denomination of the Christian Church, such as his own Catholicism, is surely significant, Bellah argues. In fact, the only thing Kennedy mentioned—as most American Presidents have subsequently done—was God, seemingly a generic enough concept that most Americans would have had no problems accepting it. The political realm is, thus, given a religious dimension, but in such a manner that specific teachings, doctrines, and identities are not perceived by most citizens to impinge upon the state. The latter is, for all intents and purposes, seen by them as secular, nor is it regarded as infringing upon the so-called separation between "church and state," something that is delineated legally in many liberal democracies. Both like and unlike specific religions, then, this civil religion is suffused with rituals that are thought to unite its citizens (e.g., playing the national anthem, celebrating Thanksgiving, prayers opening sessions of legislatures, etc.), has its own secular saints and national martyrs and set of canonical texts (i.e., the nation's founding and governing documents), all of which lead to the inevitable conclusion that the nation is allied with and informed by God.

This idea is picked up by the Yale sociologist, Philip Gorski, in his *American Covenant: A History of Civil Religion from the Puritans to the Present* (2019), wherein he argues that the specific American experiment with civil religion is ultimately a fraught one, since it tries to maintain some sort of equilibrium between America as a Christian nation and America as a secular democracy. We see this, for example, in that country's founders' desire to create a prophetic republic: one that retains something of the ethical nature of the biblical prophets with the political ideal of civic republicanism. The equilibrium, he maintains, is currently under threat on account of the cultural wars from those who want to return to one of the two extremes at the expense of a center. The current culture wars, so evident today, risk threatening this fragile equilibrium. In fact, some see the pendulum to have now swung far enough in the US that they are replacing references to civil religion with the more recent term "Christian nationalism"—using it to name much the same nationalist use of seemingly religious symbols and devises but now those that are obviously of significance to a specific segment of the (dominant) Christian population. Now, seemingly generic references to "God" are sometimes replaced with, for example, the specificity of crucifixes carried at the US January 6, 2021 Capital Hill insurrection. See, for example, Damon T. Berry's book, *Blood and Faith: Christianity in American White Nationalism* (2017) as well as Chrissy Stroop's online essay at *Religion Dispatches*: "Attack on the US Capitol Has Many Journos Finally Taking White Evangelical Authoritarianism and Christian Nationalism Seriously" (January 14, 2021).

Whether or not nations are in possession of a civil religion is less the issue for a critical student of religion, however. Rather, the category indicates that, for some, there can exist a rather benign alignment of what are for all intents and purposes largely Christian symbols and the interests of the nation-state—even if it is just a generic reference to God. We can then ask: what is the goal in referring to some things—as opposed to others—as belonging to "civil religion"? Which groups are included, and which ones excluded? To those for whom such other figures as, say, Brahma (in Hinduism) or Allah (in Islam) figure prominently, to name only two, the supposedly generic reference to God may not be all that generic after all.

The concept of civil religion allows us to witness—in detail and up-close—the social and constructed nature of society. Rather than argue over how best to separate "civil religion" from "religion," it might be more productive to imagine them as ultimately one and the same: as but another way to talk about how members of large-scale groups reproduce, entrench, and legitimize their shared identities. For all groups are—to return to the words of Benedict Anderson—communities in which members share a common set of ideas (an *imaginaire*, we could call it). One of the means by which they do this is by appealing to some transcendental force that is said to be responsible for the maintenance of the social group in question—whether that be God, the onetime US doctrine of Manifest Destiny, or even the later colonial-era presumption that social evolution had selected only some nations as civilized and privileged. On this reading, then, civil religion is no more secular than what we tend to think of as religious is sacred. They are two sides of the same coin. For if religion is a function of society, and civil religion is ultimately social, then we can conclude—to invoke Durkheim again—that these are just two ways of talking about the same thing. As such, both need to be conceptualized as what earlier scholars might have just termed social facts. That we sometimes do so for "civil religion" but rarely for "religion" itself is as interesting as it is problematic.

In this volume see: atheism/theism, church, cult, god, ritual, symbol, totem, tradition

In *Religion in 50 Words* see: authority, culture, explanation, function, identity, pluralism, politics, sacred/profane, society

6 Commentary

There exists what we might call a commonsense model that presumes meaning simply resides within things—from the intentions of authors to their texts or other cultural artifacts, in addition to a variety of natural events—and that it is then somehow broadcast or projected outward into the world. This is a model so well established that it is also found within scholarship, often with elaborate efforts to decode symbols properly, whether those of a language that is spoken/written or the symbols on material items, everything from architecture to pottery—along with human bodies and their actions, which, of course, can also be read and interpreted. The influential American anthropologist, Clifford Geertz (1926–2006), once drew upon the prior work of the British philosopher Gilbert Ryle (1900–1976) when suggesting just how complicated it is to interpret the meaning of a wink—or was it a twitch? The distinction between an origin and its coded expressions or exhibitions is so fundamental that it is entrenched in the well-established scholarly distinction of a primary source (also called a source document), on the one hand, and a secondary source, on the other (with the latter often being an elaboration upon the significance, history, context, or use of the former). In the study of religion, and especially in those subfields that are largely concerned with the study of texts, scholars are well acquainted with this somewhat ironic stance of assuming, first, that meaning is inherent in so-called sacred objects yet, second, that it can easily be misread and is therefore in need of a correct decoding by not just anyone, of course, but, instead, by an informed authority or authoritative tradition. The exercise of generating such secondary literature has often gone by the name of commentary or a (or the) interpretive tradition, sometimes with generation upon generation of textual specialists from within the group adding their own readings, layer upon layer, until this secondary tradition itself becomes part of the textual record that subsequent readers must take into account when trying to understand the meaning of some item.

The English noun "commentary"—obviously linked to such other common words as "comment" or "commentator"—is first in evidence sometime near the mid-sixteenth century, from prior French and Italian variants of the much earlier Latin. It combines "comment" and "ary," the latter a Latin-based suffix frequently used in English to signify something connected to the word that it modifies, e.g., elementary (related to or of the elements), not to mention the above-used primary and secondary. Similarly, "comment" itself derives from the Latin *commentum*, used to denote something that resulted or was devised from careful thought and attention. Perhaps it makes sense, then, that the modern word "commentary" eventually develops to refer to additional remarks or elaborations that provide supplemental insight into some original. We see this in use as early as *Pappe with an Hatchet* in 1589—a tract that many attribute to the English dramatist, John Lyly (d. 1606)— where we read: "Beware my Comment, tis odds the margent [i.e., margin] shall bee as full as the text" (413, quoting vol. 3 of R. Warwick Bond's edited collection, *The Complete Works of John Lyly* [1902]). This quotation also makes the relationship of primary and secondary clear, including the early nineteenth century, Latin-derived term "marginalia," to name comments written on the blank border or edge of the printed page.

This approach to interpretation—that is, the close linkage of so-called primary sources to an authorized tradition of secondary commentary that elucidates the meaning of the original—makes clear that meaning-making is rather more complicated than the folk model tells us. Rather than assume meaning just to radiate from things on its own, waiting for us to spot it, we see that commentary is an active, not a passive, activity. We can neither read a contemporary or long dead author's mind nor do we simply float outside ourselves and see the world as it really might be. If we think of what we now commonly call "color commentary" that we associate with watching, say, sporting events on television, we may come to the conclusion that without the comments we would not know what to look at, given the cacophony of information bombarding our senses. Anyone who has attended such events in person may know that the framing device provided by the comments (which include slow motion replays, asides, background, analysis, pre-taped interviews, etc.), not to mention the four corners of the television's screen focuses the fan's attention in a way very different from sitting in the stands in-person. This framing makes the event something that one can now experience as having a point and a narrative—that is, a distinct beginning, middle, and end—all by quite literally *making* sense of it, such as eliminating the vast majority of sights and sounds that come with the chaos of the in-person event. Thus, watching the big game at home, on television, is something that some people prefer or, conversely, this sheds light on why some claim that going to matches in person is about so much more than watching the game itself.

The larger point, then, is that a scholar's commonplace habit of distinguishing a primary from a second source, and seeing the latter's commentary tradition as somehow merely supplemental, may be part of the problem here. Without the latter reading's framing, it would be difficult to see the so-called primary text as worthwhile reading, highlighting, or even preserving, let alone as having some uniform thing called a meaning, in the singular. If anything, it now may have too many meanings to make it manageable and useful to its readers.

Commentary is, thus, part of the ongoing effort to make things meaningful in specific ways, and thus the device that makes otherwise generic things *into* primary texts that are then represented as enduring and obviously of importance. This more nuanced approach to any commentary tradition opens up a variety of options for the critical scholar. We could easily cite how liberal democratic states, for example, have complex legal traditions that interpret and apply each state's founding documents that authorizes certain readings of these texts, often known as precedents, as well as offering counter or dissenting readings that are put into the record to benefit future interpreters aiming to overturn precedent and change laws. We will instead offer a classic example from within the study of religion: the supposedly inherent meaning of a collection of texts designated as a scripture, such as the ancient Hebrew Tanakh. Though it is often called the Hebrew Bible, the latter term is a designation which itself betrays the Christian prototype used by earlier scholars in arriving at this designation. Instead, Tanakh is an acronym from the Hebrew for the books of Law (the Torah), those of the Prophets (*Nevukhim*), and the additional Writings (*Khetuvim*) that constitute the canon. Although a helpful illustration of the less than clear distinction between primary and secondary texts, and thus the crucial role played by commentary traditions in the life of the communities that we study, the Hebrew scripture hardly stands alone, despite a number of authorizing claims made about its unique origins at the hands of those seen as the community's divinely inspired patriarchs. The Torah, or first five books, are often attributed to Moses, the legendary figure who is said to have led the ancient Israelites out of slavery in Egypt thousands of years ago. It turns out that the various commentary traditions—some believed to have originally been oral but now all of which are written—are crucial and therefore hardly secondary or additional components. Indeed, one could say that among observant Jews, the Talmud—itself a commentary on the Mishnah, which in turn is a commentary upon the Hebrew Bible (both of which have generated other commentaries) is just as important, if not more so, than the Tanakh. And, given that these commentaries comprise a detailed record of readings that arose from different readers each inhabiting different periods, negotiating among different interpretations is therefore something that must be taken into account when anyone approaches the scripture for themselves. Any text comprised of separate components, written over great lengths of time by different authors and for a variety of different purposes—all of which are then selected and assembled together by yet others, long after the composition is over, and doing so for yet other, previously unforeseen purposes—are hardly coherent and uniform. To be useful they require commentators to continually address disagreements and contradictions that come to be found in seemingly foundational documents. To put it another way, it is the subsequent and continual commentary tradition that both frames the earlier text and also turns a specific text into something that is itself highly malleable because of its ongoing commentaries, moving it from its specific and historically delimited situation to a seemingly timeless work of continued relevance. It is the cumulative secondary literature, in other words, that *makes* the so-called primary literature *primary*. For without the commentaries readers would not know what to look at in that wide-ranging collection of diverse texts, nor would readers know what to do with the inevitable contradictions that they contain. Of course, even commentaries generate commentaries, which are sometimes referred to as super-commentaries.

If this is how texts actually work—i.e., multivalent things with gaps and disagreements that necessarily fail to anticipate the future situations in which they will be read and applied—we would expect to see the ongoing massaging effects of a commentary tradition whenever we find the interpretation of something carried out as an authoritative and socially formative act. As one might guess, we see comparable commentary traditions in those other groups traditionally collected together and known as the world's religions, such as in Buddhism. The latter has its own foundational documents, for example, its Theravadin school's *Tipitaka*, also known by scholars as the Pali canon, thought to date in written form to the first century BCE. In like manner, we witness a wide variety of commentaries in Hinduism, Islam (where the genre is known as *tafsir*, or commentary, in addition to the Sunna, the exemplary life of the Prophet Muhammad that the latter tradition constructs, and which augments the authority of the Quran) and a long tradition of writing Bible commentaries throughout the history of Christianity. In all of these traditions, each branch and denomination understandably possess their own approaches and thus commentary traditions. As demonstrated by the brief aside above concerning how modern nations establish, debate, and then apply (as well as overturn) laws, the focusing and fostering activities of commentary traditions are hardly unique to those groups known as religions. This suggests that scholars of religion interested in these textual traditions would be well served to look beyond the study of religion, to consider the roles played by textification, reading, and interpretation in the life of any community.

If we see secondary literature as playing a role in making the primary meaningful, then perhaps the critical scholar would be better served to start with the secondary literature rather than succumb to the temptation to see the primary as originary and merely augmented by seemingly supplemental readings. Then a genealogical reading of the secondary literature—one in which the commentary tradition is one's primary source—will shed light on how subsequent generations of readers, each bringing their own concerns and situations to the reading of their foundational texts, have reshaped that literature. This, then, provides the basis for how coming generations, with their own new concerns, approached a text that was not nearly as static as they may have thought when reading it.

In this volume see: founder, hagiography, icon, immanence/transcendence, theology, tradition, understanding

In *Religion in 50 Words* see: canon, classification, interpretation, law, politics, power, text

7 Conversion

Conversion is the term traditionally used to refer to those who move from one religion to another (e.g., from Christianity to Islam or from Hinduism to Buddhism), though interestingly one is never imagined as converting from a religion to atheism, something that is instead called "leaving religion" or "leaving one's religion." In addition, we might also note that while a person may well be called a "convert" in their new community, traditionally they are often pejoratively referred to as "apostates" in their old tradition. The latter term derives from the ancient Greek for one who "stands off," i.e., rebels or defects. Both terms, then, are ways to identify individuals or groups often with distinct political and social ramifications. Though people certainly convert to another religion for a variety reasons (e.g., reported to have been caused by a spiritual calling or, perhaps, for the sake of a marriage), we tend to romanticize the idea—especially in North America and Europe—where there is an emphasis put on the individual choice and personal autonomy, in which case conversion is said to have been done for some sort of intensely personal religious reason or reasons. Rarely, for example, do we want to talk—at least in the academic study of religion—about coercion or forced conversion; nor, for that matter, do we want to talk about the social gain and prestige brought about by conversion. For example, people rarely convert to religions in which they lose social capital. The modern emphasis on the social actor as inherently autonomous and therefore weighing options and making choices may overlook various structural factors that, despite what practitioners themselves may report, may shed light on conversion not being about spirituality, doctrine, or beliefs as much as we may think.

Since we as scholars have no access to the internal moods and motivations of those we study, all that we can examine, instead, is a variety of external justifications (either oral or written) that, in a hindsight fashion, attempt to convey and explain the prior motivations or

DOI: 10.4324/9781003196631-8

reasons behind the act. Many of these justifications border on the hagiographic (a term for the biography of a saint) or, at the very least, an *apologia pro vita sua* (an often highly stylized "defense of one's own life" and the moves one made therein—involving the classical sense of an apology). Not all scholars agree with such an assessment of our limited sources for studying conversion, however. In his *Understanding Religious Conversion* (1993), for example, Lewis R. Rambo writes of what he calls the religious quest: "Human beings continually engage in the process of world construction and reconstruction in order to generate meaning and purpose, to maintain psychic equilibrium, and to assure continuity." He asks himself, "What is authentic conversion?" To which, he responds: "my own approach to that question is unavoidably influenced by my sectarian past, but I see 'genuine' conversion as total transformation of the person by the power of God" (xii). While critical scholars of religion may be troubled with talk such as "authenticity" and have good reason to be skeptical of such phrases as "the power of God," both concepts nonetheless continue to play a more important role in the contemporary field than they perhaps should.

Instead of such approaches that are rather sympathetic to the rationales people present about themselves, more productive ones might focus on the way in which conversion problematizes identity. Rather than imagine the convert to be switching identities—moving, say, from Islam to Christianity—we can instead think about just how fluid the term is. If we imagine identity in what some would describe as primordialist terms (that is, as fixed and defined by such essential criteria as ancestry or biology), then there can be no conversion because one could, quite literally, not convert to any other religion because they lack such a primordial connection. It is for this reason, for example, that a convert to Judaism is given the title "ben/bat Abraham" ("the son/daughter of Abraham") with the new name said to establish and symbolize the new connection to the Jewish people, seen as the biblical patriarch's direct descendants. However, a more critical theory of identity, one grounded in social constructionism and the happenstance circumstances of history, maintains that identity is formed through a situated (and therefore malleable) emphasis on certain characteristics, not one that is grounded in nature; thus, to whatever extent it is a product of agency (as opposed to the result of prior structures and contexts not of one's own making), it is something that can be understood to be based on choice, often a political choice. Rather than see identity as something natural or given, based on fixed and objective criteria, critical scholars could instead focus on how identities are created and operationalized—socially, politically, and historically. Conversion, the switching of identities, allows us to witness this manufacturing process midstream and at first hand.

Etymologically, the term has a rather interesting history. Deriving from the French *conversion*, itself a derivation from the Latin *conversion-em* ("turning round"), it is a term denoting action, from the verb *convertere* ("to turn round"). In this, it is intimately related to the English term "to convert," which can be used either transitively, as in to turn a thing or oneself about or around, or intransitively, such as turning into something. We see this early usage in the late fourteenth century Wycliffe Bible, which translates the passage from John 1:38 ("Turning around, Jesus saw them following and asked, 'What do you want?'") as "Sothli Jhesu conuertid and seynge hem suwynge him, seith to hem, What seken 3e?" Interestingly, the verb here does not refer to a religious conversion (or "turning"), but to a quite literal one, retaining the original sense of the term as a physical movement or bodily reorientation. The earliest use of "convert" as a noun is now largely obsolete, and it, too, has to do with this idea of turning in position or direction. Thus, we read in Thomas Hobbes's (1588–1679) *Elements of Philosophy* (1656): "That Straight line ... which touches a Spiral at the end of its first conversion" (iii. xx. 227). It is fairly easy to see how this idea of a change in direction could eventually lead to what was perceived to be a more idealized change in character, nature, or form. For we later come to see the term used in our more customary notion of "religious conversion." Thus we read in the *Cursor Mundi*, a Northumbrian poem of the fourteenth century (ca. 1325): "Of the Conuersioun of saint Paule" (line 19477). In medieval Christianity, "conversion" could also refer to a change in status from the "secular" to the "religious" via the entry into monastic life. This latter sense concerns the movement of a church official from their role within a parish, working with the lay community to one who exclusively lived within a monastery or convent, making them "a religious." Indeed, in most of its earliest usage, "conversion" seemed to refer not so much to a switch from one religion to another, but as a movement within the Church, such as from a state of sin to one of grace, thereby symbolizing a "turn" from ungodliness and sinfulness to one of holiness—or, put more critically, a movement toward membership and standing within the community. Thus we read in John Milton's (1608–1674) *Paradise Lost* (1667): "And to them preachd Conversion and Repentance" (xi. 724).

Currently, conversion tends to be studied either theologically or historically in the wider field of religious studies. In terms of the former we could point to Rambo's aforementioned *Understanding Religious Conversion* (1993). For him, "[r]eligious conversion is one of humanity's ways of approaching its self-consciousness predicament, of solving and resolving the mystery of human origins, meaning, and destiny" (2). In like manner we find the work of the theologian Paul N. Markham, such as his *Rewired: Exploring Religious Conversion* (2007), where we read that the "model of conversion that I will offer in this book will be presented in light of Wesleyan theology and a nonreductive physicalist view of human nature" (2). Such approaches of so-called spiritual depth, not to mention claims concerning the mysteries of human meaning and destiny, however, should be far from the concerns of the critical scholar of religion. In this respect, the study of conversion from the perspective of history and historical analysis—in which we would include sociological, psychological, political etc., analyses—would seem to be more fertile for critical scholarship. We witness this type of approach, for example, in Richard W. Bulliet's book, *Conversion to Islam in the Medieval Period* (1979). In this work, he seeks to rely less on the anecdotes and self-reports that allow scholars to conclude that people simply converted to Islam without ever asking when, why, or how they did so, or—even worse—that characterize Islam as "spreading by the sword." Despite the fact that the popular conversion to Islam united the majority of peoples of the Middle East into a new religion, scholars rarely ask when and how did this happen. Against this trend, Bulliet proceeds quantitatively by focusing on the change in naming patterns as a way to chart at what points names changed to Muslim ones. This enables him to create a timeline of conversion in various areas, showing how conversion is never uniform and often not a question of personal choice, but instead, often coincides with larger structural factors, such as the weakening of centralized government in addition to rising social tensions between elements of the population that convert at different times. Just because a region (or a country) converts to a new religion, in other words, does not necessarily mean that all of its inhabitant suddenly become practitioners of the new religion, all somehow persuaded by the sheer force of the supposedly superior doctrines and beliefs. In this respect, we need to differentiate between individual conversion, which for some reason scholars often judge as heartfelt or sincere (as opposed to something based on social gain or an attempt to improve one's social capital), on the one hand, and regional mass conversion—which is described as political—on the other. Such a binary, however, is as faulty as it is oversimplified.

Any discussion of conversion also has to take into consideration the role that it plays in the academic study of religion. Although it is potentially a sensitive subject, anyone who has ever been to the annual conference of the American Academy of Religion (AAR) may notice that some scholars have converted to the religions that they study, which can lead to a preference for reverential language and other such privileging of the objects of study. Through conversion, then, scholars are able to move from so-called outsiders to so-called insiders fairly rapidly—affording more access, to be sure, but possibly precluding their use of certain (reductive or materialist) methods available to others in the field. Rather than regard these two categories (insider and outsider) as hermetically sealed, conversion shows them to be porous and, ultimately, as artificial or invented as any other category in the field. What, however, does it mean for a scholar of a particular religion to convert to the religion that he or she studies? Obviously, it means, for one thing, that the individual has found some sort of connection, or nurtured some type of affinity, with what he or she studies, something that is more than just academic. Yet, regardless of one's conversion, we would hope that one would be aware, acutely aware, of one's new scholarly voice and social interests, opening them to scrutiny as much as any other commitment the scholar may bring to their work. One cannot just pass over this in silence or pretend that it is neither unimportant nor insignificant. Case in point: Mahdi Tourage has argued that white male converts to Islam often are afforded a privileged position within the larger Muslim community (see his "Performing Belief and Reviving Islam: Prominent [White Male] Converts in Muslim Revival Conventions" in *Performing Islam* 2/1 [2013]: 207–226).

None of this, of course, is just confined to the study of Islam. Indeed, perhaps the most virulent debate between "outsiders" and "(converted) insiders" occurred in the pages of the *Journal of the American Academy of Religion* (69/1 [2001]), in which the noted scholar Robert Thurman, a onetime Tibetan Buddhist monk and Professor of Religious Studies at Columbia University, accused the scholarship of Donald S. Lopez Jr., another influential scholar of Tibetan Buddhism, of ignoring Chinese aggression against the once autonomous country of Tibet and thus minimizing Tibetan suffering. Thurman maintained that any work, scholarly or otherwise, on Tibet has to factor in the horrid treatment of Tibetans at the hands of the Chinese. Lopez, in turn, countered in the same issue by accusing Thurman of romanticizing Tibet, a larger theme explored at length in Lopez's own book, *Prisoners of Shangri-La: Tibetan Buddhism and the West* (1998). At stake, of course, is what constitutes the proper representation of Tibet and Tibetan Buddhism, a question whose various answers can be framed by the larger insider/outsider (or emic/etic) debate.

In the final analysis, then, conversion is a term that we have to understand as socially, politically, and historically conditioned as opposed to spiritually or as a process based on some sort of self-perceived inner lack and concomitant desire to adopt another religion or tradition. Sociologists who study conversion tell us that claims about persuasive doctrines and beliefs may develop as the conversion itself is happening, or sometimes after, with the process itself largely driven by increasing overlap in people's social networks. A newcomer, first introduced to a segment of a new group for innumerable different reasons only later, and incrementally, comes to feel themselves as being a member in full standing—and thus one who comes to claim to hold this or that belief. For there certainly exist many romantic and wistful accounts that accompany the journey of individuals from one religion to another (think of Paul's classic conversion narrative or that of Malcolm X's to normative Islam while on the Hajj or pilgrimage in Saudi Arabia)—including the desire on the part of many scholars to judge such reports as authentic and then merely to describe the contents of such narratives in intimate detail. However, since we cannot get inside the heads or hearts of such individuals, all the critical scholar has left are the effects and products of such conversion narratives—as well as the prior, structured conditions that may lead to the instilling of these later feelings and sensibilities. All of these conditions and effects are ultimately social, historical, and political—meaning that they can be studied by scholars interested in what makes it possible for people to identify in new ways.

In this volume see: emic/etic, hagiography, initiation, mysticism, piety, prayer, spirituality, syncretism, value

In *Religion in 50 Words* see: authenticity, belief, cognition, experience, politics, redescription, status

8 Creation/Endtimes

Traditional as well as still popular definitions tend to focus on belief in a God or gods as being among the necessary requirements for something to be designated as a religion. A quick glance at almost any dictionary will confirm this, as will a familiarity with the history of the study of religion—from late nineteenth century scholars to their contemporary successors working in what is now called the cognitive science of religion (CSR), all of whom focused on explaining *why* people believe in gods. This means that for those who support such definitions some of the heavy lifting must then be done by such terms as "God" or "gods," or what scholars once called "spiritual beings." In terms of the latter, we think of the famous example of the early anthropologist, E.B. Tylor (1832–1917) and his still well-known minimalist definition of religion as "belief in spiritual beings." Others have recently renamed this as belief in non-obvious entities, i.e., non-empirical and thus hardly natural or mundane, including such other beings as ancestors, demons, spirits, and the like. See, for example, Walter Burkert's (1931–2015) *Creation of the Sacred: Tracks of Biology in Early Religions* (1996). Although not all members of this broader group are presumed to have sufficient agency to effect the origins and destiny of either the individual or the universe, some are. This suggests that among the common traits widely assumed to be part of a religion is a focus on how the universe began and where it is all going. Since such beings are hardly assumed to be part of the historical and changeable world that humans are said to inhabit, then perhaps they are responsible for making it in the first place and have a plan for it.

Such tales are generally thought by scholars to be conveyed by a group's myths, notably those that scholars have collected together as cosmogonies (from the ancient Greek for the creation of order) and endtime tales. The latter sometimes termed apocalyptic tales (from the Greek for an uncovering or decoding) or sometimes subsumed

DOI: 10.4324/9781003196631-9

under the equally wide category of eschatology. The latter term, also derived from Greek, concerns the study of the direction, culminating point, or ultimate destiny toward which history is said to inevitably move. Both apocalypticism and eschatology, it might be worth noting, have distinct pedigrees in the history of Christian theology, with some Christians referring to Jesus Christ as "the eschaton" or the one whose eventual return will bring about the end of the world. Thus, scholars generally assume that cosmogonies and apocalypses/eschatologies are among the main types of myths told by groups, whether orally or in written form, thereby forming a specific genre of tales that, along with those presumably closely related behavioral systems known as rituals, scholars often claim to be central to religions.

We should return to the above's passing reference to symbols included in the ancient Christian text. Indicative of the study of religion as an academic field, scholars have often focused on analyzing the content of such tales, looking first to classify them according to what can be read to be their themes along with their similarities and differences from other stories, that appear throughout history and cross-culturally. Much early scholarship was concerned with this type of work, as the category of cosmogony alone should make evident. We see it, for example, as recently as Mircea Eliade's (1907–1986) once widely read book, *Patterns in Comparative Religion* (1949), with its chapters on cross-cultural water or moon symbolism, among other things. Along with the *HarperCollins Dictionary of Religion* (in its entry on cosmogony), we might be interested in identifying the procreative themes present in various Japanese creation tales (1995: 291) and then comparing that to, let's say, the sacrificial theme of at least one of the more prominent Sanskrit tales of creation, that of Purusha. In the latter, the genderless, cosmic being is cut into pieces in order to create the various elements of the cosmos, including many of the gods as well as the four-tiered hereditary social (or *varna*) system. For relevant sources, see, for example, *Rig Veda* 10.90, as found in Wendy Doniger's *The Rig Veda: An Anthology* (1981), 29–32. Then, having classified such tales based on their content or themes, scholars often move on to decode such narratives (often utilizing psychological methods), aiming to understand them as a whole, perhaps in a fashion in keeping with Charles Long's (1926–2020) analysis. In his article on cosmogony in the second edition of the still authoritative *Encyclopedia of Religion* (2005), he concludes that these tales "give expression to the religious imagination of the creation of the world" (vol. 3: 1985). As many then assume, foremost among them would be Long's onetime colleague at the University of Chicago, Eliade, such creation tales are best understood as the narratives that provide roadmaps or models for how a community establishes and reproduces itself. Long, drawing on the once influential anthropologist Bronislaw Malinowski (1884–1942), goes on to call these "a charter for conduct for other aspects of the culture" (see, for example, Malinowski's *Myth in Primitive Psychology* [1926], 29).

A focus on the content of such tales, coupled with many scholars' tendency to try to "take religion seriously," confuses an ancient Greek or Sanskrit origins tale with an actual account of how the universe might have started. This would seem to be similar to such countries as the US where creationism (ruled unconstitutional in 1987, when taught in a public school science class), but which now often goes by the name of intelligent design, is adopted as scientific. This view is still prominent among some Christians, with between 29 percent (among Roman Catholics) and 57 percent (among Evangelicals) agreeing that humans have always existed in their present form. See, e.g., the Pew Foundation's February 6, 2019, report: "The Evolution of Pew Research Center's Survey Questions About the Origins and Development of Life on Earth." Moreover, between 38 percent and 47 percent of those Americans surveyed by the Gallup polling company, in a survey conducted every few years for the past three decades, agreed that "God created human beings pretty much in their present form at one time within the last 10,000 years or so" (see the results posted at: https://news.gallup.com/poll/21814/evolution-creationism-intelligent-design.aspx).

But it is at least mostly agreed among scholars that tales about origins and ends are just that, tales. Seeing them as the site for the expression of some prior thing called "the religious imagination" hardly exhausts how a critical scholar might approach their study. Despite being popular, such an approach is rather circular (i.e., religious tales are sites of religious expression) and therefore fails to theorize just why this tendency is even in evidence. If we suspend troublesome assumptions about the inherently religious nature of certain sorts of tales, we start to see that this tendency is rather widespread. This is surely the case whether it concerns the recent past or future ("Why, when I was a kid ..." or "When summer comes I'm going to ...") let alone a time of origins or the ultimate end of history. All can be examined as narratives that are told for some sort of effect—an effect perhaps heightened considerably when their setting is the speculative dawn of history or the end of time itself, to be sure. To begin to study this, a critical scholar would do well to be reminded by the University of Chicago historian of religions, Bruce Lincoln, that the operations of the familiar are difficult to study, since their smooth functioning ensures that they are virtually invisible to us. As he makes clear in his own succinct but still provocative "Theses on Method" (*Method & Theory in the Study of Religion* 8.3 [1996]: 225–227), this is the reason why scholars should engage in cross-cultural comparative work: "The ideological products and operations of other societies afford invaluable opportunities to the would-be student of ideology. Being initially unfamiliar, they do not need to be denaturalized before they can be examined." As he concludes, the unfamiliar therefore "invite[s] and reward[s] critical study, yielding lessons one can put to good use at home."

To begin, then, imagine just one such other society—our own, but a few decades ago and thus one that is productively removed from younger readers today. Consider that nearly everyone has probably seen what they believe to be an old movie, one that one's own parents or even grandparents might have watched when it was first released but which now feels dated, whether due to the clothing, the language, etc. For our purpose, what is particularly interesting is watching an old movie that is about the future—or at least what was, when the script was written and then filmed, once considered to be that past present's once anticipated future. Consider, for example, 1989's hit, "Back to the Future Part II," in which the protagonist, having returned to 1985 from the first film's setting in 1955, ends up 30 years in his own future, in 2015—an exotic future of flying cars and hoverboards. However, the present book itself is being written six years past the film's exotic setting in 2015 and we have yet to see the flying cars that we have long been promised by futurists. Did the filmmakers get the future *wrong*? Or, perhaps this is not even the way to think about the film? Perhaps judging it from the vantage point of our present misses the point of why people before us speculated about their future, whether it was proximate or distant. Instead, and here we might think about an even older classic, the original Star Trek television series, first broadcast from 1966–1969. We might now see that the future that was once anticipated, so long ago, ends up looking an awful lot like the present from which that future was originally imagined—something hardly apparent to people at the time, of course, but obvious to those of us who are removed from their present and thus their assumptions and concerns. For despite its efforts to conjure up an image of a distant future, the episodes look to us today just like the 1960s when they were made and first broadcast. This includes not just the hairstyles but also the stories' plots, often revolving around themes of importance to the writers at the time, such as multiculturalism and issues of identity and difference, not to mention the preoccupation with the machinery and implications of space travel itself. The latter topics would have been of considerable focus in both the US and the Soviet Union throughout the late 1950s and 1960s, culminating in the first US moon landing on July 20, 1969.

Generalizing from this, we can propose that this is a feature of both creation and endtime tales. Both function as a way to address topics of relevance to the present of the teller but doing so in the more experimental space of the past or the future. The distance in time from the teller is linked to the degree of freedom (and possibly safety) to creatively address contemporary concerns in the always unfamiliar world of the past or the future. Thus, origins stories and tales of the end of the world can be read as speculative attempts to address challenges in the present, possibly resolving conflicts or contradictions familiar to the tales' tellers and listeners/readers. In this regard, it is probably no coincidence that many apocalyptic tales seem to emerge out of periods of considerable social chaos, perhaps the best known to Western readers being the Apocalypse of John, the final book of the New Testament.

As should be clear, the scholar's focus is now no longer on the tale but, rather, on the discourse on creation, or the discourse on endtimes, discourses inevitably situated in, and therefore bearing all the marks of, their present. We think here of the remarks of the scholar of Christian Origins, Burton Mack, who argues that religious symbol systems—but we can now understand this far more broadly—function "at a certain distance from the state of affairs experienced in the daily round. They articulate a displaced system (imaginary, ideal, 'sacred,' marked off) as a counterpoint to the way things usually go." Why? What he then phrases as "the inevitable incongruence" between what a group imagines as its past or future, on the one hand, and their everyday present, on the other, provides them with a shared space in which to think about that present. Now we can say that this is better or worse than that, since we have established a horizon that allows us a reference point and thus a point of comparison, thereby enabling members of groups to talk about their present in a wide variety of ways. In Mack's own words: "[i]t is the space in which the negotiations fundamental to social intercourse take place—reflection, critique, rationalization, compromise, play, humor, and so forth" (*A Myth of Innocence: Mark and Christian Origins* [1988]; citing the 2006 edition, 20). In fact, this approach can be extended to a variety of narrative techniques that groups use to make their present knowable, and thus inhabitable, through its juxtaposition with the fanciful. This is the argument of Kelly Baker, a scholar of religion, whose focus on popular culture prompts her to offer a related analysis on the role played by, of all things, the still popular genre of zombie apocalypse tales. See, e.g., her book, *The Zombies Are Coming! The Realities of the Zombie Apocalypse in American Culture* (2020). That these are hardly religious narratives, or so an old school historian of religions might argue, is obvious. Yet, inspired by a theory concerning why people shift their tales from the present either to times of beginnings or catastrophic endings, such data proves as interesting and thus useful a site as any for a critical scholar to study.

In this volume see: afterlife, commentary, East/West, magic, myth, ritual, symbol

In *Religion in 50 Words* see: belief, classification, critical, description, environment, ideology, interpretation, origin, power, redescription, society, world religions, worldview

9 Cult

There may be no better term today to exemplify how description can turn out to be a highly normative or even socially formative exercise than the word "cult." While the once prominent term "primitive" underwent significant criticism in the mid- to late twentieth century, leading scholars to avoid the term altogether today, "cult" still appears in some scholarly circles where it is frequently used to refer to ancient religious practices (let alone in the English-speaking media and in the speeches of some politicians, whether on the political left or right). Unless a persuasive argument can be made for redescribing the term in scholarship today, as a word of continued analytic value in our work, then like "primitive" it should probably be retired and thus reside solely in our field's history, as an artifact from an earlier time and thus indicative of earlier interests and assumptions.

Derived from the Latin noun, *cultus*—and overlapping with the origins of such other now common English words as "culture" and "cultivate"—the term once signified everything from the labor of farming the land and inhabiting a settled space to the training that results from an education and even devoting attention to personal care, eventually implying the results of special attention toward such activities. Eventually, it comes to designate the care associated with social membership and what we might today refer to as the ritual procedures associated with being part of a group. In this latter sense, it is akin to what some in the study of religion might now simply refer to as either worship or, better, liturgy. The former term derives from the Germanic *wurthe*, implying since Old English, being worthy of honor, such as today calling a judge by the honorific "your Worship" in parts of the English-speaking world; whereas the latter comes from the Greek, *litourgia*, a public duty or service and in English, since at least the late sixteenth century, naming the ritual component to a Christian worship ceremony. As a result of the work of the early French sociologist Emile

DOI: 10.4324/9781003196631-10

Durkheim (1858–1917), we might now conclude that all social groups, and not just those known as religions, have their cult or cultic aspect and component. This is one precise sense of the term, i.e., repetitive, public, and rule-governed behavioral settings that involve all members and thereby alert them to their status *as* members of a unified whole, doing so by means of their shared participation in the actions. Although this usage may now seem rather dated, it is not out of the ordinary to hear references to "the cult of the saints" in Roman Catholic circles, namely, the rituals associated with the commemoration and/or veneration of those figures considered to be saints along with any remaining relics thought to have been associated with them.

This curious mix of description with prescription is apparent, inasmuch as its earliest uses signify the mundane activity of tending to the land or the self/group. They could also veer into a judgmental designation for particularly fine examples of such care, ensuring that the term was never as simple as it might at first appear. In modern scholarship the term was adopted from its Christian liturgical usage and given something of its earlier Latin sense when scholars used it to designate a religion's ritual system—in particular, those religions thought to be ancient or non-dominant. Note, however, that those religions said to be dominant or widespread are often understood to have practices designated as rituals and ritual systems and not necessarily as cults and cultic activity. This again signals the term's complexly normative entailments. Early sociologists used the term as part of a once prominent classification scheme, the "church-sect typology" that dates to the work of Max Weber (1864–1920). Therein a cult was understood to be a religion that was in the highest degree of social tension with a dominant group. However, it soon came to name what some considered not just as marginal but as deviant or radical religions—hence the now common association of cults with danger and deranged memberships. This explicitly normative use of the term is commonplace in popular culture, such as magazine or even tabloid headlines. For example, a July 1, 2019, *New York Times* article entitled, "When Leaving a Religion is Like Abandoning a Cult" was devoted to the review of Amber Scorah's 2019 memoir on leaving the Jehovah's Witnesses. Thus we arrive at "deprograming" techniques that, especially from the mid-twentieth century on, were developed by so-called cult awareness experts to counter what was often characterized as the mind control techniques of those marginal groups now seen as dangerous cults.

What should be clear is that in the term "cult" we see something other than a neutral or scholarly descriptor. Instead it is a term that comes with a judgment as to the credibility or status of the items so named. The term's widespread popular usage by no means determines how it will be used by scholars today, of course; in fact, there are those scholars who have attempted to rename groups once known as cults by designating them instead as new religious movements (NRM). This change in nomenclature is still often driven by many of the same assumptions that prompted previous scholars to designate some groups as cults, however. This newer designation, whose frequency of use increased dramatically in the last third of the twentieth century, presumes, much like the earlier church-sect typology, that over time NRMs may morph into being seen as far more accepted groups. Even the more recent and sometimes preferred designation of "invented religions" —used to designate groups like Jediism or the Church of the Flying Spaghetti Monster—can be critiqued as naturalizing the undoubtedly no less invented or socially constructed nature of any social group. See Carole Cusack's *Invented Religions: Imagination, Fiction, and Faith* (2010) and the essays collected together in Steven Sutcliffe's and Cusack's edited volume, *The Problem of Invented Religions* (2016). Despite these other terms, the recurring nature of "cult," whether in popular culture or scholarship, presents scholars of religion with challenges, since whatever specific meaning is attached to the term, an unhelpfully normative sense will likely be so evenly distributed among listeners or readers as to undermine its technical use. It is for this reason that it seems advisable to drop the term from a critical vocabulary altogether, leaving us instead to study the word's usage, rather than using it ourselves as part of our descriptive vocabulary.

Should this be our approach, then we will come to see its use as an item of data, a way in which those who designate their own group's competitors *as* cults. This makes the already cited *New York Times* headline all the more curious to us, perhaps, given the apparent ease with which religions and cults (i.e., illegitimate religions) are distinguished from one other. Scholars thus will not aim to correct the public on its use of such a term but, instead, will become interested in rather new questions, inquiring why, in the English literature of the twentieth century, the term's prominence rises, spikes, and then recedes, eventually to rise again every thirty to forty years. Satisfying our curiosity about this curious pattern—and thereby helping us to answer whether it will continue into the twenty first century—will require us to be careful about identifying different or even competing uses of the term across this period. At the same time, we can ask ourselves what was taking place at each of these moments that specific uses of this one, usually normative, term helped writers of each era to name and, in some way, address, contain, or, more than likely, contest.

In this volume see: church, emic/etic, evil, icon, idol, magic, myth, paganism, sect

In *Religion in 50 Words* see: belief, comparison, definition, description, function, methodological atheism, orthodoxy, religion, status, theory

10 Dialogue

The majority of critical scholars would most likely make the argument that the term "dialogue" is probably not all that relevant to the methods that they may use to study religion. There are, however, plenty of other scholars who instead argue that their work is directly involved with promoting mutual understanding among differing groups, hence the term we now hear with some degree of regularity, "interfaith dialogue." Yet others emphasize that such conversations should also include the dialogue that opens up between scholars and the people they happen to study. The effort to establish the ground upon which this might come about often goes by the name of promoting or engaging in dialogue or, more specifically, facilitating some kind of interreligious dialogue. Although they likely do not see their work as either encouraging (or hampering) such efforts, the generally liberal attempt to bring about such pluralistic understandings among what might otherwise be competing or conflicting groups is indeed a legitimate area of research for the critical scholar. We might inquire, for example, into such things as the techniques used by the parties involved, the practical ends sought, and, just as importantly, the inevitable limits of those shared understandings and the tolerance that such dialogue is said to achieve. Nevertheless, the presumed distinction required to carry out such work—between scholarship, on the one hand, and, on the other, the practical effort to facilitate common understandings—might itself be criticized by yet other scholars, notably those who, for a variety of reasons, fail to see a sharp line of demarcation between being religious and being a scholar of religion.

Dialogue is therefore now a well-established subtext throughout this academic field. This can be explicit in, for example, a variety of liberal theological efforts, across groups, to nurture interreligious dialogue opportunities, often framed as "an encounter"—sometimes carried out under the banner of what is known as comparative theology. Or, it can

DOI: 10.4324/9781003196631-11

be implicit, for example, as some claim is the case for the modern world religions paradigm, wherein enhancing the students' empathy for, and thus shared understandings of, others is often among the intended outcomes for courses and textbooks alike. Case in point: the annual conference for the world's largest collection of scholars of religion, the American Academy of Religion (AAR), includes a program unit specifically devoted to Interreligious and Interfaith Studies. On its website this unit describes itself as "examining the many modes of response to the reality of religious pluralism (theological, philosophical, historical, scriptural, ethical, praxiological, and institutional)." Notably absent, we might point out, are all those variety of methods that the critical scholar would instead employ when going about their work. Whether or not this is seen as a desirable addition to the academic study of religion is certainly a question that needs to be addressed.

The noun "dialogue" has been in the English language since Old English, with the verb ("to dialogue," or to discuss and debate) dating to at least the very late sixteenth century. It enters the language from Old and Middle French, naming a conversation between two or more parties, but can be traced, as with so many modern English words, back to Latin and Greek, e.g., *dialogus* (Latin) and, before that, *dia* + *logos* (Greek), meaning something like "through or by means of word or speech." In earlier English uses (as well as today) it was sometimes a genre of literature, as exemplified in, among many others, the still widely read dialogues credited to Plato, the ancient Greek philosopher, in which the characters represent alternative philosophical positions on some topic and their respective conversations illustrate a debate on that topic—for example, what the just state might look like, in *The Republic*, or what it means to be pious, in the late *The Euthyphro*. Although it can also mean a generic exchange in conversation, including the name for a dramatic script, since the late-nineteenth century the word has often signified a conversation intended not just to illustrate but also to resolve a dispute between parties with different viewpoints or interests, whether individuals or representatives of competing groups. And it is in precisely this latter sense that the word makes its way into various branches associated with the study of religion.

Beginning in the mid-twentieth century we see the increasing use of the adjective "interfaith" or "interreligious" (i.e., between faiths or religions, sometimes hyphenated as a compound term) to name such conversations between members who identify with different (most often theologically liberal) religions, intended to come to a common understanding on some topic. It should go without saying that more exclusivist or maximalist versions of these groups would have little to no interest in such an activity. The result is often like-minded people talking to one another, often not asking difficult questions of one another, and in such a manner that everyone feels good about the encounter. Thus, as recently as 1961 the Reform Rabbi Balfour Brickner (1926–2005), who became well known for such interfaith work, saw the need to introduce to his readers the notion of dialogue as "[c]lergymen of varying faiths began to converse *with* one another in such controversial areas as the meaning of church-state separation, immigration, housing." We see this in an article entitled "Building Better Interreligious Relationships" published in the onetime Union of American Hebrew Congregations' former periodical, *American Judaism*. As just suggested, this activity, of course, should be sharply distinguished from overt missionary activity or conversion efforts. No one, in other words, is interested in converting others to their religion. Instead, the goal of such encounters seems to be aimed at establishing the conditions in which different perspectives on a particular topic (e.g., creation, human rights, social justice) could equally inhabit the same domain but without compromising on what each individual—as a stand-in for an entire religious tradition—sees to be essential to their identity and thus future. In this way, such efforts could be said to be ecumenical or represent a certain sort of ecumenism—yet another term, we should note, that was originally associated with the Christian church. The latter term originated in the late sixteenth century, also derived from the Greek, meaning inhabiting or being a member of the world, but one that is now often extended to name settings in which a common understanding has been established.

Driving efforts to establish an interreligious or interfaith dialogue is one's position on similarity or difference. As elaborated elsewhere in this volume, to compare does not simply mean to identify commonalities, though, historically, it has often meant mainly this. We see this, for example, in earlier generations of scholars engaging in the cross-cultural comparison of, say, myths or rituals, in order to infer something about what they claimed to be universal human tendencies. In such studies, not unlike modern interreligious dialogue, difference was a problem to be overcome or, on occasion, an inconvenience to be ignored. Perhaps nowhere was this on better display than in the World Parliament of Religions held in 1893 with the aim of creating a global dialogue of religions (and something that is still held regularly to this day). This is indicative of a larger theme in scholarship that seeks to address what could be termed the problem of difference, doing so by discovering something that could be represented as an even deeper or more foundational unity. Ultimately, that similarity, for some, was the presumably universal human nature said to be shared by all human beings—something that, despite differences in historical period, class, gender, race, etc., apparently endures, unchanged. Difference, in this model, is seen as a merely secondary and thus non-essential feature that pretty much disappears once the proper method reveals the previously unseen similarity that unites the otherwise disparate items. Given the ahistorical focus of those groups commonly designated *as* religious, it may make sense, then, that a focus on identifying and achieving such a unity is not uncommon to both scholars of religion and members of the groups they study. This is related to the desire or the habit of some scholars to treat complex groups that exist over diverse settings and historical periods *as if* they were unified and homogenous wholes. We often hear, for example, talk about "the history of Buddhism" or "Christian origins" as if a uniform, singular thing somehow moves through time, perhaps changing shape or form. Indeed, religious studied writ large, including the study of various religions, can be characterized by the effort to overcome observable differences both between religions and within religions by establishing a common understanding among potentially competing parties.

We see this, for example, in the work of those like Leonard Swidler, Professor of Catholic Thought and Interreligious Dialogue at Temple University in Philadelphia, and the founder of the *Journal of Ecumenical Studies*. According to him: "The three Abrahamic faiths have many more things in common, such as the importance of covenant, of law and faith, and of the community" (see his *After the Absolute* [1990], 123). We see here how different religious traditions are now thought to be basically the same, something that artificial rubrics like "Abrahamic religions (or faiths)" support by papering over massive difference between those traditions that sit under its rubric. Those that do not fit the rubric are seen to be either "political," "radical," or as having hijacked their traditions.

But here we see a problem—for those elements within any of the groups a scholar of religion studies that are interested in exploring possibly shared interests and assumptions hardly exhaust the various sub-groups that together are said to constitute each religion. For every constituency keen to investigate what they may have in common with those who at first appear rather different from them it is not difficult to find another whose members happily decline such advances, confident in their chosen or privileged status and equally confident in the misguided nature of all others. For scholars of religion to presume that their work advances the interests of but one of those parties or sub-groups strikes us as deeply problematic, in that it involves scholars in selecting winners and losers among the religions. As Steven Ramey has phrased it, such scholars inappropriately play favorites by normalizing one type of, e.g., Islam or Hinduism at the expense of those who identify with other parts of each of those communities but who do not see any gains from "encountering" or "dialoguing with" those who are seen to be so different from themselves as to be alien, sinful, heathen, infidels, etc. See Ramey's important afterword to Monica Miller's edited volume, *Claiming Identity in the Study of Religion: Social and Rhetorical Techniques Examined* (2015), 223–238. To put it another way, it is not the scholar's role to decide which elements of the complex groups they study count as normative or, a term often used, orthodox as opposed to "extremist" or "fundamentalist." Instead, recognizing that these subdivisions often exist within, and are therefore used by, the participants' own discourses, achieving their own interests, the critical scholar will more than likely pull their lens back a little further, studying such classifications and their practical impact. One such result will undoubtedly be to study those aspects of each group that, alienated from its own more exclusivist peers, finds affinity with yet others.

Covers of world religion textbooks often use artwork that commonly relies upon the theme of the so-called "one and the many." We think here of the popular collages of various world religions symbols or, at the other end of the spectrum, such things as a solitary image of water ripples intersecting with each other or of a flower with different pedals radiating from a center. Such imagery tell us much about the presumed unity that is supposed to be identified if only students dig a little beneath the surface differences. As optimistic or idealistic as such a view may strike readers, the critical scholar will understandably be a little suspicious before too quickly resolving difference into an ethereal unity, recognizing that similarity, no matter how appealing it may seem, is invariably established with regard to the specific choices and local priorities of the one carrying out the comparison. This would mean that we should perhaps be far more interested in what counts as a similarity worth nurturing, and thus a difference worth overcoming, along with the ones who make such choices, as opposed to simply assuming that there are indeed actual unities toward which the people they happen to study ought to be working.

In this volume see: creation/endtimes, evil, fundamentalism, hagiography, spirituality, theology, tradition

In *Religion in 50 Words* see: comparison, critical, essence, ideology, method, orthodoxy, phenomenology, religion, religious literacy, world religions, worldview

11 East/West

There may be no more criticized yet still frequently used scholarly designation than the habit of dividing the entire world between what is often called "the East" and "the West." This classification system—used to characterize both geography and people—is a good example of a binary pair, namely, that things can be designated as either one or the other, with no third choice possible. Male/female is yet another example of such a binary, but one that is increasingly seen as problematic given the rise of categories such as gender fluid or intersex. That such paired or binary concepts are widespread (think of us/them, citizen/foreigner, married/single, or insider/outsider) makes plain how handy they are in helping people to name, divide, and navigate their worlds. At the same time, however, we must bear in mind the inevitable failure of such designations—failures that can lead to the development either of new binaries or perhaps more nuanced and complicated options capable of representing the rather more ambiguous nature of daily life.

The two terms likely entered early Old English through the Middle Dutch, *oosten* and *west*, which both have a Germanic history, from the medieval Old Frisian *āster* and *westa*. The latter seems to derive from even earlier terms signifying the direction from which the sun rises, and the new day begins, and then sets, to end the day. This indicates the relation to the modern adjectives Oriental/Occidental and the nouns the Orient and the Occident with the first from the Latin *oriēns*, the direction of the rising sun and thus also linked the dawn or daybreak, while the second, also from Latin, *occidēns*, for the direction of the setting sun. This approach is a good example of a binary system for yet another reason: upon closer look it becomes apparent that each pole is empty and defined only by being not what its opposite is said to be, akin to the classic scientific definition of cold as the absence of heat. Daniel Boyarin provides a helpful example in the Introduction's opening line to his 2012 book, *The Jewish Gospel: The Story of the*

Jewish Christ: "If there is one thing that Christians know about their religion, it is that it is not Judaism. If there is one thing that Jews know about their religion, it is that it is not Christianity." It is for this reason that, since at least the 1500s, the use of the English terms "West" and "East" very closely parallel each other, with both becoming more or less popular in unison. Interestingly, the frequency of use of the related terms "Oriental" and "Occidental" are not nearly as closely tied, with the terms "Orient" or "Oriental" gaining far wider usage in the English-speaking world.

Contrary to popular thought, the pairing of East/West tells us little to nothing in particular about the places or people so named but tells us a great deal about the one who is using the designation. As with so many of the words discussed here, it may be more useful to ask who is using the term, and to what effect, rather than inquire as to what makes this or that "Eastern" or "Western." Consider that newcomers to this topic are usually surprised to learn that by "the Orient" Europeans once meant the Arab world or what was later termed the Near East, namely, that what is more recently termed the Middle East. For example, consider Napoleon Bonaparte's military campaign of 1798–1801 into Egypt and Syria, often described as the French invasion of the Orient. Or, again, it is worth noting that the famous Orient Express train of the late nineteenth and twentieth century, long associated with luxury and made even more famous in a well-known Agatha Christie murder mystery novel. Passengers journeyed from, among other cities, Paris to Istanbul (once known as Constantinople or even Byzantium), in modern day Turkey—a journey into the mysterious and exotic East, as its Europeans would have probably understood their trip. This link between the Orient and the onetime Ottoman Empire is all very surprising to contemporary readers since the term now names a rough grouping of peoples and cultures that includes modern countries across Asia, such as China, Japan, Korea, Vietnam, etc. These are often designated as the "Far East" as opposed to the so-called Near East or Middle East. Such geographic designations, of course, are all based as on proximity to "us," the so-called West. That this term "Orient" has demonstrated such slippage or elasticity over time makes clear that it is a term that has successfully been used to describe the unknown that lies to the east *of whomever is speaking*. Note that the adjective "oriental" can be used to describe everything from rugs made in Persia to a cuisine whose influences are traced to China.

The critique of the term "Orient" that many now take for granted, and which lies behind the above comments, gained considerable momentum in the light of the work of the literary critic Edward Said (1935–2003). His still influential book, *Orientalism* (1978), examined in detail a process whereby the European tradition of scholarship on the East—known as Orientalism or Oriental Studies—helped to define a "Western" sense of shared identity by defining it against what they called and represented as "the Orient" or "the mystic East." More than just a literary or scholarly movement, Orientalism was also a political tradition indebted to a long history of conflict between the states that became modern Europe and those regions that once constituted the Ottoman Empire. The "Oriental" thus became a handy European literary device for defining the limits of the known, the acceptable, the normal, and the safe against their opposites. Taking into account Said's strong critique of this representation, the onetime ease of naming regions as "the Orient" or accounting for human behavior by assuming it is informed by such a thing as "the Oriental mind" have become much criticized socio-political techniques. Indeed, his critique was also persuasive enough that, for many today, Orientalism no longer names an academic field but, instead, a way of Othering that is in need of critique, i.e., using stereotypes of other people, whether in or outside the Arab world, all in the service of generating a binary self-identity.

Despite the critique of Orientalism, the broad East/West distinction is still widely employed. This is evident in media and politics or in our field where we continue to see the division of world religions into Western and Eastern traditions. Witness, for example, the fifth edition of the late Will Oxtoby's edited book, *World Religions: Western Traditions* and *Eastern Traditions* (2 vols., 2018), as well as survey course titles in a variety of contemporary Departments. Therein, so-called Eastern traditions include Hinduism, Jainism, Buddhism, Taoism, Confucianism, etc., and the Western traditions are usually limited to Judaism, Christianity, and Islam. Oxtoby, in particular, found this way of dividing up the world to be useful. He writes in the opening to the book's 1996 first edition: whereas "we can speak in a fairly coherent fashion about the West and its role in the world," the East "is a hugely diverse region." Here we find traces of the old colonialist associations between identity, order, and unity, all of which are implicitly aligned with what was represented as the rationally ordered West. And, juxtaposed against this, difference, disorder, diversity, all of which are aligned with the mysterious East. After noting that we "could even go so far as to suggest that 'the East' is a Western construct, existing as a coherent entity only in the mind of the West," Oxtoby made it clear that this was going a little too far. Immediately thereafter he went on to maintain that, because Hinduism influenced Buddhism, which in turn influenced Confucianism, Taoism, and Shintoism, we should organize all of these under the rubric "East." We would do well to remember that each of these so-called discrete religions are the product of European scholarly cataloguing, likewise the region and history of the world organized by the category "West" is just as complex and varied. That this homogenizing clearly overlooks or just plain ignores such material criteria, such as economics (who owes what to whom?) and politics (who is authorized to exercise which power?) would all suggest that such a use of the traditional East/West division should have little use for a critical scholar.

In arguing for the East/West differences, Oxtoby quotes Rudyard Kipling's 1889 poem, "The Ballad of East and West":

> Oh, East is East, and West is West
> and never the twain shall meet
> Till Earth and Sky stand presently
> at God's great Judgment Seat.
> But there is neither East nor West,
> border, nor breed, nor birth
> When two strong men stand face to face,
> tho' they come from the ends of the earth!

The irony of a contemporary world religions textbook appreciatively citing Kipling is, for the critical scholar, too good to pass over without comment. He was, after all, among the most imperialistic and reactionary writers of his era and, according to Said, his works were intimately connected to the history and justification of the earlier British attempt to control, dominate, and thereby own and profit from huge expanses of the globe. Finding Kipling here of all places therefore provides evidence that scholarship often fails to recognize the manner in which its grand narratives of unity and homogeneity are far from free-floating, apolitical statements or neutral observations. One of the great perils of the field moving forward is the fact that we fail to recognize that it exists in large part due to the needs of the late nineteenth-century's imperial nations. Most importantly, this included their efforts to catalogue, understand, and control distant lands and peoples. Such investments make it difficult to imagine how one decolonializes the study of religion, as some write today, without offering a fundamental critique of the history and political function of the category religion itself.

By failing to take seriously and follow through on the implications of Said's critical work, this manner of designation reproduces, and in reproducing naturalizes, a system invested in finding some sort of essential difference between these two broad groups. This is all the more ironic when we consider the large number of scholars who today report having been influenced by his work but who yet discuss Western vs. Eastern religions as if they are natural markers. That "Western religions" are also known as the so-called Abrahamic faiths makes this comparative exercise evident, inasmuch as this latter title continues to be popular today among those involved in promoting inter-religious dialogue. Presumably this is on account of the common role played by the patriarch Abraham in each of these group's origins narratives, which is then used as a way to argue for a fundamental similarity among three groups with longstanding differences and outright conflicts of their own. That there are basic and, in some cases, irreconcilable differences within each of these three broad groupings is, of course, not entertained because it gets in the way of a good ecumenical story.

Given that religion is often presumed to be concerned with an essential and therefore transhistorical characteristic of the human, it may make sense that this one field is particularly prone to the sort of essentialized, binary logic that comes with the East/West pairing. That works like J. Lorand Matory's *The Fetish Revisited: Marx, Freud, and the Gods Black People Make* (2018) are now being written and published—works that, in this case, challenge readers to reconsider how European and North American scholars have traditionally understood Africa and its inhabitants as fundamentally different from, and less than, "the West"—is encouraging, keeping ever present for the critical scholar that seemingly neutral descriptive claims are far more complex, situated, and invested than they may at first seem. Moreover, the more recent north/south distinction—one that has, for some, replaced the post-World War II designations of first world/second world/third world—is sometimes now preferred by scholars interested in studying international issues (e.g., those who now work on something called "the global south"); this too is an encouraging sign, given how this designation is driven not by assumptions about such ethereal things as essential traits or unique regional/ethnic mentalities but, instead, by a people's access to and ownership of material resources or even social capital (e.g., Felix Wilfred's 2021 book, *Religious Identities and the Global South: Porous Borders and Novel Paths*). The moral of the story, then, is that while the analysis of any complex entity requires scholars to, quite literally, break them down into simpler parts or interrelated sub-components (the root meaning of the word "analyze" in fact), the presumptions driving such work matter.

In this volume see: dialogue, founder, icon, idol, liberation, meditation, myth, renunciation, salvation, soul

In *Religion in 50 Words* see: classification, comparison, definition, environment, history, ideology, identity, phenomenology, religious literacy, world religions

12 Emic/Etic

A well-known conflict in the study of religion is that between the perspective of the participant (whether we designate such people as "the faithful," "believers," "practitioners," etc.) and that of the scholar who studies them and their assorted cultural productions. Perhaps not surprisingly there exists a range of views on this topic. These run the gamut from scholars who are themselves members of the groups they are studying, and who thus see themselves as participating in some sort of mutual conversation with their tradition, to those scholars who may strongly disagree with the groups under study (such as those who study so-called religious extremists). This issue has traditionally been characterized as the insider/outsider problem, with the words "emic" and "etic" standing in as a more technical way of talking about issues of viewpoint, along with how the methods used by scholars can be influenced by the stance one adopts. Although there was a time when some framed the issue as being about working to achieve objectivity, and thus strict neutrality, today the issue is rather more nuanced than this. Very few scholars, including critical scholars, claim that the standard we ought to be aiming for is completely disinterested detachment. Despite recognition that interests are a slippery, ever-present thing and that perspective is inevitable, a critical scholar will probably still wish to maintain some methodological safeguards to be able to distinguish participant claims and accounts from those of scholarly ones. Whether or not these different viewpoints present a problem—as in the way this topic has traditionally been phrased—will depend on what a scholar aims to do when studying religion.

Reference to emic vs. etic positions derives from the study of linguistics, in which scholars regularly engage in the study of what they call phonemes and phonetics. Whereas we see the adjective "phonetic" enter English in the early nineteenth century, with the noun "phonetics," naming a branch of study, developing by mid-century. "Phoneme" did not appear until later in the century, credited to the Polish linguistics scholar Mikołaj Kruszewski (1851–1887) with its adjective, "phonemic," dating to the early twentieth century. Thus, in 1841 the philologist Robert Gordon Latham (1812–1888) observed that "Phonetics ... determines (amongst other things) the systematic relation of Articulate Sounds" (*The English Language*, 113). Both terms appear in English by way of French, but they ultimately derive from the much earlier Greek for speaking and making sounds—thus the now familiar English tele + phone meaning "sound over a distance," i.e., telecommunication; or a megaphone naming a loudspeaker. Although "phoneme" was once used in early twentieth century psychiatric practice to refer to auditory hallucinations (i.e., hearing voices), today it primarily refers to the most basic units of sound that are significant to language users and which they then combine to produce spoken language. The study of phonemes could then involve such things as how speakers physically produce distinguishable sounds, such as whether the vocal cords are needed to "voice" a particular sound or not. The latter includes the difference between making the sound represented by the English letter B as opposed to P, both of which also happen to rely upon passing air through both lips. Important to note is that by this is meant not the name that is given to each letter of the alphabet (such as identifying the letter T by saying "tee") but, rather, the sound itself as represented by that letter—or, sometimes, sounds, in the plural, such as the above example of the two different ways or pronouncing the E in "emic" and "etic." Should one be a speech pathologist helping a stroke patient regain the ability to speak, for example, then knowing the way that these discrete sounds are produced, and then combined into those multi-phonemic sounds that we call words, would be of considerable importance. But separate from the study of phonemes is phonetic analysis, which is the cross-cultural, comparative study of differing phonemic systems. Consider, for example, the International Phonetic Alphabet (IPA) that one often finds in the front of a good dictionary, itself dating from the late nineteenth century, which can be used as a pronunciation guide for all languages—even those which do not share the same phonemes. Anyone who has learned a different language may have experienced the difficulty of producing certain sounds that are local to the new language but foreign to one's own, such as native English speakers practicing the sound of the trilled, or rolled, R that is found in Spanish, or the ayin in Arabic that is a voiced pharyngeal fricative—the difficulty, of course, is that the English speaker's body (specifically, the muscle called their tongue) is untrained in producing such sounds. Should one be interested in human language itself as a phenomenon, thus aiming to compare languages, perhaps in search of the similarities and differences that might shed light on how humans produce speech, then one can imagine the utility of cross-cultural phonetic analysis.

And thus we arrive at the distinction that informs many scholars' use of these two suffixes. While emic refers to information of relevance or importance within any one signification system, etic names the stance of the comparativist who works outside of any one system, thus devising a way of working across them all. See, in this regard, the foundational work of the linguist and anthropologist, Kenneth L. Pike (1912–2000), such as his *Phonetics: A Critical Analysis of Phonetic Theory and a Technique for the Practical Prescription of Sounds* (1943) and *Phonemic: A Technique for Reducing Languages to Writing* (1947). Perhaps it makes sense then, that the International Phonetic Alphabet not only includes far more sounds than are present in any one language but also that the script it employs to represent distinct sounds cannot simply reproduce any one alphabet (e.g., ʃ is used for what in English is commonly written as "sh"). Whereas for many the former comes to be synonymous with the insider's or the participant's own viewpoint, the latter is frequently used by scholars to name that of the outsider or non-participant. Although we see occasional use of the suffixes earlier, it is really since the mid-twentieth century that these terms were widely adopted by scholars. It first moved from linguistics to the study of anthropology, wherein the study of culture was seen as analogous to the study of language, and then to a wide variety of other academic fields, among which would be the study of religion. In the latter field's earliest years, the comparative study of languages was often seen as the model for the comparative study of religion, e.g., in the once influential work of F. Max Müller (1823–1900). In all of these cases it is assumed that there are more ways for scholars to talk about the things that the people they study may say and do (or leave behind after they are gone) than merely repeating, describing, or paraphrasing them. If a scholar is interested in the reason why someone claims something, bringing to their analysis a theory about the workings of the psyche or society, for example, that may well be alien to the participant's own self-understanding or picture of the world, then it is rather difficult to overlook the gap between the insider's claims and those of the scholar who does not necessarily subscribe to their worldview. What scholars do about that gap—whether accept it or, perhaps, moderate and try to minimize it—is the difficulty of the so-called insider/outsider problem.

While some traditional approaches to this issue—as already indicated—were premised on the assumption that the outsider was truly objective and free of bias, it is not difficult today to find considerable push-back against such a so-called scientific or reductionist stance. This often involves the claim that either all viewpoints are equally biased or, more ambitiously, that religion is so foundational to the human that even so-called secular people or atheists have a (largely unrecognized) theology of their own—suggesting that, at the end of the day, we are all insiders. Recognizing that this one academic field houses both of these opposed perspectives led the Canadian scholar of religion, Darlene Juschka, to once conclude that the field is "[c]aught between ecumenicism (which is possibly disguised colonialism) and value-neutral objective study (which posits scientific epistemology as Truth)." Religious Studies, she goes on, "doesn't know just what it is. It suffers from the Jekyll/Hyde syndrome—either the cold observer or the impassioned participant." See her article, "Religious Studies and Identity Politics: Mythology in the Making," *Bulletin of the Council of Societies for the Study of Religion* 26 (1997): 8; reprinted as chapter 34 in Scott Elliott's useful volume, *Reinventing Religious Studies: Key Writings in the History of a Discipline* (2014). Calling this an identity crisis—a term sometimes used by others as well—aptly characterized the field throughout its history. It amounts to a periodic pendulum swing from early attempts to offer a naturalistic theory of religion's origins to some who today see the study of religion as an exercise in liberal interreligious dialogue meant to normalize certain ways of being religious and, thus, supportive of a particular type of pluralistic society.

To put a finer edge on this, it is not difficult to make the case that the insider/outsider distinction is rather misguided, or at least simplistic. The argument often goes that insiders might not actually have a perspective—at least not until the curious non-participant arrives with a question. Until then they are simply going about their life fully immersed in their world, in much the same manner that readers of this very text are more than likely not naturally or continually reflecting on the rules of their English grammar much less what it means to be literate. Thus, much like anthropologists from just a generation ago, who came to the conclusion that the thing too casually referred to as culture was actually the product of the fieldworker's and the ethnographer's queries (see the still important essay collection, *Writing Culture: The Poetics and Politics of Ethnography* [1986]), so, too, the thing we often name as the insider's perspective may turn out to be a collaborative creation with the outsider. The latter, after all, is the one who is asking the questions that elicit responses and making the choices about what to pay attention to and record as opposed to ignore and forget. In this model, description can be more about the descriptivist than the putative subject being chronicled. We could add to this that there is likely no such thing as a unified insider or outsider standpoint but, instead, that there are varying degrees of both, with members of groups often drawing internal distinctions of their own based on who is or is not thought to best represent the group. Consider, for example, claims about who is more or less patriotic that might characterize campaign commercials during a political contest, and we soon see that the emic/etic and insider/outsider designations are rather more complicated than some assume.

Given these challenges, we must constantly confront the ambiguity of social life while more than likely still working to demarcate our scholarly work from simply inhabiting or reproducing the lives of those they study. As suggested earlier, however, this line of demarcation, though criticized by some scholars in certain cases, is rarely undermined when scholars study groups for whom they and their readers feel little affinity. In the latter case the scholar will more than likely seek not just to describe, interpret, and understand others but will surely move from there to try to explain why someone could even see the world in such-and-such a manner. In these latter cases scholars would surely not see themselves as being in a conversation with those whom they study.

In this volume see: atheism/theism, commentary, conversion, East/West, spirituality, theology

In *Religion in 50 Words* see: authority, belief, critical, description, explanation, identity, method, methodological atheism, power, redescription

13 Evil

One of the most pressing questions in some of those social movements often known as religions is the existence and indeed persistence of what is commonly known as evil. In his *Fifty Key Words: Comparative Religion* (1971), Eric Sharpe (1933–2000) referred to evil as "all that makes man's tenure on the earth uncomfortable and insecure" (16). Instead of entertaining the notion of whether or not evil actually exists or what social function its articulation has, it has instead been more customary to define and redefine the concept in many and often conflicting ways over the last several millennia: as the absence or privation of good; as something morally inferior; as something natural (e.g., earthquakes); as something supernatural (e.g., those discourses that involve talk of various diabolic forces in the universe); and so on and so forth. Indeed, many still enroll in undergraduate courses in the subfield known as the Philosophy of Religion where they study various traditional theological (read: Christian) approaches to the so-called problem of evil. In such classes students are asked to ponder how an all-good and all-powerful god can let evil happen? Indeed, this problem of confusing philosophy for rehearsals of Christian theology, on the one hand, and, on the other, regimes of truth for settled truths is still a major issue that continues to plague that subfield. Though there are certainly those today attempting to globalize the philosophy of religion, to make it cross-culturally relevant, the discourses around the concept of evil only highlight such privileging even further.

Evil is yet another one of those terms that is often paired with—and, indeed, defined by—its opposite, in this case, "good." We witness this in the very definition of evil, as seen above, as that which is sometimes referred to as the "privation of good." Perhaps not surprisingly this is even the primary definition that the *Oxford English Dictionary* supplies for the term: "the privation of good in all its principle senses." We further witness this sharp juxtaposition between evil and good in the very manner in which the questions that many people who consider themselves to be religious ask and ones, moreover, to which so-called religions seek to provide satisfactory answers. These include: Why do bad things happen to good people? Why do the innocent (or the young) die prematurely? If there is an omnipotent God, then why do natural disasters (or horrific historical events, such as the Holocaust) happen? People have always had to struggle with such questions and, though they cannot solve them, they certainly try to convince others that they do. However, rather than see evil (and its opposite: good) as ontological categories that exist naturally in the world around us, naming actual qualities or values, it might be more profitable to regard them as relative terms and as part of authorizing discourses that seek to categorize the world for those who subscribe to them. Evil and good, on this reading, become convenient categories whereby a group's social world can be constructed and maintained, mapped out and perpetuated. Claims about something being either evil or good now function as terms for the maintenance of society—or, better put, certain forms of it. The issue, then, may not be so much how best to define evil, but to shine the torch back a little further to see who actually engages in defining the term, for whom and for what purposes, in addition to inquiring into what sort of social and intellectual work the term and the narratives surrounding it are meant to perform.

Perhaps because it plays such a large role in the history of Christianity—wherein it is related to everything from creation to redemption, from what is called original sin to the notion of free will vs. determinism, and from ethics and morality to punishment—the problem of evil is indeed foundational. In this regard, it is also intimately connected to the idea of "theodicy" (from the Greek, *theos* + *dike* = vindication of God or, better, divine justice), a still-used term coined by the German philosopher Gottfried Leibniz (1646–1716), which seeks to justify or defend the existence of a benevolent and all-knowing God in the light of the existence of evil. From its prominent role in the history of Christianity, evil—and such rational attempts to account for it—is then assumed by scholars to perform similar work in other religious traditions. And, once again, we witness how a term with a particular local history, like so many of the terms examined in the present work, is sublimated in such a manner that it is thought to be of universal import and significance.

In terms of etymology, the term "evil" has a very lengthy one. We arrive at our present usage by way of Middle English (*uvel*), Old English (*yfel*, which corresponds to Old Saxon *ubil*), Old Frisian, Middle Dutch (*evel*), Old High German (*ubil, upil*), which in turn seems to originate in an Old Germanic term. The earliest meaning of the term seems to refer to the idea of "up" or "over" in the sense that something that is "evil" either "exceeds due measure" or "oversteps" its proper limits. In English, the term seems to have originally circulated as an adjective meaning something that is morally depraved, wicked, or vicious. Thus, as early as 971, we read in the Blickling Homilies: "We sceolan..ure heortan clænsian from yflum geþohtum" (37). Likewise in the King James Bible (1611): "Some euill beast hath deuoured him" (Gen. 37:20); or in John Milton's (1608–1674) *Paradise Lost* (1667): "That space the Evil one abstracted stood From his own evil" (ix. 463). In all of these examples, amongst countless others, we see the adjective "evil" attached to nouns such as spirits, men, and eye. The term can also be stretched—again hearkening back to its original meaning of "exceeding" or "overstepping" a particular limit—to include a lack or even something painful. In this sense we read in John Locke (1632–1704) *An Essay Concerning Human Understanding* (1690), "We name that Evil, which is apt to produce or increase any Pain, or diminish any Pleasure in us" (ii. xx. 113). In this latter sense "evil" is not so much the opposite of "good," but of "pleasure," since evil here causes pain.

The term, thus, has many different meanings, though it would seem fair to say that the main one today—including its primary usage in the field of religious studies—would be that which is opposite of "good," including that which is believed to have the potential to subvert religion. This is borne out by its usage over the last two centuries, where the term appears much more frequently over the early to mid-nineteenth century. We read, for example, in the opening lines of *Putting Away Evil: The Great Essential of Religion in Four Sermons* (1820), by Rev. John Clowes (1743–1831), an English Cleric and Fellow of King's College Cambridge:

> Every considerate person, who has been accustomed to any degree of spiritual reflection, must needs have discovered that evil is the great and only enemy of man. He must needs have seen, that it is evil alone which separates man from God, and God from man.
>
> (2)

Likewise in John Wesley's (1703–1791) posthumously published *The Cure of Evil Speaking: A Sermon on Matthew XVIII: 15, 16, 17* (1829):

> But who, even among Christians regards this command [i.e., "Speak evil of no man"]? Yea, how few are there that so much as understand it? What is evil-speaking? It is not, as some suppose, the same with lying or slandering.
>
> (3)

In all of these examples, and there are quite literally hundreds of them, "evil" is often left undefined. Authors instead prefer to let the term speak for itself, as it were, by putting it in stark juxtaposition with the "good," which, more often than not, is connected to the religious position from which they speak. That there are such different definitions should lead us to the conclusion that evil functions less as something that is part of the natural world (i.e., the privation of good) so much as it does a rhetorical device, one that signals a set of values presumed to be shared by writer and reader. Indeed, the term is often associated with morality, often synonymous with "rightness" or "goodness," the latter being a term that signifies a system or a code of conduct whereby a particular social group defines what is good. What is wrong, of course, is often signified as "evil" or at least as somehow connected to evil. Though systems of morality differ from culture to culture, each one imagines its own system of morality as grounded in the natural order of things. And though philosophers and ethicists spend considerable time devoted to ascertaining morality and the ethical principles derived therefrom, we must be aware that morality—like any other discourse—attempts to authorize certain actions over others. Unfortunately too little time is devoted to the material conditions from which systems of morality derive and develop their normativity.

A case in point is *The Symbolism of Evil* (1967), by Paul Ricoeur (1913–2005), the French philosopher and professor at the University of Chicago's Divinity School from 1970–1985. In this work, Ricoeur asks, What is the nature of human will that succumbs to evil? Since the question of evil, for him at least, is inscrutable, he argues that the only way to understand the concept or the principle is through a study of its portrayal in myths and symbols. In good phenomenological fashion, Ricoeur—not unlike his interlocuter at the University of Chicago, Mircea Eliade (1907–1986)—maintains that such symbols function as ciphers through which one can have access to otherwise inaccessible, and thus inexpressible, truths. Using very Christian terms, Ricoeur argues that it is ultimately our own infallibility that leads to the propensity on the part of humans to engage in evil (again left underdefined), but that such a propensity also makes goodness possible (e.g., 247–250).

As we see yet again with this fairly well-known example from Ricoeur, the discussion of evil, and the morality that is believed to help either elevate or bypass it, is heavily grounded in Christian claims. Other groups we commonly designate as religions, for example, do not have nearly as complex a discourse, at least where the problem of evil is concerned. In addition to such philosophical (read: theological) works, we also see more historical studies on how evil is understood, but again this is often done in the context of the Christian context. Thus, in his *The Problem of Evil in Plotinus* (1912), Benjamin Apthorp Gould Fuller (1879–1956) writes that the third century Hellenistic philosopher "Plotinus goes on to say that Evil is not 'Not-being' in the sense in which rest and motion are Not-Being" (227). In the present we still witness works written on evil, but again still largely from a Christian perspective—again reinforcing our claim that this is a term with a particular history in a particular tradition. Thus: John Peter Kenney's *On God, The Soul, Evil and the Rise of Christianity* (2018) or Kevin L. Flannery's *Cooperation with Evil: Thomistic Tools of Analysis* (2019).

There certainly have been some attempts to deal with the issue of evil in other religious traditions. In her *The Origins of Evil in Hindu Mythology* (1976) the noted University of Chicago scholar, Wendy Doniger (then Wendy Doniger O'Flaherty), seeks to show how, contrary to popular opinion, Indians and Hindus do indeed possess a complex sense of evil. While we do not doubt that in the slightest—what culture, after all, does not deal with questions of good/bad and the idea of injustice—the fact that she spends her introduction discussing the term—and theodicy—shows to just what an extent she cannot help but use a loaded Western (read: Christian) term to understand others. Such intellectual contortions, we maintain, play a very significant role throughout the history of the study of religion, wherein we either think that European- or Christian-derived terms are necessarily universal, or we expend considerable energy forcing the terms and concepts of other peoples to conform to them (such as asking, "How do they say 'God'?" or "What's the Buddhist bible?"). Another more promising attempt to engage the issue of evil, less from a Christocentric point of view, may be found in Rivka Ulmer's *The Evil Eye in the Bible and in Rabbinic Literature* (1994). She takes a more folkloristic approach, connecting the idea of the "evil eye" (i.e., a gaze that conveys ill-will and bad consequence) in the Bible and early rabbinic literature using contemporary Middle Eastern folklore as opposed the Christian theological tradition.

This obsession with evil and the overwhelming treatment of the term in secondary literature associated not just with Christianity should force a critical scholar to pause and wonder why this largely Christian term is so easily thought to perform cross-cultural work. Though it has been used to examine other groups, past and present, such attempts unsurprisingly tend to resort to the default position of the intellectual tradition that gave evil—and the discourses surrounding it—such a pride of place. If so much of that tradition has been based on defining it in opposition to the good, the holy, or even the sacred, then evil becomes that which subverts. Rather than pay attention to why, when, by whom, and in what contexts such subversions are thought to happen, there is the unfortunate tendency to proceed *as if* the term "evil" actually named something. A more productive way to proceed, we submit, is to see narratives around the problem of evil as acts of authorizing discourses meant to define what is proper and allowable for members of a community. The discourse on evil, as in its earlier meaning, is very much concerned with limits and identifying anything that surpasses them. Thus, the designation tells us much about how a group ought to function by naming those occasions when it has failed. But to make such inquiries, scholars need to look beyond the claims to the discourse itself, in order to see who is producing, for whom, and for what purposes.

In this volume see: afterlife, atheism/theism, creation, god, monotheism/polytheism, myth, piety, renunciation, salvation, soul, theology

In *Religion in 50 Words* see: authority, classification, comparison, definition, ideology, interpretation, politics, power, worldview

14 Founder

As identified in a variety of other entries, the early years of the study of religion—in the late nineteenth century, when it was called either the science of religion or just comparative religion—saw a number of scholars draw upon their long-established familiarity with certain forms of Christianity. They, then, used this as the prototype to understand new and therefore unfamiliar peoples with whom they, working in universities across Europe, first came into contact through the reports and letters sent back from a wide variety of colonial outposts by those involved in the era's various imperial exercises. One of the first things that they did was ask the question "Do they have a religion?" This, of course, was influenced by the effort to find analogies to Christianity—an effort that is quite understandable, given that we all have little choice but to understand the unknown in the light of the known. The various features of others' religions were then expected to align with what Western, and largely Christian, scholars were familiar. Thus, we arrive at assorted research questions from the era: Do "they" believe in God? How do "they" understand sin? What text plays the role of the Bible for "them"? Do "they" believe in the afterlife? What is "their" way of grappling with the problem of evil? The trouble with all of this, of course, was that the prototype was not seen as a handy or even a temporary starting point but, rather, was ontologized (given the impression of permanence and thus authority) and thus held rather tightly by those scholars, as if it was the unquestioned, universal standard against which all others were not just compared but, sooner or later, judged as wanting when they failed to meet it.

Common among these prototypes was the assumption that, as with the role said to have been played by Jesus of Nazareth, all religions must have founders. That is, they must all possess individuals who first established the religion, as either the source or target of some type of divine revelation, and who, having various followers, were responsible for inspiring its expansion. That the story Christians still routinely tell themselves about the establishment and early growth of Christianity drove this should be obvious. Indeed, it drove the early designation of something that was once called an historical religion, a term of some prominence in the late nineteenth century. Namely those that, to quote from John Macpherson's English translation of Julius F. Räbiger's *Encyclopedia of Theology* (1884), "represent themselves as having a historical commencement, but that trace back their origin to a divine act" (vol. 1, 188). Despite Räbiger assuming, as was not unusual at the time, that Christianity was the absolute and thus highest expression of religion, it was gradually becoming clear that it was hardly alone in authenticating itself by means of claims concerning a founder who could (whether accurately or not, we had better add) be dated and thereby placed in historical time. The other group readily admitted to being a member of the family of world religions, when this latter category was first devised by later nineteenth-century Dutch and German scholars—in distinction to what were termed merely national religions (i.e., those that failed to expand beyond their original territory) were Boddhists, as the term was often written in the mid-nineteenth century. The latter were understood as a group whose members equally laid claim to an historical founder, known prior to his so-called enlightenment as Prince Siddharth Gautama, who was often said to have lived in what is today northeast India sometime around the sixth to fifth century BCE. His selfless acts and renunciations were said to have led to his complete liberation from historical existence, earning for him the honorary title of the one who has awakened, or the Buddha. Thus, in 1893, none other than F. Max Müller (1823–1900) would also understand "Buddhism as an historical religion." See his essay "Esoteric Buddhism" in *The Eclectic Magazine: Foreign Literature, Science, and Art* 58/1 (July): 65, a judgment shared by James. G. Frazer (1854–1941), such as in his once well-known work, *The Golden Bough: A Study in Comparative Religion* (1890), vol. 1, 59.

"Founder" in English dates to the fourteenth century and has the specific sense of a creator, that is, one who establishes or institutes something. The noun "foundation" comes soon after—with both deriving from the Old English "found," which in turn derives from the Latin *fundus* for the bottom or basis of something. Commonly associated with identifying something as a religion with an historical founder were assumptions concerning how these religions then developed, or were built up, over time. Given that they were understood to have begun with a person, their expansion from there inevitably involved what was once portrayed as a dilution or even pollution. A classic example of this may be found in the work of the early and still cited US psychologist of religion, William James (1942–1910), who writes in his *The Varieties of Religious Experience: A Study in Human Nature* (1905):

> as a rule, religious geniuses attract disciples, and produce groups of sympathizers. When these groups get strong enough to "organize" themselves, they become ecclesiastical institutions with corporate ambitions of their own. The spirit of politics and the lust of dogmatic rule are then apt to enter and to contaminate the originally innocent thing.
>
> (334–335)

We could also cite what is now a less well remembered source, an entry in James Hastings's *A Dictionary of Christ and the Gospels* (1906) written by Rev. William Morgan: "That the stream of religion flows purer at its fountainhead than at its lower reaches is a fact which the study of every historical religion confirms." As he goes on: "As a religion advances through history, it loses something of its idealism and becomes more secular, takes up foreign elements, accumulates dogmas and ceremonies, parts with its simplicity and spontaneity, and becomes more and more a human construction" (vol. 1, 165). What should be apparent is that the attribution of origins to a person—i.e., those who presumably possess the "originally innocent" inspiration—is then followed by the stifling effect of institutionalization, presupposes an unarticulated view on how groups work over time. This is certainly a highly individualist model of society, one common to much early and even contemporary scholarship, but one not without its flaws. Critics, for example, will refer to this as the so-called great man view of history (with most of these influential figures predictably said to have been males), a view once championed as accurately representing historical development—thus, much history-writing has focused on biographies or studies of an era's leading figures. Today, however, it is seen by critical scholars as a highly troublesome approach, in that it grossly simplifies social life by representing it as if it were the result of charismatic, lone actors. But is this the model of society with which a scholar ought to work? We can, instead, turn this understanding on its head and see the discourse on charismatic, lone actors as itself being a social phenomenon. Thus, when we hear tales about rugged or inspired individuals as socially formative, then both the primary focus on any group's supposed founder, let alone assumptions of the group subsequent deteriorating, to whatever extent, as it later becomes institutionalized, will be seen as an insufficient approach when writing about a group's beginnings and its changes over time.

For example, in this alternative approach, scholars will pay more attention to the many social actors and various social situations required to be able to think that a solitary individual started anything from scratch. Now, origins tales are seen as suspect inasmuch as they are understood as hindsight projects of a present whose members seek to legitimize their familiar by means of a historical narrative that portrays their present as an inevitable development from an authoritative past. With this in mind, the so-called founder who appears in an origins narrative is therefore best understood as a construct of the tale's present, a device to personify its varied members' interests as if those qualities were unified and present when the group itself first began. Moreover, it will now be assumed that every social world develops from a prior social world, and never from lone social actors—though later members of the group may find it advantageous to speak of the past as if it was the domain of influential individuals. Now those considered as individuals will be understood as but the iceberg tip of a world linguistic and cultural conventions inherited from its own past. This makes the so-called founder or great man merely a representative instance of a far more complex social situation that is best understood as always being a collaborative endeavor. Such an endeavor is comprised of, on the one hand, a variety of agents with diverse interests and, on the other, non-agential social structures that provide the conditions in which social life takes place.

If this is the approach adopted by the critical scholar, then tales of a religion's founder will themselves become our focus, instead of seeing them as something to be either trusted or possibly confirmed by yet more archeological or textual data.

In this volume see: commentary, East/West, evil, icon, idol, magic, spirituality, theology

In *Religion in 50 Words* see: authenticity, comparison, explanation, history, phenomenology, religion, text, world religions

15 Fundamentalism

Fundamentalism is yet another one of those terms with a very large semantic range despite the fact that many scholars employ it as if it were obvious what it means. While it traditionally refers to those Christians who desired to return to the "fundamentals" of their tradition, especially in early twentieth century America, it is now often used cross-culturally, to refer to any religious group that believes in, for example, a strict or literal interpretation of scripture. This is then expanded to include so-called religious extremists, those who are imagined to engage in a form of practice and overt political or even violent intervention that defies the longstanding assumption that religion ought to be about belief and not action. As with any term, however, we should be careful to examine where it came from, and, just as importantly, what sort of intellectual work it purports to do. That it is yet again a term that originated in one tradition, Christianity, and is then thought to be exportable to help scholars to understand other groups is certainly telling. By now, we hope readers are becoming aware that such movement often only goes in one direction. Terms with their points of origin in Christianity are used to understand—some would argue distort—the beliefs and practices of others, but the same thing rarely occurs in the opposite direction. So, while we might have no problem talking about a "Muslim fundamentalist," indeed we read and hear about this term on an almost daily basis— even more so, paradoxically, than we have traditionally heard the term "Christian fundamentalist"—we never, ever hear the term "Christian *salafi*." Note that the foreign-ness of that latter term is highlighted by the fact that we traditionally put it in italics or spell it with diacritics (e.g., *al-salaf al-ṣāliḥ*, "the pious predecessors")—the Arabic term to refer to the first three generations of Muslims, to whom so-called "Muslim fundamentalists" or "Muslim salafis" seek to return.

Etymologically, the term "fundamentalism" is fairly new (with the popular "-ism" suffix, referring to, among other things, a system), dating to roughly the beginning of the nineteenth century, though its root—"fundamental"—certainly goes back much earlier, at least to the fifteenth century. As an adjective, "fundamental" comes from the post-classical Latin *fundamentalis*, which denotes a foundation or a base, that which is imagined to be indispensable. In terms of the former we read in Reginald Pecock's (ca. 1392–ca.1459) *Book of Faith* (ca. 1456): "Forto leene to Holi Writt as for grounding and foundamental teching of thilk faith" (235, quoting the 1909 edition). In terms of the latter we read in *Medela Medicinae, a Plea for the Free Profession, and Renovation of the Art of Physick, Out of the Noblest and Most Authentick Writers...: tending to the rescue of mankind from the tyranny of diseases, and of physicians themselves, from the pedanism of old authors and present dictators* (1665) by Marchamont Nedham (1620–1678), a republican journalist during the English Civil War: "For [the Disease] yet continues, not in that open hostility it exercised before, but more treacherously and slily insinuates it self into the internal and fundamental parts of the Body" (ii. 36).

When we attach the suffix to the term, the idea of a foundation, grounding, or basis remains, though it is important to note it referred originally and explicitly to the teachings of Protestant Christianity, particularly in the US. In this sense, "fundamentalism"—as well as the adjective "fundamentalist," sometimes capitalized, whose increasing usage across the twentieth century predictably mirrors that of "fundamentalism"—refers to an organization, stance, or attitude that involves such things as strict adherence to doctrines and practices claimed to be *fundamental* to that tradition. These include a belief in the inerrancy of scripture and a literal acceptance of the Bible's creeds and principles. We witness this repeatedly outlined in the once influential, multi-author collection, *The Fundamentals: A Testimony to the Truth* (published between 1910 and 1915). The term also comes to designate a social and political movement among various Protestant denominations in the United States in the early part of the twentieth century. Historically, the movement is generally acknowledged to have arisen to counter what were perceived to be the pernicious effects on Christian life by the secular forces associated with liberalism and modernism. The latter could include such things as so-called higher criticism of the Bible, i.e., reading it more like an historical text. Thus we read in the Texas newspaper, *The Fort Worth Star-Telegram*:

> It is evident to every thing individual that the need of the age is not sensationalism, but fundamentalism. There never was a time

when the fundamentals of God's eternal word were needed more to be heralded from every pulpit as at this very moment.
(February 16, 1912)

In his *Religion Yesterday & Tomorrow* (1925), Kirsopp Lake (1872–1946), the church historian, writes that "[t]here has been in America some surprise at the sudden rise of Fundamentalism in the last five years" (63). Both of these sources reveal fundamentalism to be both Protestant and specifically American. In the 1980s we gradually begin to see this largely self-designated Christian term—which incidentally had originally been used positively by so-called Protestant fundamentalists—to transform into the now largely pejorative term used to describe other extremist and thus potentially dangerous movements linked to religious foundations or rationales. For example, in 1981, in London's *Observer* newspaper we read about "[t]he new, or rather very old, Islam, the dangerous fundamentalism revived by the ayatollahs and their admirers" (September 27, 1981). Or, again in 1984 in London's *The Times*, another newspaper: "It is this very process that has helped ignite the fires of Sikh fundamentalism, rather as Shiite fundamentalism was sparked off by the forces of modernization in Iran" (April 27, 1984). We now begin to see the time when the terms "Muslim fundamentalist" and "Islamic fundamentalism" begin to be used with increasing frequency in English journalism and scholarship.

Not all early uses of "fundamentalism" to denote certain Protestant movements were positive. The pejorative sense was there almost from the start, such as in Horace James Bridges's *The God of Fundamentalism and Other Studies* (1925). This work contrasts his own idea of what he calls "Ethical Religion" with that of religious fundamentalism, which he describes as having "all the sincerity of ignorance, all the zeal of bigotry, and all the radically unethical dogmatism which springs, and must spring, from the worship of mere Power divorced from the obligations of Right" (x). Indeed, the use of the term in the 1920s can be seen as at the forefront of what would come to be known as the American cultural wars. We, thus, see the term used differently by different groups, each with their own purposes or interests. In the pages of the volume 1 of the 1923 *American Review*, for example, we read—obviously in response to readers' complaints—that a

> reviewer is in sympathy with fundamentalism is not an editorial oversight .... The struggle between what is known as liberal and historical Christianity is one of the important struggles in America today. But it is carried on very largely in an intellectual fog.

> The *American Review* has no desire to support fundamentalism against liberalism.
>
> (756)

The question, then, becomes: how did this particular term, with a specific history in American political culture, then go on to become what is today imagined, for all intents and purposes, to be a universal category that can be deployed to understand any group that is deemed to be out of sync with modernity?

It would seem that since it was ready at hand to describe what many scholars of religion were already familiar with, it was only "natural" that it would be useful as the basis for identifying analogies overseas. The term was easily exported in order to help them understand differences within other religious traditions (e.g., the so-called orthodox vs. extremists). Such exportation, however, often leads to problems. For example, the fundamentals for which a segment of American Protestant argued were (and are) largely the following: the infallibility of scripture; Jesus's virgin birth; the historical veracity of his miracles; his death as an atonement for human sin; and his subsequent physical resurrection. It should be clear, then, that the term "fundamentalism," originally means some rather specific things, of relevance to some rather specific people. When we then take the term—and all the baggage that travels in its wake—and apply it to other traditions that have no conception of these specific doctrines, there is bound to be slippage. Yet, rather than pay attention to gaps, scholars usually just paper thinly over and ignore them. Thus, we hear talk of "Jewish fundamentalism," "Islamic fundamentalism" (though now eclipsed by other more preferred terms, such as "jihadism"), "Hindu fundamentalism," and the like. But while the adjective might locate the noun in various geographic and cultural locales, we are surely no clearer on the meaning let alone the contents of that noun. Indeed, we might even go so far as to argue that the same noun used in all these cases actually succeeds in deferring, and never settling, meaning as opposed to clarifying it on account of the fact that the noun, "fundamentalism," has now become far too vague.

Despite such methodological problems—problems which tend not to bother many scholars who deal with religion, we should note—there has been a general tendency to use the term as if it names something tangible that exists naturally in the world, awaiting only our recovery efforts. We witness, for example, numerous attempts to imagine the category as a useful comparative (and thus universal) scholarly tool. In his *Fundamentalism* (2nd ed., 2008), for example, Steve Bruce all too neatly tries to create a typology of fundamentalism by showing how

American Protestant fundamentalism differs from its Islamic counterpart. "We could describe the communal fundamentalism of Islam as pre-modern," he writes," and the individualist Protestant fundamentalism as modern" (9). Such a tidy differentiation, presumably based on the essentialist characteristics of some name-less Muslims "over there" and individualized Protestants "here," problematically differentiates between communal and individual on the one hand, and pre-modern and modern on the other. In so doing, it also seeks to distinguish—and this is a common theme in much of the literature dealing with "fundamentalism"—what American fundamentalists do and say versus what "militantly" fundamentalist Muslims do and say.

Perhaps the best example that imagines the term to be universal is in the once influential "Fundamentalism Project," which brought together an international team of scholars—under the general direction of the US scholars, Martin E. Marty and R. Scott Appleby—to investigate what were seen as conservative religious movements throughout the world. It was funded by the American Academy of Arts and Sciences, and ran from 1987 to 1994, producing a five-volume series of multi-authored books, with titles such as *Fundamentalisms Observed* (vol.1 [1991]), *Fundamentalisms and the State: Remaking Polities, Economies, and Militance* (vol. 3 [1993]), and *Fundamentalisms Comprehended* (vol. 5 [1995]). Note how the plural, "fundamentalisms," is now used in all of these titles, presumably as a way to signal that they are not all the same thing. However, the fact that they are all named by the one term, all comprising but local varieties, certainly denotes that they are all connected to one another (perhaps in some sort of essence/manifestation type of relationship). Even more problematic, and once again, showing just how troublesome the term is, is the fact that, as general editors, Marty and Appleby seek to bring together and then compare anything—any tradition, any text, and cultural group—that resembles what they have in mind as "fundamentalist." Roman Catholic traditionalism, for example, sits awkwardly next to Confucian revivalism, which in turn sits, equally awkwardly, next to chapters on political fundamentalism and new religious movements in Japan. The overwhelming majority of the contributors to these volumes simply assume "fundamentalism" to be an inductively generated and thus useful analytic category that is of obvious universal application. This lack of self-reflexivity—on the part of many of the authors and the editors—means that any sort of theoretical utility to the term and the approach is lost.

This, we suggest, is not good grounds for a comparative framework. The latter, as Jonathan Z. Smith (1938–2017) has repeatedly reminded his readers, ought to proceed along lines of theorizing difference as much as search for similarity. For if any two items are *seen as* comparable—in the sense that they can be placed by the comparativist into a variety of possible relationships, that make evident both similarities and differences—then the question is why should scholars regard one similarity at the expense of a variety of other differences. Too much work on comparative fundamentalism unfortunately works precisely on this model of sameness as opposed to difference. The result is that scholarly *choices* to place just this beside just that, and in this particular way, often recede into the background, allowing the similarities to appear to be obvious or natural.

In his *Holy Terrors: Thinking About Religion After September 11* (2003), Bruce Lincoln avoids the term "fundamentalism" altogether and, instead, opts to use the term "religious maximalism," which he, in turn, differentiates from "religious minimalism." Lincoln locates this distinction in the Enlightenment, which witnessed the desire to curtail the influence of religion in the public sphere—a process or set of processes that led to the foundation of the modern, secular nation-state (57–58). The establishment of the social relations and regulations characteristic of the modern nation were thus linked to the desire to have those claims, actions, and institutions designated as religious play a "minimalist" role in civil, social life, with it instead confined largely to the realms of aesthetics and ethics. Such curtailment, Lincoln argues, led to a backlash and the rise of various groups highly critical of the perceived immortality, sexual depravity, and moral laxity that emerged in society at large from religion's marginalization. Such groups, desiring a "maximalist" role for religion in society, seek to reintroduce it whenever and wherever they can and—depending on the group and the context in which it exists—by a variety of means. This approach—one that is anchored in the rise of the modern nation and the socio-political devises used to manage and assert difference—would seem to be much more useful, and thus preferable, for the critical scholar aiming to study those groups that others have traditionally grouped together as "fundamentalists." For, throughout its history, the term has clearly been indicative of a variety of clashes between competing sub-groups, suggesting that the context and stakes of these contests is far more important to examine than identifying the supposedly essential characteristics of just one of its parties.

In this volume see: church, civil religion, cult, god, salvation, sect, theology, value

In *Religion in 50 Words* see: authenticity, canon, comparison, critical, essence, history, ideology, interpretation, lived religion, orthodoxy, politics, redescription, secular, worldview

16 God

It is rather tempting to follow the lead of the entry for "God, Goddess" in Jonathan Z. Smith's edited *HarperCollins Dictionary of Religion* and offer what some might find to be an alarmingly succinct entry for this topic. There, we read that it is a "common term for the supreme deity" (1995, 389). While we probably should not speculate on the reason for that resource's curiously short entry, our guess is that a point was being made to keep the reader's attention on studying religion *as a human institution* rather than offering a detailed entry that may confirm the longstanding assumption that religion was instead all about divine beings. After all, as noted elsewhere in this volume, the still common definition of religion as belief in a god makes plain that to study religion requires one mainly to study two things: the subject and the object of such beliefs, i.e., believers and their gods. World religions textbooks, for example, will often devote considerable space to detailing these beliefs and the characteristics of these beings. But should scholars make a critical shift and, instead, see those institutions known as religions to be nothing more or less than historical, cultural artifacts, *like any other institution*, then their attention will likely move beyond believers and their gods. It will instead shift to those situations and discourses in which otherwise complex social agents are reduced to what seems to be disembodied believing minds (or hearts) that are preoccupied with their divinities. Following the early sociologist, Emile Durkheim (1858–1917), scholars will translate—as J.Z. Smith would have phrased it—people's various claims about their gods into the language of social theory, reading "God" as a (intended or not) coded reference to the collective group itself, along with what its members think to be their own society's collective needs and expectations.

Such a shift takes us away from theorizing about God or the gods, since neither are available for empirical study. Indeed, whether or not such things as divine beings exist should not even be a question that

DOI: 10.4324/9781003196631-17

is entertained in the critical study of religion, despite old school philosophers of religion being much interested in studying the so-called logical proofs for the existence of God. The latter might not be all that surprising given that sub-field's traditional adoption of many of its themes directly from the history of Christian theology. What critical scholars have available to them, instead, is the discourses developed by situated actors, always working in structured settings, who make such claims, something that can be studied in terms of who claims what and for what practical effect. In this way, we recall the famous opening line of Alexander Pope's (1688–1744) poem, "An Essay on Man, Epistle II," though quoting it here with rather more irony than Pope surely intended, along with a recognition of the now problematic discourse on Man which is its cornerstone: "Know then Thy-felf, prefume not God to scan; The only Science of Mankind is Man" (5, quoting the 1733 first edition).

So, the challenge is to resist too easily adopting the participant's stance, no matter how familiar it may seem to them. Many scholars of religion, after all, are still trained in settings where so-called God-talk is routine and therefore very familiar, from worship services commonly revolving around claims about a God to such ritualized pronouncements as the old phrase "God bless you," such as after hearing a sneeze, let alone its opposite, saying, in frustration, "goddammit" (a request, dating to the early eighteen century, for divine damnation of something or someone). Though people today saying the latter two phrases likely do not think much about each being a request for an all-powerful being to act. In just this way, such God-talk is possibly so routine today as to prompt many scholars to imagine it to be intellectually uninteresting. We can see this in the ease with which some scholars translate various designations for such beings, as if they are all manifestations of the same being and thus belief system. Case in point, local references to an all-powerful divine being in Islam, widely known as "Allah" (also used by Arabic-speaking Christians, by the way, but for a different conception of deity, of course) are often translated for English readers simply as "God" and thus: "The name of God among Muslims and Arabic people in general" (quoting the definition now offered by the *Oxford English Dictionary*). But more careful scholars may draw attention to the fact that the uppercase noun "God"—a word of Germanic origin, with versions in such other languages as German, Dutch, Icelandic, Swedish, Danish, etc., that is evidenced in early Old English about fourteen hundred years ago— has come to mean, for the vast majority of people, a very particular thing. While it of course does not have to signify this, especially for scholars who are free to re-define their terms with precision and sometimes in novel ways, the word today so frequently carries (often implicitly) specific Christian assumptions—from a being constituted by what is known as the trinity to its role in creating the universe, periodically intervening in human affairs, judging souls at the end of their physical life, and so on—that much can be lost when a scholar asserts that "Allah" is "the name of God in Islam." For the differences across communities is thereby flattened, and, as evidenced in the work of the Irish Bible scholar, Máire Byrne, and her book, *The Names of God in Judaism, Christianity, and Islam* (2011) or, before her, the bestselling British writer on such topics, Karen Armstrong (such as her work, *A History of God* [1993]), an effort to promote a particular sort of liberal theology is evidenced, at least among what such authors often refer to as the major monotheistic or so-called Abrahamic faiths. In fact, the subtitle to Byrne's book, *A Basis for Interfaith Dialogue*, makes this all too apparent.

Such efforts to achieve the ends for which only one of many theological positions' advocates cannot be confused with the critical study of religion. The latter is, instead, an academic pursuit that works not only to avoid adopting the stance of those under study but also to highlight the privilege that allows only some groups to presume their claims and ways can be universalized as if they are shared by everyone. To return to the above example, it may be obvious to readers that, of the two terms for a divine being (each with overlapping but yet also differing traits, according to those who use the terms), only "God" has such wide application for most speakers. To rephrase: most readers of this entry would likely be rather surprised to be told something like "God is the name given to Allah by English-speaking Christians" (to turn the OED's approach to defining "Allah" on its head—an approach that authorizes one word as foundational or normative by identifying local or regional variants and translations). This is because, for many readers of this text, the term "Allah" more than likely carries such specific (and, given the prominence of Islamophobia for many today, probably worrisome) connotations that it is impossible for them to elevate the term—as they routinely do with "God"—as the designation for an entire category of beings. That the divine beings discussed by other groups of people are often part of a busy pantheon of beings (from the Olympian gods of ancient Greece to their subsequent Roman counterparts to the many gods of India) makes it all the easier for English speakers to reinforce "God" or, as we just did, "god." The uppercase does significant honorific but also theological work—as the best way to organize them all, confident that saying something like Zeus or Shiva "is the name of God among Christians" constitutes what philosophers would call a category mistake (in that the former two are seen as sub-types of the latter, and thus not to be conflated with it).

That scholars sometimes so easily overlook that using "God" to translate the claims and designations of others *is equally a category mistake* is the issue that we need to keep in mind. Resisting this temptation requires not just their adoption of a rigorously anthropocentric orientation (i.e., their studies centered on human beings and their institutions) but their ability to distance themselves from what may be a commonplace of their own culture and upbringing. In fact, a degree of alienation from the familiar—something achieved by means of cross-cultural and non-evaluative comparative analysis, as many in the history of the field have argued—is likely a requirement for all critical scholarship.

In this volume see: afterlife, church, cult, evil, idol, myth, pilgrimage, prayer, priest/prophet, reformation, ritual, sacrifice, soul, theology

In *Religion in 50 Words* see: authority, belief, definition, identity, phenomenology, religion, world religions

17 Hagiography

The term hagiography, at least in contemporary parlance, has two distinct, even contradictory, meanings. The first refers to the genre, often dating to the medieval period, of writing the biography of a saint. The second meaning is more pejorative and refers to an overly adulatory or over-the-top style of writing about another person, often in such a manner that presents the subject in highly idealized and often a politically expedient manner. The two senses are certainly related to one another, but this similarity is also revealing in the sense that it shows how something in a religious (or even religious studies) context may be framed positively but from a more critical perspective such representations become rather problematic. The question, then, becomes: what to do with hagiographies? Should we treat them, as many seem to, as historical—or, perhaps, even semi-historical—accounts of actual people who lived long ago? Or do we treat them as literary fictions that are full of back-projections, wish fulfilments, and historical inaccuracies? If the latter is the case, then perhaps we should regard hagiographies as functioning as works of propaganda used to justify and otherwise legitimate certain particular positions (e.g., pro-clerical). In other words, can we read hagiographies as socially formative tales?

The issue of hagiographies also brings up that of saints. While some may tend to think of saints as synonymous with Roman Catholicism, the term—like so many whose origins lie within Christianity—has also been extended to refer to other groups. It is therefore often applied, for example, to the study of Islam where it is used to refer to Sufi "saints" (*awliyā*, a plural term that is better translated as "friends" or "companions"). Many Muslims, for example, pray to and through Sufi saints, make pilgrimages to their shrines for rain, fertility, etc. This is especially interesting when we tend to portray Islam in the classroom as an exclusively monotheistic tradition. In addition, hagiographies have also been written about the ancient Jewish rabbis recounted in,

DOI: 10.4324/9781003196631-18

for example, the Mishnah and the Talmuds. We also see saint-like characteristics applied to various historical and even fictional Hindu and Buddhist figures. So, while saints and the idea of saintship has been stretched from its original Christian context to become yet another seemingly universal and cross-cultural category, we should not forget that it is ultimately a term that possesses a distinct valence—like so many of our academic terms—that comes out of one particular religion and which is then assumed to perform useful intellectual work by helping us understand other key aspect of yet other traditions. Whether or not such local concepts can be pressed to do such general work is a matter of considerable debate, of course. For such understandings, some might add, may be less about finding cross-cultural patterns and more the result of colonialist and Orientalist contortions (what some term taxonomic, categorical, or epistemic violence).

Despite such caveats, etymologically the term "hagiography" derives from two Greek terms: *hagios* (holy) and *graphos* (writing). A hagiography is, thus, literally a sacred writing. The term, however, has a fairly modern provenance, dating to the first half of the nineteenth century. Though it is perhaps worth noting that the term "hagiographa" was used much earlier in English, as early as the seventeenth century, to denote the last of the three divisions of the Hebrew Scriptures. In Hebrew, this division is known as *Ketuvim* or "writings," as distinct from what is termed the Law (*Torah*) and the Prophets (*neviim*). Thus, we read the Church of England clergyman and author Francis Roberts's (1609–1675), in his *Clavis Bibliorum: The Key of the Bible, Unlocking the Richest Treasury of the Holy Scriptures* (1649): "The Hebrews dividing the whole Scripture into three parts, viz., The Law, the Prophets, and Hagiographa" (501, from the second edition). As far as the term hagiography is concerned, while the actual writing of so-called biographies of Christian saints dates to at least the late antique period, it was only with the development of distinct genres—something that the political scientist and south Asianist, Benedict Anderson (1936–2015) argues in his widely influential book, *Imagined Communities* (1983), was a distinct feature of the rise of the modern national consciousness—that such biographies could be labelled as such. Interestingly, some of the earliest usages of the term were pejorative, written by Protestant authors to talk about what they demeaned as "Romish" traditions. Consider Robert Southey (1774–1843), a poet and reviewer, stating in an 1821 issue of the *Quarterly Review* that: "Such tales as these are common in Romish hagiography" (476). The implication, of course, being that Roman Catholicism is less about an unmediated relationship between believer and God (as early Protestant reformers might have described the true essence of religion) and more about various intermediaries as devised by the Vatican in Rome. As early as 1856, we also see the term applied to the Islamic world, as in the English Congregational minister and writer, Robert Alfred Vaughan's (1823–1857) *Hours with Mystics: A Contribution to the History of Religious Opinion*: "In the hagiography ... of the Mohammedan world" (II.4, from 1860's second revised edition). Interestingly, a bridge between such popular usage and the academic study of religion comes by way of the person generally considered to be one of the founders of the field, Friedrich Max Müller (1823–1900), a scholar of Hinduism and the comparative study of religion; in his essay collection, *Chips from a German Workshop*, he wrote of a particular individual saying that he was a "famous name in Cornish hagiography" (III, 312).

In many ways, hagiography is to biography what salvation history (known in German as *Heilsgeschichte*) is to history. A salvation history, by way of comparison, is a way of telling an historical narrative that assumes a providential destiny driving it. The key for the critical study of religion is not to mistake the latter of each of these two terms for the former. Indeed, according to John Wansbrough (1928–2002), the scholar of Islam, so many of our early sources—regardless of the tradition concerned—are, in fact, literary texts as opposed to historical by nature, and scholars should read them as such. To rephrase, he is opposed "to that school of sanguine historiography in which the pursuit of reconstruction is seldom if ever deflected by the doubts and scruples thrown up in recent (and not so recent) years by practitioners of form- criticism, structuralism and the like." (See his "Review of Josef van Ess, Anfänge muslimischer Theologie: Zwei antiqadaritische Traktate aus dem ersten Jahrhundert der Higra," in *Bulletin of the School of Oriental and African Studies* 43 [1980]: 361–363.) In this sense, there is sometimes a tendency in the academic study of religion to present stories that are not difficult to read as works of fiction *as if* they quite literally happened. This use of the descriptive method simply to recount the content of such tales is, to invoke Wansbrough, "sanguine" in the sense that those offering mere descriptions or even paraphrases seem content to accept the veracity of the story perhaps for no other reason than because their research subjects do. Or, if such scholars maintain that these stories represent some sort of sacred manifestation or an expression of an inner experience on the part of the text's author, then they might assert that such stories need to be taken at face value, lest their so-called sacred character be lost. Reacting against such an approach, Jacob Neusner (1932–2016), the person who did more than anyone to bring the study of Judaism and Jewish texts into the fold of religious studies, once remarked of the gullibility of his colleagues:

> [so-and-so] writes articles on what time of day Pontius Pilate went to the toilet (so to speak). [Someone else] writes articles telling us the motives and intentions of figures of ancient fairy tales, as though he knew what they were thinking as they went about their affairs. [Another scholar] writes articles on the politics of Rabbi Judah the Patriarch, as though the sources at hand were stenographic reports of things people really said, or a TV camera recording of things people really did.
> (quoted in Hughes, *Jacob Neusner: An American Jewish Iconoclast* [2016], 186)

This is a real problem in the academic study of religion wherein there is a tendency to accept certain stories, myths, and salvation histories because some of the people we study claim them to be true and authoritative. While the latter is surely debatable, subjecting such stories to the types of analyses to which Wansbrough wanted to subject the earliest Islamic ones creates considerable consternation for some scholars because it is often regarded as "insensitive" to the beliefs of religious individuals. We can even add to this the fact that many scholars of religion have also adopted such a "sanguine" attitude to such an extent that if yet others examine such narrative as hagiographies or sacred histories as nothing more or less than narratives inevitably invested in issues of power, politics, identity, and propaganda, then such scholars will be accused of insulting religious practitioners by "not taking religion seriously." Witness, for example, the reception of Wansbrough's own work on the beginnings of Islam by many in the modern field of Islamic and quranic studies.

A more critical approach to the study of hagiography would be one that takes such stories less as historical or biographical accounts and more as political tracts in which authors often retroject their own ideas onto the lives of real or even fictional saints. In so doing we often see the lives of saints used as authorizing devices for the authors own interests. We see the beginnings of this as early as V.M. Crawford's 1907 translation of Hippolyte Delehaye's 1905 French work, *The Legends of the Saints: An Introduction to Hagiography*, which seeks to differentiate between hagiography and history: "The work of the hagiography may be historical, *but it is not necessarily so*" (2; italics added). Despite such a key acknowledgment, however, Delehaye proceeds (predictably, perhaps) with the notion that some, though, not all hagiographies may well have certain historical truths wrapped up in their more legendary accounts. This is a common enough approach in the history of myth studies even today, in which fanciful tales are sometimes assumed to be based on historical events that have been elaborated over time, with their many retellings. Again, this would seem for many to be the default position for these and related stories. This usually goes something like the following: while we may well know now that these stories are fictive, the people for whom they were written *believed them to be true*—therefore, scholars must read them as such, otherwise risk criticism for disrespecting the people and their meaningful tales. Indeed, such an approach that Delehaye outlines was echoed roughly a century later in a book dealing not with saints in Catholicism but, instead, in Japanese Buddhism. In his discussion of Buddhist heresiography, as found in his *Buddhist Hagiography in Early Japan: Images of Compassion in the Gyoki Tradition* (2004), Jonathan Morris Augustine writes that, while we should not get bogged down in issues of history, "if one completely ignores questions of historicity, why should one bother to examine these saints in their cultural contexts at all?"

We see two problematic issues in such an approach. The first, as already suggested, is whether or not the term "saint" is a valid cross-cultural tool that helps us to understand people other than self-identified Christians. The second is what exactly are we supposed to do with such highly stylized narratives of individuals seen as exemplary—narratives that are presented *as if* they were historically accurate accounts. Luckily, we have some precedent for how to go about this. In his *Cult of the Saints* (1981), the historian Peter Brown tries to show that the role of tombs, shrines, relics, and pilgrimages connected with Christian saints played an important social function. He demonstrates, for example, how many individuals who were living in often harsh environments relied upon saints—their perceived intercession as well as the institutions surrounding their veneration—to obtain justice, forgiveness, and to find new ways to accept their fellows. In so doing Brown successfully challenged what was, at the time, the fairly normative assumption that saint worship was largely drive by superstition among the lower classes. Brown instead argued that it was as popular among elite classes and played a large role in, among other things, patronage in the arts. On his reading, the cult of the saints (i.e., the institutionalized system of ritual practices surrounding them) replaced the late Roman imperial system of patronage, moving it toward a web of patronage relationships dominated by a class of cultural elites (including Church leadership, such as bishops).

This idea is then picked up in the work of Vincent J. Cornell, a scholar of Islamic mysticism. In his *Realm of the Saint* (1998), he argues that, in premodern Moroccan Sufism, while Sufi sainthood signaled a perceived spiritual proximity to God, just as importantly it also meant the ability to exercise social authority (due to claims of that very proximity). The Sufi saint, in other words, functioned as a "substitute of the prophets," something that, by definition, legitimated and justified the Sufis' involvement in political life. The biographies of such individuals both reinforced this, just as they made it possible in the first place. This reinforces the point made by David Brakke in his *Athanasius and Asceticism* (1998), which shows the political uses to which asceticism could be put. He argues that the Church carefully sought to integrate ascetic values and practices—i.e., austere and self-disciplined modes of living that were largely thought to be the domain of the saints—by putting them into a comprehensive vision of the church as a heavenly commonwealth, all as a way to consolidate its power. One of the primary ways they went about this was through the literature associated with hagiographies.

In the final analysis, then, we should see the genre of hagiography as we do any other sort of literary genre, namely, as something that seeks to make a point, often a political or ideological one, and then to justify and legitimate it. In the case of narratives about the lives of saints, this is often done by cloaking later ideas and interests in tales about individuals deemed by the community to possess certain status on account of their perceived holiness (i.e., their set-apartness from the usual). The mistake, however, is to treat these often highly stylized and fictional accounts as if they were simple historical narratives that could be verified if we just had the sufficient relics and other evidence—something that the academic study of religion tends to do with some degree of regularity.

In this volume see: church, cult, emic/etic, immanence/transcendence, monotheism/polytheism, myth, magic, paganism, prayer, priest/prophet, theology

In *Religion in 50 Words* see: authority, canon, comparison, culture, faith, gender, history, interpretation, lived religion, material religion, phenomenology, power, redescription, society

18 Icon

Unlike "idol" in its technical use in the field, the word "icon" has a generally positive valence. Perhaps this mirrors the more popular and widespread use of "iconic" to name something particularly exemplary, noteworthy, or paradigmatic, such as Christopher Bliss's 2010 book of photographs, *Iconic New York*, described as a "dramatic overview [that] captures the city's essence with images of its architecture, landmarks, its streets and populace." While the term retains a certain descriptive utility for many scholars, it is most often used in a rather much more specific and limited way that refers to certain painted or even mosaic symbols in what is known as the Eastern Orthodox Church. The latter represents that part of Christianity that first broke away from what continued as the Roman Catholic Church, centered in Rome, an event that is often termed the Great Schism. The latter was the culmination of a gradual process that took place from the eleventh to roughly the thirteenth centuries, with failed efforts at reconciliation following for some years thereafter. This resulted in the so-called Eastern Church, with its capital in what had long been known as the city of Constantinople, and which had functioned as the Roman capital between 330–395 CE. With the establishment of the modern nation of Turkey, not long after the fall of the onetime Ottoman Empire in 1922, the city then became known as Istanbul; however, prior to Emperor Constantine, ruling from 306–337 CE, renaming the city in his own honor, it had been previously known as the city of Byzantium. Thus we also see common references to Byzantine Christianity as well as the description of everything from a time period and an empire to an architectural style as byzantine—the latter term also possessing the pejorative meaning of something that is overly or bureaucratically complicated, not unrelated to modern judgments that something is labyrinthine, something that is intricate and puzzling. It should be added that, in this case, the East/West distinction within

DOI: 10.4324/9781003196631-19

Christianity refers to a later third century CE division in governing the onetime provinces of the Roman Empire. This history is outlined here, albeit briefly, lest we assume incorrectly that the sixteenth-century European event known as the Reformation, involving yet another split within the Roman Catholic Church that resulted in the denominations collectively known as Protestantism, is regarded as the only internal division within Christianity, as is often the case.

Within the various Orthodox Churches—e.g., Greek Orthodox, Russian Orthodox, Ukrainian Orthodox—one commonly finds a variety of front-face portraits (thus not statues), often painted on a wooden panel, in a particular two-dimensional style. Such figures include Jesus, his mother Mary (often with the infant Jesus), Jesus's initial followers/disciples, subsequent saints, as well as a variety of scenes from the biblical narrative. Though, it should probably be noted, God, or more specifically, God the Father, as well as the Holy Spirit (along with Jesus the three members of what Christians call the trinity), are not as frequently depicted in icons—an injunction in the Russian Orthodox Church dating to the so-called Great Moscow Synod of 1666. The latter is not dissimilar to the prohibition on such images that we find elsewhere, e.g., the ban on depictions of the Prophet Muhammad in modern Islam. What sets these paintings apart for some scholars, and thus inspires the use of a separate term, adopted from the devotees themselves, to name them, is the role they play in people's devotional acts, such as a participant kissing an icon as they light a candle upon entering an Orthodox service of worship. Though we do not see such behavior at Roman Catholic masses we regularly see those arriving taking a knee briefly, or genuflecting, often accompanied by making the pattern of the cross on their chest, before taking a seat—an action that is certainly comparable. Thus, for those scholars of religion from an earlier intellectual tradition, and for whom the so-called sacred was often (problematically, we will add) said to be manifested or instantiated in a variety of natural objects or symbols, such icons were of particular interest. For example, Bryan S. Rennie, a longtime commentator on the work of Mircea Eliade (1907–1986), observes that "[t]he Orthodox veneration of icons closely resembles Eliade's notion of hierophany" (see his "Mircea Eliade and the Perception of the Sacred in the Profane: Intention, Reduction, and Cognitive Theory," *Temenos* 43/1 [2007]: 79). Whether or not this is the result of Eliade's own Romanian origins and the probable impact the Romanian Orthodox Church would have had on his upbringing, we leave to others to argue—as Rennie himself does in a chapter on this very topic in Christian Wedemeyer and Wendy Doniger's edited book, *Hermeneutics,*

Politics, and the History of Religions: The Contested Legacies of Joachim Wach and Mircea Eliade (2010), which is based on a 2006 conference at the University of Chicago by the same title. Regardless, the role these images have played, and continue to play, in participants' various acts of veneration—with icons appearing in church, in public shrines, and in homes—place them centrally in a larger group of material objects used by people in their devotional lives, an area of study recently referred to as "material religion." Thus, it is not difficult to see them described as sacred objects or sacred images, with "icon" being one of the chapters in 2015's edited book, *Key Terms in Material Religion* (based on the earlier short essay, by the art historian, Robert Maniura, published in *Material Religion* 7/1 (2011): 55–57). In this case what sometimes catches the attention of the scholar is the relationship between the icon as physical artifact and the icon as idea and/or its original reference, or, as Maniura phrases it, the manner in which the "conceptual register of the iconic is in tension with the materiality of the icon as object" (2011: 52).

Though it is obvious that the term is largely used with reference to but one aspect of Christianity, it should be distinguished from the term "relic." The latter term derives from the Latin for remains—with a "reliquary" being that which is used to contain or store them—and usually signify material items said to remain from a past exemplary figures (i.e., saints). Such relics can include what are believed to be their bones, teeth, or scraps of their clothing. It is also worth noting that relics are of relevance not just to Christians but, for example, held in reverence in both Buddhists and Muslims as well.

Icons are also intimately connected to the noun "iconoclast" and the adjective "iconoclastic." The latter two terms are perhaps among the reasons why the root of each of these words, "icon," remains popular in the wider vocabulary of the field since both of these terms signify one who critiques or even destroys icons. These latter English terms date to the first half of the seventeenth century, and both derive from the Latin and, before that, the Greek. The English word "icon," for instance, derives from the Greek *eikon* for image or likeness and thus something that resembles something else. The suffix *klástes* also relies on the Greek (compare to the Latin *īconoclastēs*), to refer to one who breaks something, such as one who smashes icons. This all should be differentiated, of course, from "iconography," with another Greek suffix denoting writing or to write on some topic or, simply the study of icons. These terms, which can function semantically along a register related to the pejorative uses of such terms as "fetish," "idolatry," and even "magic" and "superstition," are traced to a critical movement within the Orthodox Church of the eighth and ninth century, in which the role played by images was severely attacked. In fact, as described by the historian of art and architecture, Cyril A. Mango (1928–2021), "[i]n 726 (or 730) iconoclasm became the official doctrine of the [Byzantine] Empire and remained in force until 780; it was revived once again in 814 and lasted until 842" (*The Art of the Byzantine Empire 312–1453: Sources and Documents* [1986], 149). Reflecting an attitude that sometimes drives iconoclasts, though written much later, we read in Henry Hart Milman's (1791–1868) 1855 book, *History of Latin Christianity*: "there can be no doubt that with ignorant and superstitious minds, the use of reverence, the worship of images, whether in pictures or statues, inevitably degenerates into idolatry" (1872, vol. 2, 343–344, quoting the third edition). Thus we arrive back at the way the issue is still framed to this day, as being one between the supposedly purer original idea or conception and its derivate reproduction in matter.

That we should not subscribe to this sort of bifurcation may by now go without saying. In fact, we may very well see the distinction as a rhetorical technique used to manage competing organizations and sensibilities, that is, as a way to authorize a non-empirical claim to exist over a wide variety of competing organizations and sensibilities. This is not unlike what we find in the case of claims of idolatry, including those who today rank spirituality ahead of what they portray as insincere and thus merely rote ritual—a rhetoric not unfamiliar to those who study the Reformation era in Europe several centuries ago. In that context, those who inhabited newly forming counter-institutions of their own represented themselves as lone individuals and free thinkers in one-to-one correspondence with what was known as the original and "Primitive Church," in distinction from the institutions of those they opposed, which were collectively known as "popery." The latter term is a derogatory early-sixteenth-century term for Roman Catholicism or so-called papists. To quote the title of a sermon from the era, preached in Southwark, England: "Popery is a Novelty, and the Protftants Religion was not only before Luther, but the fame that was taught by Chrift and the Apoftles," which can be found in Sermon VII in the collection assembled by the minister, Nathanael Vincent (d. 1697) and called *The Morning-Exercife Against Popery or, The Principal Errors of the Church of Rome Detected and Confuted in a Morning-Lecture* (1675). Though, note that the book opens with a set of twenty-five thesis statements, with VII reading: "The Pope of Rome is that Antichrist, and Man of Sin, fpoken of in the Apocalyps, and by the Apostle Paul." Thus, the common way of approaching the study of icons, as if interesting because of their inherently sacred quality or the mysterious way in which they materialize more ethereal qualities and values, may itself become the object of study for the critical student of religion.

In this volume see: animism, church, East/West, god, hagiography, idol, mysticism, prayer, ritual, spirituality, symbol, theology

In *Religion in 50 Words* see: affect, belief, classification, critical, environment, faith, history, ideology, orthodoxy, practice, worldview

19 Idol

Idol is yet another one of those terms that has a wide variety of meanings that are often specific to particular contexts. For those opposed to idols and their worship, which is referred to as idolatry—a common enough use of the term in the history of the field, and one dating to about seven hundred years ago—the word has a distinctly negative association. Indeed, Judaism, Christianity, and Islam are all predicated on eradicating idols and idol worship, which are associated with "paganism." The latter is yet another loaded term, deriving from the Latin *paganus*, originally for those living in the countryside. We see this, for example, in the Bible's book of Leviticus: "Do not make idols [Hebrew: *elilim*], or set up an image or a sacred stone for yourselves, and do not place a carved stone in your land to bow down before it. I am the Lord your God" (26:1; quoting the New International Version translation). According to the Quran: "God does not forgive associating [Arabic *shirk*, the term often translated as idolatry] others with Him, but forgives anything else of whoever He wills. And whoever associates others with God has indeed committed a grave sin" (4:48). We have to ask ourselves: How could a term with such pejorative and often hostile overtones play a role in a critical, scholarly vocabulary devoted to the study religion? One potential answer may reside in the fact that in other cultures, such as India, idols—though, of course, this is our own term for them, not a so-called indigenous term—play a large role in worship, both in temples and in the home, and there exist none of the prohibitions we just saw. An Indian scholar of religion, thus, might have a rather different conception and understanding of those items commonly known as idols than, say, a Jewish or a Protestant one. However, we should be aware of the political acts that ultimately structure and determine what makes something an idol or not. More often than not (bracketing, of course, the more popular current use of the term, e.g., "a pop idol" or someone who one might idolize), then, to call something an idol is often to demean or diminish its value and that is very much an ideological choice. It is akin to saying something like "while we worship the true God, they worship mere idols." Given the baggage that often follows in the wake of this term, it is exceedingly difficult for the student of religion to talk about idol/idols/idolatry in a manner that does not participate in the judgments as mentioned above. Indeed, it might be the case that the term "idol," not unlike "cult," is so politically charged that any attempt to retain its scholarly use may not ultimately be worth the effort.

The historical use of the term "idol" in English would seem to confirm this rather negative assessment of the term's future use. The word derives from Middle English and Old French, *id(e)le*, and *idole*, which in turn comes from the late Latin *īdōlum* meaning an "image," "form," "specter," or "apparition." The term originated in Greek (*eidos*), where it could refer to an image in water or a mirror, or one conjured up in the mind, and eventually to a material image or statue. It is in the Septuagint—the Greek translation of the Hebrew Bible/Old Testament, dating to the third century CE—that we begin to see *eidos* used to refer explicitly to a form or a shape of a deity. In this way, the term gradually began to take on the connotation of an image or similitude of a deity or divinity, often used as an object of worship, but in a pejorative sense since it was applied primarily to images of deities worshipped by those others now known as pagans. Indeed, the terms "idol" and "pagan" (or alternatively "heathen") have performed a great deal of work as the foils to what is imagined to be the proper worship of so-called monotheists. Within this context, idols have taken on the sense of false gods, fictitious divinities, and often coincide with casting aspersions on those who are believed to make and worship them. Thus, in the Christian text of 1 Corinthians 8:4, we read: "So then, about eating food sacrificed to idols: We know that 'An idol [original Greek: *eidolon*] is nothing at all in the world' and that 'There is no God but one'" (NIV translation). Here we explicitly see that in the New Testament, generally regarded to be one of the foundational documents of so-called Western civilization, things designated as idols are reduced to falsity and seen as diametrically opposed to the worship of what is believed to be the one, true God, which presumably is imagined to be idol-less.

It is in this latter sense that we begin to see the term's appearance in English, as early as the fourteenth century. Thus, in the Wycliffe Bible (dating to the period between 1382 and 1395), we read the English translation of the aforementioned verse from 1 Corinthians: "We witen for an ydol is no thing in the world, and that ther is no God but oon." In his book *Leviathan* (1651), Thomas Hobbes (1588–1679), the English philosopher, writes: "But the name of Idoll is extended yet further in Scripture, to signifie also the Sunne, or a Starre, or any other Creature, visible or invisible, when they are worshipped for Gods" (iv. xlv. 359). As also mentioned above, the term can also be applied to describe, often polemically, the images or figures of divine beings and saints, and, more generally (and generically), to any material object of worship in a Christian church. Needless to say, this usage dates to around the time of the Protestant Reformation (1517–1648). Thus we read in the polemicist Henry Brinkelow's (d. ca. 1546) *The Complaynt of Roderyck Mors* (1542): "[He] set vp in the same place another idol of .S. Iohan baptyst" (xxiv. Sig. G4). In this context, mention should be made again of the term "idolatry," which is compound word of "idol" and *"latreia,"* Greek for service or worship, once again in a pejorative sense and that makes its appearance in the Greek New Testament. As early as the early sixteenth century, for example, we read in Robert Fabyan (d. 1513), an English chronicler and author of *New Cronycles of Englande & Fraunce* (1516): "He had forsaken his Idolatry, and was becomyn seruaunt of the oonly God" (I. lxxxxvii. f. xxxviii). Or in the Tyndale Bible (1526): "We have spent the tyme..in eatynge, drynkynge and in abhominable ydolatrie" (1 Pet. iv. 3).

The use in English over the last two hundred years would seem to bear out this rather pejorative sense of the term. "Idol" and "idols" were used with some degree of regularity in the first half of the nineteenth century before largely declining over the course of the twentieth, only to find popularity again, in part due to the rise of the American TV show "American Idol," which is subtitled "The Search for a Super Star," a program devoted to finding the next singing superstar from the general populace. The television series uses the term in the same sense as a "teen idol" (a celebrity with a large teenage fan base) and thus seeks to invoke the term in a manner that is much more positive—although the implication that the new star will be worshipped like an idol still carries a rather odd subtext. Despite this, idols are imagined in so much of this literature as the polar opposite of what is taught and practiced by "true" (read: Protestant Christian) religion, in either the face of other religions or other denominations within Christianity. Thus, we read in the Irish dramatist James Sheridan Knowles's (1784–1862), in *The Idol Demolished by its Own Priest: An Answer to Cardinal Wiseman's Lectures on Transubstantiation* (1851):

> And now, Sir, what have you made of your dogma? What relation, whatever, does it bear to the Living God? What does it concern but

an idol, the work of human artifice?—and idol which, in your endeavours to establish it more firmly on its base of falsehood, you, yourself, have dashed to the earth, and shattered into fragments.
(296–297)

It can of course also be used to denigrate other religious traditions. In his *Historical Account of the Most Celebrates Voyages, Travels Form the Time of Columbus to the Present Period* (1797), William Fordyce Mavor (1758–1837), the Scottish priest and compiler of educational books, writes of his journey to China: "(w)e were places near and idol, black with the smoke of a lamp, continually burning to its honour, and daile worshipped by its deluded crew" (223). We further read in an article titled "Facts Relative to the State of the Heathen" (in vol. 7 [1802] from *The Missionary Magazine*), for example, that the "East Indian Bramins have an idol called Ganga Gramma, in honour of which pagodas are erected, and feftivals celebrated" (238). Such accounts, of course, witness European travelers predictably using language and terms familiar to them from the Bible—e.g., idols—as a way to understand the unfamiliar practices of those with whom they have just come into contact.

Idols can refer not just to other religions, but also to ideas (e.g., money, hubris) that stand in the way of what is represented as a proper relationship to God. We read, for instance, in the Church of Scotland minister Rev. R.M. M'Cheyne's (1813–1843) *Memoirs and Remains* (1852) about the concept of "self-righteousness": "[t]his is the largest idol of the human heart—the idol which man loves most and God hates most" (462). We even see this in the titles of popular books, such as Daniel J. Mahoney's *The Idol of Our Age: How the Religion of Humanity Subverts Christianity* (2018), which, as the title suggests, argues that secular humanism and the cry for social justice has meant that Christianity, at least for this author, has lost its transcendental status. In Islam, as already noted, one of the main sins is that of *shirk*, a term that literally means "association" or "associationism," in the sense of likening something (e.g., power, money) or someone (e.g., Jesus) with Allah, and which is often translated into English as "idolatry." Idolatry here, not unlike in the examples drawn from Christianity cited above, is often synonymous with polytheism, the belief in many gods and thus the opposite of monotheism.

Once again, we have to ask ourselves: How can a term with such lengthy and pejorative sense be applied in the contemporary academic study of religion, as it if were somehow value neutral or productive of useful knowledge? Even if we use the term to refer to "Hindu idols," we would seem, given the history of this term's usage, to be making an unproductive value judgement or even a theological statement on their derivative nature. Unless we are willing to take a position like that of Moshe Halbertal and Avishai Margalit, in their *Idolatry* (1992), who argue that the term is fluid because it is always defined by the shifting position of what is believed to be the normative or orthodox worship of a true God, but we still see little use for retaining the term in our critical vocabulary. For even Halbertal and Avishai must argue that, though the term is fluid, it still needs its opposite—some sort of monotheistic devotion to the "proper" God—for definition and thus utility. But if one decides to retain the term, and we do not necessarily think we should, it has to be realized that its use in the past has almost always been in the negative sense, of incorrect belief or the worship of the wrong god or gods. It therefore performs socially formative, political work, to be sure, but too often not enough consideration is given to ascertaining this work and the term is instead simply used, as if descriptively, to name something seeming to exist naturally in the world—an approach that risks normalizing the work that the term accomplishes. For this reason, we submit that "idol," and its derivatives, should be retired from the academic study of religion and, if and when encountered in earlier texts or the writings of others, alarms bells should go off for the critical scholar, inviting them to identify just what sort of work the term is performing.

In this volume see: atheism/theism, cult, East/West, emic/etic, god, icon, immanence/transcendence, monotheism/polytheism, paganism, ritual, sacrifice, shamanism, syncretism, totem

In *Religion in 50 Words* see: affect, belief, classification, critical, history, ideology, indigeneity, primitive

20 Immanence/Transcendence

A longstanding assumption in the study of religion is that those beliefs, practices, and institutions considered to be religious orbit around or somehow involve two opposed or oscillating but always intertwined states of being or, as we should probably designate them, experiences: that which is internal and that which is external. By the latter we do not just mean public, and thus empirically available for study. Rather, they are believed to be experiences and modes of existence that are overarching and all-consuming, those in which the participant can either lose or, ironically perhaps, find themselves—much as with those experiences reported to involve some sort of inward identification. Romain Rolland (1866–1944), the French author and art historian, comes to mind, who once discussed the "oceanic feeling" (in, for example, a December 5, 1927, letter to the psychoanalyst, Sigmund Freud [1856–1939]). Rolland, as with so many throughout the history of the field, argued that "true religion arose from the mystical experience of oneness with the world (*la sensation océanique*)," something he thought to be a cross-cultural constant among so-called mystics (quoting the psychologist of religion, William Parsons, in his *The Enigma of the Oceanic Feeling: Revisioning the Psychoanalytic Theory of Mysticism* [1999], 4). The terms that have traditionally been used by scholars to name the two poles of this all-consuming quality or feeling are the nouns "immanence" and "transcendence." The former begins as an adjective, "immanent," around the mid-sixteenth century, derived from the post-classical Latin term *immanens*, for dwelling or staying within. The latter term enters English in the mid-fourteenth century as a verb, "to transcend," from the Latin verb, *transcendĕre*, meaning to climb or pass over, and thus to surpass something. Immanence comes to refer to the internal realization and identification of meaning, significance, or being, while transcendence designates states or experiences claimed to exceed all measure, categorization, and thus

DOI: 10.4324/9781003196631-21

rational understanding. As the American philosopher, Louis Dupre, once phrased it in the opening line to a 1976 essay in the *Proceedings of the Catholic Theological Society of America* (31), titled "Transcendence and Immanence as Theological Categories":

> Transcendence is the religious category par excellence. It refers to that particular quality by which the source and terminus of the religious relation surpasses absolutely the mind's and all other reality .... It provides the dynamic tension without which the religious act would grow slack and eventually collapse in its own immanence.

(1)

Although these two terms gain more frequency throughout the twentieth century, we find much earlier examples that support their modern meanings. For example, as early as the 1687 English translation of the uncredited original French work, *A Moral Essay Upon the Soul of Man*, we find the following in a chapter devoted to the imagination and intellect: "That every thing which is in the Soul is Effentially Spiritual, every Modification of the Soul, and every Vital Act, being by reafon of the Immanence Effentially Spiritual" (part II, chpt. xvi, 256). And from rather earlier we read the following in the poem, a translation of an earlier unattributed Latin work by the Benedictine monk, Henry Bradshaw (d. 1513) entitled, *Here Begynneth the Holy Lyfe and History of Saynt Werburge very Frutefull for All Christen People to Rede* (1521): "O blessed Werburge and virgin pure. I beseke the mekely helpe me this day. That we may transcende this ryuer [river] safe and sure" (189, citing the Chetham Society's 1848 edition). The movement from spanning a natural object, such as a river, to surmounting or passing beyond more abstract entities, is easily tracked in English literature. A century and a half later we find the following anthem in a collection of devotions: "Thy incomparable beauty ravifhes our hearts and the joys tho hast prepared for us tranfcend all our wishes" (*Devotions. First Part. In the Ancient Ways of Offices. With Psalms, Hymns and Pray'rs; for Every Day in the Week, and Every Holiday in the Year* [1685], 39–40, quoting the fourth edition).

The title of Dupre's above-cited essay—predictably containing both terms, given that they are mutually-defining and thus often represented in tandem—provides an important clue as to why these words have often appeared in the study of religion. They become part of a participant discourse within some of the groups that a scholar of religion may study. That discourse, of course, we would term theology—more specifically, though, Christian theology. Like so many of the tools used in the modern academic study of religion, these two words arise within a specific group's own historical effort to understand and articulate their own assumptions about their group and its world—assumptions that are then universalized when trying to understand those other groups equally designated as religions. We see this as recently as the philosopher of religion, Chin-Tai Kim's 1987 essay in the North American field's main academic periodical, the *Journal of the American Academy of Religion*, entitled simply "Transcendence and Immanence," where he claims: "All theologies and metaphysical systems that posit an ultimate reality must show its double aspect as both transcendent and immanent, though some emphasize its transcendence and others its immanence" (55/3: 537). The problem that these two intertwined terms address is how a being claimed to surpass all knowing (a claim often found in Christian literature) can nonetheless be personal to the so-called believer yet, in being personal, not lose its supposed ultimacy. Thus, speculations on immanence *and yet also* transcendence are aimed at solving a theological puzzle. In this sense, it is much like the so-called problem of evil being a result of participants holding what appear to be mutually exclusive claims, i.e., that atrocious moral and natural events exist despite there also existing an all-powerful and all-living God. That the problem addressed by the intertwined concepts of immanence and transcendence is particularly relevant to Christian theology should be clear. We witness this with claims made early on by a writer such as Justin Martyr (d. 165 CE), that "no one with even the slightest intelligence would dare to assert that the Creator of all things left his super-celestial realms to make himself visible in a little spot on earth" (see the opening to chapter 60 in an English translation of *Dialogues with Trypho*). We also encounter this in those statements regularly made by some contemporary Christians concerning "Jesus Christ, my personal lord and savior." It is not difficult to read the development of the Christian doctrine of the trinity as but another way to address this same problem—one that creates yet more difficulties, however, given how quickly Christians would then add that the trinity is not to be confused with another term Europeans developed to name the religions of "others": the early seventeenth century word "polytheism," or the belief in many gods.

Since this tension exists within this one tradition, it then makes sense that, once those schooled in, and therefore conversant with, such assumptions begin to look at what they come to understand to be the religions of others. They might go looking for this same tension (and its possible solutions) elsewhere, thereby presuming (as exemplified by

Kim, quoted above) this to be a universal phenomenon. Just as earlier Europeans looked for various Christianity-based analogues in "other religions"—e.g., do they too have founders, disciples, churches, scriptures, beliefs in an afterlife—they also looked for evidence of something akin to an ultimate reality. We thus see perpetuated the notion of a universal sense of both the immanent (a personal realization of meaning or truth) and the transcendent (an experience of overarching significance). Add to that what scholars quickly came to understand as a focus on the self (and, at times, its elimination and not just its realization) in what comes to be known as, for example, Hinduism and Buddhism, we then have all we need to lend support to the earlier intuition that this is indeed a universal tendency among humankind. In fact, much of this research energy then gets focused on examining what comes to be known as mysticism, also assumed to be a cross-cultural feature of religion where these opposed experiences are investigated, experienced, and possibly resolved by elite or esoteric practitioners.

Such descriptions of participant claims, however, especially given their origins within one community's self-understanding later projected outward in an attempt to understand all others, may be of limited interest. As explored elsewhere in this volume, the search for a universal of deep or metaphysical significance might not be nearly as interesting as is the situated discourse on such a significance. Why, to rephrase, did the immanence/transcendence distinction develop in the first place and why has it so effectively been exported to other societies, *as if* it is a universal feature of what a previous generation of scholars might have just termed *homo religious* (i.e., the human as religious)? Should we go the route of social theory to address this question—as argued, for example, by the early French sociologist, Emile Durkheim 1858–1917)—then perhaps what we have here is the experience of group members who see themselves to be, to whatever extent, autonomous individuals, but who simultaneously have no choice but to be members of groups that nurture them, that long predated them, and which will more than likely outlive them considerably. As Durkheim argued and which is widely assumed today among many social theorists, that thing that we call society is not tangible in the same way as are its members' own bodies. After all, the group is the result of a set of ideas that its members share concerning a wide variety of things, from the way one dresses and with whom one associates to the foods one eats and the sounds one recognizes as language. Into this arrives rituals, which Durkheim theorized as periodic, structured events when the members unite in-person, within eyesight and earshot of each other, to reaffirm their idea of the group through engaging

118 Immanence/Transcendence

in common, routinized behaviors—as simple as something like just standing and sitting in unison. "The very fact of assembling is an exceptionally powerful stimulant," he argued, continuing: "Once the individuals are assembled their proximity generates a kind of electricity that quickly transports them to an extraordinary degree of exaltation" (*The Elementary Forms of Religious Life* [1912], chpt.7, 162, citing Carol Cosman's 2001 translation). This he termed collective effervescence, what Lasse Suonperä Liebst, at the University of Copenhagen, has described as "the affective arousal of an assembled crowd [that] creates the potential for both social conformity and group-based agency" ("Exploring the Sources of Collective Effervescence: A Multilevel Study" in *Sociological Science* 6 [2019]: 27–42). In fact, he quotes the noted US sociologist, Randall Collins as observing, even if the group is not organized around regimented shared rituals, as the Durkheimian tradition assumes, '[b]eing in a crowd gives some sense of being 'where the action is,' even if you personally are not part of any well-defined action" (*Interaction Ritual Chains* [2004], 82).

Drawing on social theory, we find a way to begin to theorize the immanence/transcendence pairing, something that is usually theologized and thereby linked to non-empirical, metaphysical issues of inwardness and eternity. Instead, the terms may arise from and thereby describe, in a fashion encoded in the language of theology, the fairly mundane, but interesting nonetheless, daily situations that all social actors inhabit: navigating between the groups with which they identify (an act presuming agency and intention on the part of the individual) and which, in turn, identify them (the result of non-agential structures). For after all, few of us picked our own names and were, instead, named by others who came well before us and who had their own hopes and dreams for us.

In this volume see: afterlife, church, founder, liberation, meditation, monotheism/polytheism, mysticism, myth, prayer, ritual, theology

In *Religion in 50 Words* see: classification, cognition, definition, environment, worldview

21 Initiation

Initiation is the act of admitting someone into a society or group often regarded as exclusive or possibly even secret, typically involving some sort of ritualistic act that facilitates entry. This can involve anything from one of the so-called mystery cults of antiquity to when someone might join a fraternity or sorority on US college campuses today. Initiations are, thus, regarded as what scholars have long termed rites (or rituals) of passage that mark entrance or acceptance into a new group or social status. In an extended sense, an initiation is often stretched, especially in the academic study of religion, to signify a transformation in which the so-called initiates are "born again" into their new role. These can include those rituals known as a baptism in Christianity, a bar or bat mitzvah in Judaism, the ceremony that marks one being a novice Buddhist monk, or even one's acceptance into some sort of other specialized or secret society, such as an honor society, a professional guild, or even initiation ceremonies to mark a hunter's first kill that we find across cultures. Many in the academic study of religion have long been interested in understanding such rituals of initiation, often through in-depth descriptive accounts of what they entail, such as their various steps and symbolic actions. Indeed, George Weckman, in an article in the journal *History of Religions* (10/1 [1970]: 62–79) titled "Understanding Initiation," calls initiation "one of the most persistent and ubiquitous aspects of religion" (62). As we shall see, this has led many scholars, especially those following in the footsteps of Mircea Eliade (1907–1986)—of which Weckman and many of his generation most certainly did—to try to categorize such rituals so as to understand their morphology (i.e., shape) as well as their relationship to that proverbial and ethereal quality such scholars knew as the sacred. A more critical approach, however, might involve looking at the social and political work that initiation accomplishes as opposed to connecting it to some sort of metaphysical transformation

DOI: 10.4324/9781003196631-22

that supposedly occurs within the individual—something to which the scholar can have no access. What, for example, does initiation confer upon an initiate? What does it let him or her do that he or she could not otherwise do? Moreover, or so the critical scholar may conclude, such ceremonies, inasmuch as they mark the border between two states or statuses, could be understood to actually constitute the two zones, inasmuch as the rites comprise the boundary, thereby defining the beginning and end of each.

It his *Rites and Symbols of Initiation: The Mysteries of Birth and Rebirth* (1965), Eliade connects, as he always did, initiation to issues of birth and re-birth that what he coined as *homo religious* (that is, religious man or human) undergoes. "All the rites of rebirth or resurrection," according to him, "indicate that the novice has attained to another mode of existence inaccessible to those who have not undergone the initiatory ordeals, who have not tasted death." Accounts such as Eliade's are, in many ways, deeply problematic for the critical scholar, trying, as they do, to take readers into some sort of experience or transformation that is usually inaccessible to one who has not had such an experience for themselves. When scholars make initiation about spiritual transformation or the like they enter into a realm of unverifiable speculation, one wherein scholars can make initiation into pretty much anything they want it to be. Despite the wide appeal of such work, scholars, we believe, can do so much better than this.

The English term "initiation" derives from the Latin *initiation* in the later sixteenth century, itself a noun of action based on the verb *initiāre*, meaning to "to initiate" in the sense of "to begin" something. This sense carried over into English where, *initially* (from the same root, we should add, and again with the sense of "in the beginning") it referred to the action of entering upon, or starting something new. Thus we read in the Church of England clergyman Thomas Brightman's (1562–1607) *Predictions and Prophecies VVritten 46 Yeares Since: Concerning the Three Churches of Germanie, England, and Scotland : Fore-telling the Miserie of Germanie, the Fall of the Pride of Bishops in England by the Assistance of the Scottish Kirk : All Which Should Happen, As He Foretold, Between the Yeares of 36 and 41* (1641): "The Church of Germanie had its initiation or beginning in Martin Luther ... in ... 1517" (3). Or, again in John Stuart Mill's (1806–1873) *On Liberty* (1859): "The initiation of all wise or noble things, comes and must come from individuals; generally at first from some one individual" (chpt. 3, 119). Eventually this sense of entering or beginning was transferred into the notion of a formal introduction into some position, office, or society by means of preliminary instruction or an initial ceremony. This often involved some sort of special (or secretive) knowledge of, or participation in, some principles or observances needed to be taught to the initiate. We see this, for example, in *A Common Apologie of the Church of England against the vniust Challenges of the Ouer-iust Sect, Commonly called Brownists* (1610), by Joseph Hall (1574–1656), the Bishop of Norwich and a satirist: "In the first of these is required indeede a solemne initiation by baptisme" (§6). Or, again, in Samuel Johnson's (1709–1784) *Letters to Mrs. Thrale* (May 25, 1780): "Bath is a good place for the initiation of a young lady." It is only in the nineteenth century that we see the word used in the now well-known compound "initiation ceremony." Thus, we read in *The Native Tribes of Central Australia* (1899), by the early anthropologist, Walter Baldwin Spencer (1860–1929): "All Australian natives, with rare exceptions, have to pass through some initiation ceremony before being admitted to the secrets of the tribe" (chpt. 7, 212). And, in *Coral Gardens and Their Magic: A Study of the Methods of Tilling the Soil and of Agricultural Rites in the Trobriand Islands* (1935), written by the Polish anthropologist Bronislaw Malinowski (1884–1942): "The instruction may take place in the course of initiation ceremonies" (vol 2, 234). We also encounter around the same time the phrase "initiation rite," as in the Austrian-born American anthropologist Robert Harry Lowie's (1883–1957) *The History of Ethnological Theory* (1937): "The instruction may take place in the course of initiation ceremonies" (234).

The role of initiation in the study of religion historically played a large role in the so-called ancient Greek mystery cults. The latter is a modern designation, we should note, used to name a collection of associations that seem to have operated outside of the official cult of the ancient city-states. Perhaps none more famous in this context are those associated with the Eleusinian mysteries where initiations were held every year for the cult of the gods Demeter and Persephone at Eleusis in ancient Greece, and which later spread to Rome. Since we have no idea what actually happened in these initiation ceremonies—as the rites and beliefs were, after all, kept secret from those not initiated into them, a key strategy for their socially formative effectiveness, to be sure—scholars are forced to rely on their interpretations of paintings and pieces of pottery, for example, that depict various aspects of the mysteries and then infer what *might* actually have happened. It seems that, for the initiated, Persephone and her rebirth symbolized the eternity of life, and those initiated would, as a result, be rewarded in some sort of notion of the afterlife. Despite that fact that we have no idea what actually happened, however, this has not stopped many scholars from making all sorts of assumptions (including speculations on the ancient use of psychedelic drugs and sex). For example, according to Carl Kerényi (1897–1973), a Hungarian scholar of Greek religion, in his *Eleusis: Archetypal Image of Mother and Daughter* (1967), the mysteries of Eleusis—and here he follows in the path of Eliade as well as the noted psychologist Carl Gustav Jung (1875–1961)—are not just important to Greek myth but, more generally and universally, to all of human nature. For Kerényi, the yearly "mysteries," and the initiations that occurred to move into and thereby join them, all revolved around the myth of the goddess Demeter's search for her daughter Persephone. This, he argues, is both a search for one woman's quest for completion but also, and more importantly, with every person's pursuit of some vague notion of authentic identity. Kerényi can do this, of course, only by explaining what *he thinks* initiates would have experienced—making plain the often-unrecognized role that sheer speculation can sometimes play in scholarship (whether it's on the past or the present, such as making claims about an author's intentions). Incidentally, Kerényi, Jung, Eliade, and a host of other scholars from this era would meet annually for a week or more each summer at the famed Eranos conference in Europe (begun in 1933 and often hosted in Switzerland or Italy), where they would discuss their phenomenological, psychological, and experiential theories about the nature of religion. It is widely acknowledged that the name for the event/group—meaning, in ancient Greek, a banquet to which members all contributed and, by the fifth century BCE coming to name a financial credit system—was suggested by the once influential German theologian, Rudolf Otto (1869–1937). While the Eranos event hardly plays the role it once did, this collection of methods is still the preferred approach among some scholars of religion, notably those who continue to understand religion as evidence of a pan-human and thus universal experience of deep meaning and significance. However, this collection of personalistic approaches will likely be seen as rather suspect to the critical scholar, if for no other reason than that they minimize historical specificity, politics, and social difference.

Speculative readings into initiation ceremonies are certainly common in this type of literature, where initiation is often seen as a code for some type of experience. Indeed, the history of the term's usage in English certainly bears this out. Used with little frequency during the late nineteenth and early twentieth centuries, it picks up considerable steam during the 1960s, often in circles associated with—at least as far as the academic study of religion is concerned—Eliade's work and the influential school of thought which followed him. Earlier in the century, though, we find an example of this approach in the table of contents to *Initiation and Its Results: A Sequel to "The Way of Initiation"* (1909), by Rudolf Steiner (1861–1925), the Austrian philosopher, reformer, esotericist, philosopher of education, and claimed clairvoyant: "History of Initiation. In Twelve Lectures: General Introduction, History of Initiation in Hindostan, Philosophy of the Eastern Mysteries, Initiation in Persia, Initiation in Greece, Ceremonies of Initiation into the Mysteries of Bacchus ...," and so on and so forth. Once again, the idea here, to be picked up by later scholars, is that initiation is one, universal thing with many different manifestations. Cross-culture comparative study of initiation rites will, presumably, lay bare the universal experience at its core—or so this approach claims.

Perhaps one of the most famous and reproduced treatments of initiation may be found in the Dutch-French ethnographer and folklorist, Arnold Van Gennep's (1873–1957) *Rites of Passage* (1960). In that work, he sought to show how a rite of passage enables an individual to leave one group to enter another. Van Gennep envisioned such rites as providing the means whereby individuals could ease, without any type of social disruption, through those difficult transitions from one social role or status to another. Based on an extensive survey of both non-literate and literate societies, he argued that rites of passage consist of three distinct, yet overlapping, elements or phases: separation, transition, and reincorporation. This three-part structure was, in turn, adopted and popularized by Victor Turner's (1920–1983) still well-known book, *The Ritual Process: Structure and Anti-Structure* (1969), wherein he argued—focusing on Van Gennep's notion of the ambiguous liminal or threshold status (i.e., as part of the transitional phase mentioned above)—for the importance of, what he called, "communitas." This latter term refers to an unstructured transitional state in which all members of a community of initiates are seen as equal, allowing them to share a common experience, usually through a rite of passage—after all, at the mid-point of the ritual, none are considered to be what they once were and yet all are not yet members of the group to which they will eventually belong. Communitas, he argued, is characteristic of people experiencing the state of liminality together. Perhaps those attending a graduation ceremony provides a useful example, with all frequently dressed the same in gowns and thus indistinguishable from one another. None of those attending are students since they have completed their classes and exams, but no one is yet a graduate, since they have yet to "walk the stage" or receive their diploma. They are, in the words of Van Gennep and Turner alike, on the threshold, making them ambiguous when understood from the viewpoint of the two opposed identities that the ceremony moves them through. In a word, they are liminal or, "betwixt and between," as Turner famously put it (see chapter 4 in his book, *The Forest of Symbols* [1967], a paper originally published in *The Proceedings of the American Ethnological Society* in 1964).

This emphasis on the social aspect of initiation tends to differ from the way in which it has traditionally been treated within the academic study of religion, which is probably related to the overwhelming influence that the Eliadean school (sometimes generalized as the Chicago school of thought) has had on the field from the 1960s onwards. As seen above, such an approach imagines initiations to be an integral part of his larger understanding of religion as somehow transporting the *homo religious* back to a time of origins, what Eliade called *in illo tempore* (Latin for "in that time"). Because participants often claim that initiation ceremonies were established by those known as "the ancestors" or the gods, such an approach claimed that the subsequent repetition of those ritual acts continually re-created the primordial moment (thus frequent references to "ritual or "sacred" time as opposed to chronological, historical time), thereby transporting the initiate to the time of origins, which centered them and gave their life meaning. More recently, we witness this in accounts such as Richard Stein's contribution, "Initiation as Surrender", to an edited volume titled, *Initiation: The Living Reality of an Archetype* (2007). According to him: "the archetype of initiation may be viewed as the process of transformation from one archetypal phase to the next" (63). Thus, in good Jungian and Eliadian fashion, he argues that, for this to happen, "the heroic attitude towards life must give way to an openness to previously unconscious aspects of the personality" (63). We thus see here even the influence of yet another member of this school of thought and one-time member of the Eranos circle: the American scholar of myth, Joseph Campbell (1904–1987)—a good example of a scholar who has had a tremendous impact on popular culture, given the widely acknowledged role his work on ritual and identity has played in influencing the Star Wars franchise's early storylines.

A rather different approach to initiation may be found in Bruce Lincoln's *Emerging from the Chrysalis: Studies in Rituals of Women's Initiation* (1981), which seeks to understand the nature of women's initiation with the broader aim of determining its form, themes, and, what he calls, its "species" (2). Not interested in experiential flights of fancy, Lincoln prefers to focus on the importance of wider social and political contexts of such rites by situating them in their historical specificity. Since women's rites do not impart a change in their hierarchical status, he argues that such initiation rituals provide compensation for women's generally low socio-political status in many societies. It strikes us that any study that examines initiation must take into consideration precisely these social and historical contexts. It is not nearly enough, in other words, to claim that such rites mystically or magically transform the initiate to other times, places, or experiential states. On the contrary, following the likes of Lincoln—and, in turn, Turner and Van Gennep—we have to study initiation's social aspects and effects. This means not understanding how such rituals transform individuals, but how they make possible certain sorts of societies with specific roles and thus identities allocated to their various members.

In this volume see: civil religion, conversion, creation, emic/etic, god, monotheism/polytheism, mysticism, paganism, ritual, sacrifice, sexuality, soul, theology, totem

In *Religion in 50 Words* see: belief, cognition, critical, experience, history, interpretation, society, theory

22 Liberation

Many are perhaps familiar with the terms "liberation theology"—a mid- to late-twentieth-century, Marxist-influenced and politically-engaged social and economic justice movement often associated with Roman Catholicism, particularly with its Latin American Church. However, when the term "liberation" is applied in the study of religion there is a better chance that it refers to what is often characterized as the objective of what are still grouped together as so-called Asian or Eastern traditions, where some people's commonplace assumptions about souls and the afterlife find few direct analogues. "Liberation," along with such other English terms as "release," "rebirth," or even "extinction," come to be a favored vocabulary for scholars looking for a way to translate a variety of terms and claims that posit the self in ways rather different from how many in Europe once took—indeed, as many in North American continue to take—things to function. Though we of course come across such things as England's mid-nineteenth century Society for the Liberation of Religion from State Patronage and Control (aimed at disentangling religion and state), not to mention the so-called women's liberation movement (dating to the mid-twentieth century and taking place largely in a variety of industrialized, liberal democratic nations), the term is certainly understood by scholars of religion as usually being accompanied by the adjective "religious" (i.e., religious liberation). We encounter this, for example, when theologians like Denise and John Carmody define the practice of meditation as "Hindu and Buddhist interior exercise aimed at liberation." See the glossary in their textbook, *Eastern Ways to the Center: An Introduction to Asian Religions* (1983), 229. This is often coupled with their companion volume devoted to so-called Western religions, and published in the same year. Such bifurcation again reinforces the all too neat scholarly categories and terms (e.g., East/West, monotheism/polytheism) that scholars have created, and continue to employ,

DOI: 10.4324/9781003196631-23

for the sake of what is, for all intents and purposes, little more than simple convenience.

The noun "liberation" is thought to have entered English from French sometime in the mid- to late fifteenth century. Prior to that, it derives from Latin (*līberātiō*) with the verb, "to liberate" not in evidence until the early seventeenth century and the adjective, "liberated," appearing a century after that. The term is based on the earlier noun, "liberate," naming a document to authorize payment as well as the release of a prisoner, which in turn is used as a verb, a century or more later, to name the action of freeing someone from constraint. It is related to the adjective and noun "liberal," i.e., to give generously or freely do something, e.g., to speak liberally, as well as the so-called liberal arts in a university curriculum, intended as less practical knowledge that may assist in creating an independent thinker and citizen. We even find the term used ironically, as a euphemism for inappropriately taking something, i.e., to liberate an item, as if the thief was doing someone a favor by taking it. In fact, we find this same sense of freeing—directly linked to the eventual Latin root, *liber* (plural: *libris*) for free or independent—across the history of the term, such as in North Carolina Supreme Court case of Bayan v. Wadsworth (1835), concerning a dispute over the proper way to provide slaves with their freedom: "The master sets free ... by this solemn declaration of his wish, that the shackles of bondage be forthwith removed, and the competent authority ascents to this liberation." See *Reports of Cases a Law, Argued and Determined in The Supreme Court of North Carolina* (1837), vol. 1, 388. In this way, the word has a history of being used as a synonym of the verb "to emancipate," itself dating to the early seventeenth century English and of Latin origins (*ēmancipāre*), referring to the act of being released from tutelage or obedience to an authority. We see this today with the legal act of a child who is still a minor being emancipated from a guardian's governance and thereby assuming authority over themselves, as would an adult. Such usage is of obvious relevance to its more modern use in such already mentioned instances as liberation theology or the women's liberation movement, not to mention the gay liberation movement of the same time. Moreover, it makes sense that during a war one will often hear of the liberation of a people or a region from an invading force, such as *la Libération de Paris* being the name of a battle, in late August 1944, to free the city (as part of the effort to free the country of France) from four years of Nazi occupation. Or, again, in 1971's Liberation War in Bangladesh, also known as the Bangladesh War of Independence, to gain autonomy from Pakistan.

128 Liberation

As far as the study of religion is concerned, we witness in the early nineteenth century a sharp rise in the use of the term "religious liberation," often with regard to English Protestant criticisms of Roman Catholic governance. Thus, in the following unattributed 1851 article from *Blackwood's Edinburgh Magazine*:

> We do not believe that any Popish government ever will give liberty to its people, nor that any Popish people will ever be fit to receive liberty .... The man whom a priest can command to send his wife and children to the confessional ... has no claims to the sympathies of a freeman—and is as incapable of civil freedom as he is of religious liberation.
>
> (vol. lxx [October]: 436)

But, as of the later nineteenth and also into the twentieth century, and with increasing interest in comparative religion, the term becomes closely associated with scholars' attempts to offer a local, English translation or synonym of what were once seen as such exotic terms from "the East." We see it as a translation, for example, of: moksha, a late eighteenth century English adaptation from the ancient Indian language of Sanskrit *mokṣa*; or of nirvana, also an adaptation from the Sanskrit *nirvāṇa* along with the Pali *nibbana*, both from the early nineteenth century. The former term is associated with what is today commonly designated as the religion of Hinduism and the latter associated with what is generally known as Buddhism. It is also worth noting that the terms used to refer to these two religions—"Hinduism" and "Buddhism"—both come into more common English usage in the late eighteenth and early nineteenth centuries. For example, in 1917 co-authors Puran Chand Nahar and Krishnachandra Ghosh, writing in their *An Epitome of Jainism*, made reference to "moksha or the state of liberation" (vol. 1, 475). According to the American occultist writer, William Walker Atkinson (1862–1932), in his 1910 *The Crucible of Modern Thought*, the Hindu equivalent to the Buddhist notion of nirvana would be "'moksha,' meaning liberation, emancipation, divine absorption, etc." (125). This is again made evident in the entry for nirvana in the 1881 edition of the fifteen volume *Library of Universal Knowledge* (see vol. X, 642), in which the Buddhist notion of nirvana, understood as extinguishing the individual self and thereby moving into a radically different mode of existence, is distinguished from the liberation of the self in Hinduism. Though, it is worth noting that different Hindu schools of thought go in their own direction on the precise understanding of what moksha actually signifies, with some claiming that it is the experience of dissolving the seemingly autonomous self into the oneness of the universe, such that they are seen as a fundamental unity. As noted above, a term such as moksha (or the related *mukti*) is in use elsewhere as well, such as in another Indian tradition known as Jainism as well as in Sikhism.

Those practicing comparative religion in its early years quickly understood that their search for analogues in the religions of others did not extend to beliefs in a life after physical death. We see this clearly in their preference for the term "liberation." The rather linear model commonly presumed in Christian theology (i.e., birth, eventually death, and then divine judgement, followed either by eternal reward or torment) fails to account for models which presuppose an almost infinite series of incrementally different rebirths. The latter coincided with a completely different sense of the self, one that inhabits and animates each successful rebirth, which, perhaps at some point, either collapses under its own weight and begins anew or which somehow is utterly dissolved and overcome. The latter results in what is claimed to be an experiential state well outside the usual language by which time, identity, and existence are discussed. Interestingly, this then becomes a difference that those specializing in interreligious dialogue have to attempt to overcome. We witness this, for example, in Diana L. Eck's curious claim that "[t]he closer counterpart to the message of resurrection is *moksha*, liberation from the long trajectory of birth and death" (see her *Encountering God: A Spiritual Journey from Bozeman to Banaras* [1993]). Eck's comment notwithstanding—not to mention the Carmodys' already noted assumption of a uniform center toward which the different paths point—it is at this point that such a term as "liberation" becomes handy, especially with its longstanding association with being unfettered and thus free. But the common scholarly focus on this term as naming the ultimate point toward which Hinduism works, much as "extinction" is used as what some designate as the goal of Buddhism, is problematic. We witness this early on, for example, see Henry H. Tilbe's (1859–1935) *Pali Buddhism* (1900, 28); and more recently, see Johan Elverskog's book *The Buddha's Footprint: An Environmental History of Asia* (2020, 25). The apparent need to find "the point" toward which these "other religions" work betrays, once again, the longstanding but, importantly, often implicit and unrecognized role that a dominant form of Christianity plays in setting the stage for scholarly efforts to compare religions. For if "we" all know that human history is working toward a final judgment and possible intervention on the part of a God, then what do "they" think about it and how do "they" talk about it? Although this is a terribly simplified and all too brief way of offering the critique, the scholarly focus on certain philosophical schools of thought, where analogues to some theme found in Christian theology might be easier to find, is the problem here that the critical scholar cannot overlook. After all, many of those people who identify with those complex traditions known as Hinduism and Buddhism, to name but two, live their lives with a much more local focus than on matters of ultimate liberation or extinction—a local focus little different, we should add, from how people worldwide carry out their lives. In this regard, a critical scholar may have some sympathies for the attempt on the part of their colleagues, in the so-called lived religion movement today, who attempt to get beyond more elite, doctrinal studies to, instead, studying the daily lives over people "on the ground," as it is often phrased. That this school of thought has some difficulties of its own does not prevent us from recognizing that the tendency for scholars to prioritize doctrinal and textual studies—and, along with them, the generally more affluent social actors involved in producing such discourses—is indeed a problem to be addressed. A continued focus on cross-cultural speculations on ultimate liberation may not be a productive way of doing this.

In this volume see: afterlife, animism, church, dialogue, East/West, meditation, mysticism, renunciation, soul, theology

In *Religion in 50 Words* see: belief, classification, culture, lived religion, text, world religions

23 Magic

Magic, both historically and in the academic study of religion, has been intimately connected to religion. Indeed, so intimately connected are the two ideas throughout the field's history that it has often been difficult for scholars to ascertain just how different they are from one another. It was often easy, for example, for a practicing Protestant—many of whom populated the early history of our field and frequently made normative judgments in its name—to claim that the practices, say, of a West African faith healer was magic or based in magic, and thus to be distinguished sharply from religion (yet alone "true religion"). It was similarly easy for such a person to mock Catholic claims that the bread and wine of the host somehow magically transforms into the body and blood of Jesus. The still common Latin parody phrase associated with magical conjuring, "hocus pocus" was once speculated by no less than the onetime Archbishop of Canterbury, Rev. John Tillotson (1630–1694) as "nothing elfe but a corruption of *hoc eft corpus* [English: this is a body] by way of ridiculous imitation of the Priefts of the Church of Rome in their *trick* of Tranfubftantiation." See sermon xxvi in *The Works of the Moft Reverend Dr. John Tillotson* (1696), sermon 26, 303. Juxtaposed against such practices, they would claim that their own beliefs and rituals were spiritually uplifting or grounded in the cool light of reason. In like manner, no orthodox Jew would consider the waving of a live chicken over their heads three times at some point during the ten Days of Repentance between Rosh Hashana and Yom Kippur, in a ritual known as *kipparot*, to be magic, though an outside observer armed with the category might, of course, have other ideas. Such examples take us to the heart of the problem involved with terms such as "magic," let alone the related "superstition" along with so many of the other words discussed in this volume. Oftentimes scholars elevate a word with an earlier and local, and by this we often mean Christian, meaning to the level of a universal category that

DOI: 10.4324/9781003196631-24

it is assumed everyone must have or exhibit. Or, if they do not, then they must either be made to have it—or scholars need to figure out how they either lost it or will eventually develop it. Alternatively, many parts of our conceptual vocabulary were originally developed as a way to differentiate, often all too neatly, what "we" do from what "they" do. The idea of "magic" certainly fits the latter. The term is traditionally defined as the application of beliefs, rituals or actions employed in the conviction that the individual can subdue or otherwise manipulate natural or supernatural beings and forces. One can see from this definition, however, just how similar it is to religion, which also tries to make sense of the world by attempting to harness what are perceived to be its positive and negative forces.

Etymologically, our word "magic" derives from the Middle French *magique*, itself from the post-classical Latin *magica* that dates to the third century CE. One can also compare our use of the term with the classical Latin *magicē*, from the Hellenistic Greek *magikē* where it was frequently used as a form of shorthand. We see this, for example, in the writings of the Hellenistic Jewish philosopher Philo of Alexandria (15 BCE–45 CE), for the phrase *magikē tēkhne* ("magic art"), which is also attested in the Septuagint, the early Greek edition of what Christians know as the Old Testament. Given its similarity, in so many ways, to the term "religion," it is worth noting—as indeed the *Oxford English Dictionary* does explicitly—that "[t]he relationships between magic, religion, and science are central to the history of the term in English. In the Judaeo-Christian tradition, magic, and esp. conjuration, are regarded as falling outside the province of religion proper." While that last sentence strikes us as rather too normative in its assessment, not to mention the tidy differentiation that it posits between what constitutes magic and what religion, we certainly concur that discourses of religion have tended to imply—whether articulated or unarticulated—discourses about magic, religion's negative "other." We encounter, especially in the premodern world, many traditions in which those discourses/practices known as magic, science, and indeed religion intersect—for example, in the Hermetic and Neoplatonic traditions of late antiquity and the Middle Ages where magic was often imagined as a precursor to the rise of modern science. Some go so far as to emphasize how natural philosophy—which also played a fairly large role in the Renaissance—functioned as a harbinger of modern science, since it was believed to be predicated on experimentation and the manipulation of the natural world (so-called natural magic), two of the hallmarks of modern scientific method. Though, of course, others argue that when we do this, there is a tendency to ignore or even remove some of the connections to those fields or disciplines that we today consider to be merely pseudo-scientific (e.g., physiognomy, astrology, even magic). Though, it is worth noting that, with the European spread of rational, scientific explanations of the natural world, the status of those things designated as magic has declined.

The English term "magic" was employed with some degree of regularity from the late fourteenth and early fifteenth centuries onwards. Therein it primarily referred to the use of ritual activities or observances with the intention of being able to influence the course of events or to otherwise manipulate the natural world, often by using what was imagined to be an occult or secret body of knowledge and techniques. Thus, we read of the doctor in the prologue to *The Canterbury Tales* of Geoffrey Chaucer (1340–1400): "He kept his patient a ful greet deel In houres by his magike natural" (104, as cited in Alfred C. Garratt's *Myths in Medicine and Old-time Doctors* [1884]). Or, again, as cited in the *OED*, consider the *Legendys of Hooly Wummen*, by the poet and Augustinain friar Osbern Bokenham (ca. 1393–ca.1464): "The myht of malgyk or enchauntement" (9340, citing Mary Sidney Serjeantson's 1938 edition). The term can often be used pejoratively, as in R.G. Collingwood's (1889–1943) *The Principles of Art* (1938): "'Savages' believe, or seem to believe, that magic can do things which we 'civilized' men believe to be impossible, like making rain or stopping earthquakes" (iv. 67). We also see this implication, as noted above, when earlier scholars of religion talk in a derogatory fashion about Catholic ritual and practice ("empty popery" it might have once been called). A secondary meaning of the term is when it is used figuratively to refer to some inexplicable and/or remarkable event that is imagined to produce some sort of enchanting or mystical quality that is otherwise inexplicable. We read of this, for example, in William Shakespeare's *Winter's Tale* (1623): "Oh Royall Peece: There's Magick in thy Maiestie" (v. iii. 39). Or, more recently, and colloquially, in the English playwright Peter Richard Nichols's (1927–2019) *A Day in the Death of Joe Egg* (1967), where a character remarks: "I wanted to bring back the magic to our marriage" (ii. 58).

The word "magic," perhaps not surprisingly given this brief etymological overview, has an equally interesting history in the study of religion, where it has always functioned as the foil to bring those things known as religious into clearer focus. More often than not, this involved attempts to stress the differences between the domains designated as magic versus religion, as if it was somehow easy to identify where one began and the other ended. Within this context, the term "magic," and thereby designating something as magic, was particularly important to early theorists of religion who were largely interested in understanding the origins of religion and, thus, how it differentiated from other related forms—like those things imagined as magical. In his once widely read book, *The Golden Bough: A Study in Comparative Religion* (1890; interestingly given the new subtitle *A Study in Magic and Religion* in its second edition), for example, James George Frazer (1854–1941) argued that many religions had their origins as fertility cults that often revolved around the sacrifice of a king. Basing his analysis on this and using a social evolutionary schema, one that was very popular in the late nineteenth and early twentieth centuries, he proposed that all of humanity progresses through a number of developmental stages. These range from a general state of magic, where nature is thought to be able to be manipulated, to religion where such manipulation begins to recede into the background. From there, he believed it would evolve into scientific thought, which for him—like so many other of these early scholars of religion who imagined their work as "scientific"—represented the apex of human development. In this regard we should also recall Emile Durkheim's (1858–1917) famous definition of religion in his *The Elementary Forms of the Religious Life* (1912) as "a unified system of beliefs and practices relative to sacred things, that is to say, things set apart and forbidden—beliefs and practices which unite into a single moral community called a Church, all those who adhere to them" (62, in the Free Press's 1965 edition of Joseph Ward Swain's translation). Most significantly for our purposes, however, is that Durkheim, in the same volume, also tried to differentiate this from magic, of which he also famously remarked that there could not be a "Church of Magic" because magic, he claimed, involves a person's (i.e., a magician's) manipulation of so-called sacred objects on behalf of lone individuals as opposed to that of the entire social group (which, for him, qualified the latter as religious). It was, after all, the entire group that formed the centerpiece of his functional analysis that sought to define the role of religion as one of the primary means whereby a society was able to think about, and in the process, to renew itself. The result is that the social cohesion of rites is largely lacking in the performance of magic—or so he argued. Both Frazer's and Durkheim's ideas were subsequently picked up by the Polish anthropologist Bronislaw Malinowski (1884–1942). In his classic works, such as *Argonauts of the Western Pacific* (1922) and *Magic, Science and Religion* (1925), Malinowski argued that magic was that which "primitives" possessed as their form of empirical knowledge. Indeed, he thought it not unlike modern scientific thought in that it allows them to understand and attempt to control nature for their own needs.

Such knowledge, he argues, allowed these groups to engage in practical work to get the results they desired.

We might say, then, that "magic" has been used in two primary ways in the history of the study of religion. First, as we have just seen, it has provided a coherent way to distinguish religion from a variety of cognate forms. While things designated as magic may have some of the traits and properties of religion (making them quasi-religions, or what others have called implicit religions, perhaps), or so this assumption goes, it lacks the social component (to invoke Durkheim's influential definition). Within this context, magic is still not infrequently put on an evolutionary scale by some, where it is imagined to be but a step on the way to science. Of course, such an approach also tends to be based on a type of privileging wherein the seemingly positive aspects of magic might be emphasized and what are perceived as its more negative ones are reduced or marginalized with the charge of being "superstitious." Indeed, the relationship between religion, as opposed to magic, and science is still on firm display in the academic study of religion, as a quick glance at the John Templeton Foundation (https://www.templeton.org) quickly shows—such as their funding of a study on so-called magical thinking among atheists (or what is also termed by its primary investigator, Clay Routledge, their secret religious lives). The second major way that "magic" can be used is pejoratively to argue that others have not religion per se, but practices and beliefs that are governed by magic. Anything that does not meet a scholar's own ideal definition of religion—which is assumed to be the "true" or "authentic" religion and the lodestar by which to compare other religions—can then be written off as "magic," "superstition," "heathenism," "barbaric custom," or, believe it or not, worse. Thus, we read under the entry "magic" in the American edition of the *British Encyclopaedia* from 1821 that magic:

> originally signified only the knowledge of the more sublime parts of philosophy; but as the magi likewise professed astrology, divination, and sorcery, the term magic became odious, being used to signify an unlawful, diabolical kind of science, acquired by the assistance of the devil and departed souls.

Such distinctions between religion and magic, while undoubtedly useful to the academic study of religion in earlier times and other eras, now seem to have little or limited utility. This is primarily because, as witnessed above, the term "magic" is highly contentious, categorically imprecise, and often comes complete with a certain value judgement involving the customary "us/them" or "we/they" binaries. If and when the term is used by a scholar today, it often takes on the second sense of the term, signifying something along the lines of that which is "inexplicable," "remarkable," or "wondrous," in which case it can be yet another synonym used to describe no less problematic experiential claims about "the sacred." We should also note in the present context that, while many still find it useful to juxtapose religion with other concepts in order to bring the former into what they consider to be clearer focus, the term or category now used to do this is not "magic," but "the secular." The latter term, however, is no less loaded than its predecessor and one that the critical scholar will surely use carefully in going about their work.

In this volume see: animism, church, cult, evil, icon, idol, initiation, monotheism/polytheism, paganism, sacrifice, shamanism, spirituality, totem

In *Religion in 50 Words* see: affect, belief, classification, comparison, definition, function, method, power, religion

24 Meditation

Much like the word "liberation," the noun "meditation," along with the verb "to meditate," has played a significant role in the history of the field. The term denotes a range of activities often associated with what many today group together as Asian (or what for some is still known as Eastern) religions. Given that scholars generally assume that such things as rituals are cross-cultural universals then the question for some scholars has been how such things are realized or manifested in different regions or historic settings and contexts. While scholars of religion in the field's early days certainly knew where such practices could be found in the traditions with which they were already familiar—i.e., in specific types of Christianity, thus allowing them to focus on such things as prayer, for example—the practices of people participating in theological systems that did not presume a creator god presented them with a puzzle. Into this entered a word they were already familiar with: "meditation."

First appearing in English sometime in the early thirteenth century—arriving from French and, before that, the Latin (*meditātio*)—"meditation" refers to the focused reflection on, extended consideration of, or serious contemplation about a topic. The verb "to meditate," is found rather later, in the mid-sixteenth century, and is related to the term, from a slightly earlier period, "premeditate," which denotes the act of thinking and thus planning ahead. While the term's early use can indeed have what readers today would understand as a religious application or connotation, it can also simply designate focused attention paid to any topic seen as worthwhile of one's reasoned consideration. For example, consider Rev. Henoch Clapham's (d. 1614) *Bibliotheca Theologica: Or, A Librarye Theological Containinge, 1. A Generall Analysis Or Resolution: 2. a Breife Elvcidation, Off the Moft facred Chapters Off Elohim His Bible* (1577): "to meditate on the works of Creation" (citing the opening line of chapter 2's "Elucidation").

DOI: 10.4324/9781003196631-25

In fact, it is the preferred English word used to entitle the still often read personal reflections of the Roman Emperor Marcus Aurelius (121–180 CE), simply referred to as his *Meditations* (the translation of a second century CE volume originally in Greek, of now unknown title, whose earliest attestation comes from a mention in a tenth century document). We also see it in the *Meditationes de Prima Philosophia* (i.e., *Meditations on First Philosophy*), the well-known title of the influential 1641 Latin work by the French philosopher, René Descartes (1496–1550). Despite this wide usage, the term often functions in relation to a form of introspection that might be distinguished from routine rational inquiry. For example, in a 1667 sermon by the English minister, William Bridge (d. 1670), entitled "The Work and Way of this Meditation," we read: "as we are to meditate on Chrift, the Son of God, fo we are to meditate on the Word of God" (*Christ and the Covenant: The Work and Way of Meditation. Gods Return to the Soul, or Nation; Together with his Preventing Mercy*, 441). The term here implies a disciplined contemplation on the significance of a specifically theological topic. Though, we should note here that for some the term "contemplation," which also dates to the thirteenth century, can itself be distinguished from mediation in the history of Christianity, with the former, e.g., the contemplative method or living a contemplative life, associated with what scholars would today simply refer to as mysticism. The close study involved with meditating on some text or topic is often differentiated from a contemplative practice focusing on knowing the divine in a fashion that can be claimed to surpass rational knowledge. As early as 1481, we read in William Caxton's translation of *Myrrour of Worlde*: "And there he was alle the nyght in contemplacion & prayer, and also slepte there" (99, citing Oliver H. Prior's 1912 edition, published by the Early English Text Society).

It is worth observing that this linkage between prayer and either meditation or contemplation continues in Christian literature for some time. It is also worth noting that mediation is often presumed to be an interpretive method where the significance of texts or events could be considered, especially with regard to their meaning for, or effect upon, the person. Thus we find "prayerful meditation and study" recommended in a sermon by the English preacher, James Parsons (1799–1877) in his *Miscellaneous Sermons* (1839), 191. We also note that Psalm 77:12 is translated as: "I will Remember the works of the Lord; I will Remember thy wonderes, and I will meditate alfo of all thy works," quoting "The fweetnefs and Profitablenefs of Divine Meditation." This translation appears in another sermon in the above cited collection by the Rev. William Bridge (416) translating a Hebrew word variously understood in English as to think, to pronounce, to ponder, or to utter. Perhaps it therefore makes sense that, with the rise of reports throughout the nineteenth century concerning the beliefs and customs of people from what was once called "the mystic East," this term "meditate" begins performing cross-cultural work that it had not previously. Now we find the noted scholar, Sir Monier Monier-Williams (1819–1899), writing in his once important book, *Hinduism*, which was published in 1877 in a series entitled "Non-Christian Religious Systems, also including volumes on Buddhism and also Islam": "A Buddhist, therefore, never really prays, he only meditates on the perfections of the Buddha and the hope of attaining Nirvāṇa" (76). It is noteworthy that Monier-Williams is here careful to distinguish prayer from meditation, given that, as he had phrased it just above: "the Buddha recognized no supreme deity." There is certainly a close link here with prayer—itself a Middle English term of French and, ultimately, Latin lineage, for a sincere request, soon associated with requests made of God, as well as formal phrasings of respectful requests made of others. In terms of the latter, for example, we read, "I pray thee, gentle Reader ..." in Thomas Harding's *A Detection of Sundrae Foule Errours, Lies, Sclaunders, Corruptions, and Other falfe Dealings ...* (1568, 43). Claims of the existence of divine being or beings capable of responding to such petitions makes the term utterly unhelpful in those situations where such beings are not thought to exist. Or, if they do, they are then assumed never to enter into relationships of mutuality or exchange with people, such as in what has long been known as deism. This is, of course, yet another helpful lesson in the limits of stretching the local to meet universal needs—yet it is something apparently many have thought possible in the case of the no less local term "meditation," what with its no less specific application throughout the history of English Christian discourse.

Since the later nineteenth century, the term has therefore come to be rather closely affiliated in our field with the study of those religions thought not to have a belief in a God, let alone a God who regularly intercedes. That is, those "religions" that lack, for example, prayers for a deity to be involved in human affairs, such as healing someone, ensuring safe travel, or "Give us this day our daily bread, and forgive us our debts, as we also have forgiven our debtors. And lead us not into temptation, but deliver us from evil ...," in the words of what Christians commonly designate as the Lord's prayer. Today we have an ever increasing number of studies in print, especially on the topic of Buddhist meditation—though, to be sure, we see the term used with regard to the study of Jainism, Hinduism, Taoism, Sikhism, as well as within the more ascetic or so-called mystical aspects of Islam and Judaism. In terms of Buddhism, for example, we see this in everything from Sarah Shaw's *Buddhist Meditation: An Anthology of Texts from the Pali Canon* (2006) and Alexander Wynne's *The Origin of Buddhist Meditation* (2007) to Edward Conze's *Buddhist Meditation* (2013) and Keren Arbel's *Early Buddhist Meditation: The Four Jhanas as the Actualization of Insight* (2017). Here the word "meditation" often stands in for ancient Pali and Sanskrit terms that might themselves be closer to the idea of properly training or nurturing one's intellect and introspection. In the case of Buddhism, this is often done for the purpose of overcoming or seeing through the apparently natural or commonsense way in which we usually perceive the world, our place in it, along with our very identity as seemingly individual social actors. Such training, taking a variety of forms—from practicing *zazen*, or so-called seated meditation, to engaging in calligraphy or even making tea is a disciplined, purposeful manner, to name but three examples—all of which appear in a tradition today closely associated with the idea of meditation. Here, the idea of meditation conveys what scholars have come to term more broadly as mindfulness, itself a word dating to the early sixteenth century, meaning to be attentive and focused (i.e., literally: full of mind, once implying a good memory but also the quality of careful attention). Understandably, perhaps, this term is also repurposed by scholars early in the field's history, to accomplish much the same work as their retooled notion of meditation. For instance, recalling Monier-Williams' collection of lectures, *Buddhism* (1889), in which the Pali and Sanskrit terms related to *sati*—signifying a variety of things, from memory to heightened awareness—are translated as "right mindfulness" (lecture 2, 44). Today, "meditation" is often used to classify a variety of techniques thought to aim at the desired outcome of this state of being mindful, as in "remembering, bearing in mind, the opposite of superficiality and of obliviousness ..., mindfulness as faculty and power ... is a factor in the Great Awakening [of the Buddha]" (citing Caroline F. Rhys Davids's *A Buddhist Manual of Psychological Ethics of the Fourth Century B.C.* [1900], 85).

More recently, the idea of meditating—or doing something in a meditative fashion— has been extended far wider than previous scholars could have likely ever imagined when they first opted to begin using a term from Christian ritual in their early work in comparative religion. A fairly major industry in self-help and self-actualization has by now developed, focused on everything from "Ironing as a Morning Meditation: Why you should break out your ironing board when you are feeling anxious" (according to a December 2019 medium.com web article) to innumerable workshops, courses, and popular books on "being in the moment." Not a few of these are aimed at achieving business success, with corporations "adopting forms of meditation that they call mindfulness to both relieve stress and also to train their employees to pay attention," in the words of the UK scholar, Richard King (as part of the opening to his public lecture, "Mindfulness and the Buddhist Tradition," given at the University of Kent in June 2017). But, as King immediately goes on:

> even in the military realm we find that the U.S. military and the Korean military are using mindfulness-based practices ... to train snipers so that they will focus intently upon their action without moral or emotional issues bringing to bear upon what they're doing but also to deal with post-traumatic stress disorder.

King's research interest, it may be guessed, is in how these originally Buddhist practices spread so widely and so successfully, to be almost ever-present in society today. Though another interest that we might have is in how these once unfamiliar, even alien and strange, practices were made familiar by an earlier generation of scholars deciding that they could be designated and then translated by means of a term once limited to devotional reflection and even prayer in Christianity.

In this volume see: atheism/theism, immanence/transcendence, liberation, magic, monotheism/polytheism, mysticism, piety, prayer, ritual, spirituality, tradition

In *Religion in 50 Words* see: classification, cognition, experience, practice, world religions

25 Monotheism/Polytheism

Monotheism, ostensibly the belief in one God (and note that the "G" is almost always capitalized in this context), only makes sense when juxtaposed with polytheism, the belief in many gods (again, often written with the lower case "g"). Often coinciding with monotheism are a host of other cognate notions, such as exclusionary claims about the existence of only one and "true" God that created the world and who is, furthermore, omnipotent (i.e., all powerful), omnibeneficient (i.e., all good), and omniscient (all knowing). More often than not, it is a term that is used positively as a self-designation, i.e., to characterize "our" religions, whereas the opposite, polytheism, tends to have a negative connotation, indicating those "less developed" religions that are "not ours." Some even go so far as to distinguish between various forms of monotheism, presumably as a way to retain the notion that, even in those cultures that apparently have several deities, there is nonetheless an indication of some notion of a supreme God among or between them all. This can then be assumed to correspond, to whatever extent, to the idea of God in Christianity, which is, after all, the unspoken norm for much comparative work throughout the field's history. Thus, we hear of terms such as: pantheism, the idea that reality is identical to the divine, from the Greek *pan* (all) + *theos* (god); panentheism, from the Greek *pan* (all) + *en* (in) + *theos* (god), namely, the idea that God or the divinity pervades everything; monolatry, the belief in many gods but the worship of only one; henotheism, a system wherein the believer worships one god without denying that others may worship different gods with equal validity; atheism, the denial of a belief in, or existence of, God; and deism, the belief in God, but the denial of miracles, revelation, divine intervention in human affairs, etc. Perhaps not coincidentally, and this is the key point here, all of these terms are the product or invention of the late seventeenth century European and Christian imagination and its concomitant desire to classify and

DOI: 10.4324/9781003196631-26

hierarchically rank the world based on what it considered to be its various and often divergent "belief systems." Though grounded in Greek terminology—perhaps as way to make such terms sound more authoritative than they actually are—there is no getting around the fact that they are "our" terms and that "we" employ them to classify the belief systems of others. The entire system of classification would seem to be predicated on the often assumed principle that monotheism is the most natural, highest, and best form of these so-called religious beliefs. That scholars still use these terms today—we think here of James K. Hoffmeier's 2015 study of the beliefs and practices of an fourteenth century BCE Pharoah, *Akhenaten and the Origins of Monotheism*—often in a manner that does not reflect upon their development and related baggage, means that there will necessarily be problems in using them unreflectively.

As may be apparent, the term "monotheism" is formed by combining the Greek prefix *mono*, meaning one, and the English world "theism," which refers to a belief in or doctrine of the divine (from the Greek *theós* for god). In like manner, the term "polytheism" instead employs the prefix *poly*, for many or much. Once again, it is worth underscoring that both of these terms did not exist prior to the seventeenth century. It is worth putting a fine edge on this point: neither derive, as we have seen with so many of the other terms in this volume, from, say, Old French or Middle English. They are modern terms that have been subsequently back-projected onto other times and places to name things that would not have been named as much. Those earlier times and places, in other words, did not know of such terms, let alone the meanings and concepts behind them. While we today might rather casually refer to the ancient Greeks or Romans as "polytheists," they certainly had no idea of the term, let alone what it meant or its implications, nor would they have self-identified as "polytheists." The same can be said for the ancient Israelites and "monotheism"—such as Benjamin Sommers's recent argument that "the Hebrew Bible is a monotheistic work and that its monotheism is not unusual for Israelite religion in the pre-exilic era" (see his chapter "Monotheism" in *The Hebrew Bible: A Critical Companion* [2016], 240).

English usage certainly attests to this. Thus, we read, for example in *An Explanation of the Grand Mystery of Godliness* (1660) by the English philosopher and theologian Henry More (1614–1687): "But thus to make the World God, is to make all; and therefore this Kinde of Monotheisme of the Heathen is as rank Atheisme as their Polytheisme was proved to be before" (iii. ii. 62). Or, again, in *Mona Antiqua*

Restaurata: An Archæological Discourse on the Antiquities, Natural and Historical, of the Isla of Anglesey, the Antient Seat of the British Druids (1723), by the Church of England priest and antiquarian Henry Rowlands (1655–1723): "The Stream of Idolatry ... deflected them [the Druids] from their profess'd Monotheism" (i. 63). Once again, we witness the always strategically useful juxtaposition between monotheism and polytheism—with each needing the other for its mutual definition and subsequent articulation. Again, in *The History of the Rise and Influence of the Spirit of Rationalism in Europe* (1865), written by the Irish historian William Edward Hartpole Lecky (1838–1903), which states, "A race whose pure monotheism formed a marked contrast to the scarcely disguised polytheism of the Spanish Catholics" (II. 227). In this latter example, we see further evidence of the ideological underpinnings of such terminology, where the term "polytheism" is attached to Catholicism, presumably as a way to refer to what might otherwise be termed its cult of the saints, something that for this author, removes it from the "pure" and "authentic" monotheism of Protestantism. The fact that some Christians are calling yet other Christians "polytheists," as a way to denigrate them as inferior, is clearly telling. We read, to draw on a final example, of this use in the Church of England clergyman and geographical editor, Samuel Purchas (d. 1626), such as his comments about Catholics in his *Purchas his pilgrimage; Or, Relations of the world and the religions obserued in all ages and places discouered, From the Creation unto This Present* (1613): "Theu built afterward ... an exchanged Polytheisme in worshipping of Saints, Images, and the Host" (ix. 43).

Monotheism and polytheism (and all the other related terms detailed above) have, perhaps rather obviously since it is based on so-called religious belief systems, played a rather large role in the academic study of religion. In its early days, the period that witnessed many scholars interested in ascertaining the origins of religion, including its original form, we witness a keen reflection on these various forms of theism. This was often done with the aim of trying to ascertain which one was the oldest and thus representative of the original form taken by what some might have termed the religious sensibility. Whereas some—most notably the early anthropologist E.B. Tylor (1832–1917)—in his *Primitive Culture* (1871)—posited animism as the original form; others, for example Emile Durkheim (1858–1917)—in his *Elementary Forms of the Religious Life* (1912)—argued that the earliest for was, instead, totemism; yet others tried to argue that monotheism was, instead, the earliest type of religion. The latter theory, known as "primordial monotheism" (or *Urmonotheismus* in German)—maintained that polytheistic and other such religious beliefs actually degenerated from an original monotheism, perhaps using the Bible's metaphor of the Tower of Babel as its precedent. The theory is perhaps best associated with the early Scottish anthropologist, Andrew Lang (1844–1912). While still maintaining an evolutionary view of religious development—as was quite popular in his day—his theory, it is interesting to note, actually went in quite the opposite direction from his contemporaries who proposed that religion progressed from simple to more complex forms. One of the biggest critics of this theory of "primordial monotheism" was the noted Italian historian of religions, Raffaele Pettazzoni (1883–1959), who, in his *The Supreme Being in Primitive Religions* (1957), argued that monotheism is but a recent development that, as others would also argue, emerged out of earlier forms such as polytheism. With its connections to various social forms, Pettazzoni further argued that the idea of a so-called monotheistic high god was ultimately a cultural one that enables specific groups to define their god in specific ways that was relevant to them (e.g., the bringer of rain, the protector of the hunt).

We witness some of these tensions when it comes to the use of later terms to describe earlier periods in a relatively recent debate in the context of early Islam. In his well-received *Muhammad and the Believers* (2010), University of Chicago historian Fred Donner argued that Islam began as an ecumenical movement of "believers" who seemed to have coalesced around the principle of the recognition of God's oneness and who were "convinced that the world around them was mired in sin and corruption" (79). Donner frequently invokes the term "monotheism" or the adjective, "monotheistic," to describe the contents of what many today would refer to as early Islam's religious beliefs, without asking what monotheism looked like in the context of the period just before Muhammad came on the scene. Reviewing the book in *Expositions* (5.2), Jack Tannous does well to note that the term "monotheism" is, as we noted above, in fact a modern European invention and, while Greek by definition and by virtue of its compound from *mono* and *theism*, does not actually appear in Greek sources before the late medieval period, that is, well after the period that Donner is talking about. Tannous, thus, asks how Christians, Jews, and Muslims in the seventh century CE could have imagined themselves as belonging to categories derived only in later centuries. While this certainly does not deny or rule out that there certainly may have been many ideas that we might today recognize as what we would call monotheistic in Muhammad's message, we should be careful to acknowledge and question the utility of so casually exporting later terms and concepts to retrofit them onto people in different times and places. Indeed, we could also say the same thing for other terms that Donner has no problem using, as if they designated concepts that exist naturally in the world, such as "belief" and "piety." This certainly highlights one of the major problems in the study of religion, namely, using later terms and categories to describe items and points of reference in earlier eras and epochs—but using them as if they name necessary and universal features of the world. Here, Tannous echoes the comments of Brent Nongbri, in his book, *Before Religion: A History of a Modern Concept* (2013), who warns us that we have to be cautious of assuming that people have always carved up the world—for example, a realm of the sacred and one of the profane—in the same manner that some of us do today. As he says: "The very idea of 'being religious,' requires a companion notion of what it would mean to be 'not religious,'" he argues, "and this dichotomy was not part of the ancient world" (94).

So, while today we might well think monotheism and polytheism to be as self-evident as such other categories as "democracy" and "freedom," the critical scholar should be aware that, like all terms, they come from somewhere and implicit in them is a number of prior contestations and struggles that often revolve around the issue of how to account for those "not like us." This, of course, is akin to Christian Europeans a few centuries ago trying to make sense of reports coming back of the almost innumerable divine beings in India, not to mention what struck them as the savior-like figure of the Buddha who certainly was not a god in their usual sense of the term. Regrettably, earlier scholars accounted for difference and otherness using imprecise terminology and sloppy, self-beneficial categories. Most significantly, at least for the conceptual pair under discussion here, is the fact that despite appearances that monotheism and polytheism are very old terms used to name concepts dating to ancient Greece, they are nothing more than rather recent inventions meant to describe the essence of things, ideas, and belief systems that predated their invention. The pair, then, presents a particularly acute example of the dangers of employing such terms without an awareness of where they came from. Though problematic, we somehow doubt that the field will opt to get rid of such terms because of the massive intellectual work that they perform in simplifying and marking difference. For the moment that we label something "polytheistic" we all seemingly know what that the term means or signifies—usually something lesser, overly complex, maybe even "primitive." The best that a critical scholar can do, it would seem, would be to be aware of their history and the problems endemic to such terms and, if and when we have to use them, to do so with caution and with an understanding of just how problematic they are.

In this volume see: animism, atheism/theism, god, idol, mysticism, paganism, soul, theology, totem, value

In *Religion in 50 Words* see: classification, comparison, critical, ideology, phenomenology, religion, world religions

26 Myth

Like the word "religion," there may be no more familiar word adapted from English vernacular to scholarly discourse than "myth." Its prominence in popular speech and writing does not make it any less of a technical term, especially when it becomes part of a scholarly vocabulary. As with so many other terms examined in this volume, it deserves some careful attention when used by a critical scholar. Most readers will understand the sometimes troublesome connotations of designating something as a myth—all depending on how one defines it, of course. Some will hear it as a handy way of identifying a falsehood, a superstition, or what an earlier generation might have even called "an old wives' tale." Yet others will use it to name the origins tales that people commonly tell one other, sometimes as part of initiation ceremonies, including those stories scholars call a cosmogony, a late seventeenth century English word from Greek *kosmos* (universe) + *gonia* (birth or "begetting") for how a system of order began. Along with these two meanings—both of which prove to be rather old and by now well-established—the scholar who digs a little deeper will find a wide variety of other inflections for the word's meaning and thus use, each of which is driven by a particular theory of society or the self. "Myth," then, is a particularly good example of how our technical vocabulary, no matter how disinterested or descriptive it may at first seem, always constitutes the tip of large and often undisclosed iceberg of assumptions and social interests. Because they are frequently unidentified—notably among those in our field who continue to wear claims of "I don't *do* theory" as some sort of strange badge of honor—there is a good chance that these assumptions and interests remain unexamined. This allows a scholar's words and thus scholarship to carry out work of which the scholar might not even be aware. We witness this, for instance, when one casually refers to something as "a myth" in distinction from, say, "a legend" or perhaps "a fable" and maybe even

DOI: 10.4324/9781003196631-27

"a fairy tale"—not to mention those things often seen today as myth's opposite: either "history" or "science."

Our modern term "myth"—whose frequency of use grew dramatically over the past century and a half—can be traced through French and, before that, Latin, ultimately to the ancient Greek word *mythos*. It appears in English as a noun only as recently as the first third of the nineteenth century, though as an adjective and as a verb it predates that by several centuries—although it is also worth noting that these latter two uses are now largely obsolete and trace to yet another Scandinavian root. Of interest is that the adjectives "mythic," "mythical," and "mythically"—all of which are directly related to the sense in which a scholar today would use the term—date to various decades in the seventeenth century. Thus, we note the claim of the Irish author and early folklorist, Thomas Keightley (1789–1872), in the close to the preface to his 1846 book, *Notes on the Bucolics and Georgics of Virgil*:

> Before concluding, I will justify my mode of spelling a word I use in this and all my other writings. From the Greek μῦθος I have made the word *mýthe*, in which, however, no one has followed me, the form generally adopted being *myth*.
>
> (vii)

For a word so widely adopted today, it may strike some readers as startling that 175 years ago it was alien enough to English readers to warrant such an explanatory note, followed by his recommendation for how to pronounce it. Moreover, combining the word with the Greek suffix *logos*, commonly used to signify the rational and systematic study of some topic (e.g., biology being the study of *bios*, a life or a lifetime) produced the now equally common noun "mythology"—adopted from Latin and later French and appearing in English in the early fifteenth century. Though sometimes used as if a synonym of "myth," it is, technically speaking, more about the study of a system of myths, such as the sub-field once called comparative mythology. In terms of the latter, see F. Max Müller's 1856 lecture by this title, included as the opening chapter in the second volume of his collection, *Chips from a German Workshop* (1902, 1–141). Quoting Keightley again, but this time from his *The Mythology of Ancient Greece and Italy: For the Use of School* (1831; no less than the eleventh edition was already published by 1858, the one from which we quote here): "These tales or fables of the adventures and actions of the Grecian gods are called *mythes*, from a Greek word signifying *fable*; and the science which treats them is termed *Mythology*" (14). He also adds in the book's preface, that the study of mythology "is closely connected with History and Philosophy; and an acquaintance with its principles is indispensable to a philosophic historian or critic, and useful even to a theologian" (vi).

But here we should stop, for alongside "myth" Keightley places both "legend" and "fable." The former word, appearing in English in the later fourteenth century, from the Latin *legenda* for an overly detailed or popular tale whose origins may be questionable. The latter term also appears around the same time, and is derived from the Latin *fābula*, with a range of meanings from narrative or story, to a discourse, or the plot of a play. But should we skip ahead to contemporary scholars, one can easily find a list of finely distinguished taxonomy of tales, in which a myth is, for instance, not at all to be confused with either legends or fables. Take the once noted British classicist, G.S. Kirk (1921–2003), for example, who distinguishes myths from legends (along with sagas) in that only the latter "is based on some kind of memory of the past, and ... [it] is described in largely realistic terms." This comes from his influential book, *Myth: Its Meaning and Functions in Ancient and Other Cultures* (1970, 32). He uses the tale from the *Iliad*, a work attributed to Homer who is said to have written in eighth century BCE, though whose historical existence is a point of debate among scholars, about the Trojan War. It is not much of a stretch to assume that some actual, noteworthy battle inspired the tale, though certainly things have been exaggerated over time. This is precisely what makes it a legend for Kirk, but in the case of myth the linkage to historical events is far more tenuous. "The gods of Homer belong to myth; they certainly do not belong to the essence of legend or saga" (33), Kirk concludes, making plain that the latter category should be reserved only for fantastical and fanciful tales not anchored in probable or historical events. Though he certainly does acknowledge that the two genres often cannot be distinguished so neatly. While he turns to tackling how folk tales differ from myths, citing the US anthropologist Ruth Benedict's (1887–1948) preference, inherited from her onetime teacher in graduate school, the noted anthropologist Franz Boas (1858–1942), to draw the line at the inclusion of supernatural elements. A tale counts as a myth when, as Kirk characterizes it, it is more than just incidentally concerned with the supernatural, whereas a narrative, as he phrases it, is based on "'serious subjects" and "deep problems and preoccupations" (37). Such distinctions remain common among scholars today. Though we might ask whether such distinctions reflect differences inherent in the tales or differences in the assumptions and interests of the scholars who happen to be engaged in such finetuning, seeing such nuanced classifications as useful to accomplish some specific work, remains for many an open question. After all, as Kirk himself admitted, at some level these tales all seem to merge into one another. Thus, we could ask ourselves: why even retain the distinctions? Or, to rephrase, perhaps we should designate them all as fables and be done with it.

Keeping in mind Kirk's thoughts on the linkage between myth and topics of supposed depth or portent, as might be predicted, scholars of religion have tended to reserve the word "myth" for a particular sub-set of tales, those that they consider to be sacred narratives. The category provides a useful way to show how their subject of study is somehow and legitimately set apart from the more mundane aspects of the world. We see this, for example in folklorist, Alan Dundes's (1934–2005) edited collection, *Sacred Narrative Readings in the Theory of Myth* (1984). No less than Mircea Eliade (1907–1986)—among the authors included in Dundes's anthology—once observed that "myth describes the various and sometimes dramatic irruptions of the sacred into the world" (see Willard Trask's translation of Eliade's still cited book, *The Sacred and the Profane: The Nature of Religion* [1959], 97). In fact, it was the cosmogonic myth that most attracted his attention, seeing it as the building block upon which a society was centered and thereby established and authorized. After all, creation stories are "the paradigmatic model for all origins," as he put it in the same volume (84). And, as might be expected, labelling such tales as *anything but* myth is utterly unthinkable. Notice that a word that is now used to name deeply consequential tales of existential truth and value retains a meaning that could not be more different from that earlier sense, cited in our opening, of lies. This meaning often credited to Plato, whose text *The Republic* (dated to around 370 BCE) famously banished poets and their fanciful stories (myths) from the just society that it proposed—an old story of the defeat of *mythos* at the coolly rational hands of *logos* that Bruce Lincoln nicely turns on its head in the opening chapters of his still important work, *Theorizing Myth: Narrative, Ideology, and Scholarship* (1999). It would be an insult, at least to many scholars of religion, to designate what they represent as deeply significant, world-building tales as being merely legendary or, heaven forbid, simply fairy tales. The baggage that comes along with the vague term "the sacred," along with Eliade's and others' problematic approach to religion (as being based on an utterly unique experience only later acted out make this approach troublesome, despite their continued popularity), should be evident by now. What this more recent development should also make clear is that, as already suggested, a scholar's terminology, including their use of the "myth," is animated by, and thereby helps to operationalize, a set of assumptions that always deserve critical attention. Sadly, they too infrequently receive such scrutiny.

Regardless of one's definition of the term, calling something a myth is hardly an innocent act. We see this, for example, in the psychoanalyst, Sigmund Freud's (1856–1939) understanding myths as being akin to shared, social dreams, i.e., coded expressions of the unconscious that allow groups of people to voice and thereby realize desires that, if actually acted upon, would otherwise be dangerous to the group's wellbeing. Or, again, the anthropologist, Claude Lévi-Straus (1908–2009), instead saw myths as symbolic expressions of a society's structure and thus order, with the study of a body of myths being rather similar to the study of a group's language. Perhaps it makes sense then, that, given much of his work's interest in exploring themes of power, politics, identity, and authority, Lincoln in the above cited book ends up defining myth as "ideology in narrative form." He goes so far in his epilogue to link this with scholarship. The latter is no less a form of narrative but one that, he argues, can be distinguished by its footnotes, i.e., its claim to authority based on prior argumentation, evidence, and a rigorous effort to "show your work," as he phrases it. This means that someone can follow along, to find your sources and test your claims, all of which can be distinguished from basing claims of authority on assertions about the gods.

The takeaway for critical scholars is that, as with all of our terminology, "myth" is theirs to define and use, though always remembering that others will be keen to determine something about the engine that drives its use. As scholars, and we think back to Lincoln's claim that scholarship makes plain its assumptions as best it can, it is our responsibility to see our tools as *ours* and thus as a means for talking about things and processes in the world that strike us as curious and therefore in need of study. Should those curiosities be shared by others, then perhaps our work can be read or a subfield can be established. But if read, and if collaborative pursuits involve others, then owning up to the assumptions that inform the vocabulary that we use and the projects that we tackle is crucial. For those projects more than likely involve moments or sites where, recalling a point often made by Jonathan Z. Smith (1938–2017), we were a little surprised by what we encountered given the challenge that resulted to the so-called commonsense that we once brought to the way we looked at the world. Whether "myth" can help make sense of that surprising situation—making it what Smith called "an occasion for thought" (e.g., in his essay collection, *Map is Not Territory: Studies in the History of Religions*

[1993], 307–308)—is something only we can answer, of course, but if so, then we had better consider carefully the work that this term can do and thus the way this tool will be defined and then used.

In this volume see: creation/endtimes, initiation, magic, ritual, sacrifice, symbol, theology

In *Religion in 50 Words* see: belief, classification, explanation, function, history, ideology, origin, primitive, religion, text, world religions

27 Mysticism

Mysticism is one of those terms that, for a variety of reasons, is thought to reside at the heart of religion. Believed to be grounded in some sort of private experience of depth and great consequence, with what is alternatively called "the sacred," "the transcendent," "the One," "the All," and the like. The mystic is often thought, especially in scholarship, to represent some form of "religious virtuoso" or "charismatic religious genius" given the authority that they derive from that experience and thus their influential status within their group. Though many might take the most important word in the previous sentence to be *experience*, we instead wish to emphasize another word, that of *authority*. The latter term—grounded in the social, the political, the material, and the ideological—emphasizes the rhetoric of experience as opposed to actual experiences, whatever that may actually name. The latter, after all, since they are claimed to be idiosyncratic and internal to the individual are, claims of those scholars engaged in the Cognitive Science of Religion (CSR) to the contrary, unquantifiable and unverifiable. Given their authority and their reliance on the rhetoric of the experiential, we often see in the historical record mistrust on the part of religious authorities to mystics, given the fact that the latter are thought to represent a threat to the status quo of the former, on account of the power they claim to derive from their special or direct relationship with the divine. Despite such unease, however, the study of religion largely validates mysticism on account of its ecumenical capability, with many scholars throughout the history of the field imagining mysticism to represent a unitary or even primal experience that is only *represented* in various cultural forms. This is yet another example of deploying the comparative method in the service only of finding similarity and thus supposed universals.

Etymologically, the term mysticism is derived from the adjective "mystic" and the common suffix "-ism," the latter of which denotes a system (e.g., capitalism or pluralism). The former word derives from the ancient Greek *mystikos*, a term that relates to what many might call sacred mysteries, with the added meaning in Hellenistic Greek of referring to the symbolic, allegorical, spiritual, esoteric, mysterious, and/or the occult. Classical Latin would seem to retain both of these senses of the term, given that in post-classical Latin (i.e., from the period of Late Antiquity), the term *mysticus* can also be used to refer to a priest, whether Jewish, Christian, or so-called pagan. Despite the fact that the term "mystic" as either an adjective or a noun dates to the early fourteenth century, the noun "mysticism" does not appear for another four hundred years. In fact, it was initially employed as a derogatory term to refer to religious beliefs characterized by a vague, obscure, or even a confused sense of spirituality. Thus, we read in *The Essential Life of the Late Learned & Pious Francis Lee* (1722): "Not to mention ye new Edition also since Publish'd by Dr Nichols, who I presume might have an Equal Aversion to Mysticism as to Popery." Or, as we read in *The works of the Right Reverend William Warburton, Lord Bishop of Gloucester, in seven volumes* (1788): "With an incredible appetite devouring the trash dropt from every species of Mysticism" (IV. 706). Or, again in the founder of Methodism, John Wesley's (1703–1791) journal from Sunday, August 28, 1827: "The same poison of Mysticism has well-nigh extinguished the last spark of life" (see *Wesley His Own Biographer, Being Illustrations of His Character, Honour, and Achievements* [1971], 185).

It would seem that in all of these early uses mysticism was a problem, something that troubled authorities on account of perceived antinomianism. Incidentally, this usage is diametrically opposed to the way in which the term is used today to refer to the timeless and thus universal essence of religion or, at the very least, its *raison d'être*. The term "antinomian" derives from the Greek *anti* ("opposed to") and *nomos* ("law")—that is, as opposed to the law—and names that which is perceived to threaten the body politic (along with its leadership). The mystic, on this reading, is someone seen as dangerous on account of the fact that they claim to derive their authority and thus their power through some special and often personal relationship to the transcendent as opposed to deriving it via the path laid out by the status quo (e.g., hierarchy, tradition, communities of textual commentary, etc.). We see this particularly in Islam where the mainstream Sunni legal tradition, especially its more conservative elements, is steadfastly opposed to Sufism—and Islamic mysticism that often attracts the interests of scholars of religion—which it labels as a *bid'a* ("innovation").

So, when do we witness the switch from mysticism as a problem to mysticism as a solution? It would seem around the eighteenth century. It is at that point that we begin to see the term expanded to include the belief in the possibility of union with or absorption into God, or some sense of an ultimate reality, by means of contemplation and self-surrender. This often involves a belief in or devotion to the spiritual apprehension of truths that are otherwise inaccessible to the intellect or empirical evidence. This mystical realm, though still imagined to be untouched by the political or the social, is said to exist far beyond or above the mundane world—said, we hasten to add, by social actors who are inextricably placed in the political and the social themselves. Thus we read in the Presbyterian minister and historian Archibald Maclaine's (1722–1804) 1765 translation of the Lutheran Church historian Johan Lorenz von Mosheim's *An Ecclesiastical History, Antient and Modern, from the Birth of Christ, to the Beginning of the Present Century*: "This female apostle of Mysticism [*sc.* Madame Guyon] derived all her ideas of religion from the feelings of her own heart" (xvii. ii. i. i. §51). Or in *Christian Mysticism* (1899), by William Ralph Inge (1860–1954): "The Gospel of St. John ... is the charter of Christian Mysticism" (ii. 44).

The use of the term over the course of the twentieth century tends to mirror this more positive meaning. In his *The Psychology of Religious Mysticism* (1925), for example, the American psychologist of religion, James Henry Leuba (1868–1946) informs readers in his Preface that mystical experiences "have played a conspicuous role at almost every level of culture" (ix). He subsequently defines that term as "any experience taken by the experiencer to be a contact (not through the sense, but 'immediate,' 'intuitive') or union of the self with a larger-than-self, be it call the World-Spirit, God, the Absolute, or otherwise" (xii). In this Leuba follows on the heels of the comments in the once influential book, *The Varieties of Religious Experience* (1925) by the American philosopher and psychologist William James (1842–1910), who argued that "ineffability," or that which is believed to be beyond description, plays an essential role in the so-called mystical experience (292–293). James, in the process, introduced the conception of the solely private nature of mysticism along with religious experience—something that would go on to play a central role in the way scholars to this day think about these concepts.

Eventually, or relatedly, this mystical experience is claimed to be the same regardless of the religion, let alone the region or historical period in question—and this is likely why it continues to play such a large and important role in the academic study of religion. Despite advances in the field over the past few generations, there remains a late-nineteenth-century tendency to find cross-cultural similarities and thus universals beneath the apparent differences. Informed by a phenomenological approach that emphasizes a common, experiential source to all religions, it became quite easy and convenient to imagine Jewish mystics, Muslim mystics, Hindu mystics, Christian mystics, among others, as all partaking in and experiencing the same transcendent reality. We see this approach as early as Evelyn Underhill's (1875–1941) once important book, *The Essentials of Mysticism and Other Essays* (1920), wherein she writes: "in every case [the mystic's] aim is union between God and the soul" (5). Such sentiments, then, produced a virtual cottage industry in ascertaining, defining, and otherwise categorizing the structures and contents of some unified thing now known as *the* mystical experience.

Various scholars, often referred to as "perennialists," have therefore tried to identify and map what they consider to be these sets of common mystical experiences across cultures and traditions. We see this in classic attempts, such as Aldous Huxley's *The Perennial Philosophy* (1945) and Frithjof Schuon's *The Transcendent Unity of Religions* (1975) and, more recently (informed by methods deriving from cognitive psychology), in the work of those like Ann Taves and Egil Asprem, such as their "Experience as Event: Event Cognition and the Study of (Religious) Experiences" (*Religion, Brain & Behavior* 7/1 [2017]: 43–62). One of the best-known attempts at such classification was provided by Walter Stace (1886–1967) who, in his *Mysticism and Philosophy* (1961), argued that two mystical experiences can be found "in all cultures, religions, periods, and social conditions" (79). The first is a universal *extrovertive* experience that "looks outward through the senses" to apprehend the One; and the second is an *introvertive* one that looks into the mind to achieve what he calls "pure consciousness." Not to be outdone, Robert C. Zaehner (1913–1974), the noted British scholar of Hinduism, once identified three different types of mystical consciousness: (1) a "panenhenic" extrovertive experience, wherein the mystic experiences the oneness of nature, (including one's self); (2) a "monistic" experience of an undifferentiated unity that transcends space and time; and (3) a theistic experience wherein lies a duality between subject and the object of the experience (*Mysticism Sacred and Profane* [1961]). All of these individuals, despite some important differences, nevertheless sought to distinguish between a universal experience and its subsequent culturally conditioned expressions. See, for example, Ninian Smart's "Interpretation and Mystical Experience," *Religious Studies* 1/1 (1965): 75–87 for a critical examination of Zaehner's approach, one that pushes back on the assumption of a universal source for all mysticism. Of note is that this approach has long been a defining trait of how the category "Gnostic" or "Gnosticism" has been used (once claimed to be a Greco-Roman or even early Christian religious group, whose emphasis on secret knowledge (Greek: *gnosis*) for the initiated was thought to be exemplified elsewhere as well). A clear example is Daniel Merkur's *Gnosis: An Esoteric Tradition of Mystical Visions and Unions* (1993), though, as David Robertson argues in his book, *Gnosticism and the History of Religions* (2021), it is also exemplified in the work of such contemporary scholars as Elaine Pagels, April DeConick, Roelof van den Broek, and others.

In most cases, those intent on studying such mystical experiences do not engage in the sort of experimentation associated with some current branches of the Cognitive Science of Religion (CSR), though it has also proven to be largely unhelpful in ascertaining the source of such experiences using, e.g., brain-imaging and other techniques. Whereas perennialists based their "findings" on the accounts that either mystics or, more often than not, their commentaries or "spiritual biographies" left behind, those engaged in CSR focus solely on the living and those who have not produced writings. This, of course, brings up a related question: Just what does a critical scholar do with mystical treatises? Do we see them as wonderful pieces of world literature, wherein artistically gifted authors wrote about their desires and yearnings? Do we imagine them as political treatises? Or, do we treat them, as many want to do, as direct transcripts of what a mystic actually experienced? Critiquing the perennialist position, scholars such as Wayne Proudfoot, Steven Katz, and Grace Jantzen (1948–2006) have argued that, even if such an inner mystical state exists, there is no possible way that scholars can have access to it, since all that we have at our disposal are the texts or claims of authors that purport to have had them. Thus, instead of searching for some vague meaning that is assumed to exist *behind* such texts, it would be far more interesting and productive to examine these texts either as works of literature or as socially formative political propaganda, and then to study the material conditions responsible for their production and subsequent dissemination in the first place, along with their practical effects (e.g., how followers use such texts). In this sense, the rhetoric of experience is, in many ways, more significant and consequential, than so-called experience itself.

In his 1994 *Mystical Languages of Unsaying*, Michael Sells examines the discourse of apophasis (i.e., and quite literally, "speaking away"), a literary technique that he argues is a common feature of medieval mysticism across Europe. The term, for him, reveals the impossibility of naming something that is ineffable by continually turning back upon one's own propositions and names. It is thus a style of writing that so-called mystics have historically employed in order to use language to get, paradoxically, beyond language (given that they often claim that their experiences transcend language). The work itself examines a set of texts (in their own languages, no less) that span over a thousand years, but the question he asks of them all is the same, namely, how they employ a particular textual strategy to speak about mystical experiences. Sells is less interested in the contents of such experiences—there is no mention, for example, of the sacred—than he is in the textual attempts to communicate such experiences. "Rather than pointing to an object," he argues, "apophatic language attempts to evoke in the reader an event that is—in its movement beyond structure of self and other, subject and object—structurally analogous to the event of mystical union" (9–10). To do this, Sells examines several mystics often thought to inhabit a tradition of apophasis: Plotinus (204–270), John the Scot Eriugena (815–877), Ibn Arabi (1165–1240), Marguerite of Porete (1250–1310), and Meister Eckhart (1260–1328). All of these individuals, he argues, sought to critique their own religious traditions while simultaneously trying to show what they considered the true meanings of their religions to be. Both of these features, Sells claims, manifested themselves in a particular way of writing that arose in specific contexts as individuals struggled with the ancient Greek notion of being. The end result is that Sells demonstrates how mystical apophasis is "a cross-cultural mode of discourse, emerging out of a variety of religious and cultural traditions and sharing key semantic features" (201). We also think here of Alex Owen's book, *The Darkened Room: Women, Power, and Spiritualism in Late Victorian England* (1989), which argues that male dominance of the Victorian-era church could be subverted by women in their role as healers or mediums who were said to channel spirits; thus, mystical appeals to private experience can be read as having the practical effect of undermining dominant power structures.

Debates about the contents and epistemological structures of so-called mystical experiences, to say nothing about whether or not the texts produced by mystics represent transcripts of some transcendent experience, therefore need not concern the critical scholar. The main issue, as just suggested, could be on a set of other focuses. Why and how, for example, did this term go from a generically pejorative one to a positive and largely ecumenical one? In this latter sense, mysticism as a category allowed scholars—at a particular time in the field's formative development—to devise a way to talk about experience that, though presumed to be unitary, was *expressed* in different ways in various cultural and social contexts. The focus, then, should be less on what mysticism, and its supposed experiences, is than on what it implies for the study of religion. Now largely an interfaith term, mysticism is often all but separated from the political and social contexts in which "mystics" function and, instead, undue attention is paid to the contents of their experiences—contents that are, by definition, unanalyzable to the scholar. When we make appeals to some sort of inner experience—regardless of whether or not such experiences existed, let alone are quantifiable—we forsake a critical examination of the authority that it grants to the speaker. When understood in this alternative manner, so-called mysticism becomes a useful political and ideological tool, one that is sometimes of potent practical effect.

In this volume see: commentary, dialogue, East/West, emic/etic, fundamentalism, god, immanence/transcendence, meditation, piety, renunciation, ritual, sect, spirituality, theology, value

In *Religion in 50 Words* see: authenticity, authority, cognition, culture, definition, experience, politics, power, redescription

28 Nones

Throughout the twentieth century, an approach to the study of religion known as the secularization thesis became dominant for many social scientific scholars of religion. It drew upon once influential theorists of religion, such as Karl Marx (1818–1883) and Sigmund Freud (1856–1939), and it maintained that beliefs and practices known as religious were seen as *compensation* for other more basic needs or desires. Put simply, the secularization thesis predicted a steady decline of religion as its function was replaced by other institutions in an increasingly diverse and differentiated society. If religion is the so-called "opium of the masses," as a classic Marxist might have once claimed, then, to continue with this one example, directly addressing the economic injustice that was assumed to cause people to believe that a powerful being would one day punish your oppressors would, or so it was reasoned, lead to religion having little to any function to play for a population. It was thus concluded that a modern, industrialized society would steadily become increasingly secular. That is not quite how things worked out, however. For many scholars of religion, Iran's Islamic Revolution of the late 1970s was the tipping point in their thinking on the irresistible pull of secularization, an event that culminated in the overthrow of the Shah, Mohammad Reza Pahlavi (1919–1980), and the installation of the formerly exiled Shi'i cleric (known by the title Ayatollah), Sayyid Khomeini (d. 1989), as Supreme Leader of Iran—a role that, such scholars noted, unified both political and religious authority. The ripples of rethinking the once prominent secularization thesis continue to this day. Scholars, notably those sociologists who once defined and then assessed religiosity by means of such measures as the frequency of church attendance, recognized that the things previously studied as religious might not really exhaust how people make meaning in their lives—with such things as "meaning making" and "world-building" increasingly appearing as the larger categories

DOI: 10.4324/9781003196631-29

under which religion was now thought to fall. Responding to the collapse of the secularization thesis by starting to see religion as but a species of a far wider family of what were also known as worldviews meant that, over the last generation or so, scholars of religion began to turn their attention to a host of activities and institutions that they would have never studied before. An earlier generation of scholars did not regard many of these activities and institutions as religious, given that they often used a commonsense definition of "belief in God" or something akin to that. It did not take long for such scholars to turn their attention to studying those who explicitly claimed *not* to be religious, such as the still prominent group of people who identify as spiritual but not religious—those known in the literature as SBNR, a designation that sees church attendance as hardly exhausting the many ways of being religious. In this regard see Robert C. Fuller's 2001 book, *Spiritual, But Not Religious: Understanding Unchurched America*.

With the decline of earlier assumptions and models prompting a newly expanded scope for scholars of religion, we come to a group that has recently come to be known by scholars and the general public as "the Nones." The latter is a convenient term to refer to those who opt for "none of the above" on surveys of religious affiliation. This is a fairly recent use of the term not yet included in the *Oxford English Dictionary*, which repurposes the Old English word for "no one" or "nobody" as well as lacking some specified quality. The irony that the term "none" is pronounced the same as "nun" (a member of a Roman Catholic religious community who has taken vows) is surely not lost on scholars of religion. In fact, in 2016 a US organization known as Nuns & Nones was founded, self-described as "an alliance of Catholic sisters, spiritually diverse seekers, and other religious elders whose mission is to create communities of care and contemplation that incite courageous action" (see: https://www.nunsandnones.org/about). Today, research into the religiously unaffiliated, or Nones, is quickly growing. We see this, for example, in Lois Lee's *Recognizing the Non-religious: Reimagining the Secular* (2015) along with the volume Lee co-edited with Elisabeth Arweck and Stephen Bullivant, *Secularity and Non-Religion* (2016), in addition to Christopher R. Cotter's *The Critical Study of Non-Religion: Discourse, Identification and Locality* (2020). The latter is a work that significantly turns away from trying to identify the content of these people's beliefs or the possible reasons for their disbelief to, instead, studying the means by which this identity is claimed along with its practical effects.

With this historical arc in mind, it is not difficult today to find a scholar of religion studying things that seem to have little to do with religion. Such scholars now regard these not as evidence of religion's inevitable decline but, if anything, its success and thus ability to morph into all sorts of areas that we might have once thought were secular. Accordingly, projects now tackled in graduate school and courses offered to undergraduate students would likely puzzle a scholar of religion from just a few decades ago. Case in point, the virtually endless "religion and ..." designation (e.g., religion and politics, religion and food, religion and sports, religion and pop culture, etc.) has exploded in the past couple of decades. This is because religion is now commonly understood as a way that people make their lives meaningful, an activity in which they engage at countless discrete, and sometimes interconnected, sites—from keeping a daily or weekly routine and celebrating certain holidays to dressing a certain way and associating only with specific people. This, a critical scholar may conclude, is part of the same trend that has turned scholars' attention to those who claim to have no religion. As counterintuitive as it may seem, if religion is about making life meaningful, and if all human beings are inevitably involved in such meaning-making, then all people are religious, whether they know it or not. Or, to rephrase it a little more delicately, just because there may be no reference to God or gods, or even an active denial of such beings' existence, let alone a lack of any attendance at regular worship services, does not necessarily mean—or so the current thinking goes—that there is nothing there for a scholar of religion to study.

It was therefore a happy coincidence to such scholars that a 2012 poll of the Religion in Public Life initiative of the Pew Research Center included a few questions containing a possible response of None, or None of the above. The context of this polling was that, as its report stated, up to "[o]ne-fifth of the U.S. public—and a third of adults under 30—are religiously unaffiliated today, the highest percentages ever in Pew Research Center polling," which marked a 5 percent jump in just a few years. Zeroing in on this trend, Pew partnered with the Public Broadcasting Corporation's TV show, Religion & Ethics News Weekly, and conducted a poll in the summer of 2012. The poll asked about three thousand randomly selected adults such questions over the telephone as "How important is it to you to belong to a community of people who share your values and beliefs—very important, somewhat important, not too important, or not at all important?" and "Do you believe in God or a universal spirit, or not?" They found that of the estimated 47 million unaffiliated adults in the

US (the majority of whom are under 50 years of age): 68 percent report a belief in God; 21 percent respond that they pray each day; 58 percent claim a "deep connection with nature and the earth"; and 37 percent understand themselves as spiritual but not religious. As the report concluded: "With few exceptions ... the unaffiliated say they are not looking for a religion .... Overwhelmingly, they think that religious organizations are too concerned with money and power, too focused on rules and too involved in politics" (find the brief report at: https://www.pewforum.org/2012/10/09/nones-on-the-rise/ and the full report at: https://www.pewresearch.org/wp-content/uploads/sites/7/2012/10/NonesOnTheRise-full.pdf).

But at this point a question might arise for a critical scholar. Are such polls descriptive or prescriptive? As anthropologists discovered more than a generation ago, ethnographies of other people's cultures (i.e., a descriptive report on their beliefs, customs, and institutions) can tell us more about the one who posed the questions and took the notes—*their* assumptions and *their* norms—than they do about the people that such writings are supposedly about. If a practice is unexpected by ethnographers, then they will likely enquire about it, understandably curious about why someone would do such a thing. But the account of "their culture" that results—as has long been known from recent studies of how earlier European authors depicted what they portrayed as "the mystic East" (a discourse now known as Orientalism) all in the service of generating a representation that served their readers' own self-definitional needs—can be demonstrated to be driven by "our" assumptions about what counts as normal or uninteresting. Thus, "their" culture could be said to be a product of "our" culture thinking about itself by means of observing "them." What, then, do we make of a survey that claims to report about empirical facts, but which cannot help but shape the data in the very questions that it poses—such as using undefined terms like "God" or "spiritual" *as if* answers to such questions tell us something specific about the world?

This critique, one for which a critical scholar may have some sympathy, is one that has been offered by Steven W. Ramey, for example in a paper presented to the annual conference of the American Academy of Religion in November 2013—the year after the Pew report was released. Instead of describing the presence of a pre-existent group, who we now happen to name as the Nones, Ramey concludes that what we have in this example is a poll, along with the subsequent scholarship and journalism that it prompted, "constructing a new group," what with the number of people, in the wake of the poll, scrambling to study the Nones, such as determining how the Nones would vote in upcoming elections and whether "they" would become a political force in US politics. And yes, it then becomes a term of self-designation (consider the above-mentioned Nuns & Nones). As a scholar of India, Ramey based his comments on the long-studied role of the Census of British India as an instrument of colonial governance, such as the one conducted by the British in 1871–1872. Among other things, it asked about the respondents' religion. "Once you ask that question," Ramey observes, "then you have to say what identifications do we allow, how do we classify these things, so you end up with disputes." Because such questions often represent or put into practice things that are taken as self-evident or obvious to those who are posing the questions, articulate thought is often not given to the way the survey itself may constitute the data in a way conducive to the pollster's own implicit interests and assumptions. For example, as Ramey goes on to note, Sikhs in India only later received their own designation as being separate from having to answer as if they were "Hindu." Thus, as reported at the time: "The census returns show that roughly calculated the Hindoos (including the Sikhs) number 140 ½ millions, or 73 ½ percent" (see the report on the 1871–1872 census that was published by the editors in *Journal of the Statistical Society of London* 39/2 [1876]: 413). Of further interest is that, because the question about religion allowed answers only for a few of what we would today designate as world religions (e.g., what the census termed: Hindoos, Mahomadans, Buddhists and Jains, Christians), as many as 5,102,823 people in India end up being designated there as "Others"—a grouping large enough to call into question any conclusion that the survey was analytically specific and thus useful.

Therefore, we may well ask whether such initiatives are an attempt, as the above cited 1876 commentary on the census phrased it in its opening, "to enumerate the people of ... British India" or is even the seemingly objective activity of merely counting already deeply implicated in (possibly competing) views on what is *worth* counting? After all, historians of the US know about the so-called "three-fifths compromise" in which representatives to the Constitutional Convention of 1787 agreed to count only three-fifths of America's enslaved population for the purpose of determining taxation and the number of elected representatives from each region (thereby resulting in greater representation, and thus federal influence, for slave-holding states at the time). If questions of value and focus drive such instruments as polls, often doing so in an implicit and unrecognized (i.e., unexamined) way, then are our own attempts to generate surveys just as deeply intertwined with possibly problematic assumptions as were earlier surveys? The latter, after all, were carried out in a period sufficiently unfamiliar to us now, which thereby assists us to see problems in what was once assumed to be natural and normal.

We may therefore come to claims about what the Nones think and will do or want and might need with more questions than those who study the Nones that they are answering by assuming such a group to exist. The discourse on some topic is seen by some as rather deeply implicated in *making* the topic seem as if it is worthwhile to talk about, let alone necessary to study. Examining that discourse itself—i.e., the assumptions and conventions that make the world appear to be naturally divided into just these discrete parts—means studying the production of an item of knowledge, something that Cotter notes in his already cited book. This may prove far more interesting given that pollsters, scholars, and journalists "have created an economy ... around a group that," as the scholar of religion Monica Miller phrased it at that same session of the 2013 AAR conference, "I'm just not quite sure exists." Miller therefore refers to this entire episode as "the curious case of the Nones" because, as she states at the close of her talk, "I don't necessarily know who they are." Thus, as she concludes, the fact that many today talk of the group as if they have always been there, waiting to be found, "speaks more to not only the public but also scholars' anxiety around narratives of religious decline." And so we return to this entry's opening arc, but now positioning not the rise of the religiously unaffiliated but, rather, our longstanding preoccupation with defining religion as belief and social affiliation, and the inevitable job of then somehow accounting for all those who fail to meet our expectations.

In this volume see: atheism/theism, church, mysticism, paganism, spirituality

In *Religion in 50 Words* see: classification, comparison, definition, faith, identity, method, pluralism, worldview

29 Paganism

Paganism is, once again, a derogatory term that has insinuated itself into the academy from prior participant discourses, wherein it probably has no business being housed. Like polytheism, it was a term originally conceived by a dominant group—that is, those identifying with a Protestant version of Christianity—as a way to refer to groups who worshipped and believed differently. Just as the term "polytheism" implies monotheism as its normative opposite, so too paganism (which is sometimes used interchangeably with "heathenism") implies a form of religion that is not monotheistic. The latter implies that which is rational, non-sensual, and, by extension, veritable and thus authentic. The term subsequently entered an academic vocabulary in what was once seen as a value-neutral, purely descriptive manner, whereupon it could be used interchangeably with other equally vague terms, like the aforementioned "polytheism," only for it to be reclaimed and resignified in recent years, as a term of self-reference by those social groups that worship nature, the earth, goddesses, etc. (so-called neo-pagans or neo-paganism, also a once pejorative term). The history of the word "paganism," however, should warn us once again that the elements of our vocabulary have real histories attached to them, that there are implications to their use, and that their meanings can and frequently do change—often radically—over time. Without an awareness of this, scholars risk repeating past mistakes, with the result that they will have considerable difficulty ascertaining a more rigorous and critical approach to the academic study of religion.

Paganism is a noun of Latin derivation (*paganismus*) comprised of "pagan" plus the common suffix "-ism," to denote a system of thought or action based on the noun in question (e.g., socialism or populism). In classical Latin, the term *paganus* referred to one who belonged to, originated from, or lived in the countryside or another similar rural community, and could even be extended to mean a civilian (as opposed to a *miles*, or "soldier"). In this sense *paganus* seems to derive from the Latin term *pagus*, meaning the country district or countryside. The term's socially formative role in distinguishing rural from settled regions and therefore people—a distinction that can easily be ranked hierarchically, as in recent discourses that demean "country bumpkins," "hillbillies," and "rednecks"—should therefore not go unnoticed. It was in the fourth century of the Common Era, in post-classical Latin, that *paganus* (both adjective and noun) begins to take on the meaning of "heathen" (again, an Old English term for one who lives well outside large population centers, e.g., out upon the heath), as opposed, say, to a Christian or a Jew. This all too tidy distinction between "Jew," "Christian," and "pagan," as we shall see shortly, is perhaps the main reason why the term became a catch-all and, at one time, a popular academic one. The fact that Jew and Christian are capitalized, whereas pagan is not, is surely also telling. Some speculate that the change in meaning was related to the notion that idolatry—i.e., "paganism"—was perceived to have continued in rural villages and hamlet settings even after Christianity had been generally accepted in the towns and cities of the Roman Empire, as its official religion. The *Oxford English Dictionary* states that since early Christians self-referred as *milites*, that is, Latin for "soldiers" of Jesus, they then applied to non-Christians the term *paganus* ("civilian, non-militant") to all those "not enrolled in the army" of God. Again, we see in the term—from the fourth century onward—how it is used for socially formative effect, to differentiate all too neatly between what one group represents as proper, and therefore authoritative, as opposed to improper beliefs and practices.

In early English usage, the term "pagan" thus denotes a person who does not subscribe to any major or recognized religion, but especially to a religious or social form that is *not* considered to be the dominant religion of a particular society and one that is often associated with a time prior to the arrival of what later became the dominant religion. A pagan—at least from the perspective of early Christianity—is therefore someone who (1) is not a Jew, and must, by definition, be (2) equivalent to a polytheist or a heathen on account of the fact that they either worship multiple deities, the wrong deity, or what are designated as idols. See, e.g., "The Golden Calf and the Idol Worshippers," an 1815 poem by Peter Pindar, a pseudonym for the English satirist John Wolcot (1738–1819). Coterminus with such terms as polytheist, pagan, or heathen are a number of moral judgments, signaled by the routine inclusion of a host of other pejorative adjectives, such as savage, primitive, unethical, overly sensual, and uncivilized, etc.—all of which are characteristics, not surprisingly, that are imagined as the opposite of those displayed by the one offering such judgments. We read, as early as 1400, in *The Death of Arthur* (*Morte Arthure*): "I sall ... euer pursue the payganys þat my pople distroyede." Or, in the English writer, Daniel Defoe's (1660–1731) *A System of Magick: Or, A History of the Black Art* (1727): "The Emperor Julian ... was perverted from Christianity, and confirm'd a Pagan, by Maximus a Magician" (i. iii. 71). Paganism, not unlike "pagan," is regarded as a non-Christian or even pre-Christian religion, that which is considered to be ancient or primitive, but note that both of these latter adjectives are, of course, used pejoratively. That is, claims about paganism are not to be regarded in the same manner as, say, references to "the *primitive* or *ancient* Church," the latter being that to which some Protestantism sought to return after centuries of what we once termed "popish superstition" (a once prominent slur for Roman Catholicism). We read, for example, in Thomas Norton's (d. 1584) translation of John Calvin's *Institutes of the Christian Religion* from the Latin in 1561: "They goe about a witty thing, to make one religion of Christianitie, Jewishnesse, and Paganisme, as it were of patches sowed together" (iv. xix. f. 158). Paganism also becomes a convenient catch-all phrase to explain a host of forces that are otherwise not clear, ambiguous, or needed for neat juxtaposition so that authors can bring their ideas (and identities) to clearer articulation. For example, in *A New Account of the East Indies* (1727), the writer for the East India Company, Alexander Hamilton (1688–1733), writes of a particular group: "Their Religion is a Complex of Mahometism and Paganism" (II. xxxix. 83). Or consider Edward Gibbon's (1737–1794) once widely read *The History of the Decline and Fall of the Roman Empire* (1781): "The divisions of Christianity suspended the ruin of Paganism" (II. xxi. 248).

The question should by now hopefully arise: Why is this even an academic term? Or, perhaps better, *how* did a word with such ideological overtones become a term of choice for scholars? Perhaps we get a glimpse of this transformation in, for example, the Anglican priest and Dean of Westminster, John Ireland (1761–1842), who could write a book with the title, *Paganism and Christianity Compared: In a Course of Lectures to the King's Scholars, at Westminster* (1809) and in which he writes that one of his goals is "a defence of the Character of the Church against the slanders of Paganism" (vi). He continues:

> [the] true causes of the decay of the Empire are contrasted with the false; the impotence of the Heathen deities, to whom the prosperity of Rome had been attributed, is exposed in the arguments employed by the ancient apologists of the Faith; and the beneficial

tendency of the Gospel is asserted, in its connection with the condition of Man in the present life.

(vii)

The seeds to answering the above questions might therefore reside in such sentiments, where "paganism" has to mean something if for no other reason than that it is necessary to bring the "true" teachings of Christianity into sharper focus. To cite another example, witness the title of a book by the Rev. Robert Adam: *The Religious World Displayed: Or, A View of the Four Grand Systems of Religion, Judaism, Paganism, Christianity, and Mohammedism; and of the Various Existing Denominations, Sects and Parties, in the Christian World. To Which is Subjoined, A View of Deism and Atheism* (1809). Paganism in these titles always refers to that which is neither "Jewish" nor "Christian" in the ancient world, i.e., that which is not "us"—it was thus a category, in other words, into which a host of vague and often ill-defined groups could be placed, without having to really define them or give them distinguishing characteristics other than to say that they worship other deities. And, with that, a scholarly comparative category was created. From the aforementioned works it is a fairly short journey to arrive at academic monographs with such unironic titles such as Judith Lieu, John North, and Tessa Rajak's edited volume, *The Jews Among Pagans and Christians in the Roman Empire* (1992) or a chapter by Sara Lipton with a title like "Christianity and Its Others: Jews, Muslims, and Pagans" in the multi-authored book, *The Oxford Handbook of Medieval Christianity* (2014). While the latter is at least aware of the work that "paganism" is doing for Christian self-formation, it is not uncommon to see in academic literature the term "pagan" invoked in such a manner that it is thought to perform real academic work with analytic utility. Instead of looking at the complexity of social formation in antiquity, many prefer to take an easier approach that involves divvying people up into imagined and discrete groups, and those which we cannot name precisely or with any degree of accuracy we call "paganism."

If the term has, over the years, gradually fallen out of favor in the study of the ancient world, recent years have seen attempts to redefine and thereby reclaim the word for all those earth-centered social movements (e.g., Wicca, Druidery, goddess religions, etc.). Now, it is sometimes referred to as "neo-paganism" with the prefix neo- being an adaptation from Greek for "new." In their edited collection, *Paganism Today: Witches, Druids, the Goddess and Ancient Earth Traditions for the Twenty-First Century (1996),* Graham Harvey and Charlotte

Hardman, for example, show that such contemporary movements are, in fact, equivalent to what scholars often designate as new religious movements (NRMs), despite the fact that their own members claim ancient origins and thus authenticity. They are, however, no less political than any other social group that appeals to religion, in the sense that, in claiming antiquity, they seek to justify their existence and their causes through, for example, claims to indigeneity and thus authenticity. Interestingly, however, for the first time in history, contemporary people refer to themselves as pagans. While no so-called pagan in antiquity, for example, would have used that term to describe themselves, or their religion as "paganism," contemporary pagans have no problems whatsoever with such a term. Consider, for example, The Pagan Federation, a UK organization founded in 1971, that is dedicated "to support[ing] all Pagans to ensure they have the same rights as the followers of other beliefs and religions" (as listed on their website) as well as the book, *Voices from the Pagan Census: A National Survey of Witches and Neo-Pagans in the United States* (2003). This once again shows how terms change their meanings over time. In the case of paganism, this means going from a derogatory category denoting a civilian, to a "heathen" and "polytheist," to a scholarly category and now a self-designation of pride.

In the final analysis, however, a critical scholar might conclude that the term "paganism" is, at least when used in the modern academy, an intellectually lazy one. Largely devoid of content, it is often employed as if it names a particular religious group when, more often than not, it is a foil for naming ourselves. If anything, it is often a pejorative term that has been given a light veneer of respectability derived from its recent inclusion in the study of religion's vocabulary. As should be apparent, however, it is a term, like so many of our terms, that probably no longer belongs there.

In this volume see: animism, idol, initiation, magic, monotheism/polytheism, ritual, sacrifice, shamanism, totem

In *Religion in 50 Words* see: classification, faith, ideology, identity, orthodoxy, primitive, society, worldview

30 Piety

Although it may seem rather dated, given the dramatic decline in its use over the past century and a half, the noun "piety"—along with its adjective, "pious" and its opposites, "impiety" and "impious"—provides a useful cautionary tale concerning how words change over time. Despite the common assumption that "there exists a continuity here, going back to the beginnings in early history, and a continuity that can be taken for granted" (1), as noted by the German scholar, Ernst Feil (1932–2015), in his opening essay to the edited collection, *On the Concept of Religion* (2000), the modern category of piety, not unlike religion, has changed considerably. How each of these words are currently employed—both in the general public and in the academy—is not necessarily an indication of how they were once used. Moreover, while their current use may tell us something about the people now using them, their ancient uses might shed light on situations long removed from us today—with the transitions in their use being of particular interest. Although "pious" has frequently been used as a rather straightforward synonym for "religious"—such as we find in the multi-authored textbook from 1931, *Religions of the World: Their Nature and Their History*, where it is noted that "the essence of religion" is said by some to be found "in the pious religious life that knows no dogma" (405). The relationship between these two words is, however, rather more complicated. In fact, it is precisely the changes in how modern speakers use such words that may attract the critical interest of a scholar, studying their strategic uses, in the plural, rather than trying to settle on what they should actually mean.

Our noun "piety" (along with "impiety") is first evidenced in Anglo-Norman English around the mid-fourteenth century, with the adjective, "pious" developing about a century later and "impious" not appearing until a century after that. The term derives from the ancient Latin *pietās* by way of the Old French *piété*, itself equivalent to

DOI: 10.4324/9781003196631-31

the related word "pity," as of the tenth century, i.e., "to take pity on," that is, demonstrate compassion toward. As defined by the *Oxford English Dictionary*, "piety" is a word used with regard to actions, thus denoting "fervent attachment to the service of God" and "the duties and practices of religion." We find this with the French reformer, Jean Calvin (1509–1564), e.g.: "by piety I mean that union of reverence and love to God which the knowledge of his benefits inspires" (quoting Henry Beveridge's 2008 translation of Calvin's still noted 1536 work of systematic theology, *Institutes of the Christian Religion*, chpt. 2: 7). The term could also be used to demonstrate "respect and devotion for parents, the dead, etc." less than a century later. Therefore, before too quickly concluding that "to be pious" is the same as saying that someone is religious, it is worth pausing for a moment to consider how these two different uses may be connected, something for which we may find some clues from the various words that these definitions put into a relationship with "piety"—such words as "action," "service," "duties," "practices," "reverence," "respect," and "devotion." Significantly, we do not find among this list those that many would today assume to correspond naturally with the no less ancient, related word, "religion," such as "belief," "feeling," "sentiment," etc.

This gap between publicly observable practices, on the one hand, and interior sentiments, on the other, was duly noted by the historian of religions, Jonathan Z. Smith (1938–2017). He observed a shift to belief as being religion's defining characteristic. "Terms such as 'reverence,' 'service,' 'adore,' and 'worship'" Smith notes, in mid-eighteenth-century definitions of religion, "have been all but evacuated of [their earlier] ritual connotations, and seem more to denote a state of mind, a transition begun by Reformation figures such as [Ulrich] Zwingli and Calvin who understood 'religion' primarily as 'piety'." See Smith's much cited essay, "Religion, Religions, Religious" in Mark C. Taylor's edited volume, *Critical Terms for Religious Studies* (1998), 271. Smith adds, even "[t]he latter term [i.e., piety] takes on a less awesome cast in subsequent Protestant discourse," citing the 1696 edition of Edward Phillips's (b. 1630) 1658 work, *A New World of English Words; or, A General Dictionary Containing the Interpretation of Such Hard Words As Are Derived from Other Languages*, where it is defined as "a Moral virtue which causes us to have affection and esteem for God and Holy Things." It is noteworthy that the original 1658 edition of Phillips's dictionary lacked entries for either "piety" or "pious," let alone "religion." The following entries were added only in later, expanded editions: (1) "Piety, Godlinefs, Devotion; alfo natural Affection of Love for one's Country, Parents or Relations"; (2) "Religion, the Worship of a Deity,

Piety, Godlinefs, Devotion; alfo the Sacrednefs of an Oath"; (3) "Religionift, one that Profeffes a Religion"; and, finally, (4) "Religious, belonging to Religion, or to a Regular Order; Devout, Pious, Godly; alfo exact, ftrict or punctual in doing one's Duty, keeping Promises, &c" (all of which are included in the dictionary's 1720 edition).

The point? In European literature across the seventeenth and eighteenth centuries we see this shift to belief, as Smith phrased it, with words previously associated with behavior, social status, and thus identity retooled to refer to a naturally occurring, inner sentiment that is only secondarily projected outward into the world. We today, of course, are the inheritors of such a shift, making us the ones who claim such things as "[r]eligion must proceed the understanding and the heart" (6), as the Unitarian missionary Richard Wright (1764–1836) once phrased it in his 1819 tract, *Essay on the Duty of Free Inquiry in Matters of Religion* (2nd ed., 1834). We might assume that if our words "piety" and "religion" have Latin origins then it must have meant for, say, ancient Romans what it means for us today. Recalling the opening to this entry, this is far from the case. Again, thinking of Smith's argument, the ancients are well on the other side of what he characterizes as the early modern shift that we moderns have inherited and which so informs our way of understanding ourselves, our neighbors, and the world. So much so that that we might find it very difficult to imagine a time when—as evidenced Phillips's 1720 edition—both "piety" and "religious" signified observable actions, practiced in specific social settings, and which carried social implications, all depending on whether they were carried out properly or not.

The irony is that many of the words from other cultures and historic periods that scholars now so unremarkably translate by the English words "religion" and "religious" can be argued to have had little to do with the modern, philosophically idealist orientation of these words for us today. Instead, many of these words—from *eusébia* in ancient Greek and, of course, *pietās* for ancient Romans to the ancient Sanskrit *dharma* along with the Arabic *dīn*—can all be understood in their earlier settings to signify a form of social identification involving what others judged to be their fellows' proper behavior with regard to their own social superiors, inferiors, and peers. It makes sense, then, that what sheds light on the meaning of "piety" for Phillips's now dated dictionary is not just devotion. Rather, we should observe, that this is itself a status inferred from an observable act, following rules, such as its earlier sense of making a vow and thus being dedicated to—but also, for example, affection for one's parents. Referring once again to one of the *OED*'s current definitions for "piety": "faithfulness to the duties naturally owed to one's relatives, superiors, etc.; affectionate loyalty and respect, esp. to parents; faithfulness, dutifulness." Thus, that earlier string of associated words (i.e., "action," "service," "duties," "practices," "reverence," "respect," and "devotion") now make far more sense, in that they name a network of behaviors, social actors, and social situations in which issues of membership and rank were navigated and worked out. Or, perhaps an example more identifiable for a contemporary reader: who must employ a title to refer to another and who gets to use their nickname—and what trouble would one be in if these two situations were confused?

This starts to get at the issues involved with designating an ancient person as being pious. Such a person was judged to understand correctly how to negotiate issues of rank, identity, place, and privilege, doing so in a complex and always shifting social world in which they sometimes occupied the inferior position. While at other times, others' behaviors toward them signified that they were now in an authoritative position—then the etymological links between "piety" and demonstrating compassion for someone else (i.e., "pity") start to make sense. It did not refer precisely to the carrying out one's specifically *religious* duty, but merely fulfilling one's general obligations with regard to the other members of one's group. This, of course, is itself a fairly useful definition of doing one's *dharma* in an ancient Indian sense of the term. In fact, the ease with which some cultural systems far afield from Europe, such as what is today known as Confucianism in China, can so easily be designated by some scholars as a religion, let alone today included in a typical world religions textbook, is surely linked to this much older understanding of piety. Indeed, the central Confucian term, *li*, is often translated as propriety—see Kurtis Hagen's essay, "The Propriety of Confucius: A Sense-of-Ritual," *Asian Philosophy* 20/1 (2010): 1–25—something, we should observe, that is curiously not all that far from one of those 1720 definitions of "religious": punctual in doing one's duty.

Those interested in all of this may even have a way to understand the discourse on religion's shift to this thing that so many of us today call belief or even faith (i.e., interior and thus empirically unavailable experience or states of mind). This is a shift that, as Smith argued, and as we have seen demonstrated in a dictionary from the time, we find taking place about three to four hundred years ago in European vocabulary. If a social theorist assumes that identity and status are not naturally occurring human traits but, rather, the result of innumerable prior situations and interactions among actors, the results of which, over time, accrue and are reinforced, such that it eventually becomes almost impossible for a person born and raised in, say, New Zealand, to see themselves as anything but a Kiwi. A handy way to authorize an identity and a status *that could have been otherwise* (had any of those situations and interactions gone a different way, such as being born in, let's say, Thailand instead of New Zealand) would be to erase the trace of those prior situations and interactions, making their contingent result seem quite the opposite: natural and thus necessary. Now the resulting identity and the status seem to stand on their own, as if they somehow sprang from the ground fully formed. We now return to Smith's observation that so-called Protestant Reformers, starting in the sixteenth century, played a large role in this shift to belief. Indeed, there might be good reason why the situations and interactions, all involving duty and obligation among ranked members within a regulated society, may have been idealized and so internalized, thereby erasing the usually observable repetition of propriety and institution, all in the service of authorizing but one of its results. Now an oppositional movement may have devised a way to represent the dominant against which it was reacting as weighted down by the stifling effect of ritual, hierarchy, and burdensome institution—what many Reformers at that time, all rebelling against the authority of the Roman Catholic Church, often referred to as "popery." The Reformers, supposedly free of such impediments, could then represent themselves as instead offering such things as free inquiry and inspired, correct readings of authoritative texts that were somehow liberated from tradition. This could include translating them into the vernacular languages of the people themselves, much as the New Testament was translated into English, and then mass produced via the recently invented printing press, by William Tyndale (d. 1536), rather than remaining in Latin, a language then of specialists in the church hierarchy. Should this be the approach to, first, delegitimize one's adversary while, second, legitimizing the alternative one is offering, then a rhetorical technique to turn such things as piety along with religion into an inner quality, from their prior life as social deference, ranked respect, and ritual propriety, would be a pretty handy devise. That the rules, traditions, ranks, and institutions remain—as they always do in any human community—will not be overlooked by the critical scholar, to be sure, but their attention will now also be given to the strategies groups use to minimize their appearance so as to naturalize their results.

In this volume see: church, icon, idol, magic, paganism, reformation, ritual, spirituality, theology, tradition

In *Religion in 50 Words* see: belief, classification, faith, history, identity, politics

31 Pilgrimage

Since many people, not to mention those groups often known as religions, attach importance to particular places—the place of birth or death of someone designated as a founder, or places seen as significant to how the group tells its own story of origins, along with those spaces where they say they feel "called" and locations where miraculous events are said to have taken place or been witnessed, not to mention shrines where a deity is said to live or be "housed"—it is perhaps only natural that people would want to visit them. More often than not, this is done as part of a larger ritual performance or as an individual act that would commonly be understood as devotion. Pilgrimage, then, is the name often given to those journeys to such places where members of the group (often now understood more specifically as "pilgrims") go, often reporting to be in search of what they consider to be a religiously or spiritually transformative experience. We see this in the annual pilgrimage (*hajj*) that some Muslims make to the city of Mecca where it is believed that Muhammad, their Prophet, received his first revelations and initiated the process of establishing a new religion, in trips for Christians and Jews to the so-called "holy land," or in journeys to a variety of shrines and sites all across India that Hindus make annually. The latter can include the so-called Kumbh Mela, which takes place every four years at rivers in India, and is often billed as the largest pilgrimage with an estimated 700,000 people involved in 2021 alone. But since the scholar of religion cannot analyze such claimed experiences, we have to look in other places for the meanings that are attached to the term. That often long-distance journeys and trips are involved in pilgrimages, for example, should alert the reader to the fact that they are, in fact, a species of the broader category tourism. Though many in the field would surely resist this observation, of course, in that it trivializes the sacred, or so some might contend. And where there is tourism there is an entire infrastructure (even industry

DOI: 10.4324/9781003196631-32

and therefore economy) based on the inevitable exchange of goods and capital, not to mention symbolic social status. Where some might see pilgrimage as "spiritually fulfilling," then, others might regard it as just another form of either regional or even international travel. What is different from, say, a trip to Jerusalem to deliver an academic lecture or sightsee and another person sitting on the same airplane going to the "holy land" to visit, among other things, what some Christians will know as the Stations of the Cross? Surely, it has to involve something other than vague notions of intent or inner experience. That they are both engaged in ostensibly the same journey to the airport in Tel Aviv means that the only way to differentiate the two actions is to rely on some other, possibly internal criteria (i.e., the intentions of the traveler). The latter, it will be recalled, has been used throughout the history of the study of religion with very little result other than invoking some authorized notion of "the sacred" and/or "experience" as some sort of default position, beyond which the scholar cannot inquire any further.

The English term "pilgrimage" derives from Anglo Norman *pilgrimage* (alternatively written as *pilrimage, pellrimage, pelremage, pelrimage, pelrinage , pelerimage, pillerinage*), all of which seem to be variants of the Old French *pelerinage* (and the modern French *pèlerinage*). As early as the beginning of the twelfth century it was used to refer to a journey, a crusade, and even the course of a person's life. Consider, for example, John Bunyan's still read 1678 text, *Pilgrim's Progress* (to be discussed in more detail below). Its primary use in English is to refer to a journey (one that usually entails a long distance and an arduous trek), sometimes to a place that a person or group deems special, or sacred, with the aim of carrying out an act of devotion once there or perhaps even returning with an artifact. The latter can also be referred to as a relic, a thirteenth century English term, deriving from Latin for something that remains after (e.g., as in a corpse being designated as someone's remains). Thus, in a sermon from 1275 collected in Joseph Hall's *Selections from Early Middle English, 1130–1250* (1920), we read: "Si Mirre signefiet ... go ine pelrimage ... and to do alle þe gode þet me may do for godes luue (XXIII, line 55).

Of course, a pilgrimage does not have to refer solely to a religious location. In William Shakespeare's (1564–1616) *The Merchant of Venice* (1600), for example, we read: "Tell me now what Lady is the same To whom you swore a secrete pilgrimage" (i. i. 120). The term could also be used to refer to a period of travelling or wandering from place to place, in the sense of either being in a period of exile or on a distant and foreign sojourn. In *Love Cure, Or the Martial Maid* (1647), a comedy by the English playwrights Francis Beaumont (1584–1616) and John Fletcher (1579–1625), for instance, we read: "To passe his tedious pilgrimage For sixteene years ... His constancy, not fortune overcame" (i. i. 125).

One of the most important and enduring works of Christian fiction centers on pilgrimage is the already mentioned *The Pilgrim's Progress from This World, to That Which Is to Come* (1678). John Bunyan (1628–1688) there recounts the allegorical story of Christian, a protagonist that functions as a metaphor for every Christian trying to make sense of this life in light of the one to come, with the story revolving around the pilgrimage from his hometown, called the "City of Destruction" (i.e., this world) to the Celestial City (i.e., the life to come), the latter sitting atop Mount Zion (a name of significance throughout the history of Judaism and thus adopted by some Christians but for their own purposes). Weighed down by a great burden, i.e., the knowledge of his own sin, he seeks deliverance from his misfortune. This burden, which would cause him to sink into Hell, is so unbearable that Christian must seek deliverance through the help of another character, Evangelist, who directs him to the "Wicket Gate" for deliverance. The subsequent struggle that ensues is meant to reflect the journey made in life by every good Christian. The rather heavy-handed Christian overtones in the work that imagines life as some sort of spiritual pilgrimage from being "born in sin" to one of release from said sin means that, once again, the term is heavily invested in one particular religious tradition, to wit, Christianity. Indeed, so important is this term to Protestant Christianity that we rarely encounter it pejoratively or written off as "popish" or Catholic. Since early scholars of religion knew, often from their own lives and upbringing, what pilgrimage was—perhaps even having gone on a pilgrimage themselves—whenever they saw people from other religions traveling or otherwise on the move in a way that was claimed to be in the name of their religion, such scholars would rather easily call it "pilgrimage" and those engaging in it "pilgrims."

But the question, then, becomes: Is this helpful? Do scholars understand the *hajj* to Mecca any better by using the term "pilgrimage" to describe it and thereby associate it with a host of other travels taken to other destinations by other people and possibly for other reasons? After all, to designate the Kumbh Mela and the *hajj*, along with a Buddhist travelling to the Mahabodhi Temple in Bodh Gaya, in northeast India (where Siddhartha Gautama is said to have become enlightened as the Buddha), as pilgrimages makes a statement about them all having a notable similarity.

It was probably only a matter of time before this term, used to refer to specific Christian journeys, was expanded to understand those found within other religions. As early as 1662, for example, we read in John Davies's (1625–1693) translation of Adam Olearius's (1603–1671) *The Voyages and Travels of the Ambassadors Sent by Frederick Duke of Holstein, to the Great Duke of Muscovy, and the King of Persia*: "Such as have gone on Pilgrimage to Mecca, to Mahomet's Sepulchre" (321). The term obviously picked up considerable steam with the rise of comparative religion, which, as we have witnessed throughout this volume, sought to find patterns in what then became known as the "world religions," often through recourse to scholars' own local vocabulary and their idiosyncratic categories. Thus, by the later nineteenth century we begin to see the term used to describe religious traditions even further afield from Europe than that of Islam. In his *Manners and Customs of the Japanese, in the Nineteenth Century* (1841), for example, Philipp Franz Balthasar von Siebold (1796–1866), a German botanist and traveler, writes: "But pilgrimage is the grand act of Sintoo devotion, and there are in the empire two-and-twenty shrines commanding such homage" (341). Again, the unfamiliar is, predictably, described using the familiar. What better way, for example, for a European Christian to make sense of a particular act than to describe it using terms and a narrative that sound remarkably similar to him, given that in his own tradition something called a pilgrimage to the "holy land" takes place. Siebold continues, in a tone not unique to writers of this era, that one of the "two-and-twenty shrines" ("the temple at Ten-sio-dai-zin, at Isye") is "conceived by the great body of ignorant and bigoted devotees to be the original temple, if not the birth-place of the sun goddess" and that "to make this Isye pilgrimage, at least once, is imperatively incumbent upon man, woman, and child of every rank, and, it may be said, of every religion" (341). Such accounts, it should also be noted, have in common the notion that all people on the so-called pilgrimage share the same thoughts and sentiments. This assumption—or, perhaps better, useful fiction—is one of the most dangerous ones that the study of religion perpetuates, often going by the name of essentialism, the view that a unified core and thus identity unites all members of a group. Surely all Muslims who go on the *hajj* to Mecca and its local environs are not automatons, all thinking and doing the same thing in unison (though, this is often the way that we are content to portray them, either in the classroom or in the introductory textbooks that students in our field use). On the contrary, they are all there for different reasons—some best described as political, some ideological, some sociological, and so on—and the moment that we say they are all pilgrims we thinly paper over such "non-religious" factors and causes. In so doing, we reduce all these factors to some ethereal motive to "commune with the sacred" or some such phrasing we can easily find in our field's literature. The key for a critical study of religion is to, at the very least, try to account for some of these material conditions of pilgrimage (or any other term for that matter). After all, some of those making the trek to a seemingly sacred site are perhaps doing it because of social pressure from their family members and friends. For is that not how groups usually function? If so, then why not in the case of those acts and occasions designated *as* religious?

The question, then becomes, is "pilgrimage" a useful term for scholars to employ to describe the travels among the people they may study? Or, is it so heavily invested in one particular intellectual (maybe even theological) tradition that, when scholars use it to describe what people across cultures and time periods do, they may do considerable damage in the service of some vague notion called cross-cultural understanding? On the surface the term certainly seems more value-neutral or objective than, say "paganism" or "polytheism," but, upon closer inspection, it seems that the term is no less grounded in one local tradition and then used *as if* it named some cross-cultural, and thus universal sentiment, need, or action. Lacking a defensible theory of religion, though, and thus a persuasive argument for the role that such travel might play, surely it does not. For this reason scholars should, once again, be cautious of how, when, where, and why they use such cross-cultural, comparative terminology. While we do not think that the term will be retired any time soon, or even that it should, it certainly is nevertheless worth reflecting upon—and worth considering what basis we, as scholars, so easily assume that all such travel is grounded on the same basis for all people, and thus requiring the same name.

The other and perhaps related, issue that pilgrimage brings up is one signaled at the outset: How is it different from other sorts of travel? When, for example, is a trip to Rome a holiday and when is it a pilgrimage to holy sites? Might not, for example, a holiday include the visitation of such sites? Is it a matter of intent? Does one have to be a devout Catholic to be a pilgrim to St. Peter's (with all others being mere tourists—and the "mere" signals that there is indeed a hierarchy here). If it is all based on intent, then how do scholars elicit or measure that, let alone what do they do with a few generations' worth of critical scholarship on what many would refer to as the illusory nature of this thing so easily called "an intention"? Simply put, why not just use the term "tourism" for pilgrimage? After all, the former may have less or at least different baggage—no pun intended—than the latter.

In this volume see: atheism/theism, East/West, emic/etic, founder, initiation, liberation, myth, piety, prayer, ritual, sect, theology, value

In *Religion in 50 Words* see: belief, classification, experience, faith, identity, lived religion, material religion, phenomenology, practice, religion, text, world religions

32 Prayer

"One of the most common practices of believers in Christianity, Islam, Judaism and other religions is prayer," or so writes David Morgan, the noted scholar of religion and visual culture, in an essay entitled "Materiality" for the multi-authored resource, *The Oxford Handbook of the Study of Religion* (2016, 282). This line, opening a section of the chapter entitled "The Materiality of Prayer," might attract our attention for at least three reasons, all of which help to make a practice commonly called prayer interesting for a whole new set of reasons. First, the word is being used here as a cross-cultural, comparative category, not unlike much of the vocabulary examined in this volume. Despite observing that "the conventions are varied" (that is, as Morgan notes, some kneel while others merely bow their heads), these actions are all instances of the same phenomenon: prayer. Second, it is clear that the term is being used descriptively, that is, to name something that people known as *believers* do. This is a designation that makes use of a certain sort of participant discourse, and therefore local to some of the people whom we study. This discourse assumes that religion is primarily concerned with those things called beliefs, and thus with *believing in*, and thereby agreeing to, certain sorts of claims, for example, the existence of gods and an afterlife or, perhaps, the claims sometimes itemized in what have been called either a statement of faith or a creed. Thus, the people whom a scholar studies are frequently classified as "believers" or even "the faithful," or sometimes as "practitioners" and "participants," although these terms have rather different inflections to them, evidence of different theories of religion driving their use. Third, and finally, in the midst of describing and then comparing prayers as sites where certain beliefs are expressed or manifested, an irony is betrayed, or better, a contradiction becomes evident. Despite being claimed to be universal, the local, particular, and thus limited nature of this term is registered by means of the key distinction between specifics and

DOI: 10.4324/9781003196631-33

vague generalities when we read the phrase "Christianity, Islam, Judaism *and other religions*" (emphasis added). That the word "prayer" has application within the history of Christianity and then, more or less, also in groups that all have their own historical relationships, is certain, but its utility to name the practices of others is rather questionable. This is made evident in the oddly generalized phrasing that ends his sentence: "and other religions." Whether we like to admit it or not, it is difficult to read as anything but a troublesome catch-all category that—in distinction from the more careful specificity used to distinguish the first three in the list—effectively groups all that remains together as undifferentiated others. In fact, while we should probably not place undue emphasis on the choice of but a few words, it is surprisingly akin to a previous era's once common tendency to divide the world between "Christians and non-Christians" (i.e., "us" and all others). We see this, for example, in the even more obviously normative textbook for missionaries written by Rev. James S. Dennis, *Social Evils of the Non-Christian World* (1898).

Despite the cross-cultural work done by much of our terminology, we see the inevitably limited nature of at least one way of practicing the study of religion. Developed from largely Christian sources at the height of the European colonial era, local terms could be stretched so as to perform cross-cultural work, despite the fact that such terms were never designed to accomplish such work in the first place. The result is that these scholars' commonsense self-understandings were used to come to terms with what they saw as the exotic practices of those people they classified as "heathens" or "primitives" (e.g., "We pray—do they?"). That so many of these much earlier, Christian-based descriptive terms remain in the field, without ever having been thoroughly retooled and redescribed, is precisely the problem that a volume such as this is attempting to tackle. Thus, the place of this word "prayer" going forward, as part of a truly critical, scholarly vocabulary, is something that needs to be addressed.

From the mid-thirteenth century Middle English verb, "to pray," the noun "prayer" is in evidence about a generation later, with the latter first used to name the words being recited (i.e., to say a prayer). Our term derives from the Old French *preere* and then the Middle French *priere*, for making a request or what, from the fifteenth century onward, is sometimes also known as offering a petition. The latter is a noun of classical Latin origins (*petition*) that is often reserved for, as the *Oxford English Dictionary* puts it, a "formal written request to an authority." Thus, the explicit idea of ranked status and power are never far from both "pray" and "prayer," meaning that it names a request—and *never* a demand or a command—made by a social actor who is mindful of inhabiting the inferior position. This is even evident in the now archaic phrase "I pray thee," inasmuch as it was once a respectful way of inviting someone to say or do something. We witness this in William Shakespeare's late sixteenth century play, *Henry VI*: "I pray thee, Buckingham, go and meet him" (Part II Act IV, Sc. 9)—something that even the one in the more powerful position could say if the goal was to soften one's authority. Accordingly, the Latin root would be very much at home in claims made in a Roman court or a request made of the Emperor, a sense of the term "petition" that is certainly retained to this day, e.g., ranging from the language of the US Constitution's First Amendment. The latter reads, in part: "Congress shall make no law ... abridging ... the right of the people peaceably to assemble, and to petition the Government for a redress of grievances" (1791)—to one adding signatures to a petition. So, the 1720 edition of Edward Phillips's 1658 work, *A New World of English Words; or, A General Dictionary Containing the Interpretation of Such Hard Words As Are Derived from Other Languages*, is on target by defining "To Pray" as: "to entreat, or befeech; to defire, or beg of," along with prayer being understood there as: "a Requeft, or Defire, efpecially fuch as if made of Almighty God." As early as the fourteenth century, an invitation by one who is socially inferior that is extended to their superiors comes to name, within Christianity at least, "direct address to the god(s), especially in the form of petition or praise (citing the *HarperCollins Dictionary of Religion* [1995], 852).

Throughout the subsequent history of Christian theology, the English words "pray" and "prayer" are widely used for formalized efforts to communicate with their conception of their deity. We witness this in English translations of the New Testament that commonly render the Greek *proseúchesthe* (*pro-* + *eúkhomai*), meaning to make a vow, to praise, even to wish for or to boast as "to pray." For example: "This, then, is how you should pray" in the New International Version of Matthew 6:9, leading to what is widely known as the Lord's Prayer. We also see it in the Church of England's *Common Book of Prayer* of 1549 that contains both prayers and the so-called order of service for ceremonies, and even in Pope Francis's book, *Prayer: The Breath of New Life* (2020), with a preface by the Russian Orthodox Patriarch of Moscow. Not only do a number of compound terms result—such as holding a "prayer meeting" or a "prayer vigil," as well as characterizing someone as "prayerful"—but a variety of types of prayers are identified, with their number differing, more or less, all depending on who is doing the classifying. These include those offering thanksgiving or blessings, those requesting God to intervene in human affairs, such as to guarantee safe travel or heal someone (i.e., intercessory prayer), and those in which God is asked for something on the part of the one who is doing the praying (not insignificantly known as petitionary prayer). Even popular discourse incorporates the term, as in saying to someone "you haven't got a prayer" used as of the early twentieth century for hopeless situations, and the common habit of saying "Amen" (an Old English term, from post-classical Latin, for "so be it" or "truly") as not only a formulaic expression at the conclusion of a prayer but also after any statement with which one strongly agrees or wishes to affirm.

It was not until sometime in the mid-eighteenth century that—predictably, given the argument offered at the outset of this entry—the word "prayer" is pressed into a far wider form of cross-cultural service. Indeed, the more familiar others' practices are to Christian scholars and readers at the time, then the more likely they were to lend their own local terms to name other people's customs. To pick but four examples: "Jewish prayer" is in evidence in English literature by at least the mid-eighteenth century; "Mohammedan prayer" appears just a few decades later; "Hindoo prayer" becomes an item of English discourse in the early nineteenth century; and "Buddhist prayer" rises in prominence by the mid- to later nineteenth century. All of these examples make profoundly evident how words reflect changing social relations and increasing contact among peoples, through both trade and conquest.

That calling something a prayer, or saying that someone is praying, "requires polytheism or theistic beliefs as a background." Thus Eric Sharpe (1933–2000) observes in his *Fifty Key Words: Comparative Religion* (1971, 48), thereby limiting how far it can be stretched, however. The term presupposes intentional actors on each end of the communication, with one requesting and one granting (or not). Earlier scholars were therefore forced to fall back on various other terms, such as "chants," "spells," "formulas," or "incantations," when identifying routinized verbal components in ritual settings that struck them as defying the assumptions common to the term's original theistic setting. For instance, consider the so-called "Vedic hymns," as described in mid-nineteenth century scholarship (and even today), understood to be recited by Brahmins (i.e., ritual specialists or so-called priests) in Hindu ritual but not to be confused, at least according to some, with prayers. That "prayer" was not easily lent to such utterances reflects the ranked nature of these concepts—a ranking not alien to the very notion of a prayer, readers may recall—given that one would never use such terms as "incantation" or "spell" to name what a member of the Christian clergy was doing during a service of worship. The term, instead, is reserved only for the doings of "superstitious" people—though, to be sure, so-called Protestant Reformers, and their later followers, were quick to delegitimize Roman Catholic ceremonies and theologies in this manner, given their general agreement that what they referred to as mere "popery" was an "enormous mass of error and superstition." The latter was claimed by the Rev. Samuel Miller (1769–1850) in the introduction to his pseudonymous book, *History of Popery, Including its Origins, Progress, Doctrines, Practices, Institutions, and Fruits to the Commencement of the Nineteenth Century* (1834, 5).

Not unlike the story of the term "magic" or "pagan," then, or certain definitions of "myth," this term "prayer" is probably of limited cross-cultural use. To put it another way, what starts off sounding like an innocently descriptive term—e.g., Morgan's opening seemingly uncontroversial claim that "[o]ne of the most common practices of believers in Christianity, Islam, Judaism and other religions is prayer"—can rather easily be demonstrated to be doing significant rhetorical work by reducing difference and complexity to universal similarity and simplicity by elevating but one local over all others. There may, then, be something to be gained by becoming comfortable with stopping short of pronouncing such a thing as "*salat* is Arabic for prayer," as a less careful scholar of Islam might suggest. Instead, we may wish to devise theoretically driven terminology of our own, should we wish to examine the role of, for example, oral or written formulaic elements within ritual settings.

In this volume see: afterlife, atheism/theism, church, founder, icon, idol, magic, monotheism/polytheism, myth, paganism, pilgrimage, ritual, symbol, understanding

In *Religion in 50 Words* see: belief, classification, comparison, faith, phenomenology, world religions

33 Priest/Prophet

Since the Bible has priest and prophets, since many Christians claim that this book (or perhaps better, this set of books) provides unerring truth, and since the majority of scholars of religion at the moment of the field's formation in Europe just over one hundred years ago were Christian, it is perhaps only natural that both of these terms—priest and prophet—have often been thought to be natural and cross-cultural categories of scholarly analysis. One could quite easily say that much of our field's history has involved searching through the textual remains of those other systems known by scholars as religious traditions to find equivalents to each, so that religion could be understood to be a universal concept and practice that all peoples of the globe share. This was the case at the field's point of origin and attempts to universalize what some see as the familiar and the local still largely continues to function as the guiding principle for much of the field to this day. Ecumenicism has meant an overwhelming focus on sameness and unity and finding analogues and similarities wherever possible between what might at first seem to be different religions. The use of these two terms, "priests" and "prophets" is certainly no different in this regard. Since "prophets" are believed to bring "revelation," and "priests" are imagined to interpret and administer it for the faithful, then all religions should ultimately possess them, in some form. And, if they do not, then perhaps scholars intent on finding similarity will find other concepts that can be forced into these categories. The result is that priests and prophets, designations local to just some, are sometimes thought to be words with universal applicability.

Prophets and priest, though intimately connected, have been construed in such a manner that they possess rather different functions. A prophet, in this view, is an individual who is regarded as being in contact with some sort of a divine being, on behalf of whom he is said to speak—indeed, throughout history they are often assumed to be

DOI: 10.4324/9781003196631-34

men, though the many counterexamples are instructive, helping scholars to see often undisclosed gendered assumptions in their work—and thus seen as delivering messages or teaching from that divine being to a community. This role of intermediary often involves, but certainly does not have to, the performance of what later generations consider to be miracles or the miraculous as evidence of the prophet's authenticity and thus authority. A crucial difference between a prophet and a priest is perhaps best summed up by the once important sociologist of religion, Max Weber (1864–1920), in his *Sociology of Religion* (1920), wherein he argues, among other things, that many prophets derive their authority from what he terms their personal charisma. The latter term is from the Greek *chárisma*, a term used in the New Testament, from a word we would today translate as grace or favor and, by extension, assumed by Weber to be a power of attraction or persuasion possessed by some who are in positions of leadership. Priests, on the contrary, often derive their legitimacy from the institution or guild of their priesthood itself. Such institutions are no less historically dominated by men in many cases, to be sure, as evidenced in movements in modern Roman Catholicism for women to gain access to administering the rituals long reserved only for male priests. A prophet can often be regarded as a threat on account of his upsetting the social and political status quo, and even persecuted on account of his unpopular warnings or teachings—a well-known line from the Christian New Testament, for example, reads: "A prophet is not without honor except in his own town, among his relatives and in his own home" (Mark 6:4 quoting the New International Version). Priests are often regarded as religious leaders who derive their authority precisely through this status quo, which in turn grants them the power to perform and thereby control access to religious rituals and the social benefits that come from participation in them. Indeed, it might not be too far a stretch of the imagination to say that priests are often seen to administer the teachings that a prophet first brings, whether by upholding them, reinforcing them, or even changing or otherwise institutionalizing them. Oftentimes, prophets are even understood to seek to undermine the status quo of such priests—think, for example, of prophets of the Hebrew Bible who warned against the simple sacrifice of animals in the Temple without proper attention to remorse and ethics. It should be clear, however, that all this talk of power, authority, and the political and ideological nature of the status quo—all of which is said to derive from their perceived access to the supernatural world—means that prophets and priests can wield considerable power within groups that have them. While much time is often spent describing the contents of so-called prophetic teachings and the sometimes complex and detailed intricacies of priestly functions, equal attention should be paid precisely to both of their relations to issues of power and authority. The critical scholar, not content with participant claims about a divine, may ask from whom does such authority derive? What do such structures of power allow priests to do, and how are those structures potentially or periodically undermined by those designated as prophets? So while priests and prophets are often thought to have simple religious functions, closer inspection redescribes them to be influential political figures.

Etymologically, the terms "priest" and "prophet" have rather different histories. Prophet is an Old English derivation of multiple origins, partly based on the Latin *prophet* and also, later, the French *prophete*, both of which seem to denote a spokesperson or interpreter (e.g., of a god). Such senses, in turn, seem to derive from the Greek *prophētes*—the prefix *pro* ("before") and *phetes* ("speaker"), naming someone who speaks on behalf of a divinity, presumably "before" an audience or a community—where it was used to denote one who proclaims or expounds upon the will of a divine being. By the time we get to the Septuagint (the second century BCE translation of the Hebrew Bible into Greek) the term *prophētes* is used to render the Hebrew concept *nābī* (which, of course, is often translated as "prophet"), a term used to denote a range of interpreters or even representatives of God, Baal or other so-called pagan deities. This early sense of the term, then, does not seem to differentiate between "good and "authentic" prophets and those who are regarded as "bad" or as somehow "inauthentic." In the Greek New Testament, the term *prophētes* is again used in this manner, where it refers to the earlier Hebrew prophets as well as to John the Baptist, who, in the narrative, comes before and "prepares the way for" the appearance of Jesus, said to be the Son of God. It can also include certain persons in the Early Church, who were imagined as inspired to utter special revelations and predictions. This Greek usage was, then, adopted in Latin as *prophēta*, under distinctly Christian influence, and used in the Vulgate (the fourth century CE authoritative Latin translation of the Bible), which was, in turn, passed down into Romance and Germanic languages. Indeed, in English the earliest uses are derived precisely from its role in Christian scriptures. Before we examine some early uses of the term, it is worth nothing that the English term "priest" derives from the earlier Latin *presbyter*, which, in turn, comes from the prior Greek *presbēteros*. Though it is worth noting that by the third century CE, the Latin word *sacerdos*, like the Greek *hiereus*, was the primary word applied to refer to the sacrificing priests of what were commonly known as the originally pagan gods. It was later used to denote the priests of ancient Israel and then also applied to Christian ministers, with the term "sacerd" (from the Latin *sacerdos*) used synonymously in English. In Old English, however, the Latin *presbyter* was usually represented by *prēost*, and could refer to a so-called pagan or Jewish priest, before becoming a generic term that could include all members of the clergy (and not necessarily just those in what many would today designate as priest's orders). By the early Middle English period, *sacerd* had become obsolete, and *prest*, like Old French *prestre*, became the current word alike for *presbyter* and *sacerdos*.

These two terms—though now thought to be universal in scope, and rather generic in their applicability—therefore have a history that is decidedly Christian. Both terms have thus been intimately connected to the Bible and biblical traditions, often involving concerns over how to "properly" or "accurately" relate the meaning of a Hebrew term with Latin and Greek cognates, before making their way into English. Though they could certainly be used to designate "pagan" or "heathen" prophets/priests, that meaning quickly took on a largely Christian veneer, which remained until the formation of the field known as comparative religion, at which point they became terms and/or concepts that all religions were assumed to have. But the term's lengthy investiture in one particular tradition, to wit, Christianity, can neither be overlooked nor denied by the critical scholar. As early as the seventh-century Anglo-Saxon Chronicle, a legal code, we read, for example: "Þær wæs Wilfrid preost [i.e., priest], þe siðon wæs biscop." And from the Lamebeth Manuscript, whose earliest manuscript we possess dates to 1225 (but its use of Old English clearly marks it as much older): "Þu scalt gan to bote and niman scrift þer of, al swa þe proest þe techet." The same can be said for the term "prophet." Thus we read in Wulfstan (d. 1023), the pre-Conquest Archbishop of York, in a work titled *Isaiah on Punishment for Sin*: "Ðas ðing gewitegode Isaias propheta be Iudean & fela hertoeacan, & eal hit aeode swa swa he sæde." From such early usages, we continue to see the deployment of both terms used in reference to Christianity, and occasionally Judaism. The latter religion, of course, is always presented in so much of this literature as the prelude to or foreshadowing of Christianity.

As with so many of the terms examined in this volume, it was only a matter of time before this rather specific Ancient Israelite and subsequent Christian usage spilled over into other religions. Whenever an individual went in front of others to engage in or lead what was believed to be religious service (i.e., worship, rituals, etc.), they became "priests." Thus we see, for example, a chapter in Abbé J. A. Dubios's *Hindu Manners, Customs and Ceremonies* (1899, translated from the French into English by Henry K. Beauchamp), entitled: "The Gurus, or Hindu Priests." The term could also be used to refer to "Buddhist priests," as in an 1883 article titled "Terms of Address and Modes of Salutation in Use Amongst the Sinhalese" by James Alwis from the *Journal of the Ceylon Branch of the Royal Asiatic Society*: "I shall now proceed to an investigation of religious titles or 'terms of address' to Buddhist priests." (vol. 3, 10 [1856–1858], 221). Such comparisons often reduce social and cultural specifics so that such individuals can simply be understood using other specific terms (i.e., either priest or prophet) as if they were universal, and in such a manner that any nuance is now lost. Other so-called founding figures can also be called "prophets." Perhaps the most famous in this sense might be Muhammad in Islam. Even this, however, is a political act because it puts him in the same category of biblical prophets, whereas in the Islamic tradition he is so much more than that, representing the pure mouthpiece of divine guidance, someone whose very purity offers an example (Arabic: *Sunna*) for every subsequent Muslim to follow, and that example, when taken as a body of literature, forms an important part of Islamic law (*sharia*). Within this context also note that in the context of the Protestant Christian tradition, that gave us so many of these "cross-cultural" terms in the first place, it never referred to Jesus as a "prophet." Immune from such comparisons, he exists as unique and *sui generis* (Latin: self-caused) to which nothing can be compared. But, of course, all those other "prophets" can easily be compared, and categorized, and ranked. According to this idea, then, with Jesus prophecy ends because he represents, for Christians, the "true end" of prophecy.

Another theme that arises with "priests" is the concept of "priestcraft," in which subsequent priests were sometimes said to have taken an originally pure and pristine message and changed it (i.e., by bureaucratizing it) to legitimate their own power. Priestcraft, in this narrative, stands opposed to "true religion." Thus we read in *The Dignity of Human Nature: Or, A Brief Account of the Certain and Established Means for Attaining the True End of Our Existence* (1812) by James Burgh: "[t]he abominable priestcraft, and horrid persecution and blood-shed, which have been the disgrace of a religion, whose distinguishing characteristic is benevolence ... pure religion" (409). Perhaps most relevantly, Protestants could accuse Roman Catholics of priestcraft because, according to their charge, Catholicism removed the teachings of the Bible from the average believer and housed it in the Church's corrupt institutions and interpretive traditions. Such a charge, of course, could also be applied to other traditions, especially among those associated with the colonial project, such as the onetime worldwide institution known as the British East India Company (in operation from 1600–1874). In his *The History of British India* (1817), for example, James Mill (1773–1836), the Scottish historian, economist, and father of the famous political economist, John Stuart Mill (1806–1873), writes: "It was the interest of the despotism and the priestcraft to join together to uphold their common tyranny over the people" (458). More modern forms of this may be found, for example, in Islamic studies where a common trope is to argue that Muhammad's original and pristine message was coopted by later male elites, in such a manner that removed the more egalitarian aspects of the earlier tradition. The obvious goal, when this critique if offered, is to bypass such priestcraft so as to return to the original message.

Like so many of our terms, then, priest/prophet—no matter how far the terms are stretched—has a history that is deeply embedded in the Christian tradition. Though it is often used by scholars in what is assumed to be a value-neutral way, the manner in which the person and role of Jesus—the main figure in the Christian narrative—is left out of such categorizations on account of his supposed uniqueness is surely telling. However, while it seems unlikely that such terms will disappear any time soon, it is surely worth reflecting on their history and potential for distortion when used too widely, with the critical scholar then proceeding accordingly.

In this volume see: church, civil religion, East/West, founder, god, icon, idol, immanence/transcendence, myth, ritual, theology

In *Religion in 50 Words* see: authority, classification, comparison, experience, phenomenology, religion, text, world religions

34 Reformation

One may wonder why a project then underway in the US by Tufts University's Freeland K. Abbott (1919–1971)—Chair of their Department of History at the time of his death—was included in both the April 1957 and April 1958 issues of *External Research: A List of Studies Currently in Progress*, published between 1955 and 1964 by the US State Department's Office of Intelligence Research and Analysis. Titled "A Comparative Study of the European Reformation and a Possible Islamic Reformation," the project is described as "[a]n attempt to establish the validity of a contemporary Islamic 'Reformation' through an analysis of basic elements in the 16th century Christian Reformation." Abbott, who received his Ph.D. from the Fletcher School of Law and Diplomacy at Tufts, worked mainly on Middle Eastern and South Asian history. A Ford Foundation Research Fellow in Pakistan as well as a Fulbright Research Scholar (1959–1960), he was also the author of *Islam and Pakistan* (1968), which Wayne A. Wilcox (1932–1974)—himself a consultant to the State Department on South Asia and onetime Chair of Columbia University's Department of Political Science—described in Abbott's death notice as "a study of the social, political, and ideological consequences of Islam in Pakistan's quest for a national identity." Wilcox went so far as to report that "Freeland Abbott stood with Charles Adams, Fazlur Rahman, Wilfred Cantwell Smith, and Aziz Ahmed as one of our few interpreters of the social ethic of modern Islam in South Asia, and especially in Pakistan." See his notice published in *American Historical Review* 76/4 (1971): 1275–1276. For those even mildly acquainted with why, say, a church historian might make reference to something called "the Reformation" (the uppercase is usually intended)—the name commonly given to a sixteenth- and seventeenth-century series of events across Europe credited with establishing Protestantism as separate from the Roman Catholic Church (the latter being the thing that was ostensibly reformed)—its association here also with

DOI: 10.4324/9781003196631-35

Islam may be a little surprising. Even more surprising is the realization that all of this was listed among projects reported on by the State Department's Office of Intelligence Research and Analysis, a branch founded in 1947, now part of the US's so-called intelligence community. Today it is known as the Bureau of Intelligence and Research, whose primary mission is described on its website as: "to harness intelligence to serve U.S. diplomacy."

But why surprising? If religion is about some sort of deeply personal, abiding, and apolitical experience, then what are we to make of the intelligence community's interest in a possible Islamic Reformation? Indeed, what might one even mean by that term? We may get some initial clues when we learn that, although part of a longstanding topic, discussions on this idea of an Islamic "reformation" gained considerable momentum in the wake of the September 11, 2001 (i.e., 9/11) terrorist attacks in the US. While we might see the odd essay prior to this latter date—e.g., the essay by the now retired Dartmouth University anthropologist, Dale F. Eickelman, "Inside the Islamic Reformation," in *The Wilson Quarterly* 22/1 (1998): 80–89—post 9/11 witnessed a virtual cottage industry on the topic in no way limited to academic audiences. In an opinion piece in the *New York Times* called "An Islamic Reformation" (December 4, 2002), for example, Thomas Friedman called for it. His piece was dedicated mostly to reporting on what was judged by the Iranian authorities to be a controversial June 2002 speech by the onetime Iranian revolutionary and then college professor, Hashem Aghajari, which in part noted that "the Protestant movement wanted to rescue Christianity from the clergy and the church hierarchy." Friedman then goes on,

> so [too] Muslims must do something similar today. The Muslim clergymen who have come to dominate their faith, [Aghajari] said, were never meant to have a monopoly on religious thinking or be allowed to ban any new interpretations in light of modernity.

We also witness this in the non-profit RAND (i.e., "research and development") Corporation's multi-authored 2004 report for the U.S. Air Force entitled, *The Muslim World After 9/11*. The report observes that the post-Reformation splintering of what was once known as Christendom, following which early nation-states began to arise, is, as yet, absent in the Muslim world. It concludes that the

> practical difference is that no one of political significance in the West has spoken seriously about the unity of Christendom for

some centuries, whereas the idea of the *umma* [i.e., the worldwide community of Muslims] continues to have deep resonance in the Muslim world.

(14–15)

We also point to the host of conferences, studies, along with scholarly and popular publications since then, on the need for a so-called reformation in modern Islam. We could easily cite a far longer list but, for the time being, consider just these, from the past fifteen years: Irshad Manji's book, *The Trouble with Islam Today: A Muslim's Call for Reform in Her Faith* (2004); the multi-authored collection, *An Islamic Reformation?* (2004); Ayaan Hirsi Ali's *Heretic: Why Islam Needs a Reformation Now* (2015); Christine Douglass-Williams's volume, *The Challenge of Modernizing Islam: Reformers Speak Out and the Obstacles They Face* (2017); Taner Edis's *Islam Evolving: Radicalism, Reformation, and the Uneasy Relationship with the Secular West* (2016); and even a book by the Emory law professor, Abdullahi Ahmed An Na'im, *Toward an Islamic Reformation: Civil Liberties, Human Rights, and International Law* (2019).

There are some writers resistant to such calls, and more so about what such calls might even mean. We think here of such pieces as Nick Danforth's January 2, 2015, essay in *Foreign Policy*, "Islam Will Not Have its Own 'Reformation': Stop Expecting a Muslim Martin Luther. No Two Religions Follow the Same Historical Path" or the Turkish journalist, Mustafa Akyol and his October 31, 2017, brief essay published by *The Atlantic* entitled, "The Islamic World Doesn't Need a Reformation: Why a Muslim John Locke Would Be Much More Useful Than a Muslim Martin Luther." In fact, Akyol's argument is that commentators have it the wrong way around: "if the Muslim world of today resembles any period in Christian history," he argues,

> it is not the *pre-Reformation* but rather the *post-Reformation* era. The latter was a time when not just Catholics and Protestants, but also different varieties of the latter were at each other's throats, self-righteously claiming to be the true believers while condemning others as heretics.

Generally speaking, the narrative around the need for Muslims to undergo a reformation is by now well established, such as the summer 2017 US State Department memo, reported on by the investigative journalism site, *The Intercept* (on June 18, 2018). According to their confirmed report: "In seeking a public diplomacy means for undermining the ideological basis for supporting the current Iranian or ISIS [so-called Islamic State of Iraq and Syria] structures, an emphasis on 'Islamic Reformation' should factor in heavily." To make sense of all this we should recall that reference to *the* Reformation (the definite article is important, here). The term once simply referred to a series of mid-sixteenth century calls for "reforms" within the Roman Catholic Church, calls that eventually resulted in widespread opposition across Europe and the eventual establishment of what came to be known as a group of Christians calling themselves Protestants. Usually it is assumed to have begun with the so-called Ninety-five Theses (though more technically known as his "Disputation on the Power and Efficacy of Indulgences") posted on a church door in 1517 by the German Roman Catholic priest and moral theology professor, Martin Luther (1483–1546), the first of many "reformers."

The noun "reformation" is based on the mid-fourteenth century English word, "reform," meaning, literally, to form over again, but soon taking on the meaning of correcting, restoring, reviving, or returning something to a prior and authoritative version. It is based on the classical Latin *reformāre*, entering English by way of French, signifying both a generic change but also a change that counts as a restoration, which is itself from the slightly early word "form" (Latin *forma*, for shape). In the study of religion, we find the terms "reform," "reformed," "reformer," and "reformist" in a variety of settings, from "Reform Judaism" (naming a particular type of more liberal, modern Judaism) to a variety of modern Reform Hinduism movements as well as various Reformed Christian churches (a subset of Calvinist Protestantism). But the still dominant sense is offered in a definition of its own by the *Oxford English Dictionary*, to mean

> 3.b. Usually with *the* and capital initial. The great religious movement of the 16th cent., the object of which was the reform of the doctrines and practices of the Church of Rome, and which ended in the establishment of the various Lutheran and Reformed Protestant Churches of Europe (with their later worldwide offshoots).

Its earliest example is that of Bishop of Chichester William Barlow's (1498–1568) *Dyaloge Lutheran Faccyons* (1531; *Dialogue on the Lutheran Factions*): "Martyn Luther ... was iugged to be syngulerly chosen of god nowe in these latter days, for a dew reformacion of the hole worlde" (46, citing the 1897 edition, with an introduction by the English clergyman, John Robert Lunn [1831–1899]). As the *OED*'s definition makes clear, then, the thing called *the* Reformation is assumed to be a specifically religious event, representing contests over specifically theological matters. These included the topic of indulgences or "permits," which one could buy from the Church to lessen one's suffering for sins in the afterlife, a practice outlawed by Pope Pius V in 1567, as part of the century-long Counter-Reformation, a response within Catholicism to Protestant critiques.

Surely, we must take seriously that the modern designation of "religion," even as recently as four or five hundred years ago—let alone such related terms as "secular"—signified something rather different than today. If we simply project modern understandings backward in time and onto the early sixteenth century and imagine the so-called Reformation as a "great religious movement," we potentially miss the point by spiritualizing a series of events that could and perhaps should be understood rather differently. For example, recall the historic origins of the just mentioned term, "secular." As recently as the 1720 edition of Edward Phillips's 1658 work, *A New World of English Words; or, A General Dictionary Containing the Interpretation of Such Hard Words As Are Derived from Other Languages* we read:

> belonging to a *Seculum*, or an Age, i.e. the space of an hundred Years; alfo relating to this World, or Life .... Alfo that is converfant in the World, without being engaged in a Monaftick Life, or to obferve the Rule of any Religious Order.

We may now recognize that, prior to taking on their modern religious connotation, such terms were used as ways of identifying a division of labor within an institution that was itself not yet religious since the term had yet to be developed in that direction. Contemporary scholars might better understand such terms as an early modern governance institution (headquartered in Rome) that, indeed, employed rhetorics and symbols of supernatural beings intervening in historical events, *but which also* managed much of daily life as well as identity and authority within an expanse of society today known as Europe. If this is the shift that a critical scholar considers making, then they could redescribe the Reformation as an early modern revolution in social legitimacy and organization. One moreover, that eventually undermined a longstanding mode of governance and thereby opened the door to social experimentations that, again for a variety of reasons, resulted in the rise of early modern nations. The latter, in turn, functioned as one of the forerunners to the modern liberal democratic nation-states that many of us today take for granted. To read backward onto this period our modern notions of religion as being uniquely apolitical and personal, because experiential, may serve to erase the disputes over authority, power, and politics that were taking place at the time. Indeed, the modern distinction between public political action and private religious feeling could itself be argued to be a creation of this era, one successfully used by the so-called Reformers to delegitimize, and thereby contest all the more effectively, prior modes of social legitimacy. In their place, they inserted new systems of authority—not unlike labeling one's own claims as "common sense" or "knowledge" and those with which one disagrees as "mere opinion" let alone "faith" or a "personal belief."

If this is the manner in which we approach a series of disputes and attacks dating to around the early to mid-sixteenth century, then things look rather different. The sort of privatization of dissent (now repackaged as "faith"), in favor of the normalization of public expressions of dominance (now known as "politics"), offers at least one potent example of how divergent and competing factions might have been managed and made subservient to a dominant force. Should this overly brief account be suggestive, then, returning to the opening of this entry, we may now have a way of dealing with the apparent surprise of seeing this notion of a Reformation being associated with Islam, let alone reports of papers and studies on the topic written for various government agencies. For now, the early modern revolution in governance that is often-described as the Protestant Reformation may indeed provide a useful model for those today who aim to identify political actors in various parts of the globe whose aims are conducive to liberal democratic and capitalist interests. They often do this by marginalizing those who are not just opposing those interests but who also fail to play by the early modern rules—e.g., that public claims operate by one type of logic while private claims are allowed to operate by those that are banned from the public square. The problem, of course, is how certain actors are seen to conflate these rules—whether so-called Christian nationalists in the US or those known by some as Muslim extremists elsewhere in the world. In this way we can arrive at contemporary debates in, for example, France, where displays of Muslim symbols are outlawed inasmuch as they are said to oppose the principle of *laïcité* (the specifically French notion of secularism, which strictly limits all religious displays to the private sphere). However, that no less public displays of, say, Roman Catholic identity are unquestioned, because they are classified *not* as religious but as evidence of the nation's heritage and culture, makes plain how all along these early modern rules have consistently cut in the favor of those in dominance and thus those who establish and enforce them.

Reformation

We, thus, might not be surprised to learn that European or North American governments have actively been involved with trying to achieve a so-called Islamic Reformation, modeled on what transpired five hundred years ago across Europe. This more critical approach, though, presupposes that we understand those prior events not as piously religious, as we today define these terms, but as socially formative conflicts that laid the basis for a certain sort of modernity that, rightly or wrongly, many of us now take for granted.

In this volume see: church, civil religion, dialogue, East/West, fundamentalism, magic, nones, piety, paganism, spirituality, theology, tradition

In *Religion in 50 Words* see: comparison, culture, history, orthodoxy, politics, redescription, sacred/profane

35 Renunciation

Renunciation, the act of rejecting or refusing something that was previously enjoyed, is a term commonly employed within the academic study of religion. It is—not unlike words such as "liberation" or "meditation"—frequently used to refer to a practice or set of austere or disciplined practices believed to be common to all those religions often grouped under problematic rubrics such as "Eastern" or "Asian." That it was a term initially used in the context of Christianity, to refer to those who renounced the devil and so-called "evils of the flesh," and often associated with the initiation ritual of baptism, should force us to ask: How did such a localized and loaded term come to be synonymous with those groups far removed from European Christianity? Of course, one way to get around such a question is to posit, in good phenomenological fashion, that all religions partake of "renunciation"— just as they are assumed to do with "prayer," "ritual," and "belief." If some think "Western" religions to be about the salvation of the human soul so that it can attain ever-lasting life in the next world, something that is achieved through the performance of faith and good works in the present one, so such a traditional approach goes, then "Eastern" ones are about renunciation in this life for the sake of ultimate liberation from it.

The term often refers to the abandonment of pursuit of material comforts, with the larger aim of achieving what is imagined to be spiritual enlightenment. The renunciate is often said to seek to attain such enlightenment through the practices associated with what is commonly known as asceticism, which is a lifestyle characterized by abstinence from all sensual and material pleasures. The latter is a mid-nineteenth century noun, from the earlier adjective "ascetic," derived from the Greek *ásketés* for a monk or a hermit. This traditionally involves a withdrawal from the world and its temptations, and the subsequent adoption of a frugal lifestyle, something that frequently coincides with the performance of what can be designated as both ritual and meditative practices. Much work in scholarship involves treating these individuals as holy men (indeed, they have often, though not exclusively, been male) who are somehow more in touch with "the sacred" than the average person, who, in turn, are imagined to look up to renunciants as religious ideals to which they should but cannot aspire. Often left unobserved in such romantic assessments—as we have seen time and again throughout the history of our field—are the political and even economic actions and implications that attend such renunciation. The social capital (i.e., status, influence, etc.) possessed by the renunciant, for example, is often so significant in some settings that it is a tempting lifestyle to adopt, especially for the impoverished or those who desire social authority or even political power. In like manner, it is not uncommon for religious (now redescribed as political) authorities to use such renunciants to further their own political goals. But this is often not recognized by scholars, given the overwhelming tendency to take the term "renunciation" at face value, as if it somehow functioned as the prototype of some religions (but not others). That it is thought to be such a major component of certain religions reminds us how our scholarly categories and terms are often little more than fictions that some continue to employ, for the sake of what is, for all intents and purposes, little more than simple convenience.

As with so many other English words, the term "renunciation" is partly a borrowing from French (*renonciacion*) and partly a borrowing from Latin (*renuntiātiō*). The former refers to an action of renouncing, i.e., giving up or surrendering a right, a title, etc. The latter names an official report, such as an official return of election results and/or the declaration of withdrawal or resignation from an office or position of responsibility. By the fifth century CE, especially within the context of Roman Christianity, it could also refer to the action of renouncing the devil, the world, and "things of the flesh." We witness usage in the first sense of the term—that is, the action of renouncing or giving up some possession—in English as early as the fifteenth century in, for example, in a 1462 letter preserved in Henry Ellis's (1777–1869) *Original Letters, Illustrative of English History* (1827, 2nd Series): "A renountiacion and relese of the ryght and title that the Corowne of England hathe unto the Realme and Crowne of Fraunce" (I. 128). And, in the latter sense—namely, that of giving up or forsaking something naturally attractive (i.e., self-denial)—as early as 1526 in *Here Begynneth a Deuout Treatyse in Englysshe, Called the Pylgrimage of Perfection* by the monk and author, William Bonde (d. 1530): "After that foloweth the dispisynge & renunciacion or forsakyng of wordely thynges"

(II. sig. Plv). Thus, in *Sartor Resartus* (1834), by the English author and historian, Thomas Carlyle (1795–1881): "It is only with Renunciation that Life, properly speaking, can be said to begin" (ix. 69/1).

In terms of religious usage, we see it, perhaps not surprisingly, used first in the Christian context, beginning in the early seventeenth century, where the term is used primarily in reference to the ritual of baptism. In *Quiet Reckoning* (1609), by the Jesuit Robert Parsons, for example, we read that "[o]ther traditions allowed by him, though not written in the Scriptures ... as for example, that of renunciation accustomed to be made in the Church before baptisme" (iii. 191). Or, again in the English translation of Louis Ellies Du Pin's *A New Ecclesiastical History of the Sixteenth Century* (1706): "Exorcism and Insufflation, as well as the Renunciation, and the Profession of Faith, and the other Ceremonies of Baptism" (II. v. 47). Indeed, we continue to witness this baptismal renunciation of the devil even today, when we encounter, for example in the pages of the journal *Church History*: "The acceptance of Christ in the Creed meant also the rejection of the devil. That rejection was not merely liturgical in the act of renunciation at baptism" (15 [1946]: 293). But increasingly over the course of the last century, the term comes to refer almost exclusively to the "spiritual practices" associated with religions seen by earlier scholars to be unfamiliar because they are "over there."

The question posed earlier is worth recalling at this point: How did a term with such a specific reference to the Christian renunciation of the devil as part of a baptismal ceremony come to designate one of the most important features of so-called Asian or Eastern religions? The turn seems to happen in the late nineteenth century, the period, perhaps not surprisingly, associated with the emergence of the comparative study of religion. We see it begin to be used to refer to "Eastern" religions as, for example, in *Unorthodox London* (1876) by Charles M. Davies (1828–1910): "Every prophet has his one distinguishing trait; and that of Buddha was renunciation" (rev. ed., 17). From such humble origins the term came to be used as the translation of the ancient Sanskrit term *sannyasa*, what is known as the life of renunciation that represents the fourth stage within the Hindu system of four life stages. Likewise, "renunciation" could also be applied to translate *nekkhamma*, an ancient Pali term that implies giving up the world and leading a life apart from it (i.e., holy, as commonly defined). In Buddhism's Eightfold Path, *nekkhamma* is the first practice associated with "Right Intention," or the proper motives that prompt one to seek what many term enlightenment.

It is not the case, we must note, that the English term "renunciation" simply names "Eastern" practices that are radically different from those in the "West." Rather, it is a term—with a distinct genealogy in Christian Europe and largely familiar from those practices of renouncing the devil and the evils of the flesh prior to the ritual of baptism—that has been repurposed and used to *translate* those terms in other languages that earlier scholars assumed to proximate it, or that function as analogues. Understanding this act of scholarly translation is the key to the entire process. It does not mean that certain Hindus and certain Buddhists do not engage in what is known locally by some as *sannyasa* or *nekkhamma*, but that such local terms have been translated into an equally local term, that of "renunciation." Such translation has allowed—and, indeed, continues to allow—scholars to domesticate a host of foreign terms by making them conform to that with which they are familiar. Potentially lost in all this translation, of course, is that the foreign terms—including their specific social, intellectual, and material contexts and conditions—do not necessarily denote that which scholars habitually refer to as "renunciation." To rephrase, these practices do not all necessarily share the same essential identity or function to all those who engage in them, despite the handy manner in which they are all grouped together and studied by scholars *as if* they do.

Take, for example, the frequent scholarly focus on renunciation in those traditions commonly known as Buddhism, especially by members of that tradition that we now refer to as Orientalism. In his *Buddhism: Being a Sketch of the Life and Teachings of Gautama, the Buddha* (1920), T.W. Rhys Davids (1843–1922), a leading British Orientalist at the time could write that it was "renunciation" that allowed the Buddha to arrive "at those conclusions regarding the nature of man, and of the world around him, at that psychological and moral system to which he in the main adhered during his long career" (40). Or, again, consider August Karl Reischauer (1879–1971), an American Presbyterian missionary interested in understanding what he assumed to be the deep connections between Christianity and other religions. In his *Studies in Japanese Buddhism* (1917) he tells of the Buddha's abandoning of his young family (as told in the popular narrative of the Buddha's life and enlightenment) to enter the "great renunciation," where we read of "his struggle with the tempter who tried to make him give up his quest" (23). More recently, in her *Jainism: A Guide for the Perplexed* (2015), Sherry Fohr devises a taxonomy of renunciation's types, informing readers that it is their respective approaches to renunciation that allows us to see differences between Hindus, Buddhists, and

Jains: "Although Hindu renunciation of 'the path of knowledge' is very different from what came before in 'the path of works,' Jainism and Buddhism are even more divergent" (8).

Renunciation, in the final analysis, should force those interested in the critical study of religion to focus on issues of translation. We have to recognize that when scholars engage in such translative acts they are taking concepts from one language—including all the social, economic, political, and intellectual baggage that goes with it (whether they recognize it or not, since words are historical artifacts)—and, ultimately, forcing them to fit into another language's system by giving it a new name and seeing it as but a species of a larger genus (a genus that is really but one species write large). That new term, of course, is no less loaded when it comes to its own set of social, economic, political, and intellectual baggage. That scholars may have no choice but to do this—for we come to understand the unknown by means of the known—they certainly can choose not to essentialize and universalize what is really only their prototype, opting to see it instead as a handy starting point and not the end.

In this volume see: East/West, evil, hagiography, initiation, liberation, meditation, monotheism/polytheism, mysticism, piety, priest/prophet, ritual, spirituality, tradition

In *Religion in 50 Words* see: authenticity, classification, definition, method, phenomenology, practice, religious literacy, status, worldview

36 Ritual

Along with "myth" there are likely few other words used by scholars of religion that are more prominent in popular discourse than "ritual," though the gaps between its various usages can sometimes be dramatic and confusing. While brushing one's teeth might count as a ritual for those who do it a few times daily, so too does the annual new year's ice water bath for Shinto devotees at the Teppou-zu Inari Shrine in Tokyo, an event begun in 1955. Into this mix, we could also add what world religions courses often consider to be more "traditional" forms, as when, for example, a devout Muslim engages in prayer (Arabic: *salat*) five times each day, thereby performing one of the so-called five pillars, or obligations and thus foundations, of Islam. Just what do these three things have in common, however, to make them what we call "rituals"? The first example, after all, might be better understood as a routine, or maybe just a habit. But notice how we, as a field, are often just willing to do this with the first example because such alternate designations would likely be seen as dismissive and therefore disrespectful of those engaging in the other two.

So just where do we put the line that distinguishes these three examples? If a habit, a routine, and a ritual were not all somehow distinguishable from each other then we probably would not need three separate words. An example of a rather precise use of the term "ritual"—a use not to be confused with a mere habit—is found among the members of the American Psychological Association (APA). They might discuss such a thing as clinically diagnosable superstitious rituals, defined as "a specific pattern of behavior that is believed to control one's performance and its outcome when there is no rational reason for this belief." But, of course, this is hardly the only way to define the term. Anthropologists, for example, have long used "ritual" to refer to an assortment of actions, sometimes revolving around so-called rites of passage—a research area notably influenced by the Dutch

DOI: 10.4324/9781003196631-37

ethnographer, Arnold van Gennep's (1873–1957) early book, *Les Rites de Passage* (1909). He argued that such ceremonials either mark or actually facilitate a change in social status or identity, such as moving an initiate from being a child to an adult—a movement that, or so theorists have argued, requires one to pass through an ambiguous middle phase, known as the liminal stage. The latter term derives from the Latin *līmen*, for threshold or edge, an earlier root from which the English "limit" likely also derives. If we add to this such things as the topic of the historian Edward Muir's 1981 book, *Civic Ritual in Renaissance Venice*, along with the so-called mating rituals of virtually any species studied by a naturalist, then we arrive at such a terminological variety that there is a very real possibility of confusion over just what is meant when we, as scholars, identify something as a ritual.

Sticking with the APA as our example, their online dictionary offers three definitions that differ dramatically from each other. They define ritual as: (1) "a form of compulsion involving a rigid or stereotyped act that is carried out repeatedly and is based on idiosyncratic rules that do not have a rational basis …. Rituals may be performed to reduce distress and anxiety caused by an obsession"; (2) "a ceremonial act or rite, usually involving a fixed order of actions or gestures and the saying of certain prescribed words. Anthropologists distinguish between several major categories of ritual"; and finally (3) "any habit or custom that is performed routinely and with little or no thought." Whereas the first has an obviously evaluative and therefore explicitly normative, diagnostic edge (placing the cause of such actions in irrational obsessions that should be cured) and the third is so generic as to be of little scholarly use, the second seems purely descriptive (i.e., non-evaluative). Indeed, the second use goes on to offer a taxonomy that covers, among others, a usage that is familiar to scholars of religion—a so-called liturgical usage, i.e., as part of a worship service—which includes all of those acts that people seem to hold as deeply meaningful to them and their so-called communities of faith. Unless a scholar offers an explicit definition each time the word is used, which of these (let alone the many other definitions we could offer here) might someone intend, when, for example, they describe the *lhasang*, a traditional Tibetan Buddhist smoke offering, as a ritual? The question in need of attention, then, is how can a word whose uses vary so widely—from it being a diagnostic for identifying a supposed psychological disorder to a mere synonym of "routine"—be of much use to critical scholars aiming for precision in their work? Moreover, we can also add to this the fact that, like all others, the word has a history all its own, and it is likely accurate to assume that people the world over whom we might describe as "carrying out rituals" are not self-designating their own actions *as* rituals. As a result, the critical scholar may recognize that here, again, we have a word that, despite its apparently innocent and descriptive uses, may actually be prescribing far more than scholars think.

"Ritual" first appears in English sometime in the latter third of the sixteenth century, though already in use two centuries prior to that was the related English term "rite." The latter, from the classical Latin *rītus* referred to a ceremony or way of acting, a practice—often but not always with regard to the domain now seen as that which is religion. We see this, for example, in a 1533 reference to "[t]his rite of chevelry" from John Bellenden's edition of *Livy's History of Rome: The First Five Books*, quoting the 1901 edition (I. i. xiii. 74). Combining "rite" with the Latin suffice, *-alis* (signifying something related to or concerning the noun being qualified, e.g., "global," "regional," or "rational"), results in "ritual," which from early on functions as both a noun and an adjective, that is, a ritual as well as a ritual act. Although the two terms come to be employed similarly, as of the mid-twentieth century, the use of "ritual" far outpaces "rite," with the latter now used infrequently and today sounding as if naming more formal occasions. For example, one would today probably not think of brushing one's teeth as being a rite though calling it a ritual would not be uncommon. The word "ritual" continues to develop long after it is first coined, with such variations as "ritualistic," "ritualization," and "ritualize" arising over the nineteenth century, with some scholars today preferring to discuss the process known as ritualization over the seemingly settled fact of something being a ritual (see below). It should be noted that, early on, "rite" and "ritual" were hardly synonymous. For example, again citing the 1720 edition of Edward Phillips's (b. 1630) 1658 work, *A New World of English Words; or, A General Dictionary Containing the Interpretation of Such Hard Words As Are Derived from Other Languages*, we find "rite" defined as "Order or Rule, to be obferved on folemn Occaffions; a Church Ceremony" while "ritual" designates "a Book containing the particular Rites and Ceremonies of a Church; efpecially of the Roman [i.e., Roman Catholic] or Greek [i.e., Eastern Orthodox]." A "ritualift" is understood as "one that ftickles [a word once meaning a referee or one who endeavors to support a cause] or ftands up for Rituals or Ceremonies in religious Worfhip." These meanings seem to be rather stable across a variety of English dictionaries from the eighteenth century, e.g., the third edition of Daniel Fenning's *The Royal English Dictionary; Or, A Treasury of the English Language .... To which is Prefixed, A Comprehensive Grammar of the English Tongue* (1768).

There is a longstanding assumption (notably present in the works of early Protestant writers) that only others have rituals, or at least have what are portrayed as unnecessarily intricate, unthinking, and thus stifling rituals—along with their equally stifling institutions and hierarchies. This is evident in the early use of the term "ritualist" just quoted above. Another example comes by way of the English cleric, Francis Mason (d. 1621), writing in 1613 in his *Of the consecration of the bishops in the Church of England with their succession, iurisdiction, and other things incident to their calling...*, which takes the form of a dialogue between a priest and a Church of England minister. "Wee are not tied to the rite of Rome," says the Protestant minister, "or any other City or Country, but only to the institution of Iesus Christ: If Rome follow this, wee will follow it with Rome; if Rome forsake this, then farewell Rome" (iii. i. 100). A scholar should be mindful that, from the outset, today's seemingly neutral, descriptive term played a role in earlier, socially formative moments, in which representations of practices familiar and unfamiliar to the writer were being compared and ranked. "We" end up seeming to possess sincere faith and right belief while "they," of course, have "the lowest level of empty ritual"—or so the Anglican evangelist and colonialist judge, Robert Needham Cust (1821–1909), once claimed of turn-of-the-era Palestinian Jews. See his now problematic tract, *On the Common Forms Which Appear in All Forms of Religious Belief* (1895), 65—where, like so many of his contemporaries, he also makes clear that original religious ideas apparently degrade over time, into mere ritual (62). Another early example is provided by the English historian, John Foxe (d. 1587) whose *Actes and Monumentes* (first English edition, 1563; also known as *Foxe's Book of Martyrs* or *The First Volume of the Ecclesiasticall History: Contaynyng the Actes and Monumentes of Thynges Passed in Euery Kynges Tyme in this Realme*). He argues that the first and second epistles of Pope Zephyrinus (d. 217) included "no manner of doctrine, nor consolation necessary for that time, but only certain ritual decrees to no purpose" (citing vol. I, part ii, 162 of the revised edition of 1853). And many of those who came long after Foxe agreed. For such writers, ritual was, in the words of the art historian, Joseph L. Koerner, to be "lumped ... together with habit and superstition .... Because it lacked speech, ritual was senseless and indecipherable" (*The Reformation of the Image* [2004], 47).

The utility of linking assumptions about what beliefs and ideas are in opposition to what can be claimed to be unthinking, brute actions and modes of organization that can be seen to hamper individuals, is also exemplified in European philosophy by means of the so-called mind/body dualism. Therein, both are assumed to be utterly distinct from one another, with the former generally taking priority over the latter. Indeed, in 1949, the British philosopher, Gilbert Ryle (1900–1976), likened the soul to a ghost inhabiting a machine. Today many scholars would complicate all of this with the notion of "embodied cognition," wherein not just the brain but the entire body is assumed to make consciousness possible. This would mean that such phrases as "empty ritual," to quote the scholar of American religion, Catherine Albanese, become a "familiar, almost hackneyed expression," one that conveys a politically efficacious view that dates to around the time of the sixteenth-century Reformation in Europe. Then, so-called reformers were intent on undermining longstanding institutions and authorized offices and figures within the Roman Catholic Church. Instead, they were intent on (1) deauthorizing the practices (i.e., rituals) associated with them, and (2) replacing them with institutions and practices of their own. See her edited book, *American Spiritualties: A Reader* (2001), specifically her introduction to the section entitled, "Knowing Through the Body: The Path of Ritual." Today, many scholars have begun to rethink ritual, no longer seeing it as the secondary site where, for example, the supposedly more important content of myths or beliefs are only later enacted. This now goes against the once prominent position that claimed rituals instead came first, classically expounded by the early British anthropologist, Fitzroy Richard Somerset, known as Lord Raglan (1885–1964), along with the so-called Cambridge ritualist school (see, e.g., Robert Segal's 1998 edited volume, *The Myth and Ritual Theory: An Anthology*). We also witness this position in Emile Durkheim's (1858–1917) still influential sociological definition of religion that posited "beliefs and practices" as an interconnected whole. Instead, the study of routinized behaviors, whether done in groups or individually are now seen as an important area of research, whether or not they are connected to things seen as being religious and even if such actions prove to be "unthinking." Indeed, many scholars now realize that the participant's conscious awareness of their actions is hardly a requirement for studying such patterned behaviors.

Among the more promising recent lines of inquiry is, as mentioned earlier and as studied in Muir's already-cited book, ritualization itself. In fact, Muir argues that the ritualization of society and politics played a crucial role in Venice's long political stability. This move from studying ritual, as a stable or isolated act, to ritualization as a process of rule-governed routinization that is linked to how authority and identity are established and negotiated, is best associated in the study of religion with the influential work of Catherine Bell (1953–2008), such as her still important book, *Ritual Theory, Ritual Practice* (1992). As she writes in her Preface, her work was influenced by an observation once made by Jonathan Z. Smith (1938–2017): ritual is *work*! Bell then elaborates: "To approach ritual within the framework of practical activity raises, I suggest, potentially more fruitful questions about the origins, purposes, and efficacy of 'ritualized actions' than are accessible through current models" in ritual studies (xv, citing the 2009 edition). Her interest is to reassess how scholars have employed this category, and to move from studying fixed nouns (e.g., a ritual) to dynamic verbs (i.e., ritualizing processes), puts her work well in line with a variety of later twentieth century, self-reflexive scholarly studies. Such works move from studying myths to the process of mythmaking itself, from tradition to acts of "traditioning", or examining techniques of identification rather than seemingly static qualities once called identities. Here we might also invoke Malory Nye's earlier call to study what he called the process of religioning rather than its product: religion. In this respect, see his 2000 essay "Religion, Post-Religionism, and Religioning: Religious Studies and Contemporary Cultural Debates," *Method & Theory in the Study of Religion* 12/1: 447–476. Thus, whatever a ritual may or may not be, it is instead the patterning of practice—its causes and effects, whether psychological or socio-political—that may strike some students of religion as far more interesting to study.

In this volume see: civil religion, magic, myth, piety, pilgrimage, prayer, sacrifice, symbol, theology, tradition

In *Religion in 50 Words* see: belief, function, identity, orthodox, practice, religion, status

37 Sacrifice

The discourse on religion has a way of taking otherwise mundane economic exchanges or even killing and giving them the appearance of transcendental value and significance. We see this clearly with the notion of "sacrifice," which is often used as if merely descriptive of certain ritual offerings of food, objects, or even the lives of animals or humans to what is believed to be a higher purpose, often to a God or gods, sometimes understood as an act of propitiation (to atone or compensate for past failings and thus a part of a worship ceremony). Students of religion will perhaps be most familiar with this from the often-complex sacrificial cult associated with the ancient Temple in Jerusalem that plays such a large (though, of course, now non-extant) role in the Hebrew Bible. Therein we encounter an elaborate set of sacrificial rituals that were administered by authorized figures (members of what are often called a priesthood) and suitable for any number of transgressions (e.g., nocturnal emissions and other unintentional sins). Although such sacrifices could indeed be bloodless offerings (including grain and wine), the most important ones tended to involve animals, whether whole or in part, and could be divided into: burnt offerings in which the whole unmaimed animal was burnt; guilt offering in which part was burnt and part left for the priest; and peace offerings in which similarly only part of the undamaged animal was burnt, and the rest eaten in ritually pure conditions. That Jesus was portrayed as critical of such practices—for example, the story in Mark 11:15–19 where Jesus interrupts commerce in the Temple's courtyard that involved buying animals for sacrifice—and given the early Church's antagonistic relationship to its representation of Judaism, it might come as little surprise that the discourse around "sacrifice" is charged and highly politicized. Beyond the Ancient Near East, however, ritual animal (and even human) sacrifices are often understood to have been common among the ancient Greeks, and among pre-Columbian

DOI: 10.4324/9781003196631-38

civilizations, in Africa, etc.; it was perhaps only natural, then, that those responsible for the early construction of the study of religion, once acquainted with such diverse instances of what have also been called "bloodletting" practices, looked for some organizing idea on which they could draw in beginning to compare the religions of the world. Thus enters "sacrifice" as a cross-cultural term of comparative religion.

This still common English noun "sacrifice" derives, in Middle English of the mid-thirteenth century, with the verb coming soon after, from the Latin *sacrificium*. The latter term is a combination that joins the terms *sacra* (things set apart, eventually signifying the quality of being sacred or holy) and the verb *facere* (to do or perform). A *sacrificus* was, thus, a priest, i.e., someone who carried out functions or sacrifices and thus the one who made things holy through such actions. In English the term initially and primarily referred to the slaughter of an animal as an offering to a deity; thus, sacrifices were what *other* people did. In terms of what *we* do, however, the term suggested surrender of an offering to the "one" and "true" God of Christianity through prayer, thanksgiving, penitence, submission, or the like. Early usages reflect this, wherein the term is used negatively to refer to so-called pagans, but favorably when referring to Christians. While the term is the same in both cases—whether naming "their" or "our" acts—its meaning would seem to derive from the intention assumed to exist behind the act. As early as 1300 in a work either called or attributed to St. Margarete, we read: "And wende to his false godes, to do sacrifise" (92). Or, again around the year 1450, we read in John Myrc's *Festial*: "Then sawe Maudelen mony pepyll comyng towart þe tempyll and þe lorde of þat contre, forto haue don ofryng and sacrefise to hor mawmetys" (205).

Yet, if violent sacrifice is what others do, Christians, who have the "gift" (read: blood sacrifice) of Jesus Christ at the heart of their religion, predictably imagine the term somewhat differently. Unlike that found in other groups, Christian theology understood by this term Jesus's offering of himself to God the Father. Early writers, such as Paul, called this an atonement—from the Greek *hilastērion*, a sin offering or expiation—as in his letter to the church in Rome 3:25. This "atonement" was accomplished by means of Jesus's voluntary death upon the cross, as payment for human sin. Presumed to be the sacrifice to end all sacrifices, Christianity therefore has the crucifixion as the archetypical sacrifice, which, as Jonathan Z. Smith (1938–2017) noted in his still important book, *Drudgery Divine: On the Comparison of Early Christianities and the Religions of Late Antiquity* (1990), is imagined as so unlike other sacrifices as to be unique or *sui generis*. Thus we read in *The Christian Life, Part Two: Wherein that Fundamental Principle of Christian Duty, the Doctrine of our Saviours Mediation, Is Explained and Proved* (1686), written by the Church of England clergyman, John Scott (1639–1695): "In consideration of Christs Death and Sacrifice he would freely forgive all penitent and believing sinners their personal obligation to eternal punishment" (II. vii. 1134). Or, again, as William Thomson (1819–1890), the Archbishop of York, wrote in his *Aides to Faith: A Series of Theological Essays* (1861): "The sacrifice of the death of Christ is a proof of Divine *love*, and of Divine *justice*" (viii. 337). It is certainly no coincidence that the Latin word *sacrificium* came to denote the central Christian ritual known as the eucharist (also called communion by some), the term derived from the Greek *eu* (well) and *charistai* (offering), and usually with the meaning of thanksgiving, and more colloquially in Christianity as the "Lord's supper." It is a ritual in which church members, under the leadership of an officiant, re-participate in the sacrifice by consuming bread and wine, considered either symbolic of Jesus's body and blood, and thus his enduring presence in the group, or, via the longstanding Roman Catholic doctrine of transubstantiation, literally understood as those two things once the bread and wine are consecrated by a priest as part of the ritual. More specifically, and perhaps telling, is that the eucharist is often referred to as a "bloodless sacrifice," presumably as a way to distinguish it from all those messy sacrifices that so-called less civilized others do that involve killing and bloodshed. We witness the movement from sacrifice as act to sacrifice as metaphor as early as 1504 in Margret Beaufort's translation of Thomas à Kempis's (1380–1471) *A Ful deuout and Gostely Treatyse of the Imytacyon of our most merciful sauyour Cryste* (but, often, simply referred to as *The Imitation of Christ*):

> For if the sacryfyce of this holy sacrament were done onely but in one place and but of one preest in all the worlde, with howe great desyre wene ye the people wolde go to that plase and to that preest to here the godly mysteryes done of hym.
>
> (iv. i. 262)

Many post-Reformation eucharistic rites refer to that ritual as a "sacrifice of praise." For example, the King James Bible (1611) translates Jeremiah 17:26:

> People will come from the towns of Judah and the villages around Jerusalem, from the territory of Benjamin and the western

foothills, from the hill country and the Negev, bringing burnt offerings and sacrifices, grain offerings and incense, and *bringing thank offerings to the house of the Lord.*

as "bringing sacrifices of praise vnto the house of the Lord." Or, in the title of the British revivalist, Henry Varley's (1835–1912), *The Sacrifice of Praise: Hymns for Congregational Use and Gospel Meetings* (1872). This broadening of sacrifices in which "we" engage, once disengaged from actual bloodletting, is not insignificant, of course. In this manner we arrive at the widespread use of the term today, to describe going without something considered to be desirable, from sacrificing a chess piece as part of a larger strategy to a sacrifice play in baseball or someone said to "be making a sacrifice" by putting their career on the backburner for the sake of a partner's aspirations.

Because blood rituals along with making offerings to deities come to be understood as cross-cultural, sacrifice has long caught the attention of scholars of religion. Indeed, there have been many theories offered as to its origins and function in human culture. Theories of sacrifice, often seen as a subset of ritual theory, are perhaps as numerous as theories of religion, with the concept of sacrifice often functioning as a convenient canvas upon which theorists, old and new, could imagine what they thought religion to be or from where it might have originated. For example, the early British anthropologist E.B. Tylor (1832–1917) proposed in his once influential book, *Primitive Culture* (1871), that sacrifices originated as gifts to the gods to secure divine favor and/or to minimize hostility amongst humans. Using a general evolutionary framework, popular at the time, he subsequently argued that, through time, such sacrificial rituals transformed into renunciation practices, wherein the ones making a sacrifice began to offer themselves (as opposed, say, to an animal) through the ritual. It was another early writer, William Robertson Smith (1846–1894), the Scottish scholar of Semitics, who argued that sacrifice originated as a type of social communion—often through the occasion of participating in a sacrificial meal—among the members of a group. Another explanation was offered by the once noted Scottish folklorist, James George Frazer (1854–1941), who, in his still read book, *The Golden Bough (1st edition, 1890)*, conceived of sacrifice as originating from magical practices associated with the ritual slaying of a king, with the aim of rejuvenating a god. The king or chief of a tribe was held to be sacred, Frazer argued, because he possessed some sort of sacred power that assured the tribe's well-being. Mention must be made of the early classic, *Essai sur la nature et la fonction du sacrifice* (1898)—translated into English as *Sacrifice: Its Nature and Function* by W.D. Halls (1918–2011)—co-written by the early French sociologists, Henri Hubert (1872–1927) and Marcel Mauss (1872–1950) and part of a school of thought associated with Mauss's uncle, Emile Durkheim (1858–1917). They define sacrifice as "a religious act which, through the consecration of a victim, modifies the condition of the moral person who accomplishes it or that of certain objects with which he is concerned" (13, citing the 1981 edition of the 1964 English translation). Yet, another functionalist definition comes by way of the psychoanalyst, Sigmund Freud (1856–1931); in his *Totem and Taboo* (1913) he argued that the ritual slaughter of an animal was instituted to reenact the primeval act of killing the father. After what Freud characterized as the primal father had been slain, however, the sons felt remorse for their action, and, thus, instituted a sacrificial ritual with the aim of appeasing their guilt for the death of the father and for the subsequent reconciliation and communion with him through a substitute victim. Finally, to conclude this quick survey of sacrifice theories, mention should be made of two more influential works. In his *Homo Necans: The Anthropology of Ancient Greek Sacrificial Ritual and Myth* (1972), Walter Burkert (1913–2015) argued that Greek sacrifices derived from prior hunting practices. Hunters, feeling guilty for having killed another living being so that they and their kin could eat and survive, tried to repudiate their responsibility via such rituals. And, in his *La violence et le sacré* (1972, translated by Patrick Gregory and published in 1988 as *Violence and the Sacred*), René Girard (1923–2015) used a Freudian approach to focus on, among other things, the role of a so-called scapegoat or the innocent offering of a sacrifice on which blame or guilt is placed, thereby functioning as a substitute victim. Since such a substitute is always powerless, Girard argues that this role helps to establish a society, inasmuch as endless cycles of socially destructive revenge necessarily come to an end.

But all these are just theories, sometimes highly idiosyncratic thought experiments that are often impossible to verify through independent, let alone repeatable, analysis. More grounded analyses may be found among some recent scholars, such as Bruce Lincoln and Nancy Jay (d. 1991). In his *Death, War, and Sacrifice: Studies in Ideology and Practice* (1991), Lincoln argues that discourses concerning practices such as sacrifice possess "very real and considerable persuasive power" to justify numerous acts, including murder. Sacrifice, for him, is not simply or solely about the killing of victims, but about creating "situations in which religious discourses are systematically used to justify and perpetuate the subordination of some classes of people to others" (xv). These can include the social and political subjugation of warriors to priests, commoners to kings, and women to men. In terms of Jay we can go to her posthumously published study, *Throughout Your Generations Forever: Sacrifice, Religion, and Paternity* (1992), wherein she examines the interconnections between sacrifice, gender, and social organization. She argues that many ritual acts function as a remedy for everyone having necessarily been born from a woman and, thus, such sacrificial rituals seek to establish an enduring paternity.

The term "sacrifice," like all of our terms, is therefore an extremely complicated one—one that demands that we not simply use it in a manner that takes it to be descriptively neutral and thus overlooks it complex history. This history has involved using the term in at least two different ways: in a rather pejorative manner to refer to the barbarous acts of others and a much more positive one that names the seemingly bloodless act of Protestant Christianity. That it is the same term, no less, is both confusing and disconcerting. Moreover, "sacrifice," like the word "religion" itself, has been used in all sorts of ways to imagine what pre-literate people might have done or thought. In this respect, theories of sacrifice often coincide with and indeed help to give definition to theories of religion, sometimes doing so in ways that are socially beneficial to the ones offering these theories (and detrimental to representations of those being theorized). It is therefore neither an objective nor a value-neutral term, but one that demands clarity when used by a critical scholar, if not sometimes actual avoidance.

In this volume see: animism, church, god, idol, magic, monotheism/polytheism, paganism, ritual, sect, shamanism, totem

In *Religion in 50 Words* see: classification, comparison, explanation, lived religion, origin, phenomenology, religion

38 Salvation

Like so many of the other terms in a scholar of religion's vocabulary, "salvation" is a word originally of relevance to a very particular group and subsequently generalized, whereupon it is assumed to do cross-cultural and comparative work often with the aim of making the unfamiliar familiar. Since many Christians understand human beings as alienated from their God—given that the original two human beings, as per their common origin tale, contravened the deity's orders and introduced into history what is known as sin—the aim of existence is to address this shortcoming. This is considered to be so onerous a task, however, that it cannot be accomplished by individuals themselves through confessing their sins or making some sort of reparation. Instead, to atone for this separation requires the selflessness of the creator taking human form as a man named Jesus and then sacrificing himself. This constitutes what, as of mid-sixteenth century English, was called a scapegoat, namely, a blameless victim in an ancient Hebrew ritual sacrifice, which represents the transgressions of others (e.g., Leviticus 16:8). As the early follower of Jesus, Paul (d. approximately 65 CE), wrote to a small Christian community in Rome: "For the wages of sin is death, but the gift of God is eternal life in Christ Jesus our Lord" (Romans 6:23, quoting the New International translation). As part of this specific view of the human condition, it makes sense to talk of salvation from the eternal torment that, again according to parts of the Christian tradition, awaits those who have not accepted the self-sacrificial act of Jesus's death by crucifixion at the hands of the Roman governing authorities at the time. That this is then a model on which early European comparative religionists draw when trying to understand theological systems unfamiliar to them, such as what a Hindu or a Buddhist might think life and human history are all about, should by now be obvious. Indeed, the point of each of these so-called great religions, as earlier scholars might have

DOI: 10.4324/9781003196631-39

phrased it, must be to diagnose the ills of existence and then to offer some way of addressing it, thereby enabling practitioners to escape it, overcome it, or, in a word, to obtain "salvation." Once again, however, the question is whether such a local term, animated by such a specific theology, can be made to work in a wide variety of other environments and contexts. A quick perusal of comparative religion scholarship will make clear that this is not a question that occupies the attention of many, inasmuch as we find plenty of claims about "salvation in Islam" or "a Jewish conception of salvation." Whether a critical scholar will be as content to just move forward and work with such an expansive use of what is actually a Christian theological concept is, however, something we should consider.

The noun "salvation" is a variation on the thirteenth century English verb "save," which derives from Old French and, before that, post-classical Latin *salvāre*. The latter has the meaning of to rescue or to deliver, later including to heal and even to retain or shelter someone or something. It is linked specifically to discourses on the soul as early as the thirteenth century, e.g., "Teche me ... How I may saue my soule," from William Langland's late fourteenth century text, *The vision of William concerning Piers the Plowman* (part 1, line 83, citing 1893's seventh edition, edited by Walter Skeat). "Salvation" results from the addition of the common English suffix, -tion, to signal a state of being related to the word so qualified, i.e., salvation is what is obtained by those who are saved. This is witnessed as early as thirteenth century English, based on the Old French *sauvacion* and, originally, the late Latin *salvātiōn*, itself also from the verb, *salvāre*. From the latter root we also derive, by the mid-seventeenth century, the noun (and later the verb) "salvage," originally designating a payment owed to someone who saved a ship from either wreckage or attack. Like so many other words, its spelling has varied greatly over the years, from the Old English *sauvaciun* to *salvatyon* in the sixteenth century. Just like "save," it too is linked early on to Christian theology, as also exemplified in *Piers Plowman*, where we find mention of "Sorwe of synnes is sauacioun of soules" (i.e., sorrow of sins is the salvation of souls, citing part 5, line 126 of the same edition). A close association between "salvation" and the fate of a Christian's mortal soul has long been established, as found, for example, in article 5 of the Church of England's *Articles Agreed Upon by the Bishops, and Other Learned and Godly Men, at the Last Convocation at London in the Year of our Lord 1552. To Root out the Discord of Opinions, and Establish the Agreement of True Religion* (1553). There we read: "Holy Scripture containeth all things necessary to salvation" (2). Or, again, in the name of the international Christian charity established in London in 1865 by William and Catherine Booth, originally known as The Christian Mission, but as of 1878, called The Salvation Army.

Keeping in mind this close linkage between souls and salvation, it should come as no surprise that early European scholars of comparative religion found it only natural to elevate "salvation" to the level of a cross-cultural universal. That "soul"—a word of Germanic roots also of direct relevance to English-speaking Christians—was put to its own early cross-cultural work should also be mentioned here, of course. For instance, "that which is the supreme desire of every Hindu soul, and the Indian equivalent of our 'eternal life,' [is] ... the beatitude of final emancipation from separate existence, in short extinction or annihilation," or so we read in an 1876 article on "Philosophy in Ancient India" in *The London Quarterly Review* (vol. 48/93, 98). That the notion of a soul carries specific connotations that were alien to many of the contexts in which early scholars put it to use should not go unnoticed by us today. In much the same way "salvation" carries specific connotations as well, suggesting why "liberation" has, at times, been preferred by scholars, at least when addressing the theological goal of so-called Asian religions. The latter, after all, are generally seen to presuppose a rather different metaphysic than the traditions that were already more familiar to earlier scholars, thus prompting them to invoke the East/West distinction. If one no longer assumes the existence of a powerful being intent on saving others, then "salvation" may not be all that useful a tool, especially if escaping the entire system, and not just improving one's position in it, is seen as desirable. This realization, however, has not stopped scholars from continuing to employ the term "salvation." Consider, for example, the title of a volume in honor of the British scholar of comparative religion and ordained Anglican priest, S.G.F. Brandon (1907–1971): *Man and His Salvation* (1973), containing chapters on salvation (and its paired concept, redemption) in a variety of world religions, including ancient Judaism, Buddhism, Islam, shamanism, Zoroastrianism and, of course, Christianity. Will Oxtoby (1933–2003), in his chapter, "Reflections on the Idea of Salvation," declares not only that religion is "virtually a universal phenomenon, a constant of culture," but, after surveying the category's origins in Christianity, then also claims far more generally that "the quest for salvation at its most general level is seen as the quest for relief from the human condition" (31)—something that comparative religion has taught us, or so he argues. In documenting the term's increasingly wider use, he then admits that "salvation" was, at that time, "in the early stages of becoming a term with adequate semantic range for comparative religion" (35), leaving the door open to whether the term can carry the weight that comparativists place on it.

What should be clear is that this weight originates in the theory of religion that drives its use. When Eric Sharpe opened his own entry on "salvation" in his *Fifty Key Words: Comparative Religion* (1971) he wrote: "The idea that man [sic] needs to be delivered, by divine agency, from ills, imperfections and misfortunes is a common one in most forms of religion" (60). Thus, in both Oxtoby's case and now here in Sharpe's, we can see that their conception of religion makes possible their view on the centrality of salvation to it. However, change the way in which "religion" is defined—there are, after all, innumerable other definitions for which one might opt—and "salvation" will no longer play such a central role, if any at all. Moreover, its related vocabulary will diminish or maybe even disappear completely from our work—such as, for example, the attendant term "soteriology," a no less Christian theological term, from the Greek *soteria*, denoting the study of claims surrounding salvation. Into this mix, we could also include the desire to find a "savior," an early fourteenth century term from the Latin, in each religion, and even the effort to write a "salvation history." The latter term is an English translation of the German *Heilsgeschichte*, used to refer to narratives on the saving work of God in human history. The latter term classically describes the biblical narrative "running on from eternity through history to eternity again, with Christ as its central and determinative point," citing the Scottish theologian, Donald M. Baillie's (1887–1954) *The Theology of Sacraments* (1957), ii. 69. Thus, the question is not whether other religions have conceptions of, and paths toward, salvation but, instead, how shall we define religion and what, in the wide world of human doings, will that allow us to study.

Selecting a definition of religion does something other than simply describing how some participants see things themselves. Since critical scholarship on religion does something other than merely paraphrase adherents' own views, the preoccupation with the need to be saved or "experiencing" so-called salvation may itself be theorized. In other words, while scholars' purely descriptive vocabulary may indeed include the term, a scholar's explanatory or redescriptive vocabulary will not. For now, the very claim that human beings need to be saved will itself be the occasion for the scholar to try to explain *why* someone would even say or think such a thing. It is not difficult to imagine a person dissatisfied but content with the world as it is rather than adopting a view of it having a degenerate nature that requires assistance from outside in order to overcome or escape it in some fashion.

In this case, it is not salvation but the discourse on salvation that becomes a problem to be understood, prompting the scholar to inquire about the origins as well as the practical effects of such a discourse. For, as Sharpe's already mentioned entry makes clear, to engage in the study of salvation, or soteriology, means learning the nuances of the participant discourse. Yet, for some critical scholars, the very existence of such a discourse is the topic to be studied—a shift that allows us not to be so focused on the finer details of the account but, instead, the fact that such a dissatisfaction with the world exists in the first place.

In this volume see: afterlife, East/West, mic/etic, evil, liberation, pilgrimage, prayer, renunciation, soul, theology

In *Religion in 50 Words* see: belief, description, explanation, redescription

39 Sect

Some words are so prevalent when it comes to thinking about how we discuss religion, whether in an academic context or more popularly, that they have often played a much larger role in structuring our discourses than they perhaps should have. "Sect," though its use has declined dramatically over the past century and a half, proves to be precisely just such a term. Frequently we see it used to refer to what is considered to be its synonym, namely a denomination. For example, Shi'i Islam is sometimes considered by scholars to be a denomination or sect of Islam, and the same for Reform Judaism within Judaism. When we do this, however, we overlook the fact that often implicit in the term "sect," but not necessarily "denomination," is the notion that what has been deemed sectarian is that which has somehow "fallen away" from what is imagined to be a stable and timeless concept of authoritative orthodoxy. Overlooked in such designations, however, are the contestations that always go into the creation of concepts like "orthodoxy" and "heterodoxy"—or "centers" and "margins"—in the first place. Despite the pejorative aura surrounding the term, we customarily assume a sect to denote a subgroup of a larger religious system, that is assumed to have broken away only *after the fact*. This often coincides with the implication that the new group or "sect" is somehow less authentic or more politically motivated then the larger group of which it was once believed to be a part. At issue in once common terms like "sect," then, are a host of related terms and concepts like "authenticity" and "orthodoxy," two words that—like "sect"—we often imagine to be natural markers as opposed to recognizing them to be politically and often ideologically motivated categories.

The English term "sect" is related to the fourteenth century French *secte*, itself derived from the Latin *secta* or "following," in the sense of pursuing a particular course of conduct or a person's guidance as an example or model. From this meaning, we get the sense of a party or

DOI: 10.4324/9781003196631-40

faction of a larger whole, including a philosophical school or a class or profession. In medieval Latin, the term could also be used to note the distinctive costume of an order or group, a meaning that carried over briefly into English before rather quickly becoming obsolete. In its earliest English usages, the term has a sense of a class or kind, often in reference to persons. Thus in Geoffrey Chaucer's (1340–1400) *The Hous of Fame* (1384): "Alderfirste, loo, ther I sighe, ... Hym of Secte saturnyne, The Ebrayke Iosephus." Or, again, in the poet and clergyman, Alexander Barclay's (ca. 1484–1552) *Here Begynneth the Egloges of Alexander Barclay...* (1530): "Joglers & pypers and scorfy waferers, Flaterers & hostlers, and other of this secte Are besy in thy chamber" (iii. sig. Nij). In terms of its place in the study of religion, "sect" could originally refer to a religious following in the sense of those adhering to a particular faith, including Christianity and Judaism. As early as the sixteenth century, for example, we read in *The Myroure of Oure Ladye: Containing a Devotional Tretise on Divine Service* (1530): "Of what secte or contre so euer they be, hethen or crysten, sarasen, or Iewe" (ii. 86, citing the 1873 edition). Or, again, in the English translation of Polydore Vergil's *English History*: "Preaching the woord of Godd and sincere secte of Christe" (I.74, from the 1846 edition). In the latter example, then, all of Christianity is referred to by the author simply as a "sect." Eventually, however, by the end of the sixteenth and beginning of the seventeenth century, the term begins to refer to a system of belief or observance that is somehow distinctive, and thus set apart, from the mainstream, often with the connotation that it is somehow different from that which is assumed to be orthodoxy (i.e., making the sect heretical). Thus, in *The Repressor of Over Much Blaming of the Clergy* (dated to somewhere around 1449), by the Bishop of Chichester, Reginald Peacock (ca. 1392–ca. 1459), we read: "Aftir the daies of the Apostlis roosen also manye vntrewe sectis of Cristen men, as the sect of Valentynyanys" (497; from the 1860 edition). Or, in Edward Gibbon's (1737–1794), still famous *The History of the Decline and Fall of the Roman Empire*: "The church was distracted by the Nestorian and Monophysite sects" (V. 1. 170). Both of these "sects," we might add, refer to early Christian theological debates on matters such as the nature of Jesus.

One of the most common appearances of the word today is its designation of a "denomination," that is a religious sub-group with a distinctive name and place of worship. For example, Anglicans, Methodists, or Baptists would be good examples of Protestant denominations. While this usage tends to be value neutral, just as common is the continuing idea that "sects" refer to groups that have broken away from the "mainstream." Now the term is certainly pejorative, in the sense that something is not a "religion," but a breakaway "sect." It is not uncommon, for example, to have the Catholic Church refer to Protestant denomination as "sects" or when, to use another example, the Anglican Church calls various bodies of Dissenters, "sects." Implicit in both of these examples is the idea that there was something originary—some set of teachings or body of faith—that various groups (i.e., the sects) have rejected and thereby broken away from. Thus, in Thomas Vautrollier's (d. 1587) English translation of Martin Luther's *Commentary on the Epistle to Galathians* (1577) we read: "The Jewes assured them selues that the Church ... should shortly be ouerthrowne: that which by an odious name they called a Sect" (f. 221). Moving into the nineteenth century, we continue to see these two uses. Sects, on the one hand, can refer to both all denominations or to a particular group, as in, for example, Ezra Stiles Ely (1786–1861), the American minister who, in his *The Duty of Every Christian Freeman to Elect Christian Rules: A Discourse Delivered on the Fourth of July 1827* (1828) could declare that "I would prefer a religious and moral man, of any one of the truly Christian sects, to any man destitute of religious principles and morality" (13). Or, on the other hand, it can be used, in its more pejorative sense when, for example, in a section entitled "Marks of the True Church" the Benedictine monk, John Manock (1677–1764), declares in his *Poor Man's Catechism: Or, the Christian Doctrine Explained with Short Admonitions* (1762) that the Catholic Church "was founded by Christ must certainly be infallible in all her decisions of faith and doctrine." Therefore,

> if the Church by our Saviour established has never erred, and it is a fact undoubted, that Catholics in no time past ever did leave the communion of that Church which was by him founded, and that all other sects left them, hence it is easy to see which is the right way.
>
> (70, citing the 1825 edition)

If Christianity was in possession of "sects," and given that comparative religion dates to Europeans frequently using their knowledge of Christian history and theology as the prototype for all religions, then it was only a matter of time before subgroups of other religions would also be described using the same terminology. We, thus, witness the term being easily transferable to account for internal divisions within other religions. In his *Development of Muslim Theology, Jurisprudence and Constitutional Theory* (1903), for example, Duncan Black

MacDonald (1863–1943), the well-known Scottish Orientalist and Professor of Semitic Languages at the Hartford Theological Seminary, writes of a Muslim "sect" known as the Kharijites, who, "being at the opposite pole from the Shi'ites, are the only Muslim sect that curses and abhors Ali. Orthodox Islam reveres Ali and accepts his Khalifate" (27). Again, we see the interplay between "orthodoxy" on the one hand and "sect" on the other, with each taking definition from the inverse characteristics and other traits of its opposite. Or, again, in Judaism, we read—most commonly in antiquity, one of the milieus from which Christianity is understood to have sprung—of Pharisees, Saducees, and Essenes (to which we could inevitably include early Christianity as a fourth "sect"). In the modern period, we frequently encounter the three "sects" of Reform, Orthodox, and Conservative Judaism. While the members of each group inevitably see themselves as the most authentic expression of the tradition and thus hardly a sect, scholars nonetheless prefer to label them all as "Jewish sects." In fact, we see the term used in describing the Egyptian Therapeutes, described there as a group of Christian hermits as "ftricter obfervers of the fabbath than any other *Jewifh* fect" (*A Univerfal Hiftory, From The Earlift Account of Time...* [1747] vol. X, chpt. xi, 484). Thus, in writing about its own movement, Reform Judaism, the *Reform Advocate* from 1937 writes that "if we remain aloof from Jewish nationalist aspirations we shall become a sect, cut off from world Israel" (11). Here, the idea is that if Reform Judaism does not adequately reflect the desires and aspirations of what is assumed to be some vague and essentialized notion of world Jewry then it will be little more than a "sect." Predictably, we also see the term applied to Hindu "sects," when, for example, an insider seeking to interpret the tradition for outsiders can title a chapter "General Character of the Hindu Sects." This Jogendra Nath Bhattacharya (1850–1899), the President of the College of Pandits in Nadiya, does in his *Hindu Castes and Sects: An Exposition of the Origins of the Hindu Caste System and the Bearing of the Sects Towards Each Other and Towards Other Religious Systems* (1896). Or, when an Orientalist does so in a similar manner, with the aim of making sense of Indian "denominations" for the benefit of English readers, as when Horace Hayman Wilson (1786–1860), the inaugural Boden Professor of Sanskrit at Oxford, writes of the Jains in his *Hindu Religions: Or, An Account of the Various Religious Sects of India* (1899): "[they] cannot be comprised within the limits necessarily assigned to this general sketch of the Hindu sects" (170).

Such divisions based on "sects" can, of course, also be used in an ecumenical way. Witness, for example, the rather peculiar and highly phenomenological discussion found in Mohammed Abu-Nimer, Amal Khoury, and Emily Welty's *Unity in Diversity: Interfaith Dialogue in the Middle East*, a 2007 publication produced by the United States Institute of Peace. They write that

> Jews, Muslims, and Christians share and identify as fellow pilgrims on a path—a path all three faiths understand to be profoundly rooted in concepts of truth and peace .... [A]ll three believe in the validity of revelation as a sign from God and struggle to maintain unity in spite of splits in their populations (Reform/Orthodox, Shiite/Sunni, Protestant/Catholic).
>
> (19)

While they do not technically use the term "sect" here, their meaning is quite clear: all three so-called Abrahamic religions have divisions—"splits" to use their term. Historically, of course, the three divisions mentioned here can also be understood to have absolutely nothing to do with one another, indicating that grouping them together as "Abrahamic religions" is itself an effort to create the impression of similarity for an author's own socially formative purposes.

What, then, does a critical scholar do with this term "sect," one that has played such a formative role in structuring how we think about religions? It is certainly worth pointing out in this context that a quick survey of its use over the last two hundred years shows a gradual diminishment, which would seem to mean that the term is slowly disappearing or being retired as other terms find favor (e.g., whether denomination, or even new religious movement [NRM]). This is probably for the best since the term easily implies a certain orthodoxy/heresy binary, with "sects" often associated with the latter category. This means that its use inevitably naturalizes certain participant claims as to whether or not groups are mainstream or not. It is clear, then, that the term, like so many of our terms, is highly political. Very rarely does someone refer to themselves as being a member of a sect, for example. Rather, it is an identity that larger and thus dominant groups—those whose members imagine themselves to somehow represent the superior and originary form of the religion in question—ascribe to subgroups.

In this volume see: church, cult, magic, myth, mysticism, paganism, reformation, sacrifice, tradition

In *Religion in 50 Words* see: authenticity, classification, orthodoxy, politics, power, society

40 Sexuality

"Sex and religion are two of the commonest concerns of mankind," although they are often opposed to one another, inasmuch as one is presumed to be physical and the other spiritual. Thus wrote the English comparativist, Methodist minister, and onetime missionary, Geoffrey Parrinder (1910–2005) in the opening line to his book, *Sex in the World's Religions* (1980). Despite how common they apparently are, if this very book was being written just a generation ago, there is a rather good chance that "sexuality" would not have been included in the list. Or, if it was, it most likely would have entailed a survey of the role of sexual practices or imagery throughout the world's religions. Like many world religions textbooks, that entry likely would have included reference to the symbolism—no doubt shocking or perhaps even titillating to some sensibilities—of the *lingam*, associated with the Hindu god Shiva (indicative of a phallus), and the *yoni*, representative of the goddess Shakti (and signifying the vulva), engaged with each other, as if in mid-copulation. There was a time, in fact, when such imagery would have prompted observers to conclude that devotees for whom such devotional objects were important actually worshipped them.

We see the latter, for example, in a note appearing in William Hodges's (1744–1797) *Travels in India, during the years 1780, 1781, 1782 and 1783* (1793): "The Lingham is the great object of fuperftition among the followers of Brahmah, it being the general fymbol of regenerative nature" (94, quoting the 1794 edition). While accusations of idolatry have certainly diminished, the assumption that sex is properly understood as part of the process of reproduction remains. Thus, as reflected in as recent a title as *Sex, Marriage, and Family in World Religions* (2006), sex and sexuality have often been included in the orbit of comparative religion mainly with regard to the normative role played by heterosexuality—though practices that diverged from this presumed or even hegemonic norm certainly caught scholars' attention as well. Consider here the role played in Indian society by those known as *Hijras*—a Hindi word, though sometimes used pejoratively by some (and thus replaced by other terms today, such as *khasuaa*)—that is, intersexed or transgendered individuals. Lieutenant Richard C. Temple (1850–1931) described them in 1882 as "a class of eunuchs, who dress up as old women and obtain a living by singing ... songs at births and marriages .... They go about generally three together with a drum" ("Some Hindú Folksongs from the Punjáb," *Journal of the Asiatic Society of Bengal* 51/3: 187). Attention is also given to such southern Indian goddesses as Renuka—also known as Yellamma, Jogamma, or even Holiyyamma—whose devotees include men who present as women. As scholarship on sex and gender in particular, and identity more broadly, has become more nuanced and critical over the past few academic generations, it has become apparent that sexuality is about far more than sex and gender. Instead, the term is about how society works and how its members designate and thereby understand and value each other (or not). Most scholars now recognize, to quote the anthropologist, Lucinda Ramberg, that those who report calls from Yellamma to come serve her,

> withdraw from sexual relations with their husbands and leave untenable marriages. They take the path of divine service out[side] of gendered kin obligations, which are otherwise extremely difficult to escape in this rural context, where endogamous relations remain the most powerful arbiter of social belonging.
> (quoting her 2019 blog post "Divine!" at The Immanent Frame: Secularism, Religion, and Public Life)

An entry in a book such as this on the place of the word "sexuality" in the critical scholar of religion's vocabulary would have to follow suit and make apparent that it is about so much more than what a previous generation might have once thought.

"Sex," early on also written as "sexe" or "seex," appears in English in the late fourteenth century. One such early example can be found in the Middle English of the so-called Wycliffe Bible, dated to about 1382 or thereafter. Though the term therein does not correspond to a word in the Hebrew text, which only includes the words *zakar* (male or man) and *neqebah* (female or woman), we read: "Of all þingez hauyng soule of eny flesch: two þou schalt brynge in to þe ark, þat male sex & female: lyuen with þe" (Genesis 6:19: "of all the things having a soul of any flesh: two you shall bring in to the ark, that male sex and female, living with you"). Like so many of our other key words, it enters

English from French, originally deriving from the Latin *sexus*, which is itself of obscure origins. Indeed, some argue that it derives from earlier terms signifying to sever or divide things up, hence its later application to what is portrayed as a fundamental way in which biological species are internally divided. From early on it denotes a person's reproductive identity, sometimes even a way of referring to their genitalia. Over time the term is extended to other members of the animal and plant kingdom, such as we see in John Maplet's 1567 book, *A greene forest, or A naturall historie vvherein may bee seene first the most sufferaigne vertues in all the whole kinde of ... plants*, making reference there to plants having "both sexes and kindes" (in the Preface to the Second Book, 28). With the late eighteenth century and the addition of the common suffix *-ity* we find the noun "sexuality" used as a variation of the early-seventeenth-century adjective "sexual." Thus, we find references to the "sexuality of vegetables" and plants in general, as in John Claudis Loudon's 1865 book, *An Encyclopaedia of Agriculture* (248). We also find the word naming an expression of a person's sex, as in Edward Moor's (1771–1848) wry comment in 1834: "The ardent fanaticism of convents is of necessity often blended with unconscious sexuality, that would if recognised shock the virtuous aspirant" (*Oriental Fragments*, 220). We then witness a host of variations and expressions from "the weaker" or "the fairer" sex, to "sex education" in the nineteenth century and even "sexy" in the late nineteenth century as well as "sexist" in the mid twentieth. The term "sexuality" is often presumed to name an emitted quality that constitutes an expression of an inner sexed identity, and it is now certainly a common part of the English language, increasing in its frequency of use during the second half of the twentieth century.

Part of that increase is linked to its close pairing with "gender." The latter term derives from the French and, before that Latin, sharing a root with the word "genre," a term whose own use increases even more dramatically over just the past forty years. One's sexual identity was long thought to name "the natural ... distinction in human beings and animals," as phrased in A. Knutson's doctoral dissertation at the University of Lund (Sweden), *The Gender of Words Denoting Living Beings in English and the Different Ways of Expressing Difference in Sex* (1905), 1. However, a person's gender—i.e., whether one behaved in a fashion judged to be more or less feminine or masculine—was seen to be socially conditioned and possibly variable. If gender acknowledged gradations, sex implied for most people a non-negotiable distinction firmly anchored in biology and evidenced in the simple fact of anatomical differences. Thus a man could portray feminine traits, and vice versa. But this is no longer the case, what with a number of scholars now considering both gender and sex to be products of the various ways that human beings perform or identify themselves. This latter position benefits in a fundamental way from Judith Butler's work, e.g., *Gender Trouble* (1990) and *Bodies That Matter: On the Discursive Limits of Sex* (1995). We should, of course, acknowledge that (sometimes heated) debates on these matters continue in both scholarship and daily life in the early twenty-first century, as exemplified at various levels of government in the US, concerning such basic issues as who is allowed to use which public bathroom. These so-called bathroom bills, introduced into a variety of state legislatures, sought to police identity.

Today, the once strict binary that distinguished females and males from one another, and which then also represented any variation on heterosexuality as, quite literally, a perversion, has been greatly complicated. Initially this was done by means of the increasingly wide acceptance of homosexuality as a natural and thus legitimate sexual orientation—though, we must add, there remain some groups who exert effort trying to "unteach" or "deprogram" homosexuality, especially associated with certain conservative Christian groups—and then with recognition of a variety of more nuanced distinctions across the spectrum of sexual identity. How the various so-called mainstream world religions view these matters—whether such works are written descriptively or, as is often the case, prescriptively—is likely the main place where the scholar of religion will find these issues addressed in the field. We witness this, e.g., from David Shneer and Caryn Aviv's edited volume, *Queer Jews* (2002) and Scott Siraj al-Haqq Kugle's *Living Out Islam: Voices of Gay, Lesbian, and Transgender Muslims* (2014) to Gillian Frank, Bethany Moreton, and Heather R. White's co-edited collection, *Devotions and Desires: Histories of Sexuality and Religion in the Twentieth Century United States* (2018). The latter includes essays by Andrea R. Jain (on sex and religion in the practice of yoga) and Judith Weisenfeld (on celibacy and same sex desire in an early twentieth-century movement led by Reverend Major Jealous Divine, who died in 1965). The critical scholar will likely approach things differently than just chronicling religious responses to, or views on, sexuality—let alone advising members of the groups that they study on how they ought to conceive of sexuality. Much like the last volume just cited, they may think of religion and sexuality instead "as categories that create and impinge upon each other" (3). Such a position avoids assuming that both categories refer to a stable substance that is expressed in either this or that way, and is then treated in either this or that way. Though such assumptions have not entirely disappeared from the academy (let alone the wider public), it is much more productive to think of both sexuality and religion, among a variety of other ways of talking about the human and its features, as governing techniques that discipline and thereby shape social actors in specific ways and for specific effect.

This shaping, for lack of a better word, is accomplished by defining and then distinguishing proper from improper, allowed from forbidden, normal from deviant, and mainstream from extremist. Just as it is the *discourse* on religion, and not the fact that we then end up talking about an assortment of things *as* religion that the critical scholar may wish to examine, so, too, it is the *discourse* on sexuality that will likely attract the critical scholar's attention. The latter term is, thus, one more site where the limits of the acceptable are asserted and, to be sure, contested as well. As Michel Foucault (1926–1984) persuasively argued in his influential work on the history of sexuality—the first of its volumes published in France in 1976—it is the discourse on sexuality that turns mere behavior into something seen as risqué or desirable, maybe even forbidden and thus something to be denied and avoided instead of something to be obtained and experienced. He asks:

> What are the links between these discourses, these effects of power, and the pleasures that were invested by them? What knowledge was formed as a result of this linkage? The object, in short, is to define the regime of power-knowledge-pleasure that sustains the discourse on human sexuality in our part of the world.
> (*The History of Sexuality* [1990], vol. I, 11, citing Robert Hurley's translation)

Thus, as he sums it up: "The central issue, then ... is not to determine whether one says yes or no to sex ... but to account for the fact that it is spoken about," that is, that it is an item of discourse, knowledge, and thus governance.

While Foucault's work is hardly the only source for this shift—which entails rethinking sexuality as the product of an historical, and therefore changeable, discourse including performance, assumptions, institutions, ways of thinking, material artifacts, etc.—it has certainly had wide ramifications throughout scholarship, not least being scholarship on religion. The turn away from debating the best or the right way to define religion and, instead, examining why such debates even take place and why a specific zone of human behavior and association are so consistently designated (and then managed) *as* religious owes much to Foucault's work some fifty years ago. And for a critical scholar comfortable with making this shift with regard to religion, one would think that the same shift in approaching sexuality would promise just as interesting and far-reaching results.

In this volume see: idol, immanence/transcendence, value

In *Religion in 50 Words* see: authority, classification, definition, gender, identity, orthodoxy, politics, power, race, world religions

41 Shamanism

Despite the fact that shamanism is thought to be an ancient practice, perhaps even regarded in some quarters as one of the older, if not oldest, forms of religion, its use in English only dates, perhaps surprisingly, to the eighteenth century. Regardless of when the concept, if not the actual word, came into existence, shamanism today is often defined as an archaic religious form that involves a practitioner (i.e., a shaman) who is thought to interact with a—or better "the"—spiritual world. This is often done by means of trances or other altered states of consciousness, including through the use of narcotics, with the aim of somehow harnessing them in this world for purposes of healing the sick, protecting crops, and so on. The romanticism of the term, especially the primary idea that the shaman is imagined to have some direct and unmediated access to and thus experience with "the sacred," has, needless to say, been an endless source of fascination (if not actual obsession) for some scholars interested in religion. Indeed, there even exists an international academic journal, *Shaman*, published by the International Society for Academic Research on Shamanism (ISARS), wherein anthropologists, archaeologists, historians, religious studies scholars, and psychologists all seek to study and account for this practice in its—and this should immediately alert the critical student of religion—many diverse "forms." Such "forms," in good phenomenological fashion, often imply an unchanging essence that links the various instances or versions altogether. Shamanism is, thus, thought to be a universal though archaic form of religion that is often claimed to coincide with Indigenous groups throughout the globe, regardless of their temporal period or geographic locale.

Again, despite the supposed antiquity of the practice—with articles in the aforementioned journal finding shamanistic practices scattered around the world and existing as early as the Iron Age, if not before—we should probably enquire initially into what the term does or, at the very least, it claims to do. It would seem, then, that "shamanism" is little more than an attempt on the part of European and other scholars to group together any number of perceived practices taking place outside of the orbit of so-called world religions that involve attempts to conjure the spiritual world for mundane usage. It really is that vague. Once defined in this rather open-ended manner, it can then be conveniently located wherever the researcher looks for it. Rather than regard it as a "religion" (that is, an "-ism," i.e., Shaman-ism, placed alongside Buddhism or Hinduism), or even as one of the points of origins of religion, we should perhaps better regard it as yet another attempt on the part of scholars to impose a taxonomic rubric on a variety of diverse forms that may well have nothing in common with one another. All of these forms, moreover, are argued to revolve around some amorphous experience that the practitioner (to wit, *the* shaman) is believed to have had.

We witness this in the very ambiguousness of the term. It is unclear, for example, from where the word initially derives, though it does exist in German as *schamane* and in French as in *chaman*. Earlier attempts to derive it from the Persian term *shemen* (used to refer to an idol, or the temple for an idol) or an adoption from the Chinese *sha mên* (an ordained member of a Buddhist fraternity) seem unlikely. Yet others have argued that the term derives from the Russian *šaman*. Regardless of its origins, the term was first used in English in the late eighteenth and early nineteenth centuries to denote a priest or priest-doctor among various northern peoples of Asia, but especially those tribal groups associated with the Uralic and Altaic regions of Siberia. Thus, in the twenty-seven-volume *Penny Cyclopaedia*, published between 1833 and 1843, we read that it is a form of religion associated with "heathens": "They [Samoyedes] are heathens, and profess the religion called Shamanism" (XX. 382). Or, framed somewhat more positively, if equally in an exotic manner, we begin to see it in a more positive light as, for example, in *The Middle Kingdom: A Survey of the Geography, Government, Education, Social Life, Arts, Religion, &c* (1848) by Samuel Wells Williams (1812–1884), the American missionary and Sinologist: "The form of Budhism prevailing among the Mongols and Tibetans differs more in its state and power than in its doctrines; it is called Shamanism, or *Hwang kiau*, the Yellow doctrine, from the color of the priestly robes" (II. xviii. 258). Interestingly, less than twenty-five years later, we witness the term extended to apply to similar practices of yet other peoples in different parts of the globe, but especially to Indigenous communities in North America. In 1870, for example, in his *Alaska and Its Resources* by the American natural historian William

Healey Dall (1845–1927), we read: "The belief in shamánism is universal among the natives of Alaska, Eskimo as well as Indians" (88). With this, we now see Shamanism name a particular religious form common to small, tribal groups wheresoever they may be located.

This jump from the Uralic and Altaic mountains to North America is considerable and demands comment. It would seem that a set of "archaic" and indigenous practices believed to exist in the former context could then be used to translate what were understood as similar practices among other peoples, if for no other reason than that they, too, were imagined to be "archaic" and Indigenous peoples—presumably sharing universal features with all such peoples. This stretch of the term to include all these diverse peoples therefore seems to be based solely on the fact that they are all imagined to exist on what would seem to be, using the language of the late eighteenth century, a similar level or spectrum of development. Because of this, it is assumed by scholars—then as well as now—that they must all have access to the same "experiences" derived from a similar, if not universal, Indigenous religious system. Moreover, given the fact that there has always tended to exist in the field of religious studies a wistful romanticism when it comes to the "spiritual" traditions of Indigenous peoples, many of which are often thought to represent earlier and thus purer forms of religiosity that do not have the same impersonal, bureaucratized infrastructures of later "organized" religions, they are believed to share the same unmediated access to "the sacred." These experiences—to this day—are often collectively labelled "Indigenous spiritualities," still revolving around the assumption that they are all *still* somehow similar to one another.

Perhaps one of the most egregious examples to which "Shamanism" has been put may be found in the work of the influential historian of religions, Mircea Eliade (1907–1986), especially in his monograph simply titled *Shamanism: Archaic Techniques of Ecstasy* (1951 in French, with the English translation appearing later in 1964). Clocking it at over six hundred pages, the work is certainly one of Eliade's longest, and to this day among one of his more popular. In the book, he seeks—working on the assumption that the term "Shamanism" names a universal category—to provide a "historical" study of its different forms around the world. In the foreword to the book, Eliade, in typical fashion, argues that the sacred is something that is *sui generis* and therefore cannot be reducible to, or explained by reference to, anything else. He uses this opportunity as yet another occasion to differentiate the expertise of the scholar of religion (understood by him as an interpreter and conservator of the sacred) from that of other social scientists. While the psychologist, sociologist, or ethnographer seek to make the case for studying shamanism psychologically, sociologically, or ethnographically, all of which ultimately reduce the shaman's experiences to other non-religious factors. It is the "unique" gift of the student of religion to be able to see and explain the shaman's experiences for what they *really are*: an irreducible experience of that ill-defined universal, "the sacred." In like manner, Eliade argues, in phrasing he repeats throughout his many works on religion, that "although the historical conditions are extremely important in a religious phenomenon (for every human datum is in the last analysis a historical datum), they do not exhaust it" (xx). Working on the assumption that a hierophany—a term he coins, from Latin, for "the appearance (*phanos*) of the sacred (heiros)"—is structurally similar no matter where or when it appears, he subsequently goes on to argue that shamanism, as a so-called archaic technique of ecstasy (to use the book's subtitle), combines "at once mysticism, magic, and 'religion' in the broadest sense of the term" (xxv). Indeed, the shaman, again according to Eliade, is someone who is able to "manipulate" the sacred and stand apart from their communities on account of "the intensity of their own religious experience" (8).

Despite, or perhaps better because of, Eliade's basic triangulation of the shaman, religious experience, and "the sacred," many have followed in his footsteps in analyzing the structure and extent of shamanism. In his Foreword to *Shamanism: An Encyclopedia of World Beliefs, Practices, and Culture* (2004) edited by Mariko Namba Walter and Eva Jane Neumann Fridman, for example, the noted historian of religions, Lawrence E. Sullivan writes: "Shamanism serves, in this respect, as a parable for religious life more broadly in our day" (ix). Indeed, as the editors write in their own Introduction to that *Encyclopedia*: "Shamans are globally distributed and shamanism is an ancient spiritual practice" (xi). Once again, we see the connection between shamanism and spirituality (and not necessarily religion) on the one hand, and the fact that it has come to signify a universal condition that takes place beyond the confines of what are assumed to be more organized religious forms. A more sober analysis may be found in Graham Harvey's *Shamanism: A Reader* (2003), where it is at least recognized that there are possible problems involved in such universalizing suppositions. In fact, Harvey writes in his opening that scholars would be well served to be aware of "the implication of the use of the word shaman outside of Siberia" (1).

Further demonstrating what a vague term "shamanism" is, we should not be surprised to see it picked up in various contemporary new age spirituality movements. In the twentieth century, for example, many of its practitioners in Europe and North America, such as those interested in such concepts like "alternative" spiritualities, have adopted elements from what they understand as shamanism. Interestingly, they are often recycled and reduced from scholarly, comparative works like those found in Eliade and other phenomenologists, not to mention the popular writings of those like the new age figure Carlos Castaneda (1925–1998), who claimed to have been initiated into the rituals of shamanism. Along with other Indigenous religious practices, recent years have witnessed the rise of the "neo-shamanism" movement, which can often be grouped together with other more recent developments, such as neo-paganism. So, while the term seems likely here to stay, a critical scholar should be cautious in its usage, especially given the fact that it often has a very specific cultural reference despite efforts to use it to name some universal phenomenon that is connected to the equally murky concept of "Indigenous spirituality."

In this volume see: animism, cult, East/West, immanence/transcendence, magic, meditation, mysticism, paganism, piety, soul, spirituality, value

In *Religion in 50 Words* see: authenticity, classification, cognition, definition, description, essence, experience, indigeneity, interpretation, phenomenology, primitive, sacred/profane, world religions

42 Soul

Yet another Christian theological term that earlier comparativists applied far and wide in their efforts to understand others, the word "soul" has a central place in the history of the study of religion. Whether it deserves that place is, of course, a question that a critical scholar may want to consider, especially given the rather particular baggage that tends to come with the term. Often working closely with the word "belief" (i.e., "I believe that my soul will outlive my body"), as well as the idea of "salvation" ("my soul has been saved"), the soul seems to have been a natural topic for scholars of religion to study. However, this became more complicated once they made a shift and tried to do something more than (i) merely paraphrase the claims made by the people whom they happened to study, and then (ii) universalize the claims of a small segment of the population by looking for analogs in other cultures and historical periods. This second move—for example, posing such a comparativist question as "how do they say 'soul' in Hebrew?"—presumes that either the reality or at the very least the idea identified by an English word such as "soul" is a universal. This is an assumption shown to be problematic as soon as one adopts a different local tradition as the normative starting point and then goes about posing such an alternative question as, e.g., "how do you say 'karma' in English?" The question likely makes little sense because almost any English reader who understands the definition of this term and something about the context of its origins or usage (i.e., Sanskrit and southern Asia) will imagine "karma" to be a concept so localized to, e.g., Hindus or Buddhists, and thus of little comparative use. This is because "karma" is understood as a term related to a very specific metaphysic, where the universe is presumed to be governed by rather different theological laws than those familiar to, say, Christians. Thus, the English listener would more than likely not hear this term as having any deep, universal significance for all human beings, let alone for themselves—as if "we" needed a word of our own to name a reality that "we" had somehow failed to recognize in our daily lives. We witness this when we come to a claim such as that of the once prominent American occultist and writer, William Walker Atkinson (1862–1932), a popularizer of research produced by those working in early comparative religion. "Strictly speaking 'Karma' is the Law of Cause and Effect as applied to the life of the soul, the law whereby it reaps the results of its own sowing" (from his book, *Reincarnation and the Law of Karma* [1908], 222). A critical scholar will quickly recognize much going on that a descriptivist might not, such as the role this word "soul" plays for Atkinson's English readers. It functions as if it is universal when, in fact, it is no less local an idea than the unfamiliar (e.g., "karma") that he is trying to describe to his readers. While this may be an effective, perhaps even inevitable, cognitive technique when confronting new information, it is hardly helpful in scholarship when it results in normalizing but one local as if it is transcendent and self-evident. Rethinking the ease with which "soul" is sometimes used by scholars of religion is a task we need to address.

For those to whom "soul" is a familiar term it will more than likely imply a very specific set of assumptions and relations that are not universalizable—even if others in their comparative work make claims about an ethereal something that is said to animate the body. It is not just the assumption that bodies have an immaterial essence that lives beyond physical death. More than likely it is that this substance is often thought to retain the traits of the individual while moving to some new type of existence in which it will be judged for the life it lived, earning for it either eternal reward, in a place called heaven, or eternal torment, in a place called hell. Holding the whole system together is the assumption that there exists a just creator that governs the universe who sets the moral standards for human conduct, and, equally, a demonic figure who reigns over the souls that are damned in hell. While the former is usually known as God, the latter is known in Christianity as Satan or the Devil, deriving from the ancient Hebrew *śāṭān* for an adversary or, in some parts of the Hebrew scriptures, for a member of the heavenly host who tests human beings, such as the Book of Job and the trials undergone by the protagonist. We then also sometimes find claims about souls that have somehow not transitioned to this existence after death, and who continue to roam the earth. Such claims, usually not sanctioned by church hierarchies, that souls are often considered to be tormented in some manner (i.e., ghosts or spirits), perhaps on account of unfinished business, should also be added to this concept of "soul." But even if this all sounds rather familiar to the reader it is hardly cross-cultural. For even in those groups who also presuppose some sort of unified self that merely inhabits a body—e.g., the Sanksrit-based termed *ātmán*, used in some Indian schools of thought to refer to this animating force—can differ so drastically from the story above that it would be rather sloppy to just conclude something along the lines of "atman means soul in Hinduism." It is precisely for this reason that a more careful comparativist will devise a term of their own making, e.g., "self" (itself a technical term with a complex history of its own, to be sure) that is capable of including all those assumptions and claims that seem to be shared across cultures and historical periods. Such a position avoids merely elevating any one local term as if it is capable of also naming the entire family of concepts.

The noun "soul," used more prominently throughout the nineteenth century than now, is a rather old word, dating back to early Old English "salwle" and "sawal," and includes a wide variety of spellings over the years. It has Germanic roots, implying an oath that one might make based on one's future salvation and coming to be associated later with life and, thus, a life force thought to inhabit and live beyond the body. We see a variety of related terms, from Old Saxon and Old High German to Old Icelandic and Old Swedish, with *Seele* being the modern German equivalent, *sál* in Icelandic and *själ* in Swedish. Of note is that the modern French term, *âme*, reflects a rather different trajectory, deriving instead from the Latin *anima*, meaning life and breath as well as mind, feeling, or as we would say, spirit, and from which we also derive the English "animal" and "animate." The often-associated term "spirit," from the Middle French *espirit* and, earlier, the classical Latin *spīritus*, enters English around the early fourteenth century, also linked to a similar semantic range, with more abstract senses deriving from the earlier association with breathing, breathe, and life. English speakers, then, have two words, of very different origins, that do much the same work: "soul" and "spirit." (Though thought to be synonyms by some, for others, such as some Victorians, the former was said to be one's "true self" whereas the latter was said to be the animating force of all life.) From "spirit" we see "spiritual" in evidence by the late fourteenth century, "spirituality" not long after, and even such variations as "spirited," by the sixteenth century. All these related terms refer to something with vigor, enthusiasm, or energy. It can even be used to refer to distilled alcohols, i.e., to drink spirits or, in the UK, "surgical spirits" referring to an antiseptic that, in North American, would be designated as "rubbing alcohol."

"Soul" is more closely associated with a person's presumed essence, though to be "soulful" (a mid-nineteenth century variation) indicates one who is considered of deep emotion. By the mid-twentieth century, it characterizes a genre of music, "soul music," closely associated with African American culture. Examples of such singers include Sam Cooke (1931–1964) and Aretha Franklin (1942–2018), who was widely known as the Queen of Soul. "Soul food" long predates its current linkage to staples of traditional southern US, and more particularly African American, cuisine. Indeed, the term appears as early as the late twelfth century where it is used as so-called nourishment for the soul, and refers to the Christian ritual of the eucharist, or communion. In his posthumously published *Two Treatises More ...* (1703), for example, Thomas Lawson (1630–1691) refers to the eucharist as "the Soul's Food" (vol. II, 167). Its applications can also be seen in sympathetically referring to someone as a "poor soul" or, respectfully, as a "pious soul." The term can also be used in those phrases that refer euphemistically to dying, i.e., "to give up the ghost" or "to give up the soul." It can also be used to emphasize the absence of anyone (i.e., "not a single soul") or as a way of referring to a single person, and "immense airliner with hundreds of souls on board," as in *The Times* of London (December 30, 1983: 8/6). The last use often concerns tragedy, such as when Michel J. Mooney's referred to "the Titanic's 1,517 lost souls" in his memorial article published in *Mariners Weather Log* 36/1 (1992: 18). Regardless of the variation, the linkage between "soul" and a Christian theological notion of a person's immaterial and eternal essence endures. Witness, for example, the concluding line to a prayer included in *Rebels not Saints: or, a collection of the Speeches, Private Passages, Letters, and Prayers of those persons lately executed, viz. T. Harrison, J. Carew, J. Cook and H. Peters* (1601): "Lord Jefus receive my Soul, Lord Jefus into thy Arms I commend my Spirit" (31). More recently, but with the same idea, see Elisa Romeo's 2015 self-help book, *Meet Your Soul: A Powerful Guide to Connect with Your Most Sacred Self.*

That members of other cultures, now and in the past, also posit the existence of a nonphysical, animating force must be acknowledged, of course. So common was this once thought to be that the early anthropologist Edward Burnett Tylor (1832–1917) proposed animism, a belief in spiritual beings, as the original and thus simplest form of religion, from which all others, no matter how complicated or eventually bureaucratized, developed over time. As Tylor reasoned, in his once influential book, *Primitive Culture* (1871), early human beings must have misunderstood a dream, taking it instead as evidence that a part of the body travels during sleep, concluding that it also outlives the body, leading to such developments as so-called ancestor worship and offerings for the dead. As these early comparativists noted, we do indeed find a wide variety of names used to make reference to what is presumed to be the invisible impulse that animates the individual. Recognizing the dramatic differences in narratives and meanings that surround this term should prompt a critical scholar not only to be careful generalizing and too quickly drawing broad theological conclusions about something called "the soul" but also to recall that "religion" is itself a no less local a designator. In this way, we might be wary of assuming that such references to an immaterial substance are somehow inherently theological and thus religious by nature. To put it another way, that "soul, spirit" received an entry in Eric Sharpe's *Fifty Key Words: Comparative Religion* (1971), one that itemized some of the ways that various "primitive" and then also contemporary religious people have conceived of it might miss the point entirely. Perhaps such entries should be included in political science handbooks, what with the interest over the past fifty years or so in the idea of the self—its historical rise across European modernity and its various socio-political effects. Instead of theologizing that which is assumed to distinguish the individual from his or her social setting, the very idea of the individual itself, now seen as an historical product, is indicative of the specific social circumstances that led to its rise, that concerns the scholar. What we could now call the detheologized self can then be understood as a building block for the kinds of mass social identities that many of us today take for granted, such as nationalism. See, for example, the work of Canadian philosopher, Charles Taylor's *Sources of the Self: The Making of the Modern Identity* (1989) as well as a variety of works on such topics as the history of privacy and domesticity, e.g., Michael McKeon's *The Secret History of Domesticity: Public, Private, and the Division of Knowledge* (2006). Such identities function as necessary fictions that makes possible a sense of autonomy in a world in which human beings are, whether we like it or not, social through and through.

These long-, and dare we say over-, used words "soul" and "spirit" provide an ideal opportunity to redescribe what it is that a scholar of religion does. This includes everything from what we study to the relevance of our work and whom our readership might be. We should be caution of limiting our scholarship to the descriptive and discursive limits of those whom we study by using primarily theologizing categories. When approached in a different manner, such terms and categories can be demonstrated to be fundamental components of daily social life. In the midst of incredible conformity—from the schedules their members each keep to the ingredients with which they cook and the styles of clothes they wear—societies often presuppose a domain for the social actor that is, to whatever extent, set apart from the group. If the critical tools of religious studies tell us anything—and we here have in mind Emile Durkheim's (1858–1917) sociological approach to studying the various ways of sacralizing otherwise mundane things—it is that these seemingly essential, ethereal qualities are actually products of prior routinized practices taking place in specific social situations. If so in the case of the ideas of the sacred and the profane, then perhaps also with that immaterial substance that everyone supposedly has—their soul.

In this volume see: afterlife, animism, god, immanence/transcendence, mysticism, piety, ritual spirituality, theology

In *Religion in 50 Words* see: belief, description, essentialism, practice, primitive, redescription, religion, sacred/profane

43 Spirituality

Spirituality, like religion, has now become one of the most important, and we dare say overused, words in the academic study of religion's conceptual vocabulary. Not surprisingly, then, the term connotes different things to different constituencies, and, without a consensus on the intellectual work it performs, the term offers yet another window onto the field's imprecision and continued investment in theological categories. The latter then have simply been recycled into a new and scholarly context. The term thus demands a critical rethinking, and failing that, we might go so far as to suggest that it has no place—at least as an analytic category—in academic study. Historically, the term has been used interchangeably with religion, in the sense that it is assumed to demarcate the spiritual, that which is connected to the "soul," and the experiential, that which is imagined to be distinct from the body. Used in this manner, the term functions as yet another way to protect religion in the academy by making it immune from scholarly study. Since we have no way of knowing if a soul even exists, let alone in good Neoplatonic fashion, that it somehow functions as the essence of the individual, studying so-called spirituality proves impossible. But if spirituality, for some, underscores religion, for yet others it connotes a distinct form of individual and highly personal experience. We witness the latter, for example, in the now common phrase, "I'm spiritual, but not religious" (SBNR) that is distinguished from the creeds, rituals, and institutions of so-called organized religion. It is in this latter sense that it is most often used today, such as those who see in spirituality something that can take place *outside* the confines of more normative religious institutions and practices. This is the opinion, for example, of Paul Heelas and Linda Woodhead in their *The Spiritual Revolution. Why Religion is Giving Way to Spirituality* (2005). Here it is important to recognize that this distinction is only possible should one define each term in such a way as to determine their opposite. The term, in other words, has had a lengthy, and often

DOI: 10.4324/9781003196631-44

contradictory, set of usages. Any word that can be used in so many ways, all of which have no verifiable referent, should cause a critical scholar to pause and reevaluate its place within their vocabulary.

Spirituality derives from the noun "spirit," a term which refers to the animating or vital principle presumed to animate human beings (and perhaps other animals). Derivative of the Old French *espirit*, which itself comes from the Latin word *spiritus* (soul), that is formed from the verb *spirare* (to breathe) and the suffix *-itus*. In the Vulgate (i.e., the late fourth-century Latin translation of the Bible), the term *spiritus* is used to translate the Greek *pneuma*, a term initially used by ancient Greek philosophers to refer to "heat" or "warm air," and subsequently used by the authors of the New Testament to refer to "soul" or "spirit." It was also used to translate the Hebrew term *ruach*, meaning "breath," "wind," or "spirit." The term "spirituality" is likewise derived from Middle French *spiritualité*, and from the late Latin "*spiritualitatem*," which, in turn, was also derived from Latin *spiritualis*. "Spirituality" was originally used to refer to an institution, "the Guardian of the Spiritualities," the person or body responsible for the ecclesiastical jurisdiction of a bishopric or archbishopric while a see (from Latin for seat or dwelling, for the position of the Pope) is vacant. Thus, we read in Act 13 of the *Statutes of the Realm* (Acts of the English Parliament) from 1571: "Parlyament ... shall bryng from such Bysshop or Gardyan of Spiritualities [*v.r.*Spyrytualtyes] ... a testimoniall of such Assent" (IV: 546). From this, the term could be extended more generally to the spiritual or ecclesiastical realm or sphere, such as the jurisdiction of church authority, or the clergy, along with those possessions or benefits belonging to the church or clergy. Thus, from the designation of a legal jurisdiction the term could also then be used to refer to a realm that was different from the jurisdiction of so-called worldly authorities along with their materials, actions, and interests.

It is this latter meaning that would seem to be the one that is most common to this day. Thus we read in a sermon, *The Spirituality of the Divine Essence* (1806), from the Rev. John Styles (1782–1849), who informs his audience that the "spirituality of God" is important for at least three reasons. "First, As it affords us exalted ideas of the glory and majesty of divine perfections. Secondly, As it tends to the destruction of idolatry; Thirdly, As it prescribes the nature of acceptable worship" (30). Or, in his *Selection of Hymns Adapted for Divine Worship* (1818), the English Baptist Christopher Anderson informs his reader that

> The nature of God as a *Spirit*, forms the foundation of all Christian worship. In every approach to his sacred presence, the principal

consideration must be that of his spirituality; because each of his perfections suppose him to be a spirit, and they all center in this.

He continues:

> From places, your attention must be turned to persons, and whatever anxiety you may feel about the superiority of Gerizim to Jerusalem, must now be transferred to that spirituality of mind, without which God cannot dwell in you, nor you in his holy habituation.
> (3)

It is in this sense—the immaterial, the ahistorical, and thus the pure, undiluted, and authentic—that the term is primarily used to this day. In fact, during this time it has often been part of an explicitly theological vocabulary, e.g., Robert J. Wicks's *Handbook of Spirituality for Ministers* (1995) or Carol Ochs's *Women and Spirituality* (1997). It is also in this sense that the term, like so many others, also crossed over from Christian theological discourses to an academic discourse. We witness this at least as early as Mircea Eliade's "History of Religions and a New Humanism," the opening article in the inaugural 1961 volume of what was then the new journal, *History of Religions*. Therein he writes that one of the reasons behind the new journal is the fact that "the Westerners are being increasingly led to study, reflect on, and understand the spiritualities in Asia and the archaic world" (2). Here the term "spiritualities," once again, seems to be used interchangeably with "religions." This latter is common in the field where we encounter books with titles (listing only those from academic presses), such as *Pentecostal Spirituality: A Passion for the Kingdom* (2003), *Celtic Spirituality* (2000; in the series *Classics of Western Spirituality*), *Ignatian Spirituality in a Secular Age* (1984), *Women and Spirituality* (1997), and *Islamic Art and Spirituality* (1987). While all of these titles refer to what many would characterize as Western religious traditions, the term can also be used—as evident in Eliade's usage—in reference to so-called non-Western ones as well. We read, for example, titles like: *Eastern Spirituality in America: Selected Writings* (1987), *Hindu Spirituality* (1999) as well as *Buddhist Spirituality: Indian Southeast Asian, Tibetan, and Early Chinese* (1994), and *Korean Spirituality* (2008). Implicit in all of these titles, and the contents of their volumes, is the typically phenomenological assumption that spirituality names a universal category, immune from mundane forces. It is, moreover, something that manifests itself somewhat differently not just in different genders but also in different historical periods, in different regions, as well as

248 *Spirituality*

in different religious traditions. We never see entertained the idea that the term may well be little more than a rhetorical technique to promote certain interests (e.g., class, ideological) at the expense of others.

One of the more common uses for "spirituality" in recent years has been in the context of those groups and movements associated with indigeneity. This makes plain that the term can also have a valence with regard to power, often being aligned with those who do not occupy central positions. Thus, we hear concepts such as "Native American spirituality" (especially in the United States) or "First Nations or Indigenous spirituality" (in the case of Canada). This term can refer to a sense of romanticism or wistfulness on the part of commentators in the sense that such communities are sometimes imagined as having different social (and thus religious) structures than those associated with the world religions paradigm. However, it is also a usage that is potentially paternalistic inasmuch as it can recycle the old trope of the primitive, one that was so common in a much earlier iteration of the field. In his Introduction to *Native American Spirituality: A Critical Reader* (2000), for example, Lee Irwin writes that an "embodied, committed Native person" provides a

> sense of authenticity [that] rings true in the writings of this volume, where Native authors write first and foremost as Native people. The sense of personalization is a refreshing early spring wind, a Chinook, melting some of the ice and snow of a long hard winter of overly rationalized theory-making that has largely depersonalized the community and spirituality of its participating members.
> (7)

Irwin here uses spirituality in two senses: (1) to name a religious tradition that is represented as authentic and thus unlike that found among non-indigenous populations; and (2) invoking the term as used above, to name a personal experience, one that while unique to the indigenous community (presumably *all* indigenous communities), is nevertheless recognizable to the non-indigenous reader.

Whether or not it is opposed to religion, in all of these examples that which is "spiritual" is constructed in direct opposition to that which is historical, mundane, and social. It is thus difficult, by extension, to analyze using the tools offered by disciplines found in the human sciences of the modern academy. Much like trying to study an experience, how does one understand that which does not exist within a body? If not locatable, the term risks becoming nothing more than a metaphor, used to name pretty much whatever one wants to. Lacking any specificity, the term's status in our scholarly vocabulary is questionable at best.

Despite such problems, many scholars persist in the desire to keep it as part of the field's conceptual vocabulary, using the term as if it is a neutral descriptor of actual states of affairs or sentiments. In her article "Is There a Future for Religious Studies As We Know It?: Some Postmodern, Feminist and Spiritual Challenges" (*JAAR* 70/2 [2002]), Ursula King, the German theologian and scholar of religion, invokes the postmodern critique of individualism and dualism. For her, "certain scientistic, empiricist, and positivistic epistemologies" hold out hope for what she calls "new possibilities for a more holistic and organic understanding of human existence at both personal and social levels" (370). By this, of course, she means nothing more nor less than making room for spirituality. Also, in the pages of the *Journal of the American Academy of Religion*, we find an essay by Robert C. Fuller (the author of the 2001 book, *Spiritual, but not Religious: Understanding Unchurched America*) entitled, "Spirituality in the Flesh: The Role of Discrete Emotions in Religious Life" (75/1 [2007]). He also seeks to study spirituality, but in a manner that is found "in the flesh." Again, though, the term "spirituality" is left undefined, and thus undetermined. He nevertheless imagines it to be an important first step towards what he characterizes as a truly inter-disciplinary understanding of lived and material religion. "Although it is true that religion is a prime instance in which culture exerts considerable sovereignty over biology," he argues, a "truly interdisciplinary understandings of human spirituality must nonetheless include an appreciation of the bodily substrates of human spirituality" (27).

It is also worth calling attention to the fact that, after the Second World War and the growing disillusionment with mainstream religious expression, the domains known as spirituality and religion become increasingly disconnected from one another. Spirituality, now in complete contrast to its initial usage as defining that which comes under ecclesiastical control, comes to denote this vague sense of a subjective experience. We now see the rise of a "spirituality" industry, sometimes called New Age Spirituality and modeled, intentionally or not, on self-help literature. This industry combines psychology (often pop-psychology), mystical and esoteric traditions (such as Sufism and Kabbalah, Islamic and Jewish mysticism respectively), and what is represented as Eastern religions. They are all decontextualized and then blended in such a manner that, for some, offers a compelling response to what is perceived to be the growing forces of the secular, all the while simultaneously participating in the commodification associated with neo-liberal capitalism during this period. We see this, for example, in everything from websites such as "Spirituality and Health," subtitled "The Soul-Body

Connection," with self-help articles such as "Mindful Weight Gain in Pregnancy" and "Radical Intuition: 3 Ways to Be True to Yourself." We also witness it in the integration of a Zen sense of mindfulness into contemporary business culture. We think here of Jeremy Carrette and Richard King's *Selling Spirituality: The Silent Takeover of Religion* (2004) and James Dennis LoRusso's study, *Spirituality, Corporate Culture, and American Business: The Neoliberal Ethic and the Spirit of Global Capital* (2017). With its emphasis on personal authenticity, personal meditation, and mindfulness, the modern consumer is able to be "spiritual, without being religious"—what some critics might characterize as a low or even no cost form of religion suited to the modern, consumer age. In this category, we have the rise of modern-day gurus, like Deepak Chopra, and Eckhart Tolle, who encourage their disciples to reach their true selves by means of radical self-disclosure to themselves. We also see this, for example, in Shirly MacLaine, the actor-cum-spiritual coach, whose 2008 book *Sage-ing While Age-ing* recommends:

> Once we find the feelings, we can hang on to them, then we change. We become more balanced. That is truly channeling one's own perfectly balanced soul. Once that happens there is no need to fight or be angry about anything. Such negative feelings fall away, and possibly so does our negative DNA.

In the final analysis, spirituality—not unlike other key terms in the field, like experience and the sacred—should, ideally, be retired from our conceptual vocabulary. Such terms, while frequently used by some of the people whom we may study, provide scholars with little to no analyzable content. It instead defers meaning to something that is imagined to exist beyond the observable, the mundane, and, thus, the here-and-now. And this deferral strikes us as prone to ideological abuse. However, it is on account of this ambiguity that such terms ultimately remain part of our vocabulary. For their imprecision allows many to cordon off certain features of human production as somehow being "special" or immune from explanation or redescription. Since critical scholars are probably not able to retire such terms from the field at large, we encourage them to see such words for what they are. They are little more than rhetorical devices whereby social actors attempt to justify and/or legitimate certain very human claims by appeals to what others recognize, from habit, as something transcendent.

In this volume see: animism, East/West, mysticism, nones, soul

In *Religion in 50 Words* see: comparison, culture, essence, identity, lived religion, material religion, religion, sacred/profane

44 Symbol

That an English speaker cannot tell the difference when hearing the words "symbol" and "cymbal" begins to tell us something about the complexity of how the former term might be used by scholars. For without hearing them each used in context (i.e., "The drummer played the cymbal"), or seeing them in written script, they are identical. This is despite the fact that someone claiming that each word symbolizes—a key term here—something entirely different. If we add to this the once dominant approach to the study of religion that claimed it to be a private experience that was only later expressed, then one can imagine the prominent role played by this term "symbol" throughout the history of the field. For many years a standard course in Departments of Religious Studies was often titled something like "Myth, Ritual, Symbol," seemingly invoking the three domains in which these religious expressions were said "to take shape": in narrative, in behavior, and in systems of abstract representation. (This might be a succinct way of describing the supposed field of symbology, in which it is said Prof. Robert Langdon worked—the fictional protagonist of Dan Brown's once popular series of novels, which includes *The Da Vinci Code* [2003].) For example, a student might study the small colored dot that appears on the middle of the forehead of some people in India and now elsewhere, known as the *bindi*, and is surely bound to ask: "What does it mean?" This very question—a question of semantics or meaning—presupposes at least one approach to how those things called symbols are said to work. They are claimed to correspond to, and thereby directly represent a source, an association from which they gain their meaning. To return to our example of the *bindi*, if we follow Parvesh Handa's book, *Home Beauty Clinic* (1989), then we will conclude that it is "a symbol, not only of beauty but of your *Suhag* too—an indication of a married woman .... Likewise, *bindi* is [also] a symbol of good luck and purity," adding that "[t]oday even unmarried women use *bindi*" (60).

This approach to how symbols work—sometimes known as the correspondence theory of meaning or of truth—might strike a critical scholar as surprisingly traditional. It would seem to presume the existence of stable referents and equally stable relations between the supposed source and its variously coded expressions. Such a model presupposes a type of realism that the ambiguity of "symbol/cymbal" already begins to undermine, suggesting that the activity of making meaning is rather more complex and nuanced than we might at first think. For a scholar of religion who claims that religion comprises a unique experience that predates culture and defies language, then such an approach may prove rather appealing. Now the cross-cultural study of religious symbolism can, in a fashion very much at home in the earliest years of the field in the late nineteenth century, help us to discover similarities that might themselves allow scholars to infer something about their otherwise unseen source. A more critical approach, however, might be tempted to look elsewhere in the human sciences for help in devising an approach to understanding the workings of symbols and meaning making, perhaps now redescribed as the study of signs and signification.

Given how this entry began, perhaps we should observe that the English word "cymbal" dates to Old English, c. 825 CE, and refers to the name for an instrument, deriving from Greek and then Latin and later the Old French *cymble* or *cymbal*. The word "symbol" occurs in English only much later, at the end of the fifteenth century, deriving from the late Latin *symbolum* via French, originally linked to the Greek *súmbolon*. A "symbol," thus, refers to a tally, a permit, or a mark of some sort that indicates another thing, such as a permit signifying someone's legitimate status or a document as proof of identity. Perhaps, also worth noting is that an earlier, but now obsolete use, named a portion or contribution someone would make, perhaps to a shared meal. By the mid-seventeenth century we see such variations as the adjective "symbolic" and the noun "symbolism," with the verb "symbolize" coming slightly earlier. In fact, the no longer used "symbololatry," akin to "idolatry"—the latter a pejorative judgment against those said to worship mere representations—also develops in the early nineteenth century. Thus, we read: "The Pietists, and afterward the Rationalists, rebelled against symbololatry and lifeless orthodoxy" in the Swiss Protestant theologian, Philipp Schaff's (1819–1893), *The Creeds of Christendom: The History of Creeds* (1877, 336). This last term provides a helpful insight into how "symbol" makes an appearance in the study of religion. If one presupposes a domain of human experience that somehow corresponds immediately to a pure and original source, then any material item that is said to represent it—such as a text, an image, a sculpture—might be judged to be an insufficient or derivative copy, or even a counterfeit that is not to be confused with the authoritative original. If we recall the rhetorical techniques employed during the so-called Protestant Reformation—with what the reformers saw as unnecessary bureaucracy and thus the illegitimate authority of Roman Catholic church leadership—it should make sense that this use of the term "symbol" could be a handy one to draw upon, now akin to the word "idol." "Any higher view of the authority of symbols is unprotestant," Schaff adds in the just-cited title, "and essentially Romanizing. Symbololatry is a species of idolatry and substitutes the tyranny of a printed book for that of a living pope" (7). In 1694 we find the English minister Robert South (1634–1716) using financial accounting as an analogy: "Words are the Signs and Symbols of Things; and, as in Accompts, Ciphers and Figures pass for real Summs; so ... Words and Names pass for Things themselves" (*Twelve sermons preached upon several occasions*, vol. 2, 451). As long as we presume something called "things in themselves," i.e., essences, to exist, then their secondary representations can be handy reminders, but also poor substitutes and therefore always open to criticism by those advocating for yet other coded ciphers of the always absent original.

The study of symbols took on new significance with the rise of comparative religion, now no longer imagined as a poor or unauthorized copy. We can cite no better example than Mircea Eliade's (1907–1986) once famous book, *Patterns in Comparative Religion*, published originally in French in 1949 as *Traité d'historie des religions* and then translated in English by Rosemary Sheed in 1958. For a recent assessment of the (to some, controversial) work, see Laurie L. Patton's "Mircea Eliade, *Patterns in Comparative Religion* (1949; trans. 1958)" in *Public Culture* 32/2 (2020): 385–396. In a fashion not much different from works published a generation before his book first appeared, Eliade searches the world over for all of the moon symbolism that he can find, for example (see chapter 4), or, to cite but one more, all of the symbolism of the center, what he and others call the *axis mundi*, Latin for the axis of the world (chapter 10). As outlined in the book's foreword, that which he often referred to as "the sacred"—an ill-defined term, to be sure, but the source of religion nonetheless, or so he regularly claimed—cannot be known directly *but only through the many diverse ways that it is manifested throughout history*, whether in cultural acts or natural events. It is only from studying the various *forms* that the sacred takes, what he coined as hierophanies, that the careful scholar who has done their comparative homework, collecting as many examples as possible, can infer something about the sacred itself. Such a scholar works toward this "sacred" inductively by identifying its various patterns, as it were, hence the title of his book. Eliade's aim is "to examine as closely as possible the pattern to be found in cosmic hierophanies, to see what we can discover form the sacred as expressed in the sky, in water, in vegetation, and so on" (xx).

That Eliade should be preoccupied throughout much of his work with religious symbolism now makes sense, since these are presumed to be the only means for studying the inexpressible source for all religion: the sacred. We see this again in his 1952 essay collection, translated into English in 1961 as *Images and Symbols: Studies in Religious Symbolism*. The same approach is often still used with, for example, the standard world religions introductory course where diverse instances of religious life and practice are surveyed descriptively and comparatively. "We" have rituals and so do "they," and thus we can infer something about religion in general. We also see this in the long-standing distinction among some scholars in the field between using "religion" in the singular and in the plural, with detailed, historical studies of the latter (the religions) thought by some to establish the basis for claims about the former (religion, as a human universal). Thus, a once popular textbook such as Catherine L. Albanese's *America, Religions, and Religion* (1999) can accurately be judged to making a claim about religion in general from studying its various historical representations.

This more traditional approach to the study of symbols may be unsatisfying, however. This is in part the result of it reproducing both a commonsense model for how meaning works, and that it also repeats a participant's own claims for the uniqueness of specifically religious symbols. Consider the comments of the University of Chicago-trained Jeffrey B. Pool in his book, *God's Wounds: Hermeneutic of the Christian Symbol of Divine Suffering*, published in 2009 in the Princeton Theological Monograph Series. Were they unattributed, they might very well have been written by Eliade himself:

> although a symbol may be a religious symbol, a religious symbol may and usually does also possess political, social, economic, or even racial features. These other symbolic features may become objects of consideration when examining a religious symbol, but only insofar as their relations to the religious heart of the symbol may be traced to them.

He then goes so far as to claim that *all* symbols, regardless the type, have a religious dimension (see vol. 1, chpt. 1, "Delimitation of the Problem: Describing the Concept of Religious Symbolism"). A more critical approach may rely on a different intellectual tradition in honing the use of the term "symbol"—possibly even retiring it altogether, due to the baggage it yet carries in popular and scholarly discourse alike. One might instead opt for terms such as "sign," "signifier," "signified," and "signification." Although these, like any words, can be variously defined, it is the tradition linked to the twentieth-century academic field known as Semiotics that we have in mind. The latter term, from the Greek *semeiotikós*, refers to the interpretation of signs, even symptoms, where the potentially arbitrary relationship between signifier (e.g., the word "cymbal") and signified (a circular metal object) is studied. Now the goal is not so much to correctly interpret the meaning of some symbol, something also known as the practice of hermeneutics. Rather, the aim is to study the process by which meaning making takes place, and in terms of which a correct from an incorrect interpretation is distinguished by language users. Thus, the issue is not whether "symbol" or "cymbal" is correct in some given instance but, given the ambiguity, how do language users and linguistic systems police their symbol systems so as to avoid the ambiguity that, apparently, is woven into their very heart of all representational systems. If we generalize from spoken and written language to all other sites of meaning making then we might now just call it all signification, something taking place all throughout culture—from how one dresses or to how we behave and how our groups are organized. If so, then we can see the need to provide a more technical understanding of the topic than the folk model that each of us probably just presumes and therefore uses in daily life.

Now we may understand the thing we call culture as a site where social actors are constantly establishing and negotiating (and not just inferring) significance, i.e., what is worth paying attention to and thus worth doing, remembering, teaching, etc. If we presume that social groups are not uniform and homogenous but are instead internally ranked and therefore diverse, with contests and contradictions of their own, then negotiating significance takes on a much more complex look. How members, for example, "read" each other and the worlds they inhabit are linked to internal disputes and struggles for the right of certain subsets of the group to represent the group itself. In this way, a so-called symbol or sign can be understood as merely the tip of an always messy social process, as opposed to some item that naturally means either this or that. Thinking of the contemporary US, the so-called confederate flag associated with the Civil War (1861–1865) remains a useful example of the complexity of symbols, open to different readings with each prompted by rather different social interests and contexts. The flag, then, can either be a sign of "pride in one's heritage," as its advocates will often say; or, for yet others, a potent racist image representing a nostalgia for a world premised on the institution of slavery. How some generic item can come to signify anything, let alone such seemingly diametrically opposed meanings as evidenced in the case of this one flag, is what a more complex approach to symbolism aims to examine.

In this volume see: commentary, emic/etic, icon, idol, myth, reformation, ritual, theology, tradition, understanding

In *Religion in 50 Words* see: authority, classification, comparison, essentialism, experience, interpretation, origin, orthodoxy, phenomenology, politics, power, redescription, society

45 Syncretism

Depending on one's academic generation, the term "syncretism" may or may not be familiar. It is a word once used by scholars to name a social blending or the mixing of groups, what some might today instead refer to as hybridity, creolization (a term borrowed from Linguistics), or even the now prominent intersectionality. "The bringing together of two or more religious traditions or practices to create something quite new" (117), as phrased by the classics professor, Gary Reger in his essay "Ethnic Identity, Borderlands, and Hybridities in *A Companion to Ethnicity in the Ancient Mediterranean* (2014). It is included in the present list because of the way that its use represents important gains in the field while, ironically perhaps, also making plain how such advances can, whether intended or not, also entrench long-standing but problematic assumptions. Its use, including the reasons behind its use and what it was thought to accomplish, therefore strikes us as a cautionary tale for critical scholars of religion. As Rosalind Shaw and Charles Stewart rightly note when opening their introduction to the essay collection, *Syncretism/Anti-Syncretism: The Politics of Religious Synthesis* (1994): "'Syncretism' is a contentious term."

The word itself became more prominently used in English around the mid-seventeenth century, with significantly increased usage across the twentieth century. The term is related to the French *syncrétisme*, itself derived from the Latin *syncrētismus* and, prior to that, the ancient Greek *synkretismos*, signifying a strategic alliance or even a reconciliation. We see this, for example, in an often-cited passage from *Moralia*, written by the first-century Greek philosopher Plutarch:

> we must be careful especially at such times to associate familiarly with our brothers' friends but avoid and shun all intimacy with their enemies, imitating in this point, at least, the practice

of Cretans, who, though they often quarrelled with and warred against each other, made up their differences and united when outside enemies attacked.

The passage closes: "and this it was which they called 'syncretism'" ("On Brotherly Love," 19, line 490 B, citing William Clark Helmbold's 1962 translation).

Though it has obviously ancient origins, from the outset it is crucial to keep in mind that "[t]he term 'syncretism' is *our* category for questioning and selecting certain phenomena in the history of culture and of religions" (35). Thus wrote the historian of religions, Carsten Colpe (1929–2009) in his chapter "The Phenomenon of Syncretism and the Impact of Islam" in the edited collection, *Syncretistic Religious Communities in the Near East* (1997). Indeed, as Peter van der Veer observes: "like many terms used to describe aspects of religion, indeed like the term 'religion' itself, it has a peculiar Western history" (185). See his "Syncretism, Multiculturalism, and the Discourse of Tolerance," in *Syncretism/Anti-Syncretism: The Politics of Religious Synthesis* (1994). Thus, the range of related words—such as the noun "syncretion," the personal noun "syncretist," the more prominent adjective "syncretistic," and the verb "syncretize"—are all employed by those scholars concerned to identify and then study a set of processes. These include: (1) of social merging, whether of opposites that are logically combined, akin to a synthesis as part of what philosophers might term the dialectical process—as in the "Our Monthly Crypt" column in *The Monthly Magazine* (July–December 1839, vol. II): "the art of concentrating and reconciling all the scattered rays of truth, dispersed among all sects and parties" (223); or merely (2) of different cultures or systems that appear to be randomly comingled—as in William Fleming's (1791–1866) *Vocabulary of Philosophy* (1857): "*Syncretism* is the jumbling together of different systems or parts of systems, without due regard for them being consistent with one another" (503, quoting the 1860 edition). That the latter usage often comes with either an implicit or explicit judgment, based on the assumed priority of supposedly pure and authentic things (as opposed to those things that are "jumbled together" with no rhyme or reason), cannot be overlooked. In the words of the philosopher of religion, Tinu Ruparell, the discourse around syncretism "has aroused a great deal of suspicion and opprobrium since the sixteenth century and continues to be a highly charged label today"—especially so in the theological area in which he works: inter-religious dialogue (see chapter 8 in the *Wiley-Blackwell Companion to Interreligious Dialogue* [1995]).

In the study of religion the term has, since the mid- and later nineteenth century, been used with specific application to the influence and development of religion that have been impacted either by prior religions and wider cultural factors or those that are contemporary to the religion in question. Early on it was mainly used by scholars with reference to Greco-Roman religions, as noted by Eric Sharpe in his *50 Key Words: Comparative Religion* (1971). He defines it as those "in which deities and practices from various parts of the world were freely combined" (71). As the scholar of Hellenistic religions, Luther H. Martin has observed, the term can be traced at least to the German historian, Johann Gustav Droysen (1808–1884), such as his three volume work, *Geschichte des Hellenismus* (1836–1843; English transl. *The History of Hellenism*). In Martin's words, the term occurs in his "description of Hellenistic culture as 'the east and west mixture of people' occasioned by the conquests of Alexander the Great in the fourth century B.C. and by his policy of Hellenization which was continued by his successors" (277) See his "Of Religious Syncretism, Comparative Religion, and Spiritual Quests," *MTSR* 12 (2000). From there the word, coupled with an interest in the recombination of prior influences, is used more widely throughout the late nineteenth century. The early anthropologist, Andrew Lang (1844–1912), writing on the ancient Egyptian dynasty of Thebes: "the process of syncretism, by which various god-names and god-natures are mingled, so as to unite the creeds of different nomes and provinces, and blend all" (*Myth, Ritual and Religion* [1887], vol. II, 118, quoting the 1901 edition).

Thus, scholars had developed a way to explain why, for example, ancient Roman religion looked an awful lot like the previous ancient Greek religion, given their similar pantheons of gods—despite their new names, they played similar roles or features. Claiming that something was a syncretistic religion then, meant that "it is a religion which consists of a combination of elements taken over substantially unchanged from earlier faiths, and without any distinctive character or new contribution of its own" (as quoted from the US Lutheran-Missouri Synod periodical, *Theological Quarterly* 16/2 [April 1912], 115). This quotation, it is important to note, arises from an anonymous article rebutting the proposal that Christianity too should be considered as a syncretistic religion—a position that the anonymous author, writing in a periodical affiliated with a specific Protestant denomination, concludes to be "a libel of the grossest kind and an act of the basest ingratitude to God for His unspeakable gift" (116). After all, as the short essay goes on to ask, how can Christianity have benefitted from influence coming from *any* of its forerunners, let alone contemporaries, given "the vagaries of the perverted mind and imagination of fallen man?" Such was the 1912 reply to a prior article, by the Rev. Nicholaus Martin Steffens (1839–1912), a Reformed Church pastor and Professor of Theology, entitled, "Is Christianity a Syncretistic Religion?" that was published in *The Christian Intelligencer*—a weekly newspaper of the Protestant Reformed Dutch Church of America, from 1830–1920. Steffens had argued—at least according to the current author's quotations—that "the old teachers would never have consented that Christianity pure and simple has to be looked upon as a syncretistic religion." Why? Steffens goes on:

> They objected to a mixture of different tendencies in Christianity because they believed that they had found in their system the correct conception of Christianity; hence they feared an adulteration of the genuine article by an admixture of less valuable materials.

To which he adds: "The new theologians," of which he clearly counted himself a member, "however, have no scruples of this kind" (114).

This view of syncretism as "corrupting Christianity" is also seen in Abram Herbert Lewis's (1832–1908) book from the era, *Paganism Surviving in Christianity* (1892), 22 and 194. It betrays long-held assumptions within European (and largely Christian-based) scholarship about religion. More specifically, it also assumes that Christianity was so unique as to have descended from the heavens fully formed. To offer an argument that either it was somehow at least *influenced* or, the even more audacious claim, *caused* by, factors in its context or prior circumstance struck many at the time and even some today as utterly unthinkable. For the more historically inclined scholar, this shift in perspective was very appealing. In this context, we arrive at the late-nineteenth and early-twentieth-century's turn toward trying to understand such a thing as early Christianity within its own social and historical setting. This was then coupled with the effort of *not* taking participant disclosures about such things as how the group was established as determinative of scholarship. Instead, the challenge was to read such claims as later members' efforts to craft a narrative of origins that suited their own situated purposes and interests. The move toward understanding what was previously seen as pure and homogenous as, instead, being internally diverse and plural was, as some of the above citations make clear, seen by many as a form of irreverent criticism. The controversy that results might be similar to how an ardent royalist might hear claims that the so-called Queen's English is not just one among many forms of the language (and thus no better, nor worse), but that it is itself a so-called creole comprised of words and rules derived from a wide number of prior languages—though it certainly is a version that is authorized by the influence of the monarchy and its associates. This is a radical shift in how some approach the topic of identity, one that firmly contextualizes what was formerly seen to be ahistorical and uniform, having simply and wholly manifested itself at a certain place and time. And because, as Anita Leopold writes in her 2004 introduction to an anthology on the topic, "[m]ost syncretistic formations go unnoticed as they appear as the natural results of interaction," keeping the inevitable hybridity of social life uppermost in our minds is no small accomplishment (*Syncretism in Religion: A Reader*, 4). Thus, to be able to identify—again, using the history of Christianity as an example—the blending and adaptation of previous Jewish and Greco-Roman influences became, for earlier scholars, an effective measure against treating their object of study as *sui generis*. In its place, they humanized religion.

As the opening paragraph to this entry has already suggested, this gain might not be so dramatic as scholars first thought it was. Unlike how we phrased it above, syncretistic approaches did not so much explain borrowing and blending but, instead, simply described its presence in material that was once thought to be pure and original. Among the problems was the early failure to appreciate that, regardless the scale of one's analysis (i.e., whether studying a family or a nation-state), any group is always and already a result of sometimes evident and other times unexpected precursors. This seemingly more dynamic theory of social change presupposes a problematic series of assumptions, inasmuch—to return to the just used example—such apparently uniform prior things as "Judaism" and "Greco-Roman religion," let alone the "Greek" and "Latin" languages, supposedly exist as uniform and obvious things that, much like prior primary colors, can be mixed to produce a new shade. But as anyone who has gone to the paint store well knows, which blue? Which yellow? Let alone how much of each to then produce which of the many greens that our mixing can create? Moreover, if, as in our example, early Christianity was indeed a syncretistic product of prior elements, then those earlier elements too must be syncretistic products of yet prior influences, influences which themselves are blends of yet earlier factors. That is, as important as this shift may have been for scholars over one hundred years ago, and as much as today's work on social change may require this earlier shift first to have been made, modern theories of identity find little to be added by concluding that a certain situation or practice "is syncretistic." Why? Because the critical scholar likely now sees the word as synonymous with the word "culture" itself. That is, all social moments can now be seen to be complex blends of yet earlier situations, combined in purposeful or quite possibly unanticipated ways. This makes it all a blend—and thus anything *not* seen as a blend is concluded to be, as evidenced with "the Queen's English," something that has been sufficiently authorized as to be seen as self-evident and thus *as if* it is pure. Thus, the Judaism and the Greco-Roman religion, let alone the Greek and Latin, to which we just referred are themselves generalizations created, for our purposes, from numerous varieties of each. This of course, leads to the question: Where did Jewish or Greco-Roman identity begin and the other end in the first century CE Mediterranean region? This becomes an especially difficult question to answer if we try to avoid anachronistically projecting a modern sense of identity backwards in time, as if, for example, all Jewish people currently understand, and have always understood, themselves in a particular manner. Or, simply taking the compound nature of the designator "Greco-Roman" seriously, it should be more than obvious that this is an abstract, ideal type that is generated by the observer more than describing actual people who were once "on the ground." The differences between classes or genders within any ancient Greek setting, let alone differences (and outright conflicts) between the autonomous city-states and regions that comprised part of the history of what we today know as Greece, should make evident the difficulty of so simply assuming some sort of uniform thing called "Greco-Roman identity."

As van der Veer, quoted earlier, goes on to write, the term "syncretism" is therefore hardly a neutral or merely descriptive designator, for it "refers to a politics of difference and identity and that as such the notion of power is crucial in its understanding." "At stake," he continues, "is the power to identify true religion and to authorize some practices as 'truthful' and others as 'false'" (185). He thus concludes that "syncretism" is a term that functions much as does "multiculturalism" in some social settings today: as implicitly having already eliminated groups which have not been deemed legitimate, authentic, or, as in his modern analogy, tolerable. To put it another way, discourses on syncretism participate in contests of what Edward Shiappa, a professor of communications, has termed representational correctness (see his 2008 *Beyond Representational Correctness: Rethinking Criticism in Popular Culture*). To conclude, for example, that C is a syncretistic product of the prior elements A and B—as we see with Ron Geaves quick example: "Sikhism came into existence as a syncretic mixing of elements of Hinduism and Islam" (*Keywords in Religious Studies*

[2006], 101)—the person making such a claim must have already sifted through the many possible variants of both A and B. This would, in turn, imply that, for whatever undisclosed reasons, such a person would have settled on establishing their own normative limits to A as well as to B, something necessary just to be able to even talk about such things. Relatedly, there are certainly those scholars today who would argue that, for example, modern Hindu nationalist movements, let alone those Muslims who employ organized violence to achieve political ends, are both aberrations of these two world religions, thereby denying them entry to what is said to properly constitute each. And, with such a scholarly act, the scholar interested in understanding the precursors to something known as Sikhism has just created their own versions of both Hinduism and Islam. We thus arrive at the possibly ironic, and perhaps unintended, but very real linkage of an approach seemingly interested in change and variation over time to issues of power and supposedly uniform identity. Or, to appeal again to the classicist Gary Reger, when he cites the example an ancient "traditional local religious festival transmogrified by the incorporation of 'outside' elements" (118). What he describes as syncretism in the classical sense, we clearly see how the term functions: as a way for those working to establish and police a social boundary—and to thereby separate the familiar inside, *as they wish it to be*, from the alien outside—to name and address what strikes them as anomalies and importations.

Frequently in the study of religion we read statements such as Mircea Eliade's (1908–1986) that "The complex figure of the *fravashis* [the Zoroastrian name for a person's essence, also naming benevolent spirits] appears to be the result of a long process of religious syncretism" (332 n. 67). See his 1978 *A History of Religious Ideas*, vol 1. Or, again and more recently in 1993, Diana Eck: "what goes by the name of New Age religion today is an informal religious syncretism" (*Encountering God: A Spiritual Journey from Bozeman to Banaras*, 196). We should recognize that nothing much has been said other than that these things exist, inasmuch as existence is now presumed always to entail mixing and blending. Such mixing and blending, in turn, is often opposed, policed, and managed, in the hopes of crafting the impression of a so-called unpolluted and thus seemingly pure, ideal, and authorized instance of something. Studying where such efforts are expended, whether successfully or not, will tell us much about how those engaging in such policing conceive of themselves, their identity, their place, and those against whom they are defining themselves. For the process of blending that once went by the name of syncretism—often assumed to be an intentional activity and thereby leaving unaddressed the implicit and unplanned intermixing that more than likely happens all of the time—is now seen as an inevitable aspect of daily life. For this reason, syncretism, no less than the various other terms that are currently favored by scholars when studying this process (e.g., hybridity, etc.), is best seen as a participant rhetoric that is used in local and always strategic acts of identification and distinction. Hence, its close association with such troublesome terms as authenticity, originality, purity, let alone with impurity, contamination, diluting, and the like. However, should the scholar have an interest in this process then "syncretism" must always be seen, as Colpe wrote above, as *our* term, used for *our* analytic purposes, by which *we* isolate from the innumerable interrelated moments of its larger setting a specific belief, practice, or institution that attracts *our* attention. All this is done, moreover, for the purpose of an examination that is carried out by *our* admitting into consideration these *and just these* prior factors *as if* they constitute this thing that we so easily call the (prior or current) "context" from which something is said to result. This makes "context" yet another seemingly neutral descriptive term that effectively hides the speaker's choice, editing, and framing. All of these acts are required to convert, for a time, the unbounded situation that is any daily life into a seemingly manageable setting, or context that scholars can conceptualize and discuss.

In this volume see: emic/etic, founder, sect, spirituality

In *Religion in 50 Words* see: authority, classification, comparison, critical, culture, essence, identity, interpretation, pluralism

46 Theology

There has surely been no more central and ongoing debate throughout the history of the study of religion than its relationship to theology. Given the fact that the academic study of religion is now about a hundred and forty years old at most, the already well-established tradition of studying religion *from within* the religions themselves could not but impact this newer field. For some, this impact has been beneficial and constructive, but for others it has been detrimental. Drawing the line between the two fields, while in theory an easy undertaking, has proven to be rather difficult. Advocating for interfaith dialogue and so-called mutual understanding of faiths, for example, is no less a theological pursuit than is missioning. The former is often considered to be an academic enterprise, but we would argue that is little more than a theologically liberal enterprise. The admittedly old debate of "religious studies vs. theology" strikes some today as settled, and they charge those who continue to pursue it as *passé*. Surely, however, there is a crucial difference between those who focus on *people* and their actions, and those whose object of study remains the contents of religion. Appealing to a favored terminology of the scholar of Christian Origins, Willi Braun, the critical study of religion can be said to differ from other scholarly pursuits inasmuch as it is strictly anthropocentric, something that tends to be much different from those who engage in theology, regardless of how it is defined. The one focuses on historical and cultural production by firmly situating "religion," always seeing it as an all too human affair, the other, in contrast, alienates historically- and culturally-situated products from these very forces and factors, something accomplished by studying them *as if* they are stand-alone, self-generated items of obvious interest or value.

Combining two ancient Greek terms, *theos* and *logos*, the noun "theology" originally referred to "speaking and writing about the Olympic and pre-Olympic gods, as done by [the ancient Greek authors] Homer

DOI: 10.4324/9781003196631-47

and Hesiod" (see the 1995 *The HarperCollins Dictionary of Religion*, 1067). Or, in a much earlier characterization, the English independent minister, Rev. Charles Buck (1771–1815), could write in his *A Theological Dictionary* (1826), such stories referred to "the heterogenous fables, of those poets and philosophers, who wrote of the genealogy and exploits of the gods of Greece" (582). The word first appears in English, deriving from Latin *theologia* via the French *théologie*, in the fourteenth century, where it is used specifically in Christian contexts. According to its linguistic roots it literally means the rational or systematic study of God's existence and nature. Though, as *The HarperCollins Dictionary of Religion* goes on to specify, the term is expanded during Europe's medieval era to include commentary on all things believed to be a result of God's works. It's adjective, "theological," dates to the sixteenth century while the nouns, "theologian" or "theologue" (as in one who engages in theology), date a little earlier. Being a theologian was traditionally a professional position, working for either a church or training the clergy. The theologian's duty was, according to the once noted Professor of Sacred Rhetoric at the Andover Theological Seminary in Massachusetts, Rev. Edwards Amasa Park (1808–1900),

> to pay a rational regard to the opinions which have been entertained by Christians in past times ..., to address himself [sic] with fresh ardor to the writings of the fathers, and to derive from them a strengthened assurance in their and our fundamental faith.

See his "Duties of a Theologian," an address to the Theological Society of Dartmouth College on July 24, 1839, 3–4.

The word "theology" signified an academic exercise carried out and debated by elite members of the group with various traditional branches. The latter included: historical theology, "occupied with the development of the kingdom of God as an object of science," according to Heinrich Andreas Christoph Hävernick's (1811–1845) posthumous 1852 work, *A General Historico-Critical Introduction to the Old Testament* (1); dogmatic theology, which produces "the standard of dogma," as phrased by Rev. Robert Owen (1820–1902) in his 1858 *An Introduction to the Study of Dogmatic Theology* (vi); the closely related systematic theology, which "present[s] ... the doctrines which the Scriptures yield to the advancing insight of the Church," as defined by Elias Henry Johnson (1841–1906) in his 1891 *Outline of Systematic Theology* (36); moral theology or Christian ethics, which is "confined to the duties of man [sic] to God, to his neighbour, and to himself" as put in the appendix to the *Eighth Report of the Commissioners of Irish*

Education Inquiry (June 2, 1827, 152); and the related practical theology, which "occupies itself with the whole circle of studies directly preparatory to the exercise of the office of a Christian teacher," including the study of pastoral care and church law, as noted in the appendix of Francis Lieber's *Encyclopædia Americana* vol XII (1832, 595). As defined in its entry in the Roman Catholic *The Concise Dictionary of Theology* (3rd ed.), theology is understood as "the science of God," and thus "the methodical effort to understand and interpret the truth of revelation ... us[ing] the resources of reason, drawing in particular on the disciplines of history and philosophy" (citing the 2013 edition). We likely should recognize, however, that a Greek Orthodox or a Protestant resource could reasonably rephrase it. We might also note a specifically Jewish theology (a term of increasing use in English from the mid-eighteenth century on) or an Islamic theology (a term not used in English much at all until the early and mid-twentieth century, replacing the much earlier "Mahometan theology," to say nothing of what was once called "Hindoo theology." On the latter, see vol. 1, part 1 of Thomas Maurice's (1754–1824) book, *The History of Hindustan: Sanscreet and Classical, From the Birth of Brahma* (1793, 293). We also encounter the term Buddhist theology, such as in the appendix to Julia Corner's (1798–1875) *India: Pictorial, Descriptive, and Historical*, where she comments on Buddhism's "remarkable cosmogony, which is but part of their theology" (1854, 472). This book nicely represents work from that time by, for instance, wildly mischaracterizing the lives of distant others by claiming that "nearly every trace of Buddhism, as an actual faith or worship, has long since disappeared" (465).

Such a *variability* in theology, based on which dogma and assumptions are made to determine the parameters of the study or be in need of defense, becomes the issue once a skeptical and non-confessional study of religion develops in the later nineteenth century. Despite the latter, older work being subtitled "an impartial account," the distance between Jonathan Z. Smith's *The HarperCollins Dictionary of Religion* (1995), on the one hand, and Rev. Charles Buck's *A Theological Dictionary* (1826), on the other, is not merely chronological. Recall the latter's above-quoted characterization of ancient Greece's "heterogenous fables," which differs markedly from its assessment of the Christian message, as evident in its entry for Truth: "For this truth [i.e., the so-called Gospel truth of Christ] we ought to be sincere in seeking, zealous in defending, and active in propagating; highly to prize it, constantly to rejoice in it, and uniformly to be obedient to it" (590). Buck is not to be criticized for writing as such, for his adoption of such a polemical attitude toward others is understandable given his aim to authorize one to the exclusion of all others. Consider how his entry for "Catholic" explicitly challenges the "Romish" habit of claiming a preeminent status—"in the strict sense of the word," he concludes, "there is no catholic church in being; that is, no *universal* Christian communion" (81). When compared to Smith's resource the difference is dramatic and difficult to overlook. The latter's entry on "Catholicism, Roman" (189–190) neither offers an assessment nor attempts to undermine Catholic claims and, instead, provides a description. It reads, in part, "[t]his term *catholicism* designates a general ideal of the entire Christian religion expressing its desire for wholeness …. For Roman Catholicism, such wholeness centers in the historic community of Rome." This strikes us as the key difference between a theological pursuit and one carried out from within the academic study of religion. Whereas the former is normative with regard to the ultimate or necessary value of the items being discussed, the latter engages in description, comparison, interpretation, and explanation of the same items. It does this, moreover, by conceiving of them, for the purposes of such study, as situated and thus contingent human productions. Nothing more and nothing less.

Traditionally, this difference was signaled by the scholar of religion's conscious adoption of what was called a methodologically agnostic stance. This was aimed to suspend normative judgments by bracketing out so-called truth questions (e.g., Does the law of karma really govern the universe and determine one's rebirth status?) But the manner in which such scholars can often be demonstrated to still play "accidental favorites"—as phrased by Steven Ramey in his 2015 Afterword to *Claiming Identity in the Study of Religion*—by, for instance, merely paraphrasing some participant claims *as if* they are established descriptive fact. This can undermine this longstanding way of distinguishing these two scholarly practices, especially when one takes into account more recent redefinitions of theology. For the understanding so far established would likely be contested by a number of scholars who today identify both as theologians *and* as scholars of religion. They would certainly see no contradiction between these two. We witness this, for example, in those contributing to Clayton Crockett's essay collection entitled *Secular Theology: American Radical Theological Thought* (2001). While admitting in the opening of the Introduction that the book's main title "produces a superficial confusion," Crockett argues that the presumed opposite domain to the theological, i.e., the secular, is in fact originally a theological notion. This, for him, makes the longtime and rather harsh distinction between the secular study of religion and a theological approach, misleading if not inaccurate. We all inhabit, to use his words, the same "shared world of human experience"—one presumed to involve both "human and divine meaning and value" (1).

Contributors to his volume advocate for what some might call a theology of immanence or even a form of post-secularity. The latter position claims not only that religion pre-dates the constraining and privatizing rise of secularism, but that recent efforts to historicize secularism open the way to a theological renaissance. As a result, the contributors maintain such things as:

> [t]he secular is what outgrows religion: it looms on the incomprehensible horizon of memory as what's left when religion is loosened from the fossilizing effects of memory and fades into hope .... The secular is not merely secular. Nothing is secular that is not at the same time symmetrical with something religious.
> (11)

This is from the opening chapter, "Theology and the Secular" by the French Protestant theologian, Gabriel Vahanian (1927–2012). We admit that some may not know how to read such claims. While many critical scholars would likely agree that the sacred/secular binary is itself an historical product and, furthermore, that its seemingly opposed poles mutually inform one another. They might, however, hesitate to universalize just one of these two poles by presuming that religion or religious affectations somehow preceded the establishment of the binary. Instead, thinking about how binaries work, one might likely reply that whatever it was that preceded the modern sacred/secular, or religion/politics, binaries, it certainly was not religious—at least as we moderns conceive of the term. Some might conclude that such recent critiques of the traditional religious studies/theology distinction are based on a sort of magical thinking whereby such critics project but one component of modernity backward in time, by dehistoricizing and thereby universalizing it. This is much like someone trying to argue that, prior to the invention of cooking people just knew their food to be raw, i.e., as if the concept raw was somehow untethered from the meaning that it gains in specific relation to the idea of something being "not raw," i.e., cooked. Should we moderns wish to back project such ideas, anachronistically, that is certainly our prerogative. However, the failure to see ourselves as the ones doing this, by assuming these designators name some sort of pre-discursive reality (i.e., saying that the secular is a religious notion) would certainly strike the critical scholar as rather poor historical work.

We need to acknowledge that we live in social worlds alien to a period prior to the invention of the sacred/secular distinction. In the latter, people more than likely made reference to powerful beings believed to govern the universe and probably engaged in all sorts of regulated, communal practices or ceremonies that were seen to have relevance for such beliefs. This does not take away from the critical conclusion that such claims or activities, if treated by the scholar in a rigorously historical manner, should *not* immediately or just naturally be designated *as* religious. However, the moment that such a designation is presumed to be in a one-to-one fit with a reality on the ground, either now or in the past, is the moment when one has side-stepped the requirements of an anthropocentric approach. One then proceeds to do something other than critical scholarship—whatever one wishes to call it. Theology is certainly among the options.

The traditional sense of theology as a uniquely religious discourse is probably not sufficient to name the many different approaches that study "religion" in an extra-anthropocentric manner. This is why a distinction once proposed by the longtime and vocal participant in the religious studies/theology debate, the Canadian scholar Donald Wiebe, may still have some use for the critical scholar. We refer, in particular, to his 1984 essay, "The Failure of Nerve in the Academic Study of Religion," *Studies in Religion/Sciences Religieuses* 13/4: 401–422. He differentiates between Confessional theology and confessional theology (the upper- and lower-case are intended). The former identifies discourses carried out from within traditional denominations or so-called religious traditions. The latter, in contrast, include those approaches not usually seen as theological—given its usually narrow definition—but those that broader humanistic approaches that nonetheless presuppose, for example, the actual existence of such extra-historical things as the sacred. In the latter we might include studies that presume that the idea of the religious somehow predates and establishes the secular to those claiming that a universal essence inhabits all things named as religious. We might also include as "confessional theologians" all those scholars who maintain that the designators they employ—such as the categories myth, ritual, magic, tradition, scripture—float free of their own interests. This would include those who think that a careful reading of a text can help the scholar to time travel to the minds and intentions of distant and long past authors. The distinction remains but the lapses that it helps us to identify (and hopefully avoid) are now seen by some to be far wider and more pervasive than what classical theology ever attempted to name.

In this volume see: church, commentary, emic/etic, god, tradition

In *Religion in 50 Words* see: authority, belief, classification, explanation, ideology, interpretation, law, methodological agnosticism, orthodoxy, redescription, religious literacy, worldview

47 Totem

"Totem" is a term different from many of the others discussed in this volume. This is owing to the fact that its derivation, as will be discussed shortly, is neither Christian nor European; instead, it derives from the language of the Ojibwe First Nation (a subgroup of the larger Anishaabe people) of North America. However, despite this change in point of origin, the term is no less problematic since, in many ways, it still functions—not unlike "mana," the onetime popular scholarly term but of Polynesian origins—as the plaything for earlier European theorists of religion to name and imagine a host of supposedly universal issues that they deemed relevant to the study of religion. They often did this, of course, in ways that were contradictory or just plain romantic and misinformed. Like all of the other terms then, "totem"—and the religious form most associated with it, "totemism"—is a local term (only this time local to the Ojibwe First Nation), whose meaning has been expanded upon, by European theorists as opposed to Ojibwe ones, to function as a universal category of analysis employable to account for what were believed to be a host of cross-cultural forms.

Reading from their armchairs in Europe, a host of early theorists—from James George Frazer (1854–1941), Emile Durkheim (1858–1917), and Sigmund Freud (1856–1939), among others—were enthralled by the term. In particular, for what they thought it stood for and what it therefore contributed to their theories of religion. It was invoked as a catch-all phrase and often in tandem with an often overlapping term that was also becoming popular in circles associated with the study of religion around the exact same time: animism. Totemism and animism thus became linked in the minds of many as synonymous with the pre-historic origins of religion, with the former term often regarded as the belief in a spiritual being, a sacred object, or some symbol that serves as an emblem of a social group (e.g., variously known as a family, a clan, or a tribe). As we have seen time and again, these theorists

DOI: 10.4324/9781003196631-48

were taking an example of a specific religious form contemporary to them, one that they considered to be the most "primitive" and then subsequently extrapolating it into the distant past as a way to explain what their idea of the earliest humans would have believed/practiced. They used the formula: modern primitive = the species at its origins, sometimes referred to in earlier scholarship as "the childhood of the species." The totem, which obviously functions as the central component of an approach then known as totemism, is often an animal or other natural figure that is said to spiritually represent a group of related people, such as a clan.

The term "totem," as already mentioned, derives from the Ojibwa *nindoodem*, meaning "my totem" or "my clan." This, in turn, is believed to come from an Algonquian root that has the sense of "to dwell together," as can also be seen, for example, in the Ojibwa term for village (*oodena*). The term initially appears in English associated with early anthropological literature of the nineteenth century. A rather earlier attestation comes from 1791 in John Long's (d. ca. 1791) *Voyages and Travels of an Indian Interpreter and Trader*:

> One part of the religious superstition of the Savages, consists in each of them having his *totam*, or favourite spirit, which he believes watches over him. This *totam* they conceive assumes the shape of some beast or other, and therefore they never kill, hunt, or eat the animal whose form they think this totam bears.
>
> (86)

Though Long described these First Nations as "savages," as did many European writers at time, many subsequent descriptions, as problematic as they continue to be, tend not to be quite so overtly racist. For example, consider the following in *The Song of Hiawatha* (1855), by the American poet and educator Henry Wadsworth Longfellow (1807–1882): "From what old, ancestral Totem, Be it Eagle, Bear, or Beaver, They descended, this we know not" (xiv. 189). Such attestations imply that the "totem" is an emblem, often an animal or other natural object, believed to represent a clan or other social unit. Perhaps most famously such totems were found on large, monumental carvings common among First Nations on the coasts of the American Northwest and Southwest British Columbia in Canada. Many of these so-called "totem poles" were dismantled, shipped across the Atlantic, and subsequently reassembled in the museums of Europe (such as the impressive collection of totem poles and other Indigenous artifacts today at the University of Oxford's Pitt Rivers Museum). In these museums, aided by the then latest anthropological reports, many of the early theorists spun their imaginations to account for the origins, function, and future of religion in modern society.

It was only a matter of time that the term, originally localized to this one geographic region (and then North America writ large), was extended to include all other "tribal" groups *believed* by scholars to be in possession of similar practices or beliefs. Now South Americans, Australian and New Zealand Aboriginals, Polynesians, Africans, and so on were all imagined—at least by those Europeans doing the categorizing in metropoles such as Paris, London, Oxford, and Berlin, often those who had never set foot in the places of which considered themselves to be the experts—to be "totemists." Or, depending upon the theorist, such groups were said either to have evolved from it or into it, thereby functioning as yet another problematic example of applying the then recent theory of biological evolution to understand social change among human communities. The rationale seems to be as simple as it is now understood as insulting: groups around the world are arranged according to tribes that then seem to have some sort of symbol or set of symbols that represent the group; therefore, they must all somehow be "totemists," believing the same things and engaging in the same set of practices. Thus in 1879, the banker, politician, and scientific writer John Lubbock, (1834–1913), in his *Origin of Civilisation*, could now see totemism in other places: "in Australia we seem to find the totem, or, as it is there called, kobong, almost in the very moment of deification" (2nd ed., 184). Perhaps this is made even more explicit in the 1849 statement of James Cowles Prichard (1786–1848) in J.F.W. Herschel's *Manual of Scientific Enquiry: Prepared for the Use of Her Majesty's Navy; and Adapted for Travellers in General* (1849): "The institution of the *Totem*, as it was termed among the North American nations, has its counterpart among the nations of Australia" (435). It is perhaps worth noting, to get a sense of the time period of the work, that in the same volume Charles Darwin (1809–1882) wrote the chapter devoted to "Geology." The essays in the volume also nicely show the triangulation between colonialism, tourism, and the need for our predecessors to understand "others" who were then seen as unfamiliar and even exotic.

So, what sort of intellectual work were such words as "totems," "totemism," "totemic," "totemite," and "totemists" expected to perform? Well, without putting too fine a point on it, these categories could be used for almost any purpose—anthropological, religious, social, artistic/aesthetic, all of which, of course, were ultimately as ideological as they were political. In 1905, for example, the Scottish anthropologist

Andrew Lang (1844–1912) argued in his *The Secret of the Totem* that "[i]n marrying a woman of his totem, but not of his set of classes, a man does not break the law of Arunta exogamy" (69). While he was interested in the social aspects of totemism in terms of endogamy/exogamy here, he could also posit in some of his other works that the same group of Australian aboriginals also worshipped a single, powerful and creative high God, something that he concluded must be the original form of religion. He posited this idea of a high God in opposition to his contemporaries who had posited animism—such as the aforementioned E.B. Tylor (1832–1917)—ancestor worship, or other such forms. Their evidence? *None whatsoever*, except for the odd anthropological report, a comfortable armchair, and much imaginative thought experimentation. That scholars just a generation or so later found all of this idiosyncratic, speculative work highly problematic should, of course, be noted.

Totemism, as part of a theory of religion, perhaps took on new life a few decades later with the publication of Durkheim's *The Elementary Forms of the Religious Life* (1912). He boldly declared that it was the simplest and thus earliest form of religion and, as such, was worth an intimate study. His interest was not simply historical, however, but to discern principles he thought generalizable to modern, industrialized, and highly diverse societies. "But primitive religions do not merely aid us in disengaging the constituent elements of religion," he wrote, "they also have the great advantage that they facilitate the explanation of it" (19, in Swain's 1915 translation with the Free Press). For if we understand totemism, the most simple and primitive religion known to humankind (at least according to Durkheim's formulation), then we are permitted to witness "on the ground" as it were, the origins and function of religion. The latter is perhaps most famously encapsulated in his statement that the symbol of the totem is society personified: "If it is once the symbol of the god and of the society, is that not because the god and the society are one" (236). But, of course, totemism is simply the concept onto which Durkheim projects his theories. While it is impossible to ascertain that this is the most primitive form of religion—though a critical scholar would hardly even use such language today—it cannot be denied that Durkheim's very important functionalist and still relevant analysis did not, paradoxically, need any presumption about totemism being the oldest and most primitive religious form.

And this is something that virtually all early theorists of religion have done. For instance, others connected "totemism" to biology, with it being understood as an attempt to satisfy basic human needs—as seen, for example in Bronislaw Malinowski's (1884–1942) theory. Or that totems were ways to control the otherwise uncontrollability of the natural world, as for example in the theory of A.R. Radcliffe-Brown (1881–1955). Though, of course, the issue for us today is not which one of these theorists got the totem "right." On the contrary, it is to see how a term—not unlike "shaman"—was a local word of relevance to a specific group for a particular purpose. Then, in the hands of European comparativists, it took on a life far beyond anything that, in this case, the Ojibwa First Nation could have imagined. The issue, then, is not what is totemism—it can, as seen here, mean almost anything to anyone, dependent upon the work to which they put the category. More interestingly, we might ask ourselves: How has totemism, variously defined, been used and abused to name any set of activities *believed* to be religious and simple, as practiced by groups *designated* as tribal and *imagined* as such by earlier scholars.

Indeed, the subsequent use of the term bears this out. With fairly broad usage spread out over the course of the mid-twentieth century, the term is now rarely used, at least as a so-called technical term in the contemporary study of religion. Like shamanism, however, it has certainly been picked up by the new age spirituality movement, where we witness titles like *DIY Totemism* (2008), or *New Paths to Animal Totems: Three Alternative Approaches to Creating Your own Totemism* (2012). Interestingly, there is often a correlation, between when a term goes out of favor in the study of religion and when it is picked up by New Age Spirituality (a point made by Steven Wasserstrom in his book, *Religion after Religion: Gershom Scholem, Mircea Eliade, and Henry Corbin at Eranos* [2000, 238]). Regardless, however, the term "totem" offers a cautionary tale for the critical scholar in how terms become dislodged from specific contexts. Then, without careful retooling and redescription, they come to be used to try to create a universal category, into which scholars can then lump other beliefs, actions, groups, etc. that they deem relevant. While we may owe a debt to those who founded the comparative study of religion, and who went about their work in this manner, but surely this is *not* the way to go about creating a critical study of religion today.

In this volume see: animism, cult, East/West, emic/etic, icon, idol, immanence/transcendence, magic, myth, paganism, ritual, sacrifice, shamanism, soul, spirituality, tradition

In *Religion in 50 Words* see: classification, comparison, culture, definition, description, function, history, indigeneity, phenomenology, primitive, redescription, religion, sacred/profane, society, world religions

48 Tradition

To the question "Why do you do it that way?," it is not unlikely that the answer might simply be "Well, because it's a tradition." Such a reply is, in fact, a bit of a dodge, for the person has actually responded by saying "I do it that way because I have done it that way in the past." What is missing is an account for *why*, of all the various ways that, say, a cuisine could be prepared, or a holiday marked, one has *continued* to do it in this and only this way. Despite doing something one way in the past, there are of course all sorts of reasons why it could be done differently in the future, whether to address what might be perceived as a past shortcoming or because the activity is somewhat arbitrary in how it is accomplished each time. In yet other cases, human beings seem rather more regimented in their practices, doing something in a routine manner again and again, sometimes so much so that the method will be closely monitored by authorities for the least deviation, whether something done daily or annually. We think here of some brahman ritual specialist in India, who are reported to monitor the rituals performed by other brahmans, engaging in rituals of their own to address the mistakes of others. In this regard, see Brian K. Smith's 1996 essay, "Ritual Perfection and Ritual Sabotage in the Veda," *History of Religions* 35/4: 285–306. It is certainly at times such as this, as per the opening of this entry, that practitioners attribute the systematicity of their actions to this thing that they call "tradition"—or sometimes "the weight of tradition," or "the force of tradition," as if what is perceived as accumulated past practice had a momentum all its own. Should outside observers arrive to witness these practices, year-in, year-out, there is a relatively good chance that they may notice a curious discrepancy between a claim of regularity and how things are actually done, thereby noticing plenty of unaccounted for variation in the supposedly regimented behavior. This suggests that a scholar would be well served to hear claims about tradition rather critically, for while they do not account for *why* this rather than that repetition takes place, such claims might sometimes be reserved more for the realm of rhetoric than actual practice, thereby lending the impression of routine and uniformity where variation might actually be the case. But why? That is the critical scholar's question to answer.

The noun "tradition" is first seen in Middle English sometime around the late fourteenth century. The adjective "traditional" appears in the mid-sixteenth, the noun "traditionalist" one hundred years later, and the noun "traditionalism" and the verb "traditionalize" as recently as the mid-nineteenth century. Our term is a variation on the Middle French *tradicion*, or the action of handing something over to another, and derives ultimately from the Latin *trāditiō*, used for delivering or even surrendering something to another, thus coming to have the more abstract application meaning of conveying knowledge. Early on it has a specifically Christian application—yet another term in our scholarly lexicon with such a history—concerning passing on theological knowledge, doctrine, and belief. Thus, the late fourteenth century Wycliffe Bible translates the Greek *parádosin tōn presbutéron* as "the tradiciouns, or statutis, of elder men" (Matthew 15:2; "the tradition of the elders" in the current New International Version's translation). In fact, the role and authority of Church tradition, and thus the role played by its hierarchy and institutions, was among the key points of dispute in the so-called Protestant Reformation of the sixteenth century, in which tradition was seen as stifling and oppressive. Such a critique, however, must be engaged in carefully, of course, since both sides in any dispute will surely want to marshal the authority of the past in support of its current interests and practices, making claims about tradition something on which almost all parties draw. The point here is that the past, the archive to which traditions are traced, is rather more complicated than it at first appears. It does not simply lead in a direct and unambiguous line into the present and, because of this, the past houses all sort of practices that can be elevated to the status of authoritative precedent, all depending on the present social actor's needs.

Offering an explanatory theory as to *why* this set of actions is seen to constitute a standard worth either repeating, as opposed to others, has not often attracted the attention of scholars of religion. There is a long-standing tendency in the field to take some participant claims at face value, thereby legitimizing the self-understanding of the specific people being studied by merely offering a description of their own account of their practices and their past. It may go without saying that this was quite a problem when later scholars found that their predecessors often only queried elite males in the groups under study, leaving large segments of these communities silent at best or, at worst, wholly absent in the scholarly record. While scholars of groups seen to be controversial or dangerous would surely never be content with merely chronicling their member's self-perceptions, the study of religion is filled with scholarly works that offer little more than paraphrases of what participants already report. This is surely due to the uncritically high regard given by many scholars of religion to the particular actions, institutions, and beliefs they may study. After all, if the claims and actions were seen as controversial to the scholars and their readers, then the claims and actions would likely have been designated as something other than religion—for example, "idolatry" in an earlier era or "cults" and "extremism" today.

It is for this reason that a book such as *The Invention of Tradition* (1983), edited by the noted British historian of nationalism, Eric Hobsbawm (1917–2012) and the English historian of Africa, Terence Ranger (1929–2015), caught the attention of an earlier generation of critical scholars of religion. In its various essays, readers were provided with a way to *explain* the continued existence of practices designated *as* traditions rather than just describing them or even celebrating them. Such explanatory accounts tend to undermine the authorizing role of the rhetoric of tradition, inasmuch as it is historicized. In this respect, see Hugh Trevor-Roper's (1914–2003) often cited opening chapter in the volume, "The Invention of Tradition: The Highland Tradition of Scotland," which argues that "the whole concept of a distinct Highland culture and tradition is a retrospective invention" (15). When such "traditions" are placed into the contingency of history, they suddenly lose their luster of necessity, inevitability, and essential meaning. This suggests another reason why those scholars of religion who demonstrate sympathies for the people and practices under study may wish to avoid such historical and explanatory analysis, in favor of mere description and chronicling. Returning to Trevor-Roper's work, it is difficult to continue to treat the kilt as a symbol of deep and abiding Scottishness when we learn that later Scottish identity is a product of much earlier Irish migration, beginning as early as the fifth century. Moreover, citing late-eighteenth-century sources, we also see that it was a mid-eighteenth-century English industrialist, Thomas Rawlinson, who invented the kilt, from prior garments that were far larger and worn on the torso as well, for his laborers to wear. While this does not take anything away from its modern use in *articulating* a national identity, its concurrent role in *legitimizing* that identity, as if it stretches back into the archaic mists of time, is certainly undermined.

Of interest is the ease with which "tradition" is, at least for some, now synonymous with religion itself. Indeed, many today even prefer to use the term "religious tradition." The term is more akin to the word "ritual" in earlier English sources. Thus, we read claims about "religious tradition" in eighteenth-century documents that reference elements of the liturgy or the order and elements of worship, for example. This was later juxtaposed to assumptions of religion's proper "individualistic spirit," thereby making so-called "religious tradition" somewhat stifling. We see this, for example, in Samuel Max Melamed's (1885–1938) essay, "Historic and Unhistoric Judaism" in the monthly magazine, *The Jewish Forum* 1/8 (1918): 462. By the mid-twentieth century the likelihood is that, when qualified by the adjective "religious" it provided another way of talking about what are also termed the world's religions, with Islam, Buddhism, Taoism, etc., all qualifying now as religious traditions (in the plural). As recently as the late 1960s and early 1970s we commonly find references to the earlier sense, such as "this religious tradition of social criticism" in, e.g., Helen C. White's *Social Criticism in Popular Religious Literature of the Sixteenth Century* (1966), 41. At the same time we start to see a new use, such as Paul Younger's ambiguously titled book, published in India, *The Indian Religious Tradition* (1970)—ambiguous inasmuch as it concerns traditions specific to Indian religion. Or, again in W. Widick Schroeder's methodological claim, in *Cognitive Structures and Religious Research: Essays in Sociology and Theology* (1970): "A social scientist who wants to understand a religious institution, a religious idea, or a devotee of a religious tradition must empathize with the institution, belief, or person" (5). Moreover, in *An Introduction to the Psychology of Religion* (1971) by the English psychologist, Robert H. Thouless (1894–1984), we read: "An attitude that may well be changed is the one adopted towards other religions and towards variations within one's own religious tradition" (132; citing the third edition). This use is now very familiar today, e.g., in Thomas G, Plante's effort to identify "spiritual and religious tools common among all of the major religious traditions that can be used by contemporary professional psychologists in clinical practice" (from his 2008 "What Do the Spiritual and Religious Traditions Offer the Practicing Psychologist?" in *Pastoral Psychology* 56/4: 429–444). Or, again, in Birgit Stammler's comment that "[c]ontrary to European or North American countries, Japan has never been dominated by one religious tradition to the exclusion of all others" (in her chapter, "Japanese NRMs," in the 2014 edited resource, *The Bloomsbury Companion to New Religious Movements*, 53).

But what accounts for this shift? Many would cite the Canadian scholar of Islam, Wilfred Cantwell Smith (1916–2000), and his influential *The Meaning and End of Religion* (1962). There, he criticized the ease with which what at least he claimed to be two otherwise distinct things were inappropriately lumped together, as if they were the same, whenever the word "religion" was used by either scholars or the general public. Instead, as his title conveys, he recommended doing away with the term "religion" and replacing it with "faith in transcendence," on the one hand, and "the cumulative tradition," on the other. The first was understood by him as the source for all religion, placing Cantwell Smith squarely in the field's still dominant personalistic or individualistic school of thought. The latter, or so he argued, was the secondary and public site where that prior faith was expressed in history. Unfortunately, as he concluded, the latter, inasmuch as its elements—what we commonly call myths, rituals, and symbols—could be seen or heard, etc., they were inappropriately assumed to exhaust all that religion was. After all, as he opens the chapter entitled "The Cumulative Tradition": "The man [sic] of religious faith lives in this world" (154, citing the 1991 edition) and "this world," being social, economy, historical, etc., inevitably changes over time. Hence Cantwell Smith's choice of the adjective "cumulative" to qualify "tradition," lending to his work the appearance of historicity, while the careful reader understands it still to be firmly anchored in the presumption that the source of religion was a timeless and personal sensibility: faith.

We should recall here Raymond Williams's observation that "tradition" can easily take on a negative connotation when used as part of a modernist discourse, in which it is represented as backward. See his 1976 *Keywords: A Vocabulary of Culture and Society*, 319–320 (citing the 1983 edition). Thus, the earliest uses of the term with regard to religion aimed to deauthorize the foundation of one set of practices and institutions, in favor of another. Over time it has been used more descriptively, akin to naming longstanding practices, and, very recently, as a way to lend the appearance of empirical rigor to work that nonetheless places the source of religion outside history. But, as already noted, few have made the shift to explaining *why* certain practices not only come to be repeated and given authority over the present and the future, but *how* continually changing practices are given a thin veneer of antiquity. In terms of this we might note Vaia Touna's 2017 book, *Fabrications of the Greek Past: Religion, Tradition, and the Making of Modern Identities*, in which not tradition but the process of traditionizing and thereby authenticating is examined in a variety of case studies. For example, she looks at a newly renovated "traditional Greek village," not far from Mount Olympus, which has been built in a fashion to look "traditional" so as to satisfy the expectations of tourists, which is just up the hill from the "new" village, by the same name, where most of the people who work in the "old" village's shops and restaurants actually live. To make this shift a critical scholar must turn their attention from the past to the present during which claims about tradition are circulating, in search of the criteria and interests that always direct contemporary social actors' choices. The archive of the past—a term we have borrowed from Michel-Rolph Trouillot's (1949–2012) still important little book, *Silencing the Past: Power and the Production of History* (1985)—is a large and hectic place, with many options. Think, for example, of how many different ways some of the words included in this volume have been spelled over the years (in Middle English alone: tradicioun, tradicyon, tradycion, tradycyon, etc.) But not all continue to be relevant to us today. Accounting for this will mean turning from studying tradition or traditions to the discourse on tradition, seen not as an innocent repetition of obviously important past patterns but, rather, as an active selection and willful reproduction that always takes place in the present. "For what reasons?" and "to what effect?" are the questions that the critical scholar will now ask. Thus, it will require us always to remember that, despite Tevye, the lead character in the well-known 1964 musical (and the 1971 film adaptation), "Fiddler on the Roof," opening the show by singing about tradition, it is always the present—its actors and their choices and social interests—that is being referenced.

In this volume see: church, commentary, immanence/transcendence, myth, piety, reformation, ritual, symbol, theology

In *Religion in 50 Words* see: authority, belief, identity, indigeneity, origin, orthodoxy, politics, power, practice, religion, society

49 Understanding

Although a common enough word in the English language, in the study of religion (as well as throughout the Humanities) "understanding" traditionally implies a rather specific conception of the item under study and the proper approach to its study. In many ways, the term is not unlike "phenomenon," a word whose scholarly orbit often includes unarticulated phenomenological assumptions about religion's essence and its varied manifestations. To say that one "studies religion in order to understand it" can also denote assumptions about the object under analysis. The result is that we should be aware that the term implies a theory of meaning that may require further scrutiny.

The term has a lengthy history, dating back to Old English and Germanic languages. The modern word "understand," as both a noun (one's own understanding) and verb (to understand a message) combines the prefix "under-" with the word "stand," also derived from an Old English and previous Germanic term for adopting an upright posture. The meaning of the latter term could also extend to other ranges of meaning, such as: existing or occupying a position or a status (i.e., to stand for election or to have standing in a lawsuit); a view on a topic or one's subject position (one's standpoint); the act of advocating in support of a cause (i.e., to take a stand or to stand up for something); a device used to elevate something (a music stand to hold sheet music or a bandstand); or a small place of business akin to a booth or a stall (i.e., a newsstand selling newspapers and magazines). Thus, to understand something—designating for us today that act of comprehending or interpreting something correctly would seem to be linked to a much earlier sense of occupying a place within a particular setting or amongst others in a common situation.

Colloquially, the effort to understand something may simply be thought of as synonymous with examining, studying, or analyzing an item or a topic. In this sense, we could propose the seemingly uncontroversial claim: "critical scholars aim to understand religion." But, in its more specific, technical usage, the term can generally be linked to a history of modern German philosophical work that has influenced the field. We refer specifically to the German term *Verstehen*, which results in a sense very different than what it means to analyze something. The latter term derives from the Greek, by way of Latin and then French, for dissolving or breaking something down to its more basic, constitutive elements. According to the English philosopher David E. Cooper, in a chapter of the edited volume, *Verstehen and Humane Understanding* (1996), *Verstehen* refers to:

> the constellation of concepts—life, experience, expression, interpretation, understanding—which, according to Wilhelm Dilthey are essential to the study of human affairs, thereby showing that 'the methodology of the human studies [*Geisteswissenschaten*] is ... different from that of the physical sciences'
> (95; quoting H. P. Rickman's *Dilthey: Selected Writings* [1986], 177)

As already noted with the term "phenomenon," the use of "understand" in the study of religion comes with very specific baggage. It implies that the study of religion must be essentially a hermeneutical or interpretive exercise, inasmuch as human behavior and the systems within which human beings live and interact, are presumed to be inherently meaningful. This also implies that their proper study requires scholars to understand that meaning—both in the sense of comprehending it and in the sense of empathetically re-experiencing it for themselves.

As Cooper rightly concludes, this influential approach is indebted to Dilthey (1833–1911), a wide-ranging German Romantic scholar associated with the influential work of the earlier German theologian, Friedrich Schleiermacher (1768–1834). Dilthey edited the latter's letters (which began in 1859), his uncompleted multi-volume biography, *Leben Schleiermachers* (the first of which was published in 1870), and continued to advocate for, and develop, Schleiermacher's hermeneutical program. As observed by the historian of religions Hans Penner (1934–2012), "Schleiermacher sought for a theory of understanding that would unify the various methods for interpreting texts, grammars, and rhetoric" (in Penner's chapter "Interpretation" in the 2000 *Guide to the Study of Religion*, 58). Given that the interpretation of meaning, and its personal experience within the mind (or heart?) of the interpreter, would not so easily succumb to Enlightenment rationality and skepticism, the Romantic era's reaction to such critiques found in both experience and meaning a handy refuge. Here, we might also agree with Penner's onetime colleague, Jonathan Z. Smith (1938–2017), that when we look through the archives we find the strategic redefinition of a variety of words, by the mid- to late eighteenth century (e.g., terms such as "reverence" and "adoration") that were once used mainly in relation to ritual. Such words, referring to social and observable situations, now came to be used as if they referred to, in Smith's words, "a state of mind." He concludes that this shift in usage, and thus conception, marked "a transition begun by Reformation figures such as Zwingli and Calvin who understood 'religion' primarily as 'piety'," but now no longer signifying the classical sense of proper behavior in ranked social settings (see Smith's "Religion, Religions, Religious" from Mark C. Taylor's edited volume, *Critical Terms for Religious Studies* [1998], 271). As Smith continues, we arrive at Schleiermacher's preference in his works for the German term *Glaube*—translated usually as "faith" (*glauben*, to believe)—over the equally possible German term *Religion* (plural *Religionen*)—for example, Schleiermacher's major work in systematic theology, *Der christliche Glaube* (1830; English, *The Christian Faith*).

With Dilthey, the implied distinction between what is often represented as the meaning-centered and thus interpretive human sciences, on the one hand and, on the other, the causal or mechanistic natural sciences is treated in far more detail. Both are seen as practices known as *Wissenschaft*—German for the systematic, rational, or academic study of a topic—from *Wissen* or knowledge plus *-schaft*, the activity of producing or carrying out something, along with its practitioners or community. This is a much broader term than the contemporary use of the English "science" and is certainly one that hearkens back to one of the field's earlier names: the Science of Religion. See, for example, F. Max Müller's *Lectures on the Science of Religion* (1872), which, in a suitably Renaissance style, is seen to study the various manifestations of the enduring human spirit. As a result, its practitioners are said to risk doing a terrible injustice to those whom they study if their approach relies upon the reductive methods of the latter academic pursuit (traditionally termed *Naturwissenschaft*). We now begin to see the intellectual tradition into which much of the history of our field is placed, at least by some of its most influential members. Religion, being an essentially human meaning-making activity, is mistakenly studied if it is seen as anything but religion, in and of itself, and thus something which is irreducible to anything else. Because of this, religion must be interpreted and thereby understood by the scholar.

This latter term, "understanding," at least in this influential tradition, thus implies the requirement for the interpreter to carefully learn and then work within the meaning system, thereby inhabiting the meaning world of the people under study. Here we might see links with Clifford Geertz's (1926–2006) more recent advocacy for what he termed the thick description of interpretative anthropology. In this way, the scholar is thought to be able to re-experience for themselves, *if reading things properly*, either the otherwise lost meanings and existential situations of long dead peoples, as encoded and available in their surviving artifacts. This is how Mircea Eliade (1907–1986) described the method of his so-called New Humanism in a 1961 essay by that title. It is also the way that others maintain we can access the often overlooked experiences of non-dominant and therefore marginalized peoples, as best illustrated in the field's current lived religion and material religion approaches. While one might merely imply that to understand one's material is akin to studying or analyzing it, to others the use of that term signals a very specific set of assumptions about what it is that a scholar of religion is studying and how to go about those studies.

At this point, we should perhaps pause and resist too quickly agreeing to the claim that the field is inherently hermeneutical. The later, an early eighteenth-century English term from ancient Greek by way of Latin and then French, was originally associated with the Christian effort to interpret their own scriptures. We see this, for example, in the Protestant Bible scholar and philologist, Eduard Reuss (1804–1891), writing in *History of the Canon of the Holy Scriptures in the Christian Church* (1884). According to him,

> the speculative school, of which Clement was one of the first and most brilliant representative ... revived the hermeneutic method of the profound and hidden meaning which had already corrupted the theology of the Jews and was henceforth to invade that of the Christians.
>
> (90, citing David Hunter's translation from the French)

The term has now also been extended far wider, to the study of virtually any meaning system (for an overview, see *The Blackwell Companion to Hermeneutics* [2016] as well as *The Cambridge Companion to Hermeneutics* [2019]). Should such readers not already be cautioned by just the prominence of notions as intentionality and experience in the *Verstehen* tradition, then consider again Reuss's just quoted thoughts on what he represents as the corruptions of, by his time, an already very long tradition of detailed interpretation and commentary on the Hebrew Bible by Jewish writers. The latter working with text for what we should recognize to be rather different reasons than why Reuss and his Protestant contemporaries might have been reading what, in distinction, they called the Old Testament (e.g., searching for foreshadowings of Jesus as the promised messiah). Should we adopt an interpretive approach that seeks to recreate the participant's experience of meaning, a contest will inevitably take place over how best to read a text, i.e., from whose point of view and for what purposes.

This economy of readings and meanings is therefore highly competitive. This is especially the case for texts presumed to float free of their writers (such as those attributed either to deities or, as in constitutions, supposed self-evident) and thus those that are put to work authorizing this way of allocating status and resources over the many other possible ways. We may certainly be keen to study these systems in considerable detail, learning of their histories and their intricacies, along with just who has been working with them (and who has not). In this sense, we should retain an interest in seeing each as an item of study rather than presuming that any one of them can provide some sort of privileged access to what Eliade once termed the camouflaged sacred, let alone to the supposedly pure and uncorrupted original intention, meaning, or experience.

The critical study of religion is not so much a site to determine the correct meaning of a text or a relic, and neither is it the place to adjudicate between multiple interpretations. On the contrary, it undergoes a shift, and becomes a domain where one can engage in the historicization of meaning. Some might just term this semiotics, an English term that, while dating to the later seventeenth century, today names a modern academic field that dates to the mid-twentieth century. By the historicization of meaning we hope to convey the sense of coming to see what we commonly call meaning and that we often assume to be somewhere in the head, or perhaps in the text (or the mind of the author), as instead being a product of contingent situations and social actors. The latter use such inventions as routinized and enforced rule systems—which include vocabularies and grammars—that make it possible to "read" an artifact in either this or that way. And so, to borrow a quotation from the American philosopher Hilary Putnam (1926–2016), "meanings ain't just in the head" (from his 1975 essay "The Meaning of Meaning" in *Language, Mind, Knowledge*, 131–193, in support of a position known as semantic externalism, by which the meaning of something is established by public factors, to varying extents). Meaning is now seen as the product of a social and therefore always observable and negotiable system, one that can itself be studied and compared to the standards and results of its competitors. The goal in such an approach, moreover, is not to inhabit the system in an effort to recover, appreciate, or conserve its contents. Rather, it is to study its workings and the processes that, when successful, so authorize its products that its users often mistake them for being timeless and self-evident. This is not unlike someone lost in a foreign country who resorts to reciting their requests for directions in the language that they happen to speak but doing so loudly and slowly in the hopes of being understood.

Contrary to the classic approach of aiming to understand the items or peoples whom they may study, doing so from within those meanings, we should adopt a rather different approach. This one would always look for the manufacturing history that is assumed to come with all human actions and artifacts. To quote Bruce Lincoln, writing in a 2006 essay titled, "How to Read a Religious Text: Reflections on Some Passage of the Chandogya Upanisad," such scholars will therefore "treat the 'truths' of these texts more cautiously (and more properly) as 'truth claims'," which are themselves made within the conditions of what he has elsewhere termed regimes of truth (on the latter see the last of his "Theses on Method"). "Such a stance obliges us," he continues, "to inquire about the human agencies responsible for the texts' production, reproduction, dissemination, consumption, and interpretation." This means, as he concludes, that, rather than aim to recover the meanings or the so-called lived experiences for ourselves, either to cherish or even contest and disagree with them, critical scholars will instead ask about the manufacturing process itself. This means posing what Lincoln has called some irreverent questions: "Who is trying to persuade whom of what...? In what context is the attempt situated, and what are the consequences should it succeed?" (*History of Religions* 46/2: 127).

In this volume see: emic/etic, symbol, value

In *Religion in 50 Words* see: authority, critical, interpretation, method, redescription, religious literacy

50 Value

Value is what measures the worth of something, often in the sense of, at least in common usage today, how much something costs. For example, what is the value of, say, that painting or fancy car? When applied to religion, including the academic study thereof, the noun—not surprisingly, perhaps—tends to refer to the nonmaterial (i.e., spiritual) value associated with beliefs and practices. In this sense religion is ostensibly all about value, sometimes even described as that which is concerned with the Ultimate Value, with the uppercase used purposefully—as in the terminal value, of which none other can be greater. Just as often, it can be used to express the more relativistic plural "values," the latter term often being synonymous with ethics. For example, the phrase, "she has good religious (or often used with a specific religion, like Christian) values," meaning that the person in question is a moral, ethical, and thus upstanding Christian (or Jew, or Buddhist, or whatever the case may be). The term, however, is certainly vague, once again pointing to some ambiguously specified referent beyond itself. Despite the interest in religious values in the field and, presumably, how to study them "properly," however, the critical scholar might finally conclude that value is always something imposed from without by social actors who always have a stake in the game. Nothing, after all, is considered to possess or emit intrinsic value in and of itself. When we talk about value, in other words, we—the interpreter—are the ones assigning and adjudicating worth, whether of the economic or spiritual nature.

From the Anglo-Norman *valu* (including variants, such as *valeu, valew, valwe, walue*) and Old French *valuwe*, the term has a wide semantic range. In use in English for several hundred years but with the related "valuable" and "valuation" dating to the early fifteenth century and "evaluate" dating to just over a century and a half ago and "evaluation" a century before that, with though "evaluative" and "evaluator" being early to mid-twentieth-century developments. The term's meanings can include worth, price, material worth, fair equivalent, reputation, and even personal merit, the latter of which can also include the "importance of a person of social standing." Thus, in the *De Officio Pastorali* of John Wyclif (d. 1384), we read: "Also god is so skileful þat he wole not þat men chaffere but in þingis whoos valu þei knowen" (414). The term then came to denote the material or monetary worth of something, referring to the amount at which something may be estimated in terms of a medium of exchange, such as money or goods, or some other similar standard.

> The man who wanted to buy salt, for example, and had nothing but cattle to give in exchange for it, must have been obliged to buy salt to the value of a whole ox, or a whole sheep at a time.

Thus wrote the Scottish economist and moral philosopher Adam Smith (1723–1790), in his *An Inquiry into the Nature and Causes of the Wealth of Nations* (1776).

In the domain of the personal (and thus of religion, or so common usage demonstrates), however, value has a somewhat different connotation. Now it is less interested in the monetary or economic value of something, including what can be used in exchange for something in an economic (but largely capitalist) system of exchange. We now have discussion of the religious or spiritual values that the religious practitioner ostensibly internalizes from his or her religious tradition—or rather emits by means of the tradition. Such values can include charity, generosity, and compassion. Indeed, if anything, religious values tend to be defined in stark opposition to material ones, despite the fact that they share the same name. So we read in the *Sermons on the Dignity of Man and the Value of the Objects Principally Relating to Human Happiness* (1802) by the Rev. George Joachim Zollikoffer, the "Minifter of the Reformed Congregation at Leipfick" (as translated into English by the Rev. William Tooke, F.R.S [1744–1820]):

> The value of virtue is likewife in the fecund place far more unchangeable than the value of all other goods and advantages. The values of our riches is regulated by our wants and the wants of fociety in which we live.
>
> (239)

In like manner, we read about the importance of not just understanding but also appreciating the value of a particular doctrine over others.

Thus: "The foregoing pages have been employed in tracing the peculiar religious value of a Doctrine, which has brought upon its professors more reproach than any other" (65). These are the words that the Unitarian minister Edward Higginson (1807–1880) used to refer to his own tradition of Unitarianism in his *Christ Inimitable: Or, The Religious Value of the Doctrine of Christ's Simple Humanity* (1837).

Religious values would thus seem to be of a different order altogether. For example, in issue 37 (1932) of *Religious Education Bibliography*, a journal put out by the United States Office of Education, we read about the summary of an article titled "Making Religion Meaningful" by Roy A. Burkhart (1895–1962), Senior Minister of the First Community Church in Columbus, Ohio. Summarizing an article that appeared in the *International Journal of Religious Education* (8 [1932]), he writes that it "[p]resents criteria which are designed to help the religious educator, not only to test the religious values of a given program, but also to aid him in so planning a program that a religious level may be attained" (19). This idea of religious values as part of the teachings that religions provide to the faithful, to make them into what is imagined to be better people, approximates how the term comes to be used in the study of religion. Here, once again, we see a crossover from theological to academic domains without any real reflection on how the term was used in the previous context and then again in the new one.

So-called religious values are thus often believed—and then studied—to reflect the beliefs, practices, and even experiences of a particular religion. These are often claimed to have their sources in the text (or texts) held to be sacred to each of the respective religions. Thus, if one wants to learn about Christian values, one presumably reads the Bible; Muslim values are found in the Quran, just as Buddhist values are located in the various sutras of the canon. Such ancient scriptures, then, are claimed to lead directly to distinct ideas applicable to pressing social issues in the present (such as abortion, homosexuality, gay marriage, and even divorce). After all, those opposed to such issues today not infrequently cite "religious values" as one of the main factors animating or informing their opposition. Indeed, in some countries, so-called religious values can determine the law of the land (think of Saudi Arabia, which, until very recently, has prevented women from driving and does not let women go out unless in the company of a husband or other male guardian). Thus in J. Mark Halstead and Michael J. Reiss's *Value in Sex Education: From Principles to Practice* (2003), we read: "Religious believers need no arguments to be voiced in favour of taking religious values seriously, both generally and with particular reference to sexual ethics and behaviour" (86). This is then juxtaposed with the values of "agnostics and atheists," who "might be tempted to ignore religious values but this would be a mistake" (86). Such a framework also figures highly in the academic study of religion where it is often assumed that if one understands the values of religious people (whether in general or of particular religions), one is somehow better positioned to grasp their patterns of cognition, systems of belief, and rationale or motivation for their actions and associations. Not infrequently we find scholarship on religion that tries to modify so-called traditional values, as in, for example *Sacred Rights: The Case for Contraception and Abortion in World Religions* edited by Daniel C. Maguire (2003), professor of Moral Theological Ethics at Marquette University. In his Introduction, and using a rather typical world religions approach, Maguire states that his volume seeks

> to counter the undue and deceptive monism because the classical wisdom traditions that we call the world's great religions have considerably greater depth and breadth .... On the subjects of contraception and abortion, there are 'pro-choice' as well as 'no-choice' positions solidly grounded in these religions.
>
> (4)

Once again, we see how scholarship on religion seeks to steer the reader into appreciating religion, or at least certain forms of it. It does this, moreover, while showing that when religious people subscribe to positions that those, in the West, do not read as liberal enough or which are judged to be out of sync with modernity, it is often because they do not fully appreciate the vast diversity of the so-called religious voices.

In an article in the journal *Ethics* (45/3 [1935]), titled "The Place of Ultimate Values in Sociological Theory," the sociologist Talcott Parsons (1902–1979) argued that, for the social sciences, a meaningful theory had to include the question of so-called ultimate values. These, by their very nature and definition, included questions of metaphysics—something that seems to have been picked up afterward with some degree of regularity in the academic study of religion. Thus, in his *Theory of Value* (2001), Roy W. Perrett, the scholar of Indian philosophy, can write of the term *moksa* (naming the release from the cycle of rebirth),

> in Indian philosophy and culture ... not only denotes the ultimate (or a very high grade of) reality but also the ultimate value, and therefore to make ethics a means to its attainment is only to provide motivation but also justification for being moral.
>
> (391)

Here we see the conflation, so common throughout the field, of religious values with ethics or authorized systems of action. Thus, the Australian philosopher, Graham Oppy can opine, in his *Reinventing Philosophy of Religion: An Opinionated Introduction* (2014), that "everybody knows that Hindus and Buddhists and Jains and Jews and Christians and Muslims and Taoists disagree with one another about divinity, salvation, ultimate Reality, ultimate values, the meaning and purpose of human life, and much else besides" (10). Implicit is that each religion possesses not just its own worldview but also its own ethical system based on such values. Indeed, as has become increasingly popular over the years, finding their shared values can aid in getting different religions—or, at the very least like-minded participants form the different religions—to talk to one another in interfaith dialogue venues. Of course, this is in complete juxtaposition to those like the writer Ayn Rand (1905–1982), who argued in her essay "The Objectivist Ethics" (1961), that it is survival—and not high minded ideals—that is the ultimate value of all organisms, becoming "the final goal or end to which all lesser goals are the means" (16).

Before proceeding, we should likely consider how strategically useful this discourse on ultimacy can be, regardless of what noun it qualifies. We think here of much earlier claims that Christianity was the "ultimate religion," as in the onetime Bishop of Gloucester, William Warburton and, in his 1742 book, *The Divine Legation of Moses Demonstrated*, he asserts that "Judaifm was *preparatory* to *Chriftianity* and *Chriftianity* is the *ultimate end* of *Judaifm*" (vol. 2, Part II, Book VI, sec. 6, 636). Thus, claiming something to be ultimate—not unlike the German theologian Paul Tillich's (1886–1965) still influential definition of religion as faith in an ultimate concern—is an authorizing tactic that removes an item from history and thus contestation, inasmuch as nothing can, by definition, succeed or follow it. Thus, in the case of Warburton and those who also participated in a discourse later known as *praeparatio evangelica* (i.e., the work being done prior to the revelation of the Christian message, for its proper receipt by people), one religion inherits, yes, but also culminates and thereby tops and ends all others. And, in the case of Tillich, any other concern (which, though important, are by no means ultimate) is dwarfed by the ill-defined one signified by anyone opting to use his preferred term. And many have used it throughout the history of the field precisely because, as Patrick Q. Mason, in his chapter, "Violent and Nonviolent Religious Militancy," correctly described it, the term has "elasticity" (*The Oxford Handbook of Religion, Conflict, and Peacebuilding* [2015], 216). While this might make the adjective "ultimate" useful to the social actors whom we may study, it is hardly a good quality in a scholarly, analytic term. In other words, in academic discourse precision is a guard against ideological excess.

Regardless of how the term "value" is used, it is important for the critical scholar to bear in mind that the act of assigning value to beliefs, practices, and institutions is an historical and thus situated human act. According to this view, no item, regardless the sometimes vigorous claims of those for whom they are dear, has an inherent value in them. It is therefore always human actors who assign, and invariably reproduce and also contextualize, a value. Indeed, the term "value" is often used to attribute a supposedly ethereal quality to items as if they were natural and eternal qualities. They can now be read as a code for a prior economy of social interests and investments that find the item in question to be useful in efforts of promoting and authorizing precisely those same interests and investments. This is why a critical scholar should never mistake the claim of value for the rhetoric that assigns the value. It is the latter to which we should be attuned and not the latter. For it is in the former sense that we witness members of social groups talking about their worlds and the latter sense in which scholars study such claims.

In this volume see: dialogue emic/etic, symbol, tradition, understanding

In *Religion in 50 Words* see: authority, belief, classification, comparison, critical, definition, explanation, faith, ideology, interpretation, power, redescription, world religions, worldview

Appendix
A word on etymologies[1]

Words define words, in an endless cycle. As such, words derive from yet other words, which change over time, sometimes subtly or even dramatically. For the scholar, there might be something gained by knowing about these changes and trying to understand them in the light of other shifts in the wider social world of those who use them. Words, after all, do not float free of their usage, nor are they used apart from those who exist within the social acts of speaking and writing them—activities that are hardly idle or disinterested. There are reasons for talking or creating a text, after all, as well as effects to both, whether intended or not—among the reasons might be dissatisfaction with some of the work being done by a scholarly field's key terms.

We are here reminded of Jonathan Z. Smith's (1938–2017) point that the King James Bible, like Shakespeare's plays, is an Elizabethan text. Despite this, only the English of the former is presumed to be transparently meaningful to modern readers since the latter usually comes with a hefty scholarly apparatus in the footnotes, to help readers make sense of what sometimes reads like a foreign language. (In fact, in the Fall of 2015 it was reported that the Oregon Shakespeare Festival had decided that Shakespeare's English was just too difficult for contemporary audiences to decipher, so it commissioned playwrights to translate the English-language plays into an English that moderns might understand.) As Smith goes on, "the word 'let' often means to stop somebody from doing something, and the word 'prevent' at times means to let them go ahead and do it." His point? "One gets odd moral conclusions by reading the King James Bible without such footnotes, and yet our mutual lie is that it is infinitely accessible while Shakespeare is accessible with difficulty" (from his Afterword to *Studying Religion: An Introduction* [2019], 125). The lie of which Smith writes is the hard work that scholars often hide from their students and their readers, making something that took years to acquire or figure out seem almost effortless and self-evident. This, or so he argues, does not benefit a field that tackles the study of something (i.e., religion) that so many people think is equally self-evident and effortless to understand. In part, this volume has been our attempt to address this shortcoming. Doing so requires us to make the roots and the changes more apparent, and it is within this context that each of the previous entries opens by offering an etymology, providing at least a glimpse into the historical derivation and uses of the terms included.

While neither of us are etymologists (and knowing our readers likely are not as well), we have relied on the work of those who have enabled us to provide insight into some of the twists and turns of the words so important in our work today. But, with the entry on origins in mind, we resist seeing any of these as definitive. Instead, these entries are suggestive and representative of the archival materials that happen to remain and that have come to the attention of the curious etymologist. Indeed, the very word "etymology" comes into English around the fourteenth century, by way of the Middle French *ethymologie* (and as is so common, from the Latin *etymologia* and prior to that the ancient Greek *étumología*). According to the Oxford English Dictionary, early on the term came to be used in the sense of providing an account of a word's origin by explaining its composition. Among the OED's early examples is Richard Sherry's 1550 *A Treatise of Schemes & Tropes*: "Etymologie or shewyng the reason of the name." So, contrary to discourses on origins that posit a linear development from some pristine source, we advise seeing these as exemplary and representative of a far sloppier history, comprised of the many other words that inhabit the sometimes overlapping and shifting orbits of the words in question.

For more details on what we have offered in the preceding entries we of course advise interested readers to stop by the OED for themselves, to explore the proposed derivations and examples of what John Locke once (ungenerously, mind you) called "a web of perplexed words" (*An Essay Concerning Human Understanding*, vol. II, Book III, 32, quoting the 1813 edition).

Note

1 This appendix, like the introduction, appears in both this volume and in *Religion in 50 Words*.

Index

We leave it to readers to see the main entries in this volume for topics of interest and then to follow the suggestions at the close of each entry for supplemental readings elsewhere in the book. The items indexed here are therefore the mostly contemporary scholars mentioned throughout the present volume as well as the critical concepts that are each discussed in detail in the previous volume, *Religion in 50 Words: A Critical Vocabulary*, and which are also relevant to the entries in this book. (Because all entries concern the study of religion there is no entry for "religion" in the index.) Following this model, this volume's main entries are likewise indexed in *Religion in 50 Words*, allowing the two volumes to work more smoothly together.

Abbott, Freeland K. 194
Adams, Charles 194
affect 118
   religious affectations 269
Ahmed, Aziz 194
Akyol, Mustafa 196
Albanese, Catherine 210, 254
Ali, Ayaan Hirsi 196
Almond, Philip C. 16
Anderson, Benedict 36, 40, 99
Appleby, R. Scott 92
Arbel, Keren 140
Armstrong, Karen 96
Arweck, Elisabeth 162
Asma, Stephen T. 17
Asprem, Egil 157
Augustine, Jonathan Morris 102
authenticity 26, 37, 47, 51, 122, 135, 144, 167, 171, 189, 190, 223, 226, 247, 248, 250, 258, 262, 264
authority 21, 30, 32, 42, 45, 84, 103, 127, 152, 154, 155, 160, 161, 176, 184, 185, 189, 190, 198, 199, 202, 210, 246, 253, 277, 280
Aviv, Caryn 231

Baker, Kelly 56
belief 2–5, 20, 23, 25, 37, 51, 52, 88, 94, 112, 116, 139, 142, 146, 156, 162, 166, 173, 175, 199, 201, 206, 209, 236, 239, 242, 271, 291
   belief system 17, 20, 95, 143–4, 146
   shift to belief 174, 176, 224
Bell, Catherine 210
Bellah, Robert N. 21, 38, 39
Benedict, Ruth 150
Berry, Damon T. 39
Boas, Franz 150
Boyarin, Daniel 67
Brakke, David 103
Brandon, S. G. F. 220
Braun, Willi xi, 265
Broek, Roelof van den 158
Brown, Peter 102
Bruce, Steve 91
Bulliet, Richard W. 49
Bullivant, Stephen 162
Burkert, Walter 52, 216
Butler, Judith 231
Byrne, Máire 96

Campbell, Joseph 124
canon 5, 31, 36, 39, 43, 44, 290
Carmody, Denise 127, 129
Carmody, John 127, 129
Carrette, Jeremy 250
Castenda, Carlos 238
classification 3, 23, 59, 67, 143, 157
cognition 20, 157, 240, 291
  cognitive science of religion (CSR) 15, 21, 52, 154, 157, 158, 279
  embodied cognition 210
Collingwood, R. G. 133
Collins, Randall 118
Colpe, Carsten 258, 264
comparison 10, 12, 15, 53, 56, 64, 66, 75, 92, 100, 129, 132, 135, 183, 213, 268
  comparative religion 2, 4, 84, 128, 129, 140, 180, 191, 213, 219, 220, 221, 225, 228, 240, 253, 259
Conze, Edard 140
Cornell, Vincent J. 103
Cotter, Christopher R. 28, 162, 166
Cristi, Marcela 38
critical 6–9
  critical study of religion xii, 2, 6, 20, 95, 96, 100, 181, 205, 265, 275, 286
  criticizing religion 2, 6, 102, 260
  critique 22, 56, 68, 69, 70, 130, 159, 164, 193, 249, 277
  higher criticism 89
  social criticism 279
Crockett, Clayton 268
Crook, Paul 19
Cusack, Carole 60
culture 7, 54, 57, 75, 76, 81, 82, 91, 97, 156, 164, 199, 215, 220, 249, 252, 255, 258, 262, 278, 291
  culture studies 8
  culture wars 39
  popular culture 56, 59, 60, 124, 163
  visual culture 183

Danforth, Nick 196
Darwin, Charles 18
David, Caroline F. Rhys 140
Davids, T. W. Rhys 204

DeConick, April 158
definition 3, 10, 33, 67, 78, 94, 95, 103, 133, 132, 134–135, 144, 152, 160, 175, 197, 207, 210, 216, 217, 221, 226, 239, 270, 291, 292
  commonsense 162
  minimalist 20, 52
description 3, 5, 9, 10, 17, 24, 47, 51, 58, 68, 77, 90, 91, 92, 104, 111, 118, 136, 145, 146, 156, 171, 179, 180, 181, 207, 215, 240, 258, 259, 268, 277, 278
  thick description 285
Dilthey, Wilhelm 283
Doniger, Wendy 53, 82, 105
Donner, Fred 145, 146
Douglas-Williams, Christine 196
Dundes, Alan 151
Dupre, Louis 115
Durkheim, Emile 33, 38, 40, 58–59, 94, 117, 134, 144, 210, 216, 244, 271, 274

Eck, Diana L. 129, 263
Edis, Taner 196
Eikelman, Dale F. 195
Eliade, Mircea 14, 53, 81, 105, 119, 120, 122, 124, 151, 237, 247, 253, 254, 263, 285
Elverskog, Johan 129
environment 19, 102, 219
essence 20, 21, 33, 92, 100, 104, 146, 150, 155, 172, 180, 234, 240, 241, 242, 245, 253, 263, 270, 282
experience 12, 14, 15, 29, 42, 56, 74, 86, 100, 114, 117, 120, 122, 123, 129, 151, 154, 156–160, 175, 177, 178, 195, 232, 234–237, 245, 248, 249, 251–253, 283–284, 285, 290
  human experience 253, 269
  human nature 29, 49, 65, 86, 122, 192
  lived experience 287
explanation 8, 46, 77, 169, 215, 221, 237, 250, 259, 261, 268, 272, 274, 278
  reduction 24, 35, 76, 105, 181, 192, 236, 237

faith 23, 36, 65, 89, 169, 175, 183,
  195, 199, 201, 224, 225, 266, 280,
  284, 292
  Abrahamic faiths/religions 65, 71,
    96, 227
  faith community 207
  faith healing 131
  sincere faith 209
  synonym for religion 32, 63, 64,
    227, 259, 265
Febvre, Lucien 25
Feil, Ernst 172
Finke, Roger 31
Fitzgerald Timothy 24
Flannery, Kevin L. 82
Fohr, Sherry 204
Foucault, Michel 232, 233
Frank, Gillian 231
Frazer, James George 85, 134, 215, 271
Freud, Sigmund 114, 152, 161,
  216, 271
Fridman, Eva Jane Neumann 237
Fuller, Robert C. 162, 249
function 1, 20, 38, 40, 56, 70, 78, 79,
  81, 83, 102, 106, 126, 160, 161,
  174, 181, 188, 204, 215, 216, 217,
  243, 271, 273, 274

Geaves, Ron 9, 262
Geertz, Clifford 41, 285
gender 28, 53, 65, 67, 189, 217,
  229–231, 247, 262
Gennep, Arnold van 123, 125, 207
Girard, René 217
Gorski, Philip 39

Hagen, Kurtis 175
Halbertal, Moshe 113
Hardman, Charlotte 171
Harvey, Graham 17, 22, 170, 237
Hastings, James 86
Heelas, Paul 245
Hobsbawm, Eric 278
Hoffmeier, James K. 143
Hubert, Henri 216
Huxley, Aldous 157

ideology 2, 24, 55, 103, 110, 144, 151,
  154, 160, 169, 180, 189, 194, 197,
  216, 248, 250, 273

ideological excess 293
  myth is ideology in narrative
    form 152
identification 28, 31, 114, 162, 174,
  211, 264
indigeneity 17, 21, 22, 109, 171, 234,
  235, 236, 238, 248, 272
interpretation 41, 42, 43, 44, 45, 77,
  88, 188, 226, 255, 267, 268, 283,
  285, 286, 287
Irwin, Lee 248

Jain, Andrea R. 231
James, William 86, 156
Jantzen, Grace 158
Jay, Nancy 216–217
Johnston, Jay 8
Jung, Carl G. 122
Juschka, Darlene 76

Katz, Steven 158
Keeney, John Peter 82
Kerényi, Carl 122
Kim, Chin-Tai 116
King, Richard 141, 250
King, Ursula 249
Kirk, G. S. 150, 151
Klassen, Pamela E. 18
Kugle, Scott Siraj al-Haqq 231

Laack, Isabel 17, 22
Lang, Andrew 145, 259, 274
law 30, 43, 45, 127, 155, 185, 290
  canon (church) law 36, 239, 267
  civil 37
  of exogamy 274
  Islamic law 192
  of karma 240, 268
  Torah 43, 99
Lee, Lois 162
Leopold, Anita 261
Leuba, James H. 156
Lévi-Straus, Claude 152
Liebst, Lasse Suonperä 118
Lieu, Judith 170
Lincoln, Bruce 54, 93, 124, 125, 151,
  152, 216, 287
Lipton, Sara 170
lived religion 130, 249, 285
Long, Charles 53, 54

300 *Index*

LoRusso, James Dennis 250
Lopez, Donald S. 50
Lowie, Robert Harry 121

MacDonald, Mary N. 21
Mack, Burton 56
Malinowski, Bronislaw 54, 121, 134, 275
Mango, Cyril A. 107
Maniura, Robert 106
Manji, Irshad 196
Marett, Robert Ranulph 20
Margalit, Avishai 113
Markham, Paul N. 49
Martin, Luther H. 259
Marty, Martin E. 92
Marx, Karl 2, 12, 161
Mason, Patrick Q. 292
Matory, J. Lorand 71
material religion 106, 249, 285
Mauss, Marcel 216
McKeon, Michael 243
Merkur, Daniel 158
methodology 14, 23, 24, 28, 276, 283, 285
  contemplative 138
  methodological agnosticism 25, 268
  scientific 132
  "Theses on Method" 55, 287
Miller, Monica 66, 166
Monier-Williams, Monier 139, 140
Moreton, Bethany 231
Morgan, David 183
Muir, Edward 207
Müller, F. Max 75, 85, 100, 149, 284

Na'im, Abdullahi Ahmed An 196
Neusner, Jacob 100–101
Nongbri, Brent 146
North, John 170
Nye, Malory 211

Obayashi, Hiroshi 14–15
Oppy, Graham 292
origins 20, 21, 29, 41, 88, 188, 218, 271
  of religion 18, 20, 21, 85, 134, 144, 235, 271
  tales 56, 87, 148

orthodoxy 25, 66, 91, 113, 131, 223, 224, 226, 227, 252
Otto, Rudolf 122
Owens, Alex 159
Oxtoby, Willard 69–70, 220, 221

Pagels, Elaine 158
Parrinder, Geoffrey 228
Parsons, Talcott 291
Parsons, William 114
Patton, Laurie L. 253
Penner, Hans 283
Perrett, Roy W. 291
Pettazzoni, Raffaele 145
phenomenology 4, 10, 14, 81, 122, 157, 201, 227, 234, 238, 247, 282
Pietz, William 20
Pike, Kenneth 75
pluralism 63, 155
Pool, Jeffrey B. 254
politics 18, 69, 70, 86, 101, 122, 152, 163, 164, 165, 199, 210, 262, 269
  body politics 28, 37, 155
power 8, 15, 16, 20, 36, 70, 90, 103, 112, 140, 152, 154, 155, 159, 164, 184, 189, 190, 192, 199, 202, 215, 232, 235, 248, 262, 263
practice 30, 88, 126, 133, 138, 164, 183, 188, 198, 201, 208, 211, 231, 234, 237, 254, 257, 261, 264, 276, 277, 279
Proudfoot, Wayne 158
primitive 18, 19, 21, 54, 58, 107, 134, 144, 145, 146, 168, 169, 184, 215, 242, 243, 248, 272, 274
Putnam, Hilary 286

race 65, 144, 254
  racism 18, 256, 272
Radcliffe-Brown, A. R. 275
Rahman, Fazlur 194
Rajak, Tessa 170
Ramberg, Lucinda 229
Rambo, Lewis R. 47, 48
Ramey, Steven W. 66, 164–165, 268
Rand, Ayn 292
Ranger, Terence 278
redescription 9, 198, 221, 243, 250, 275

Reger, Gary 257, 263
Reischauer, August Karl 204
religioning 211
Rennie Bryan S. 105
Ricoeur, Paul 81
Robertson, David 158
Rolland, Romain 114
Ruparell, Tinu 258
Ryle, Gilbert 41, 210

sacred, the 24, 83, 119, 136, 146, 151, 154, 159, 177, 178, 181, 202, 234–237, 244, 250–254, 269, 270
Said, Edward 69–71
Schleiermacher, Friedrich 283
Schuon, Frithjof 157
Scorah, Amber 59
secular 32, 35, 36, 38–40, 48, 76, 86, 93, 112, 136, 161, 163, 198, 249, 268–270
  post-secular 269
  secularism 199, 229, 269
  secularization thesis 161, 162
Segal, Alan 16
Segal, Robert 210
Sells, Michael 158–159
Sharpe, Eric J. 2–7, 78, 186, 221, 222, 243, 259
Shaw, Rosalind 257
Shaw, Sarah 140
Shiappa, Edward 262
Shneer, David 231
Smart, Ninian 157
Smith, Brian K. 276
Smith, Jonathan Z. xi, 92, 94, 152, 173, 211, 213, 267, 284, 295
Smith, Wilfred Cantwell 194, 280
Smith, William Robertson 215
society 23, 25, 27, 36, 38, 54, 55, 75, 79, 93, 94, 119, 141, 152, 161, 168, 176, 198, 229, 273, 274
  as constructed 40, 117, 134, 151, 216, 229
  individualist model 86
  pluralistic 76
  ritualization of 210
  secret 119
  theory of 146

Somerset, Fitzroy Richard (Lord Raglan) 210
Sommers, Benjamin 143
Spencer, Herbert 18
Stace, Walter 157
Stammler, Birgit 279
Stark, Rodney 31
status 16, 23, 48, 59, 65, 103, 112, 119, 123–125, 133, 154, 174–178, 184, 189, 202, 205, 207, 252, 268, 277, 282, 286
status quo 154, 155, 189
Stein, Richard 124
Steiner, Rudolf 123
Stewart, Charles 257
Stroope, Chrissy 40
Stuckrad, Kocku von 8
Sullivan, Lawrence E. 237
Sutcliffe, Steve 60
Swancutt, Katherine 17
Swidler, Leonard 65

Tannous, Jack 145, 146
Taves, Ann 157
Taylor, Charles 243
Taylor, Mark C. 10, 173, 284
text 5, 253
  canonical 39
  careful reading of 270
  components of 44
  foundational 45, 176
  primary 43
  as source of values 290
theory 47, 57, 75, 144, 215, 248, 261, 265, 277, 282, 283, 291
  correspondence theory of meaning 252
  evolutionary theory 18, 19, 273
  "I don't *do* theory" 148
  just war theory 5
  of religion 18, 20, 76, 145, 181, 221, 274
  social theory 94, 117, 118
  undisclosed 32, 148, 189, 263
Thurman, Robert 50
Tillich, Paul 292
Touna, Vaia 280
Tourage, Mahdi 50
Trevor-Roper, Hugh 278
Trouillot, Michel-Rolph 281

Turner, Victor 123, 125
Tylor, Edward Burnett 19, 20, 52, 144, 215, 242, 274

Underhill, Evelyn 157
Ulmer, Rivka 82

Vahanian, Gabriel 269
Veer, Peter van der 258, 262

Wallace, Ruth A. 38
Walter, Mariko Namba 237
Wansbrough, John 100, 101
Wasserstrom, Steven 275
Weber, Max 59, 189
Weckman, George 119
Wedemeyer, Christian 105
Weisenfeld, Judith 231

White, Heather R. 231
Wiebe, Donald 270
Wilfred, Felix 71
Wilkinson, Darryl 17, 22
Williams, Raymond xi, 1, 7–9, 280
Woodhead, Linda 245
world religions 10, 14, 18, 66, 69, 85, 165, 180, 206, 231, 235, 263, 291
   courses 220, 254
   paradigm 30, 63, 248
   textbooks 21, 66, 70, 94, 175, 228
worldview 27, 75, 162, 292
Wunn, Ida 21
Wynne, Alexander 140

Zaehner, Robert C. 157

For Product Safety Concerns and Information please contact our EU representative GPSR@taylorandfrancis.com
Taylor & Francis Verlag GmbH, Kaufingerstraße 24, 80331 München, Germany

www.ingramcontent.com/pod-product-compliance
Lightning Source LLC
Chambersburg PA
CBHW050838230426
43667CB00012B/2055